SABOTAGE!

SABOTAGE!

An In-Depth Investigation of the 1943 Liberator Crash that Killed Polish General Sikorski

CHRIS WROBLEWSKI
AND GARTH BARNARD

GRUB STREET • LONDON

Published by
Grub Street
4 Rainham Close
London SW11 6SS

A CIP record for this title is available from the British Library

ISBN-13: 978-1-911667-90-2

Design by Myriam Bell Design, UK
Printed and bound by Finidr, Czechia

CONTENTS

This book is dedicated to crash victims of AL523; those who perished, the sole survivor, the saboteur, first responders, witnesses and lastly their families who lived with the sorrow and stigma surrounding this event for so many years. All were victims swept up by events that were not of their choosing. May you all finally have closure.

ACKNOWLEDGEMENTS

The authors could not have undertaken this project without the assistance of several individuals who helped this book transition from concept to reality. Our deepest appreciation and thanks to the publisher Grub Street, contributors Richard Beaumont, Adrian Scrope, Peter Urbański, David Walker and Jack Waterfield; for research assistance Benoit De Mulder, James Fowler, Gill Chesney-Green, Mark Krason, Chuck Parsonson, Natalie Schmidt and Paul Sheehan; for translations Stanley Urban and Christina Zehaluk; for their encouragement and advice navigating the complex world of publishing Kyle McNeil and Paul Morgan; for his machining skills Peter Brown; for construction and workshop use Jeff Gray; and Leigh Barnard for her patience with Garth's aviation history pursuits.

The authors further acknowledge the following sources. AeroAntique.com, *After the Battle*, AirCorps Library, aircraft-reports.com (Sicuro Publishing), B-24 Diving Center, DW (Deutsche Welle), eFlightManuals.com, Experimental Aircraft Association EAA, flight-manuals-online.com, GBH Archives, Mach One Manuals (Matthew Savage), San Diego Air & Space Museum, Steven Galicia, The National Archives TNA, timeanddate.com, Stellarium, vintagetin.net http://vintagetin.net/B-24Witchcraft/J/.

Illustrations from Experimental Aircraft Association/Tony Bingelis. Used with permission from EAA.

Illustrations from The National Archives documents contain public sector information licensed under the Open Government Licence v3.0.

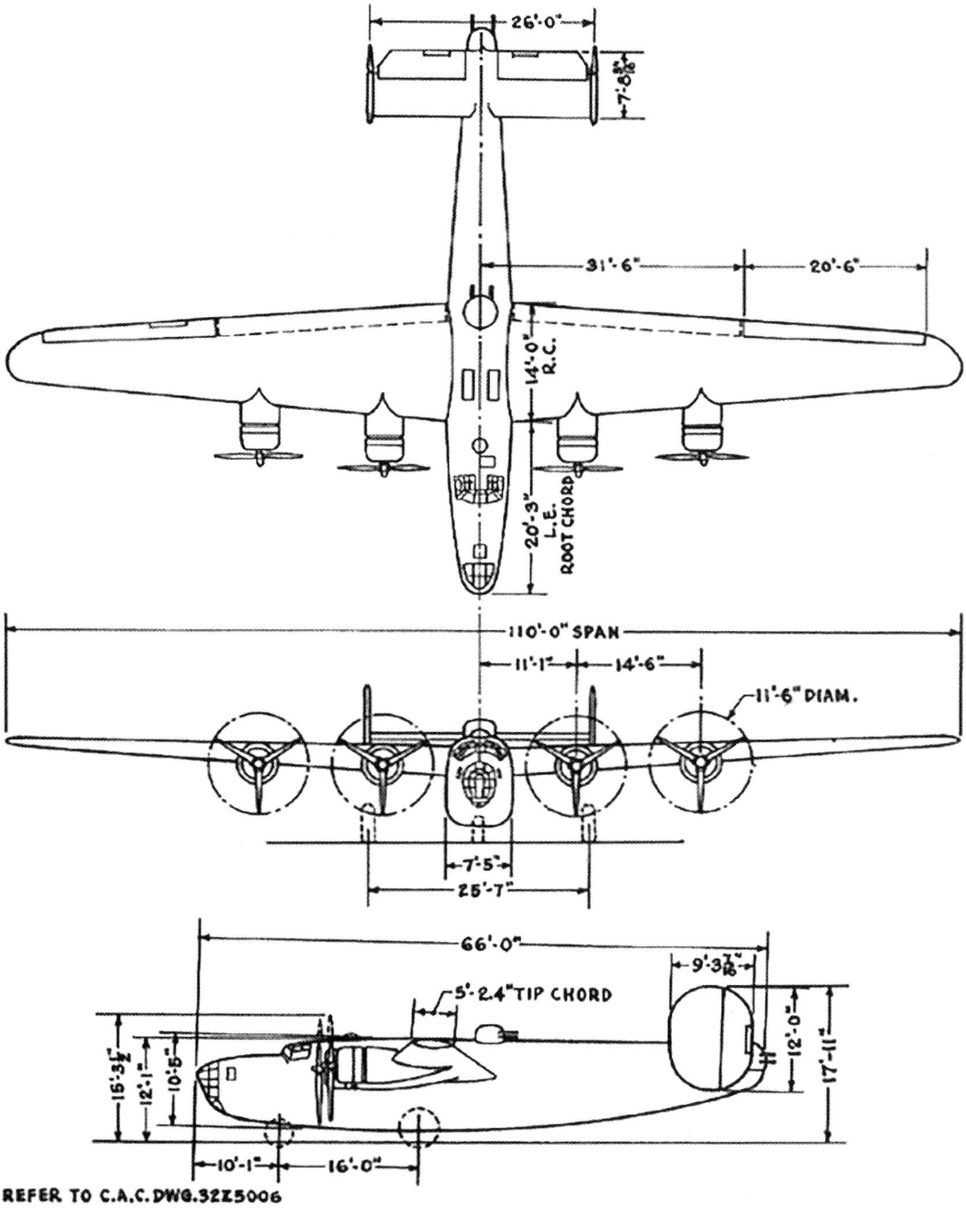

REFER TO C.A.C. DWG.32Z5006

INTRODUCTION

by Chris Wroblewski

In the late evening of 4 July 1943 an RAF Liberator II, registration AL523, lifted off from Gibraltar's North Front airfield; on board were seventeen passengers and crew including General Władysław Sikorski, the commander-in-chief, and prime minister of the Polish government-in-exile. Moments later the Liberator's elevator locked causing it to plunge into the sea approximately 700 yards off the eastern runway. The crash killed General Sikorski and most aboard with the exception of the pilot, Flight Lieutenant Eduard Prchal, who survived though severely injured.

Controversy immediately surrounded the crash, was it pilot error, a technical fault, sabotage, or assassination? A court of inquiry could not fault the pilot nor determine how AL523's elevators became locked after take-off as the pilot asserted while Polish officials considered the inquiry's conclusions unsatisfactory. Over many years several theories have been put forward as to why AL523 crashed, all of which remain unproven. Recent information has since come to light suggesting that AL523 was sabotaged in a covert and unlikely manner.

This new information presented itself after Garth Barnard's *WW2 Air Crash Detectives* episode aired in 2015 when he received an email from a Mr Peter Urbański who resided in Australia. Peter claimed his father Bronislaw Urbański was responsible for sabotaging AL523. Initially guarded and hesitant when Garth pressed for more details of his father's involvement in Sikorski's death, Peter offered him the opportunity to read his biography about Bronislaw titled *To Live Well is to Hide Well.* After reading Peter's narrative Garth agreed that sabotage was the only possible explanation for AL523's crash. Garth noted that Bronislaw's sabotage was simple in its execution lacking a lengthy convoluted narrative so often found among implausible sabotage and assassination myths. Bronislaw had told his son that he had tucked a green cleaning rag into a flight control while standing on a ladder. What Garth could not figure out was how a cotton cleaning rag caused AL523's crash. In 2018 Peter crossed paths with me after replying to a comment on the 'Kresy Siberia' Facebook page regarding Sikorski's death. As with Garth he was guarded in his correspondence and offered me an opportunity to read the biography about his father. Upon reading how the Liberator's flight control was sabotaged I was initially confused with Bronislaw's description of putting the rag in a flap. After familiarizing myself with the circumstances of AL523's crash and Prchal's claim that his elevators jammed I realized that what Bronislaw had tried to describe was an elevator. Peter later confirmed that his father did not know the English word for this control surface. After giving some careful thought as to how a cotton rag could potentially jam a Liberator's elevator, I wrote an illustrated theory and posted it on the 'Kresy Siberia' Facebook page and shortly afterwards Peter shared the document with Garth.

In 2019 Garth and I connected and began corresponding through email, messenger and Skype. During our correspondence Garth described how his new eyewitness accounts differed with the court of inquiry findings. Through these new accounts plus research from his 2015 Gibraltar visit, Garth had begun to form a hypothesis that pointed to human factors surrounding the accident's circumstances. With my elevator sabotage theory, this provided a new technical perspective of the crash which helped rule out several unlikely technical scenarios proposed by other researchers which further reinforced Garth's hypothesis. In August of that year Garth gave a talk to the Rugby and District Royal Air Force Association about the Sikorski crash, it was here that he first presented the sabotage theory and presented my illustrations through visual graphics. Garth summarized his impression of the audience response to his lecture:

> "As I got going, I noticed a few of the old boys slouch in their chairs, fold their arms and cross their legs in a way that would suggest they were going to be force fed a load of bull for the next hour. But as I concluded I noticed they were all sitting forwards, thumbing their chins. I got a long clap and a few shouts of bravo too!"

The use of graphics had helped immensely in that a picture tells a thousand words, the audience saw immediately how plausible it was to shove a rag in the elevator and have it shift in flight. Secondly it was an independent view from an aviation expert.

First impressions of this method seemed implausible but detailed research and testing has since proved that not only was the sabotage method possible but the only probable cause that locked AL523's elevators after take-off. In my thirty-six years as a licensed Canadian aircraft maintenance engineer, I have serviced and repaired both light and heavy aircraft types. My background includes troubleshooting many types of aircraft flight control systems some of which were similar in layout to the Liberator II. Years of experience taught me that seized components or objects obstructing the movement of flight controls often multiplied effort at the pilot's control column making it stiff or difficult to operate. It was through this experience along with some outside the box thinking that I was able to demonstrate how AL523 was potentially brought down by an act of sabotage.

No attempt in the writing of this book was made to calculate the weight and take-off performance of a Consolidated Liberator II as there has already been much published analysis of that subject related to AL523. Garth and I chose instead to focus on the fact that AL523 was seen to take off, fly for sixteen seconds during which it climbed, levelled off, descended, and struck the water. Being an aircraft mechanic I chose to examine the crash from the perspective of aircraft components and systems. While writing this book it was further appreciated that many readers lack an understanding of how aircraft operate but rest assure this is not a lengthy technical dissertation about theory of flight or aircraft system fundamentals. Technical descriptions have been simplified as much as wherever possible to give the reader a rudimentary understanding of how pilot actions and aircraft systems interact, along with a basic explanation as to how those systems work. Where performance data was required to emphasize an idea or abstract concept a well-founded source was referenced and cited. Liberator enthusiasts will also note that many images are from various models as it was not always possible to obtain specific illustrations of certain Liberator II or LB30 items. It should be noted that both designations refer to the same aircraft type, the first being British, the second American.

This book does not focus heavily on the political intrigue surrounding events that led up to the 4 July 1943 crash, that subject is extensively covered in other published works, but instead focuses on two specific areas. The first covers the sabotage method and technical aspects of the crash which have never been examined in detail or

General Władysław Sikorski.

put into logical context. The second presents historical air crash investigator Garth Barnard's new eyewitnesses which lend further perspective to the accident. In addition several questionable myths and stories that conflict with events surrounding the crash are examined and debunked. The individuals responsible for these controversial myths were historian David Irving, playwright Rolf Hochhuth, and Jerzy Klimkowski who are referenced throughout the book. These individuals' unsubstantiated claims and allegations in the 1960s about the crash of AL523 suggest Sikorski's death was due to either the pilot's smuggling activities, an assassination plot approved by Churchill, or that one or both pilots were co-conspirators who deliberately crashed the aircraft. Rather than give these individuals a new platform outlining their controversial theories and ideologies it was decided to focus instead on specific allegations of each as it related to the crash. Lastly much invaluable information was sourced from Carlos Thompson's book *The Assassination of Winston Churchill*. Thompson's tenacious and unbiased research in the late 1960s brought him in contact with many key individuals associated with different aspects of the Gibraltar accident and investigation. Subsequent interviews with these individuals offered unique perspectives to those found within the pages of court of inquiry testimony. Garth and I hope this information sheds new light on the crash of AL523, the death of General Sikorski and absolves the pilot Eduard Prchal of any ill-perceived negligence.

PRINCIPAL CHARACTERS

Anders, Władysław: General Commander of Polish II Corps in the Middle East.

Bailey, Lieutenant Commander William: Royal Navy clearance diver who dove on the wreckage of AL523 during recovery and salvage operations.

Beaumont, Flight Lieutenant Alan: Flying control officer, Air Headquarters RAF Gibraltar. Was aboard RAF rescue launch HSL 181 during recovery of the crash victims.

Buck, Flight Lieutenant John: British Air Ministry, Accidents Inspector. Examined AL523 wreckage in detail during salvage operations.

Capes, Flight Lieutenant Renault: Flying control officer, Air Headquarters RAF Gibraltar. On the evening of 4 July 1943 observed AL523 take off and pass his position in the control tower at North Front airfield.

Cazalet, Major Victor: British liaison officer to General Sikorski. AL523 passenger, killed.

Ciechanowski, Jan: Polish ambassador to the United States from 1941 to 1945.

Crabb, Lieutenant Commander Lionel: Royal Navy clearance diver who dived on the wreckage of AL523 during recovery and salvage operations.

Falk, Squadron Leader Ronald: Chief test pilot, RAE Farnborough. Expert witness during court of inquiry on flight characteristics of the Consolidated Liberator.

Hammond, Leading Aircraftman James: Assisted Wing Commander Stevens in examination of AL523's wreckage.

Herring, Squadron Leader Wilfred: AL523 co-pilot, missing and presumed killed.

Hochhuth, Rolf: German author and playwright. His 1967 play, *Soldiers: An Obituary for Geneva*, alleged Winston Churchill had ordered the death of General Sikorski and that the pilot had deliberately crashed AL523. Hochhuth at the time believed that Eduard Prchal had died in the United States; unbeknown to him Prchal was still alive. Prchal won a libel case against the London theatre which staged the play.

Irving, David: British author, historian and Holocaust denier. His 1967 book *Accident* suggested overloading had caused the crash, that the pilot Eduard Prchal, his crew and passengers, had been illicitly smuggling contraband. Irving further suggested the Gibraltar crash, Montreal accident, and mid-Atlantic incendiary bomb scare were all somehow connected. Lastly he tried to insinuate there had been a plot instigated by Winston Churchill to kill Sikorski but the publisher William Kimber & Co Ltd refused inclusion of that theory. In a 1969 German language revision of the book Irving removed references to smuggling and overloading instead suggesting the crash was an assassination plot approved by Churchill in support of General Anders' opposition to Sikorski.

Kelly, Sergeant S: Flight engineer. AL523 crew member, killed.

Kleczyński, Lieutenant Colonel/Wing Commander Bohdan: Polish air attaché to Washington. Staged the discovery of an incendiary device on General Sikorski's aircraft while over the Atlantic in March 1942. Polish sources refer to Kleczyński as a lieutenant colonel whilst British sources refer to him as a wing commander.

Klesnil, Josef: Captain, Czech Airlines. Post-war had flown with Eduard Prchal at Czech Airlines as his co-pilot.

Klimecki, Brigadier General Tadeusz: Chief of Polish General Staff, Polish Army. AL523 passenger, killed.

Klimkowski, Major Jerzy: Served as aide-de-camp to General Anders in the Middle East. Led an anti-Sikorski faction in Polish II Corps, was arrested for conspiring to assassinate Sikorski and imprisoned in the UK. After the war he was among the first to return to Communist-dominated Poland and actively engaged at the height of the Cold War in a campaign to smear General Anders' name and agitate against the Polish government-in-exile in Britain. In 1965 he published *Katastrofa w Gibraltarze. Kulisy śmierci generała Sikorskiego* (*The Disaster in Gibraltar. Behind the scenes of General Sikorski's death*) that alleged Churchill sanctioned Sikorski's assassination, and that AL523's co-pilot was a British agent who deliberately crashed the aircraft, jumped out before impact and swam away. A British government investigation in 1969 determined David Irving and Rolf Hochhuth had used elements of Klimkowski's story in their narratives.

Knowles, Stoker 1st Class Sydney: Royal Navy clearance diver who dived on the wreckage of AL523 during recovery and salvage operations.

Kulakowski, Adam: Civilian. Secretary to General Sikorski. AL523 passenger, missing and presumed killed.

Leśniowska, Mrs Zofia: Civilian and member of *Pomocnicza Służba Kobiet* (Women's Auxiliary Service), daughter of General Sikorski. AL523 passenger, missing and presumed killed.

Llewellyn, Wing Commander Thomas Henry: Commanding officer of No. 511 Squadron's Liberator Flight.

Łubieński, Lieutenant Ludwik: Polish liaison officer Gibraltar. Was the last person to see Sikorski alive before boarding AL523.

Mason-MacFarlane, Lieutenant General Frank Noel: Governor of Gibraltar from 31 May 1942 to 14 February 1944.

Martin, Douglas: Company Quartermaster Sergeant. British Special Operations Executive (SOE) wireless operator. Claimed to have witnessed from a cliffside balcony AL523 land on the water the night of 4 July 1943.

Maisky, Ivan: Soviet Deputy Minister of Foreign Affairs and ambassador to Great Britain. His aircraft landed at Gibraltar on the morning of 4 July 1943 and departed a few hours later.

Mitkiewicz, Colonel Leon: Chief of the Polish Military Mission to the United States.

Moore, Sergeant Norman: Fitter II. No. 511 Squadron Maintenance detached to RAF North Front Gibraltar. Sergeant Moore oversaw the servicing of AL523.

Perry, Flight Lieutenant Arthur: Air Headquarters RAF Gibraltar, aide-de-camp to Lieutenant General Mason-MacFarlane.

Prchal, Flight Lieutenant Eduard: AL523 pilot, sole crash survivor.

Prokop, Jaroslav: Radio operator/navigator for Czech Airlines. Post-war had flown with Eduard Prchal at Czech Airlines.

Protasewicz, Lieutenant Colonel Michal: Aide-de-camp to General Sikorski, later head of the Polish Sixth Bureau in London.

Quayle, Major Anthony: Aide-de-camp to the governor of Gibraltar.

Rechka, Josef: Captain Czech Airlines. Wartime friend of Eduard Prchal, both had flown with No. 310 Czechoslovak Squadron during the Battle of Britain. Was at Gibraltar the evening of the crash. Post-war both flew for Czech Airlines.

Sach, Squadron Leader Jack: A Flight commander, No. 511 Squadron. Testified at court of inquiry that VIPs on occasion refused to follow regulations.

Scrope, Lieutenant Colonel Adrian: Assistant Quartermaster General to General Clutterbuck, 1st Division, Eighth Army. Was present on North Front airfield the night of 4 July 1943, was told of an altercation between AL523 flight crew and passengers.

Sikorski, General Władysław: Polish prime minister in exile and commander-in-chief of the Polish Armed Forces. AL523 passenger, killed.

Skarbek, Krystyna (alias Christine Granville): Member of Polish intelligence organization Musketeers, Polish agent with the British Special Operations Executive (SOE). Sent coded radio message to Bronislaw Urbański to position himself in Gibraltar for Sikorski's stopover during his Middle East visit.

Slessor, Air Marshal John: Commander-in-Chief, RAF Coastal Command. In 1950 he became Marshal of the Royal Air Force.

Stevens, Wing Commander Montague: Technical officer, Air Headquarters Gibraltar. Observed recovery of AL523 wreckage and inspected recovered components.

Swabey, Flight Lieutenant Leslie: Pilot with No. 511 Squadron. David Irving claimed Swabey had overheard Prchal say he had lied during the court of inquiry.

Thompson, Carlos: Writer and TV producer. Wrote *The Assassination of Winston Churchill* (1969) which challenged and refuted allegations made by David Irving in his book *Accident – The Death of General Sikorski* (1967) and German playwright Rolf Hochhuth's 1968 theatre production *Soldiers* which suggested Prime Minister Winston Churchill had authorized the assassination of General Sikorski.

Urbański, Bronislaw: AL523 saboteur. Member of Polish intelligence Musketeers organization, Polish resistance group OW-ZJ, and agent with British Special Operations Executive (SOE).

Walker, Leading Aircraftman Charles: AC1 airframe mechanic. Witnessed loading of cargo aboard AL523 on the evening of 4 July 1943.

Waterfield, Jack: AC2 mechanic. Witnessed AL523 departure from North Front tarmac and take off on the evening of 4 July 1943.

Watson, Squadron Leader Wallace: A Flight commander, No. 511 Squadron after Squadron Leader Sach. Was squadron Liberator instructor and had instructed Prchal on type. He had flown AL523 prior to switching aircraft with Prchal.

PART I

THE CRASH OF AL523

CHAPTER ONE
POLITICAL UNREST

On 24 May 1943 General Władysław Sikorski set out on an inspection tour of Polish forces in the Middle East to reassert his authority, calm agitation, and put to rest all rumours about plots against him. Much of the unrest towards Sikorski centred around his diplomacy with the Soviets which to many within Polish diplomatic and military circles was considered weak and concessionary. On 30 July 1941 Sikorski had signed a Polish-Soviet alliance in London with Soviet ambassador Ivan Maisky known as the Sikorski-Maisky Agreement which unfortunately did not ensure that areas of Poland taken by the Soviets in 1939 would be returned. Sikorski would be heavily criticized for not insisting on settling the border issue before signing the alliance.[1] He instead believed a unified non-communist, numerically strong Polish force of 100,000 or more fighting alongside the Soviets was the only option in re-establishing Poland's pre-war borders and independence.[2]

In August 1941 Stalin nullified the Russo-German Molotov-Ribbentrop Pact of August 1939, which saw tens of thousands of Polish prisoners of war and citizens released from Soviet labour camps and granted 'amnesty'. Desperate to secure Allied aid Stalin allowed the Poles to form an army under General Władysław Anders on Russian territory with promises of Soviet food and arms. The terms of the alliance angered three of Sikorski's ministers who had resigned on 25 July because of its ambiguous wording. They objected to restoration of relations between Poland and the Soviet Union having not been based on guaranteed restoration of Poland's eastern borders, only inferred borders to be agreed upon later. The ministers also opposed the use of 'amnesty' in relation to Polish citizens in the Soviet Union. It suggested that the Poles, who were deported by the Soviets during the military occupation of eastern Poland, were guilty of a crime.[3]

The eastern border issue would plague Sikorski's tenure as commander-in-chief and prime minister up until his death. During Sikorski's last visit to Washington in late 1942 the Polish National Council in London on 2 December adopted a resolution demanding post-war restoration of Poland's eastern frontiers within the 1921 Treaty of Riga. Pro-communist sentiment in the United States reacted with hostility in the press terming the resolution 'chauvinistic'. Anti-Sikorski sentiment among American Poles was equally hostile viewing Sikorski's endorsement of the National Counsel's resolution incompatible with his defence of the Polish-Russian pact and a violation of Poland's rights within the Treaty of Riga.[4][5] Though the agreement had freed thousands of Polish soldiers it angered army officers who could not forgive the Soviets for their invasion on 17 September 1939. While Sikorski held a guarded faith in Stalin and Soviet guarantees, General Anders saw his commander's decisions as misinformed and ill-advised.[6] By 1943 Anders' Middle East army would become Polish II Corps.

On 13 April 1943 Radio Berlin announced the discovery in the Katyn Woods of mass graves containing remains of Polish officers. These victims were part of 21,892 officers and public officials captured by the Soviets in 1939 and murdered between April and May 1940.[7] Sikorski demanded an investigation by the International Red Cross, as did simultaneously the Germans. Unwilling to risk their alliance with the Soviet Union the British government's foreign secretary Anthony Eden convinced Sikorski to withdraw the request and agree instead to an independent inquiry.[8] In response the Soviets on 25 April 1943 broke off diplomatic relations with the Poles accusing them of allying with the Germans in order to extract concessions on border issues. A great many Polish army officers in the Middle East were already hostile towards Sikorski citing his blind willingness to let Poland's eastern provinces be the price for a Soviet alliance. His failure to address the Katyn massacre further stoked their hostility. In the month prior to events at Katyn this rising acrimony was such that on 3 March 1943 General Anders sent his acting chief of staff Colonel Kazimierz Wiśniowski as envoy to General Sikorski with a letter expressing his views and those of the Polish army in Iran that he should give up his post of premier and confine himself to military affairs by remaining commander and chief.[9] Rumours circulated that several officers within the Polish II Corps favoured replacing Sikorski with Anders, that his Middle

East visit was to relieve Anders of his command, and that Sikorski faced possible assassination.[10] Sikorski's tour lasted for over a month, during this time he and Anders apparently settled their differences and cleared up misunderstandings.[11] According to Anders during their discussions about Katyn, Sikorski started coming around to the views that Anders held of the Soviets.[12] On 18 June Sikorski flew to Beirut for ten days rest, the tour's heat, tension and political pressure having been a heavy physical and mental strain. On 28 June 1943 he flew from Beirut to Heliopsis Egypt.[13] The next day Sikorski received a telegram from Churchill conveying congratulations on the successful outcome of his trip: "Am delighted to hear from Casey[14] of general success of your visit. Shall be glad to welcome you home."[15] On 2 July, while in Cairo, Sikorski cabled his gratitude: "Many thanks for message. Success of my visit largely due to your constant support and understanding of Polish problems. Look forward greatly to seeing you."[16] That same day he contacted his ambassador in Washington and told him of his plans upon his return to London.[17] Before leaving on his Middle East tour Sikorski had asked the British and American governments to intercede with Stalin and arrange a meeting between him and the Soviet leader as he was eager to re-establish a united front against Germany.[18] Once back in London Sikorski intended to advocate to Prime Minister Churchill and President Roosevelt, through Poland's ambassador Jan Ciechanowski in Washington, to affirm their support for him to negotiate an agreement with the Soviet government. If Sikorski obtained this support, "he was determined to fly to Moscow in order to make a supreme effort to clear up Soviet-Polish misunderstandings in direct talks."[19] Prior to his 24 May Middle East departure Sikorski had discussed with Anthony Biddle, the American ambassador to Poland's government-in-exile, of being opened minded to diplomatic initiatives intended to mend the break in Polish-Soviet relations over Katyn. A draft of the initiative was finalized on 29 June by William Standley and Archibald Kerr, the American and British ambassadors to the Soviet Union.[20] On the morning of 3 July 1943 Sikorski and his entourage departed Cairo on a four-engine Consolidated Liberator II registration number AL523 for a return trip to the United Kingdom with an overnight stop in Gibraltar that afternoon.

ARRIVAL AND DEPARTURE

In the late afternoon of Saturday 3 July 1943, AL523 approached Gibraltar's North Front airfield, turned onto its final approach and set down at 18:37. The Liberator taxied to the airfield's north apron where a group of dignitaries and ground staff stood in the afternoon warmth. As Sikorski disembarked, he was greeted by the governor of Gibraltar, General Mason-MacFarlane; plus Air Commodore Sturley Simpson, Admiral Edward Collins; the Polish military mission chief in Gibraltar, Lieutenant Ludwik Łubieński and a host of other officers. Afterwards Mason-MacFarlane led Sikorski and his entourage to waiting cars that drove them to the governor's residence. As the motorcade left officers of the RAF station's No. 27 ADRU (Air Despatch and Reception Unit) boarded AL523, checked off its passengers and cargo against the aircraft manifest and searched for contraband or unauthorized passengers.

In attendance was No. 511 Squadron's maintenance unit commanded by Sergeant Norman Moore, he and ten airmen were to service the Liberator. Sergeant Moore asked AL523's captain, Flight Lieutenant Prchal, and flight engineer, Sergeant Kelly, if the aircraft was serviceable. Both replied that the Liberator was in perfect order. Moore had his senior corporal, William Davis, put a continuous guard on the aircraft. He further instructed Davis that an airman was to remain on the aircraft throughout the hours of darkness, keeping near the rear entrance hatch. In addition to the RAF guard a British army sentry from No. 2 Platoon, Independent Company, King's Regiment, Gibraltar was posted, the sentry being relieved every two hours by another.

That evening Sikorski and his party dined with the governor at his residence and afterward retired for the night. Towards midnight Ludwik Łubieński drove down to the airfield with Sikorski's private secretary Adam Kulakowski to retrieve decorations and ribbons left on AL523 that Sikorski wished to confer on some of the

Consolidated Liberator II AL522 pictured on North Front airfield. This aircraft was identical to AL523 and flown to Gibraltar to assist investigators with technical details of the crash. (After the Battle *No. 20)*

Sikorski inspecting a contingent of Polish troops at Government House Gibraltar on the afternoon of 4 July 1943. (After The Battle *No. 20)*

Gibraltar officers the following day. At the airfield, the pair were barred by two sentries. After explaining their presence, they accompanied Łubieński and Kulakowski to the Liberator where an RAF airman inside the aircraft retrieved a briefcase, the pair then drove back to the governor's house.

The following morning at 07:00, Soviet ambassador Ivan Maisky arrived at Gibraltar; his aircraft – a BOAC Liberator III G-AGFR[21 22] – was later parked near AL523. The Soviet party was brought to the governor's residence where Mason-MacFarlane arranged their accommodations in a distant wing of Government House far from Sikorski and his entourage. After breakfast Maisky was taken on a quick sightseeing tour before departing Gibraltar at 12:03.[23] At 13:00 in the garden of Government House Sikorski inspected a Somerset Light Infantry guard of honour standing to with its regimental band.

He then presented General Mason-MacFarlane and Admiral Sir Frederick Edward Collins with a traditional Polish decoration, the Order of Polonia Restituta. Afterwards there was an official luncheon given by the governor attended by his three service commanders. Later in the garden of Government House, Sikorski inspected ninety-five Polish soldiers evacuated from Spain and waiting for transport to Britain. He then spent the remainder of the afternoon with British War Minister, Sir James Grigg being shown Gibraltar's tunnels and defences. Sikorski's next engagement was at 18:00 in the Gibraltar Garrison Library Garden to commemorate the 167th anniversary of the American Independence. His daughter Zofia in the meantime went into town accompanied by Lieutenant Łubieński to buy a few small items and gifts for her family and some southern fruit which was hard to get in England.[24] Two hours later he returned to Government House for dinner where a message from Flight Lieutenant Prchal said take-off was scheduled for 23:00.

Sikorski and his entourage arrived at North Front that evening accompanied by Mason-MacFarlane and his senior officers. With AL523 ready to depart passengers began boarding while Sikorski shook hands with the governor and his party before being last to climb aboard. Shortly after Sikorski entered, the Liberator's engines were started one by one. AL523 taxied slowly to the runway's far end and sat for several long minutes as Prchal ran through his take-off checks. Satisfied that AL523 was ready, at 23:07, he opened the throttles to forty inches of boost. As the Liberator accelerated his co-pilot, Squadron Leader Herring, took over the throttles and opened them to forty-eight inches at Prchal's order. Mason-MacFarlane and several of his party wandered to the edge of the runway and waved to the Liberator as it roared past then climbed upward, blue flames pulsing steadily in the darkness from each exhaust. The governor and others had begun to leave when they noticed the Liberator's navigation lights had stopped climbing and begin to descend. They waited a moment expecting the lights to rise again as was normal for many Liberator take-offs, but they did not. The aircraft continued downward, its engines abruptly stopping before it struck the sea.

Also watching AL523's take-off from his watch office was the flying control duty officer. Seeing the Liberator's navigation lights suddenly descend and hearing its engines stop before impact he rushed to his phone and called the Area Combined Headquarters who dispatched two air-sea rescue launches. In the meantime, six airmen launched a small rescue dinghy and rowed toward the crash site. Several minutes later search lights atop Gibraltar's eastern cliffs began to sweep the waters. The rescue dinghy reached the crash site within fifteen minutes and found two survivors, one was Brigadier Whiteley MP, the other Flight Lieutenant Prchal wearing an inflated life jacket. Twenty minutes later both rescue launches arrived off the end of the eastern runway. The two survivors were transferred to a launch, Brigadier Whiteley died shortly afterward. Two more bodies were recovered, General Sikorski and his Chief of Staff General Klimecki. Both air-sea rescue launches continued to search for survivors until 04:20. Of the seventeen passengers and crew only eleven bodies were eventually recovered, five being never found including Sikorski's daughter Zofia Leśniowska. That five victims were never recovered was not unusual given the strong ocean currents off Gibraltar's eastern runway. For example, on 31 October 1942 at 09:23 a No. 511 Squadron Liberator II, AL516, crashed into the sea 200 yards off the runway end in daylight. Of thirty-four occupants seventeen were fatalities two of which were never found.[25] Had the crash occurred at night the number of missing may have been higher.

From 5 July to 16 July, debris and wreckage were recovered and brought to Gibraltar's Gun Wharf dock. From here it was inspected then dismantled and moved to the northern side of the airfield close to Spanish Road where it was further examined by investigators. On 7 July 1943, a court of inquiry into the crash of General Sikorski's aircraft was formally opened at Air Headquarters in Gibraltar.

COURT OF INQUIRY

Thirty original documents and transcripts of testimony from The National Archives' AIR 2/9234 detail the court of inquiry's proceedings and findings and are presented in their entirety in the appendix. Readers are strongly encouraged to first read through these transcripts for context as these will be referenced to throughout the book. A court of inquiry into the accident was held in Gibraltar on 8 July 1943 and adjourned on 19 July. Air Commodore Philip Simpson summarized the inquiry's findings on 24 July. Air Marshal Sir John Slessor re-convened the court in England at RAF Coastal Command Headquarters on 3 August 1943, the proceedings closed on 8 August with Slessor summarizing the inquiry's findings and conclusions on 11 August. The court considered that Flight Lieutenant Prchal was in no way to blame for the accident, nor was any reason found for the elevators becoming locked. On 1 September the Air Ministry drafted an official communique and sent it through the Foreign Office to the Polish government-in-exile's London ambassador Count Edward Raczyński. The communique stated that "after most careful examination of all the available evidence, including that of the pilot, it has not been possible to determine how the jamming occurred, but it has been established that there was no sabotage". The Polish Council of Ministers on 3 September objected to the communique's wording of there being no sabotage. The Poles redrafted the communique along lines similar to the British version amending the last line to read, "but it reached the conclusion that there was no question of sabotage". This proposal was communicated to the Air Ministry but was not incorporated. The official British communique was published on 21 September 1943 with the same reassurances about the absence of sabotage and a testimonial of Prchal's capabilities as a pilot.

It should be noted that a court of inquiry is not a trial to establish guilt or innocence; there is no magistrate, jury, prosecution, or defence. The purpose of a court of inquiry is to establish the facts of an accident and to make recommendations to prevent recurrence. It is an internal fact-finding investigation

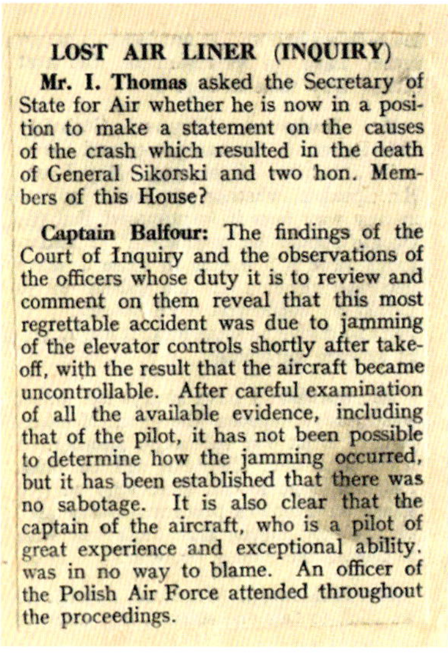

LOST AIR LINER (INQUIRY)

Mr. I. Thomas asked the Secretary of State for Air whether he is now in a position to make a statement on the causes of the crash which resulted in the death of General Sikorski and two hon. Members of this House?

Captain Balfour: The findings of the Court of Inquiry and the observations of the officers whose duty it is to review and comment on them reveal that this most regrettable accident was due to jamming of the elevator controls shortly after take-off, with the result that the aircraft became uncontrollable. After careful examination of all the available evidence, including that of the pilot, it has not been possible to determine how the jamming occurred, but it has been established that there was no sabotage. It is also clear that the captain of the aircraft, who is a pilot of great experience and exceptional ability, was in no way to blame. An officer of the Polish Air Force attended throughout the proceedings.

AIR 2/9234, 16A (The National Archives)

established primarily to assist in maintaining operational effectiveness and does not explicitly attribute blame. This policy avoids criticism that deceased or seriously injured personnel, in particular those who are unable to account for their actions, are blamed. It also protects the interests of individuals alleged to be involved and maintains the necessary separation between service inquiries on the one hand, and disciplinary or criminal investigations on the other. A court of inquiry panel consists of a president and at least two other members; however for complex inquiries, as determined by the convening authority, it may be appropriate to appoint additional or specialist members.[26]

PART II

A NEW PERSPECTIVE

CHAPTER TWO

A SABOTEUR AND METHOD REVEALED

In the evening twilight of 3 July 1943, a tall, uniformed figure calmly walked across the dusty floodlit apron of Gibraltar's RAF North Front airfield; parked nearby was AL523. As the figure made his way towards the Liberator a large white-coloured Wellington bomber lumbered past, the low-slung tail pivoting side to side as the aircraft crept from the runway onto the crowded apron, its twin engines throwing up clouds of dust obscuring the plodding figure. Rummaging among trolley accumulators, oil bowser carts, work stands, and wheel chocks the figure retrieved a step ladder. He brought it over to the Liberator where several airmen busied themselves finishing the last of their servicing tasks. Setting it next to the nose he climbed its few rungs and began wiping the cockpit windshield with a cotton rag. He then climbed down, walked over and peered thoughtfully at the massive undercarriage, the broad engine nacelles and propellers, shining a torch into shadow-darkened corners, all the while wiping at smudges and stains. He moved toward the fuselage wiping here and there, slowly making his way towards the back. At the rear he set the ladder beneath its tail, folded the rag, climbed up and quickly tucked it into a small alcove beneath the elevator then resumed wiping with another. Moving to the other side he continued toward the aircraft's nose

Bronislaw Urbański. (Peter Urbański)

cleaning randomly, stopping occasionally to examine an item before moving on. After returning the ladder he calmly walked among a group of de Havilland Mosquitos parked behind AL523 casually stooping beneath their low-slung wings and side-stepping tailplanes, his receding figure fading among angular patchworks of dull shadows. How this person was able to approach AL523 unchallenged and inconspicuous suggests his actions went unnoticed, were ignored by the guard and airmen, or taken in stride as part of the normal goings on with the Liberator and activities of a military airfield. That mysterious person was Bronislaw Urbański.[27]

Bronislaw Urbański was born in 1912 in Piotrków, Poland. In the mid-1930s he found employment with the AVA Radio Company in Warsaw and worked for cryptologist Maksymilian Ciężki. It was here he learned cryptology, wireless transmission, and worked on the Polish copy of the Enigma cipher machine. He later joined the Polish Military's Section II, cipher and intelligence bureau as an officer in the Border Protection Corps (*Korpus Ochrony Pogranicza* or KOP). The KOP patrolled Poland's borders and gathered intelligence. Bronislaw often attended meetings between Polish intelligence and British MI6 representatives, among whom were Colonel Colin McVean Gubbins and Major Peter Wilkinson of MI6 S. In July 1939 Bronislaw was in attendance when MI6 and Polish intelligence met secretly in Pyry Forest near Warsaw. At this meeting a Polish-replicated Enigma machine and cipher material were given to French and British military intelligence representatives. At this meeting Urbański was introduced to Piotr Jan Ryback, a member of British intelligence who was of Polish descent. Ryback acted as translator and liaison and would become Bronislaw's partner in future operations. With the invasion of Poland on 1 September 1939, Bronislaw was tasked with a platoon of soldiers to escort the British military mission, Colonel Colin McVean Gubbins, Major Wilkinson, the Polish army Marshal Rydz-Śmigły, General Adrian Carton de Wiart, Piotr Ryback and the Polish Cipher Bureau out of Poland into Romania.[28] Efforts to reach the Romanian border became chaotic as more and more Polish army units withdrew south. Though the British military mission, Polish Cipher Bureau and others escaped over the border, Bronislaw, Ryback, and the platoon were unable to. Left

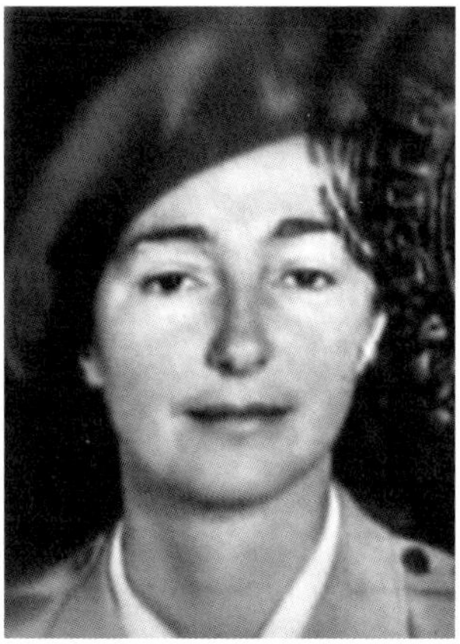

Krystyna Skarbek, alias Christine Granville.

with few options they hid and eventually surrendered to the Germans rather than the Soviets.

Many removed their rank, changed clothing, and made new dog tags for fear of being shot by Soviet forces if discovered to be Polish officers. Urbański and Ryback were in time separated with Bronislaw sent to Stalag VB. While at this compound he suffered a fractured skull when struck with a rifle butt by a guard. In early 1942 while working as a farm labourer near Stalag VB Bronislaw managed to escape. In time he made contact with Polish operatives and soon joined the Musketeers – the Polish intelligence organisation formed in October 1939 in Warsaw by Captain Stefan Witkowski.

Here he reconnected with Piotr Ryback who had also escaped imprisonment. During these early days he was directed by the SOE through Krystyna Skarbek (alias Christine Granville) who also sent instructions to him from the Musketeers. Operations with the Musketeers also saw Bronislaw working with the Polish Resistance Group OW-ZJ (*Organizacja Wojskowa Związek Jaszczurczy* – Military Organization Lizard Union). Up to mid-1942 he and Ryback planned and carried out assassinations of Nazi officials, the OW-ZJ providing communications, documents and equipment.[29] After 1943 Bronislaw continued espionage and resistance activities in Poland and Czechoslovakia throughout 1944 to May 1945 where he took part with American forces in the liberation of Holýšov concentration camp. In April 1946 he met and married a German woman and emigrated to Adelaide Australia in November 1949 where the couple raised three children. Bronislaw died on 11 August 1984.

The circumstances that brought him to Gibraltar revolved around a growing dissatisfaction and hostility towards General Sikorski's brand of politics. This dissention had grown since the signing of the Polish-Soviet alliance. Much of the dissent towards Sikorski was found within the Polish army in the Middle East under the command of General Anders.[30] Further dissention simmered within the ranks of the Musketeers, with the group had operatives throughout Europe and long-standing connections with British MI6.

As commander-in-chief and prime minister of the Polish government-in-exile, Sikorski had grown increasingly worried about the Musketeers' political influence. Earlier in May 1941 he had withdrawn support for the Musketeers. Sikorski saw

Witkowski's organization as a threat to Poland, highly secretive, and possibly collaborating with the Nazis.[31] Sikorski had learned that Witkowski had sent resistance cell leader Lieutenant Szadkowski on a clandestine mission to the USSR. Szadkowski was to contact General Anders with instructions to collaborate with the Germans against the Soviets.[32] These instructions were allegedly issued by Polish Field Marshal E. Rydz-Śmigły.[33] The Polish Home Army in August 1942 suspected Witkowski of collaboration with the German military intelligence service Abwehr, and Gestapo. In April 1942 General Sikorski was pursuing his own policy of detente with Stalin. Many senior officers in General Anders' army were incensed with Sikorski's apparent willingness to let Poland's eastern provinces be the price for an alliance with the Soviets against the Nazis. In March 1942, an alleged assassination attempt was made on Sikorski when an incendiary bomb was found on his plane. Another alleged attempt in December 1942 saw the engines of his aircraft suddenly lose power on take-off.

Krystyna Skarbek had by now been recruited into MI6 Section D as a courier taking propaganda into Poland from Hungary. However, the Polish II Bureau based in England questioned the reliability of the intelligence data she brought back as it often came from the Musketeer resistance group. Resistance groups in Poland did not trust Krystyna because of her Musketeer associations. The Polish II Bureau was further distressed that Krystyna bypassed them and sent information to British intelligence. On 18 September 1942, the Polish Home Army's military court issued a death sentence on Witkowski which was signed by the Home Army's commander Brigadier-General Tadeusz Komorowski and approved by his deputy General Stefan Rowecki. Stefan Witkowski's execution was carried out by a group dressed in German gendarmerie uniforms.[34] Afterward the Gestapo arrested Musketeers in Warsaw, Krakow, and other cities. It was suspected that Rowecki or II Bureau had tipped off the Gestapo.[35] The assassination of Witkowski, betrayal of Musketeers to the Gestapo, and the unresolved Polish borders issue upset surviving members including Urbański and Krystyna Skarbek. It was at this juncture that Urbański found himself in Iran in early 1943 under a false identity in Polish II Corps. In April 1943 he was assigned to wireless signals duties during Operation Vulcan where the Allies struck Italian and German forces in Tunis, Cape Bon, and Bizerte from 22 April 22 to 12 May 1943.

Rumours began circulating that Sikorski would be assassinated by a group of extremists led by General Anders' aide-de-camp Captain Klimkowski during his forthcoming Middle East visit in June. In March 1943, Krystyna was approached by

Captain Klimkowski. Aide-de-camp to General Anders.

Klimkowski who was fanatically anti-Sikorski, anti-Soviet and held extreme right-wing views; they met in Cairo's Continental Hotel. There had already been an abortive coup to replace Sikorski with General Sosnkowski in early 1943. In April the mass graves of Polish officers were found in the Russian forest of Katyn. Though Sikorski demanded a Red Cross investigation the British government pressured the Poles to withdraw the request. This further drove Klimkowski and factions within II Corps to conclude that Sikorski had betrayed Poland by selling it to the Soviets and Britain through his passivity and slowness. They felt it was necessary to cooperate with the Nazis against Soviet territorial ambitions.[36] Throughout this period, Krystyna passed instructions and helped organize efforts by surviving Musketeers and factions within II Corps to eliminate Sikorski. It was sometime after Krystyna's meeting with Klimkowski that she contacted Urbański by wireless to position himself in Gibraltar; the playing of three songs from a Polish VI Bureau radio station by a faction member in London would be his signal to move on Sikorski. Urbański's movements after 12 May are unknown, but it is presumed that he made his way to Gibraltar at some point in May, under the guise of a bodyguard transferred to protect Sikorski prior to his Middle East trip.[37] Klimkowski appears to have had no knowledge of an assassin positioned in Gibraltar and years later – in an effort to smear General Anders' name and to agitate the Polish government-in-exile – would allege that AL523's co-pilot was a British agent who deliberately caused the accident, jumped into the water and swam away immediately after the crash, and that Prchal was a participant in this plot.[38]

In *To Live Well is to Hide Well*, Bronislaw Urbański had told his son: "I was one of a dozen bodyguards for Sikorski." To date no known records, Polish or otherwise, refer to bodyguards having been assigned to Sikorski while on Gibraltar. Governor Mason-MacFarlane's statements and biography make no mention of bodyguards assigned to Sikorski during his 25 May and 3 July visits. Liaison officer Lt Ludwik Łubieński with the Polish Military Mission on Gibraltar also made no reference to bodyguards for the same dates in his memoirs. Łubieński does note that on 25 May Sikorski had gone for two private walks with no mention of attendant bodyguards.

In the first instance Sikorski accompanied Mason-MacFarlane alone on a personal tour:

> "After dinner and breakfast, the governor took the general alone without witnesses (because it is a strict secret and highly guarded) around Gibraltar's fortifications and various underground installations, which were already supposedly magnificent and nearing completion. There was still the threat of a German invasion."

In the second instance Sikorski invited Łubieński to walk with him:

> "After dinner in a family – so to speak – atmosphere, the general lay down, the people around went for a walk, and Mrs Leśniowska for tennis. The weather was beautiful and warm. So the general, after getting up, suggested that we go for a walk to the seaside, because he wanted to talk to me without witnesses about my work, about the Military Mission and about people who have already passed this way and may still pass. Only the general's adjutant, Lieutenant Ponikiewski, went with us, but he stayed away and did not hear the conversation at all. After the walk we sat on a bench by the sea. The general was in high spirits, rested, and clearly glad to be out of London and to have mostly purely military, less political, work ahead of him, and to be among his troops. He did not hide, however, that he had been warned that this inspection could be fraught with consequences and that he might even face some 'dangers'."[39]

Use of Polish guards to protect Sikorski was not unheard of and first proposed on 30 April 1942 by security officer Captain Kaminski of the Polish GHQ who supervised all security measures concerning protection of Poland's commander-in-chief. This new protocol came after an incendiary bomb incident in Sikorski's aircraft over the Atlantic on 21 March 1942. Polish guards were posted in May 1942 to Sikorski's residence in England at Iver Lodge, Buckinghamshire. The property sat adjacent to the Duke of Kent's residence whose security was overseen by a contingent of local British constabulary. Two British military policemen already assigned to protect the general were augmented by three non-commissioned Polish soldiers, Sergeant Stanislaw Heller, Corporal Jan Winklarz, and Lance Corporal Tadeusz Strzesinski. Though armed the Poles were required to dress in plain clothes and could call upon British policemen at the Duke of Kent's residence for assistance day or night if required. Along with protecting Sikorski at his residence the three guards also accompanied him while travelling by motor car and when staying in London.[40]

Twelve bodyguards protecting one dignitary seems excessive for such a heavily defended location like Gibraltar, Churchill only ever travelled with one. Sikorski's accommodations at the governor's residence, called the Convent, was guarded by armed British sentries and the Gibraltar constabulary. In addition British Field Security Sections since 1942 had been operating counter-intelligence operations to intercept saboteurs and infiltrators from Spain. Were twelve Polish bodyguards assigned to Sikorski for the duration of his 1943 inspection tour? If so were they dispersed in small groups at destinations from Gibraltar on through the Middle East? It is currently unknown if security protocols changed in early 1943 to incorporate additional guards for Sikorski's forthcoming Middle East trip with its inherent safety concerns. If indeed this is the case then given the contingent size assigned to Sikorski in England a presumed minimum of at least three guards may have been utilized as an additional security measure at the Convent during his May–July 1943 Gibraltar transits. Similar numbers might have been posted in advance at key Middle East locations in Egypt, Iraq and Lebanon. It remains unclear as to the numbers recruited nor how many bodyguards were utilized while Sikorski transited through Gibraltar or during his Middle East tour.

FLIGHT LIEUTENANT EDUARD PRCHAL

Flight Lieutenant Eduard Prchal.

Eduard Maximilian Prchal was born on 1 January 1911 in Dolní Břežany near Prague. He joined the Czechoslovak Air Force in October 1930 as part of his required national military service and was sent for flight instruction to the 41st Aviation Regiment at Prague-Kbely. On 15 October 1931 he was posted to the 4th Air Regiment's 14th Observation Squadron based at Hradce Králové. On 16 May 1932 he was promoted to corporal and graduated 1 November 1932. Upon completion of his two-year military service he chose to remain in the air force and was promoted to sergeant on 16 July 1933 and completed night-flying training on 1 July 1934. Prchal was posted to the 14th Air Regiment at Olomouc on 31 August 1934, then No. 5 Squadron of the 84th Air Regiment based at Brno from 16 April 1935 to 28 May 1937 when his air force service period finished. He remained a reservist and had accumulated 1,040 flying hours of which 300 were at night.

On 1 June Prchal joined Baťa, a Czechoslovak company based at Zlín which had production facilities in other countries and a commercial aircraft fleet to service them. Over the next two years he flew 1,260 hours for Baťa. With the German occupation of Czechoslovakia in March 1939, the Czechoslovak Air Force and civilian air fleets were grounded and disbanded. Prchal left Baťa on 22 June and went to Poland with other Czechoslovak airmen. From Gdynia they travelled by ship to France arriving on 30 June.

In France the Czechoslovak airmen were given the choice of enlisting with the French Foreign Legion for five years or deportation back to Czechoslovakia. Prchal joined the Foreign Legion with the rank of soldat. With the declaration of war he joined the Armée de l'Air at Châtres, Seine-et-Marne on 2 October 1939 and was soon sent on a Bloch MB.152 fighter conversion course. During this period he was promoted to the rank of corporal-chef (staff sergeant). With training completed on 27 December 1939 he was posted to GC I/8 an operational fighter squadron based at Hyères on the western front flying Bloch MB.152 fighters. During the Battle of France Prchal flew sixty operational hours and achieved three aerial victories, two of which were shared.

Prchal was in Bordeaux when France capitulated. Two days later, on 22 June after flying a light communication aircraft to Bayonne he and other Czechoslovak military personnel boarded the HMS *Queen Emma* bound for Plymouth, England. Czechoslovak pilots who escaped from France joined the Royal Air Force Volunteer Reserve and were in time sent on Supermarine Spitfire and Hawker Hurricane conversion courses. Prchal went on a Hurricane conversion course and was later posted as a sergeant to No. 310 Czechoslovak Squadron at Duxford on 12 July 1940 flying the Hurricane Mk I. During the Battle of Britain Prchal achieved four aerial victories two of which were shared. During his second aerial victory he was wounded and belly-landed his damaged Hurricane on a beach three-and-a-half miles south-east of Hornchurch, Essex. Prchal was awarded the Czechoslovak War Cross twice for his achievements during the Battle of Britain.

On 1 March 1941 Prchal was promoted to flight sergeant and posted on 6 March to No. 55 Operational Training Unit (OTU) where he served as a fighter pilot instructor. On 16 July he was posted to No. 54 OTU at Church Fenton and sent on a night-fighter course then later posted to No. 255 Squadron at Hibaldstow on 12 August where he trained on twin-engine Bristol Beaufighters. Approximately ten hours of instrument instruction was given at the start of a night-fighter course though most pilots were already very skilled instrument flyers before arriving at an OTU. Classes were made up primarily of older pilots having much operational experience including a lot of instrument flying with Bomber Command, Fighter Command, and Coastal Command. Night-fighter pilots operated under instrument conditions nearly all the time, particularly in winter. Every mission required some use of instruments as visibility was very bad particularly at higher altitudes while flying through cloud.[41]

Prchal was posted to No. 68 Night Fighter Squadron at High Ercall on 16 September 1941 receiving a commission on 19 December rising to pilot officer then to flying officer on 10 January 1942. Prchal flew only four operational patrols for a total of 5.1 hours; in October two of forty-eight patrols with a further two of twenty-three patrols in November 1942.[42] The squadron flew only one patrol in December 1942. Winter saw the squadron fly a reduced number of operational patrols between January and February 1943 with patrol activity increasing in March and April. Prchal and other pilots when not on patrol maintained their night-interception skills through squadron practice sorties involving night-flying tests, cross-country flights, night and dusk landings, GCI (ground-controlled interception) practice and calibration, searchlight co-op practice, AI and Uncle (airborne radar interception) approaches, Granny Homing or GH (Gee-H, radio navigation system) practice, air tests and local flying. On 23 April he transferred to Transport Command and was posted to No. 116 Squadron at Heston where he remained until 3 June. Prchal's next posting was to No. 1425 Flight at Portreath, Cornwall where he flew the twin-engine Lockheed Hudson Mk III flying military personnel at night from Portreath UK to Gibraltar and Malta and back. Between 17 June and 30 December he made twelve flights to Gibraltar and fourteen flights to Malta amounting to 183.20 flying hours. On 22 December 1942 he was promoted to flight lieutenant and transferred to No. 511 Squadron at Lyneham where he flew passengers, freight and VIPs to the Middle East and Far East in the four-engine Consolidated Liberator II.[43] At the time of the 4 July 1943 Gibraltar accident Prchal had accumulated 292.10 hours flying the Liberator, 171.20 of those hours at night.[44] Also during this period he had made nineteen flights to Gibraltar with the Liberator.[45] After recovering from his injuries sustained there Prchal returned to flying with No. 511 Squadron from September 1943 through to January 1944. In February he was posted to the RAF's Atlantic Transport Group based at Dorval, Canada. From 10 February to 9 May 1944, he flew Liberator and Douglas C-47 aircraft to North Africa along a southern route through the Bahamas and Brazil to destinations as far as Karachi, India (now Pakistan). During this period he accumulated a further 232 flying hours of which 103 were night flying. [46]

UNDERSTANDING AN UNCOMMON SABOTAGE AS TOLD BY CHRIS WROBLEWSKI

When first reading Peter Urbański's work *To Live Well is to Hide Well* I struggled to understand how a simple green cleaning rag externally stuffed into the elevator of a Consolidated Liberator could potentially jam or lock them after take-off. Examining pictures of Liberator tail assemblies I could see no possible way that a cotton rag might jam an elevator from outside the aircraft. Perhaps Peter's father, Bronislaw, was unclear and had instead gained access inside AL523 and somehow jammed or fouled a cable, pulley, chain, or lever? An examination of Liberator technical manuals and elevator-control system diagrams revealed several potential points of sabotage, but each would have involved noisy, time-consuming access. Even if our saboteur had managed to jam some internal elevator component it would have been immediately evident to the flight crew during pre-flight function checks; AL523 would have never departed. I had to ask myself how could the elevator-control system be sabotaged in such a manner that allowed it to function normally then suddenly jam in flight? There appeared to be no obvious method, was it even possible? The only way it seemed to gain a better appreciation and understanding of the accident was through the surviving pilot's testimony.

As an experienced aircraft technician, after much thought and research I had to consider the possibility that a simple cotton rag could have caused AL523's crash. You might say what, how? A cotton rag brings down a fully loaded 54,000-lb (twenty-seven-ton), four-engine transport, impossible! That was my initial impression, but many years fixing aircraft has taught me small things sometimes cause big problems. That being said, I have worked on maintenance issues where flight controls have been compromised by ceased components or objects obstructing their movement which often multiply effort at the pilot's control column, as I have stated earlier. With this in mind, a closer examination of the external structure of a Liberator's elevator, particularly where it met the fuselage, revealed a triangular-shaped alcove. Protruding through this alcove was a thick control tube, or torque

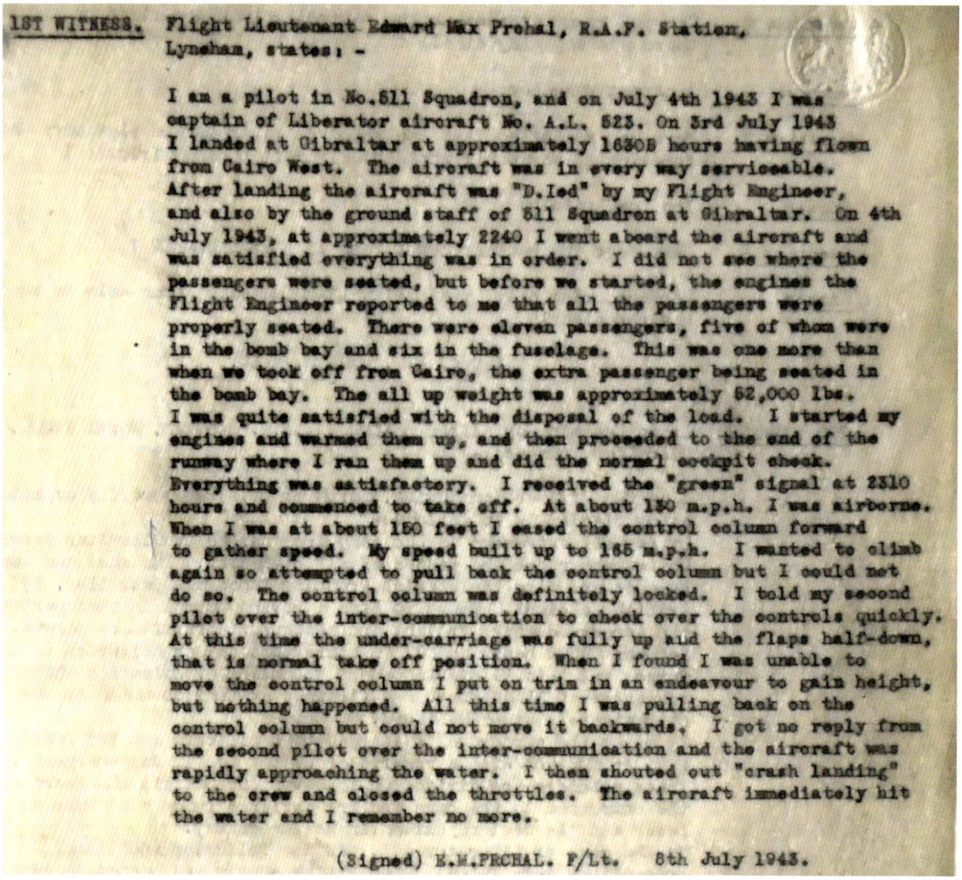

1ST WITNESS. Flight Lieutenant Edward Max Prchal, R.A.F. Station, Lyneham, states: -

I am a pilot in No.511 Squadron, and on July 4th 1943 I was captain of Liberator aircraft No. A.L. 523. On 3rd July 1943 I landed at Gibraltar at approximately 1630B hours having flown from Cairo West. The aircraft was in every way serviceable. After landing the aircraft was "D.Ied" by my Flight Engineer, and also by the ground staff of 511 Squadron at Gibraltar. On 4th July 1943, at approximately 2240 I went aboard the aircraft and was satisfied everything was in order. I did not see where the passengers were seated, but before we started, the engines the Flight Engineer reported to me that all the passengers were properly seated. There were eleven passengers, five of whom were in the bomb bay and six in the fuselage. This was one more than when we took off from Cairo, the extra passenger being seated in the bomb bay. The all up weight was approximately 62,000 lbs. I was quite satisfied with the disposal of the load. I started my engines and warmed them up, and then proceeded to the end of the runway where I ran them up and did the normal cockpit check. Everything was satisfactory. I received the "green" signal at 2310 hours and commenced to take off. At about 130 m.p.h. I was airborne. When I was at about 150 feet I eased the control column forward to gather speed. My speed built up to 165 m.p.h. I wanted to climb again so attempted to pull back the control column but I could not do so. The control column was definitely locked. I told my second pilot over the inter-communication to check over the controls quickly. At this time the under-carriage was fully up and the flaps half-down, that is normal take off position. When I found I was unable to move the control column I put on trim in an endeavour to gain height, but nothing happened. All this time I was pulling back on the control column but could not move it backwards. I got no reply from the second pilot over the inter-communication and the aircraft was rapidly approaching the water. I then shouted out "crash landing" to the crew and closed the throttles. The aircraft immediately hit the water and I remember no more.

(Signed) E.M.PRCHAL. F/Lt. 8th July 1943.

Witness statement.

tube, which connected the two elevators. This tube imparted simultaneous up or down movement to both elevator surfaces through internal control rods inside the fuselage.

Of further significance were the structural U-shaped end ribs of the elevator and its opposite stationary fairing. These U-shaped end ribs faced each other forming a wide double U-channelled cavity between the elevator and its stationary fairing with a narrow, finger-sized gap between them. It is within this U-channelled cavity, just behind the control tube, where I suspected Urbański placed his green cotton rag. From there I envisioned the rag migrating rearward as airspeed increased, compacting under an air load in the narrowing U-channel and locking the elevator to the stationary fairing surface.

The theory as to how I believe AL523 was sabotaged is described in three parts on the next pages. Part One describes through illustrations the basic operation

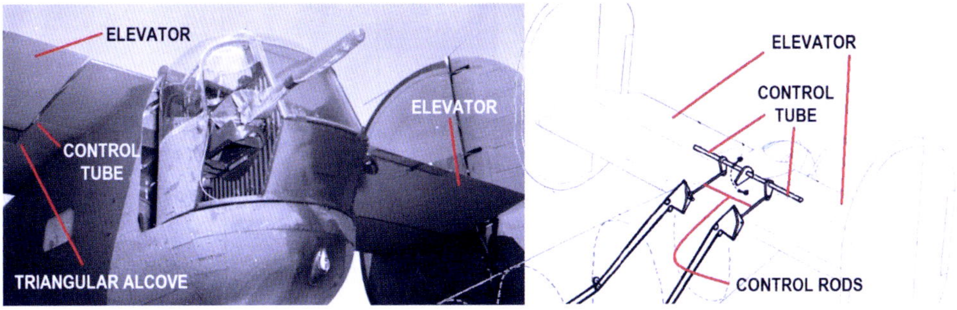

Elevator diagram.

of an elevator and outlines how AL523's were potentially sabotaged. Part Two considers Prchal's statement that only his elevator control was locked and not his aileron or rudder controls. Part Three is a short description of the Liberator's flight control lock system and how it was suspected as a possible cause but eliminated by investigators. Each part is described in layman's language and referenced with simple illustrations.

PART ONE: ELEVATORS, STALL AND A COTTON RAG

Appreciating that many readers do not have an aviation background five illustrations have been provided to explain in layman's terms how elevators affect flight and how AL523 was sabotaged.

Control column movement verses elevator movement.

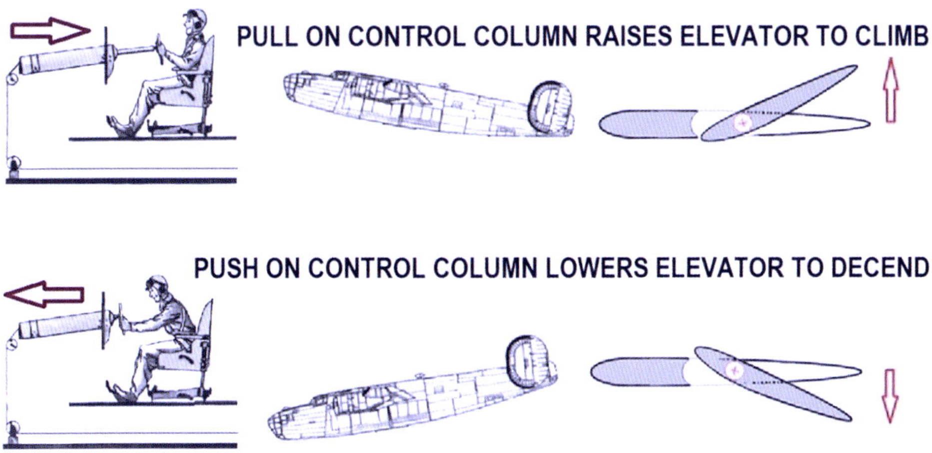

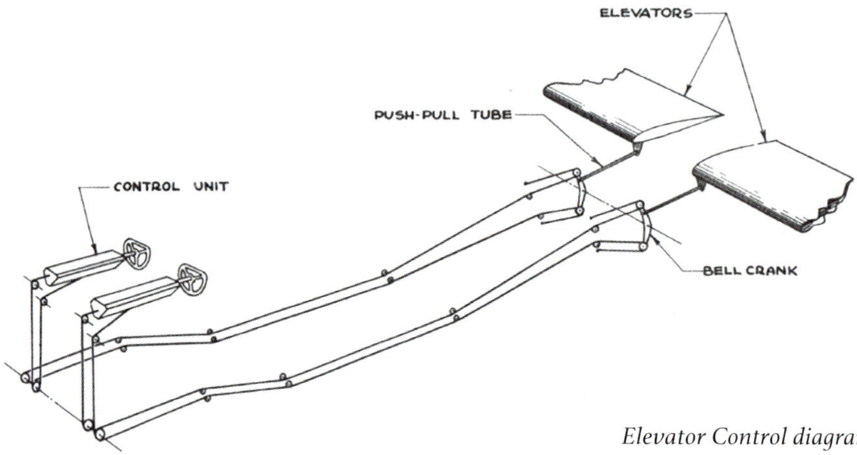

Elevator Control diagram.

Stall

One aeronautical term the reader will come across repeatedly through the course of reading this book is the word 'stall'. The ability of the Liberator's wings to generate lift is affected by raising and lowering of the aircraft nose through use of elevators. This ability to generate lift can be lost if the nose is raised too high which can induce a stall. So what is a stall?

The shape of an aircraft wing causes air to move faster over the top than at the bottom. As the speed of the air increases, its pressure decreases. This results in a lower air pressure on top of the wing than the pressure on the bottom. This difference in pressure provides lift which enables the aircraft to fly. Simply put

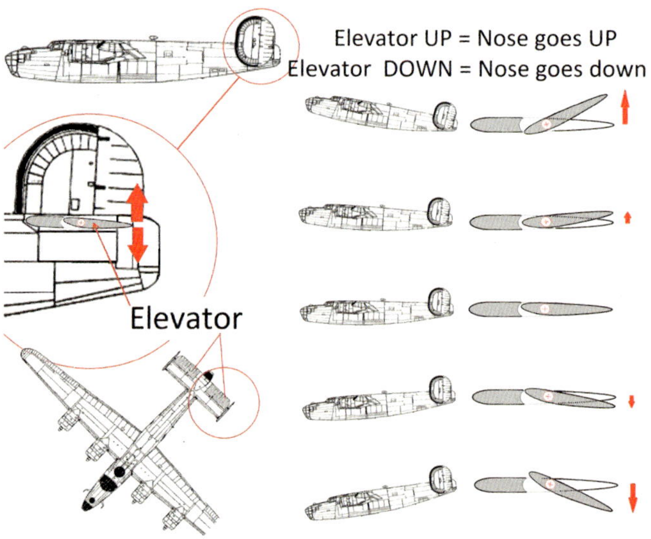

Basics of how an elevator influences aircraft flight.

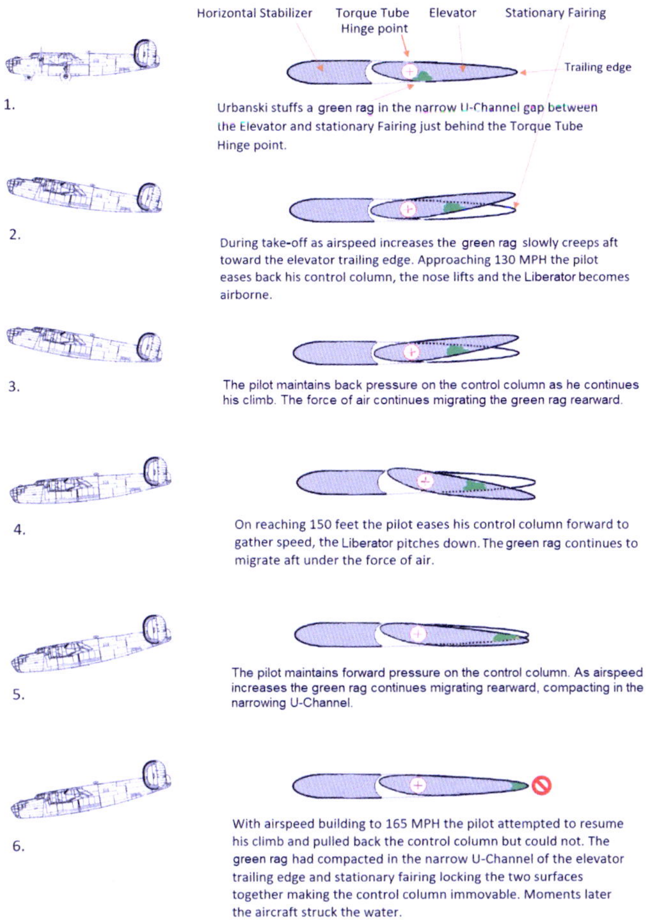

Rag movement in elevator U-channel during flight.

Rag movement in elevator U-channel during flight.

the higher pressure beneath the wing overcomes the lower pressure over the top resulting in lift.

A stall is basically a reduction of lift experienced by an aircraft. This reduction of lift is due to a breakdown of smooth airflow over the wing into a turbulent airflow resulting in a decrease in lift. This condition can occur when the wing's angle of attack is increased too much. This is known as the critical angle of attack which is typically around fifteen degrees. The Liberator's wing design was able to accommodate slightly higher angles of attack.

Left uncorrected a stall will cause the aircraft to fall. A pilot's first sign of an impending stall are sluggish flight controls which become less responsive due to changes in airflow and buffeting, conditions that pilots are trained to recognize. A stall is easily corrected by pushing the aircraft nose down to reduce the angle of

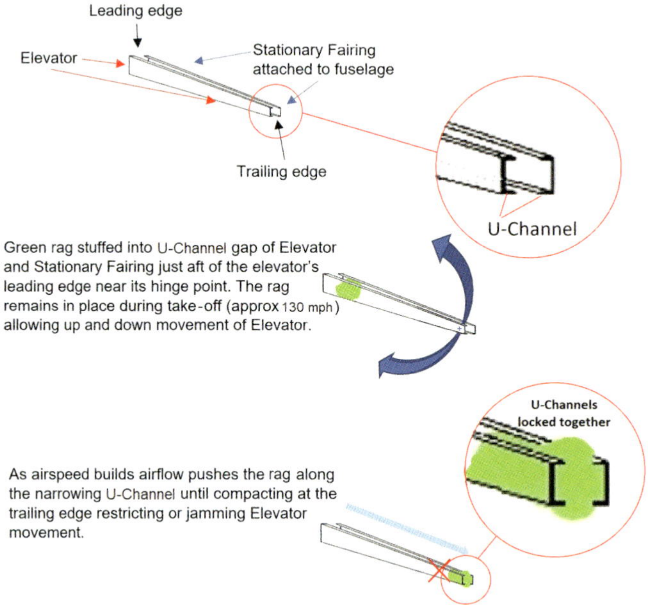

Left: *Illustration of rag compacting in U-Channel.*

Below: *Pictorial representation of diagram locations. (Library and Archives Canada Photo, No. 3583435)*

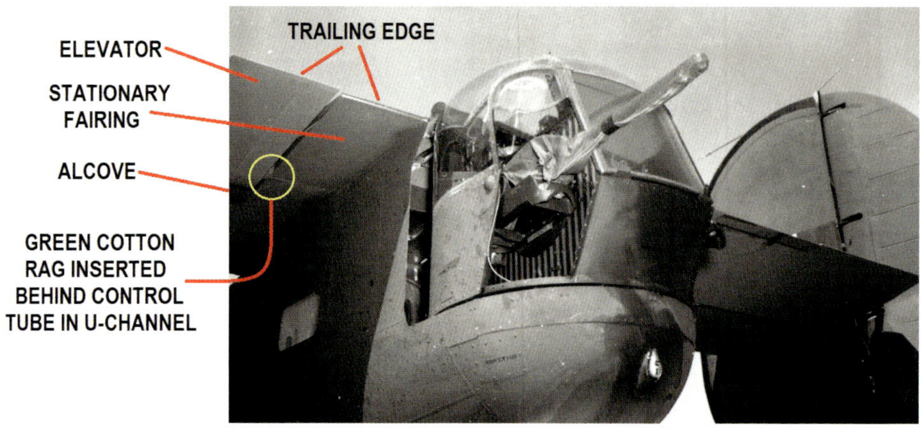

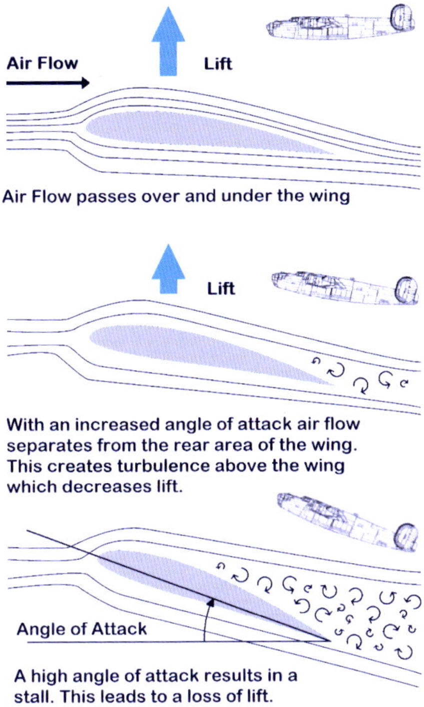

Stall diagram. (DW Deutsche Welle)

attack. This condition is more serious at low altitudes when taking off or landing. If not immediately corrected the wing loses lift and the aircraft will start to fall.

The Cotton Rag

There is little information regarding cotton rags used to service aircraft during the Second World War. What little there is can be found in a 1944 United States Army Air Force journal that reference them as *Wiping Cloths Cotton spec. no. DDD-C-503, Stock no. 7100-249000.*[47] Further journal references relate to safety precautions and incidents of negligence where rags had fouled engine and flight controls, caused engine compartment fires, and blocked fuel, engine oil and hydraulic systems.[48] Close examination of wartime films and photos of aircraft servicing show their use in virtually every aspect of maintenance and repair. Their sizes appear to be similar to a kitchen dish towel measuring approximately twenty inches by thirty inches.

The US government's Director of Procurement specification for wiping cloths stipulated:

> "That cloths for wiping purposes shall be of an absorbent fabric which shall weigh from 2 to 9 oz. per sq. yd. Each cloth must have an area of at least 2 sq. ft., and no cloth shall be longer than 30 in. or narrower than 10 in."[49]

A quick history of cotton cloth manufacturing reveals that in the early 20th century cotton mills in the United States sought to upgrade waste cotton fibres into saleable products. The first method involved bonding short cotton fibres (fibre waste) with latex and resin; these products were used mainly as industrial wipes. British-manufactured cotton cloth presumably followed suit with this method.

Recent research shows cotton to have a moderate shear strength. In 2015, shear strength experiments were carried out at the University of Zagreb on five sections

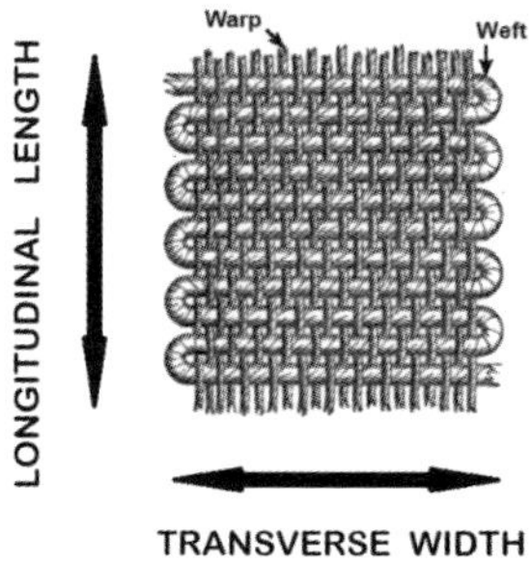

Warp and weft. (Alfred Barlow)

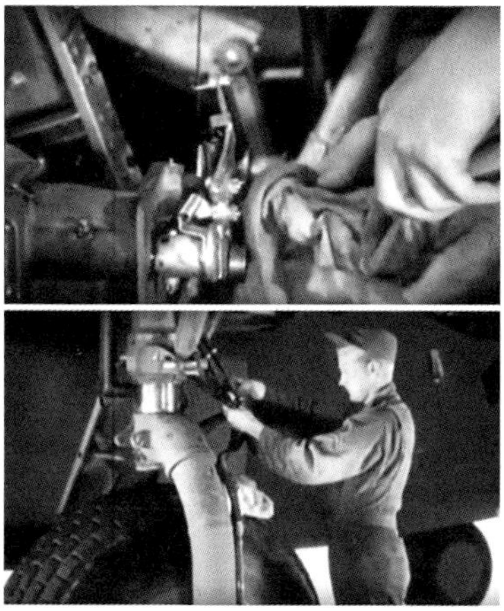

Cloth use in 1943 USAAF Training Film 'B-24 Liberator 50-Hour Inspection Hydraulics'. (San Diego Air & Space Museum)

of cotton cloth of different weave densities. Each were subjected to a shearing force against their weft and warp from zero through to ninety degrees in a tensile measuring instrument and recorded at fifteen-degree increments. The cross-woven threads of cotton cloth are known as weft and warp. During manufacture the lengthwise or longitudinal warp yarns are held stationary in tension on a frame or loom while the transverse or widthwise weft is drawn through and inserted over-and-under the warp. For the experiment, sections of cotton cloth were cut 125 x 75 mm and fastened in clamps of the test instrument at a separated distance of 25 mm. One clamp was stationary and the other movable with the test cloth subjected to a force acting in the plane of its fixed side until rupture (see images on next page). Trial results showed shear strengths rising in pounds-per-square-inch against the cloth's weft and warp at 0 degrees and peaking at 45 degrees. Approaching 90 degrees the shear strengths began to drop as the cloth began to fail.[50] The results from the trial are shown below; these have been converted from MPa (megapascal) to PSI (pounds per square inch).

Shearing force degree angle vs shear strength in pounds per square inch.

SAMPLE	0° – PSI	15° – PSI	30° – PSI	45° – PSI	60° – PSI	75° – PSI	90° – PSI
S18	69.61	81.22	248.01	577.25	203.05	84.12	75.41
S20	92.82	104.42	291.52	659.92	258.16	123.28	104.42
S22	110.22	165.34	323.43	751.29	348.09	149.38	118.93
S24	129.08	201.60	395.95	777.40	403.20	221.90	143.58
S26	150.83	232.06	464.12	841.21	526.48	284.27	188.54

Though the precise weave density of the cotton rag used to jam AL523's elevator is unknown, trial results show that similar cloths, in a controlled setting and environment, have a moderate pound-per-square-inch shear strength in the low to mid hundreds. It would not be unreasonable to assume that an industrial cotton rag bundled or folded upon itself and stuffed into a narrow space, like the area between a Liberator's elevator and fairing near the trailing edge, then subjected to a shear force from elevator deflection, would see a multiplied shear strength due to

Liberator II undergoing servicing in the Far East. Note large cotton rag in the hand of the airman. (© IWM CI 271 Imperial War Museum)

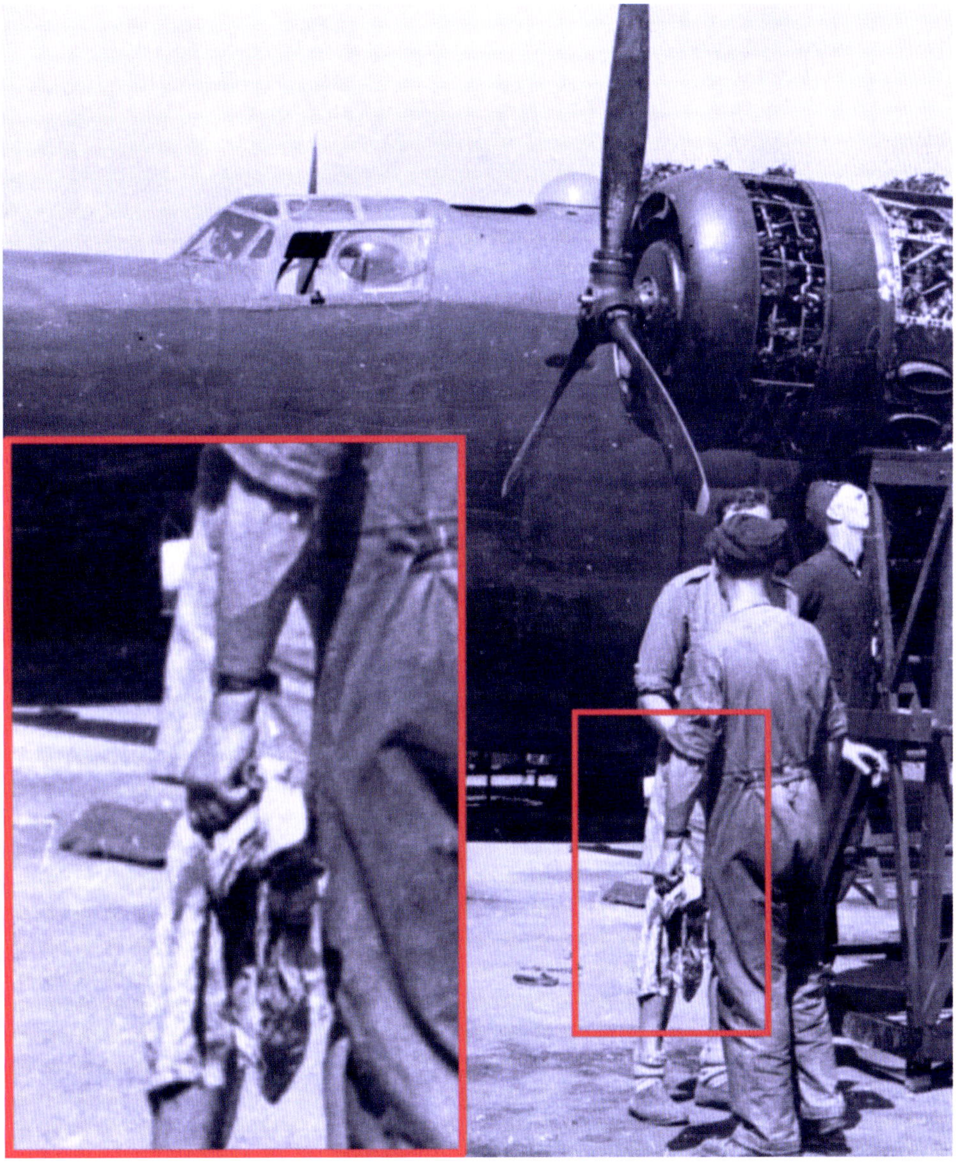

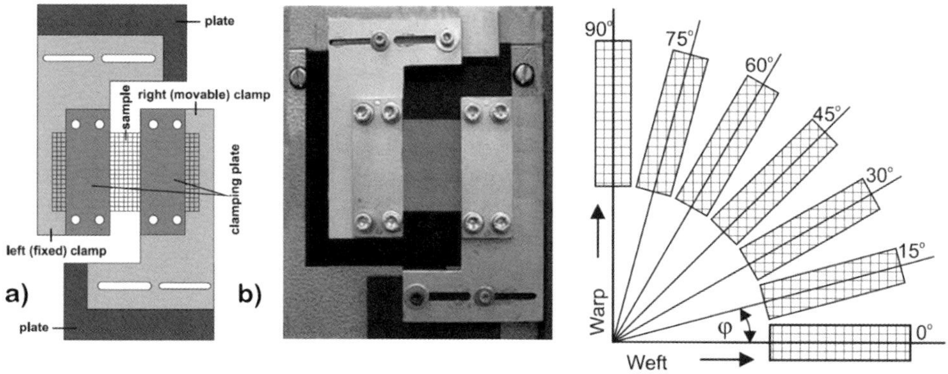

Sample testing in clamps: (a) schematic view, (b) photo of test unit. Right: Schematic view of directions (angles) applied to specimens. (Journal of Engineered Fibers and Fabrics *Volume 10, Issue 4, 2015)*

innumerable folds being compacted one upon the other. The shear strength under this condition is incalculable but would likely reach pound-per-square-inch values in the low thousands rendering the elevator immovable.

PART TWO: USE OF RUDDER AND AILERON

To further emphasize that some type of foreign object debris (FOD), such as a cotton cleaning rag, may have locked AL523's elevators I refer to the court of inquiry testimony found in National Archives document AIR 2/9234. Prchal during the inquiry repeatedly emphasized that his elevators were immovable. Not once did he say that his aileron or rudder controls were locked during his testimony.

> QUESTION 13: How did you keep Liberator AL523 straight during its take-off run on this occasion?
> ANSWER: By throttles first and then rudders.
> QUESTION 14: Can you state how much rudder you used?
> ANSWER: A very slight amount.
> QUESTION 15: In previous evidence you stated that rudders, ailerons and elevators were definitely functioning correctly when the aircraft became airborne. Why are you so certain of this?
> ANSWER: First of all I had to pull the aircraft off the runway by a considerable

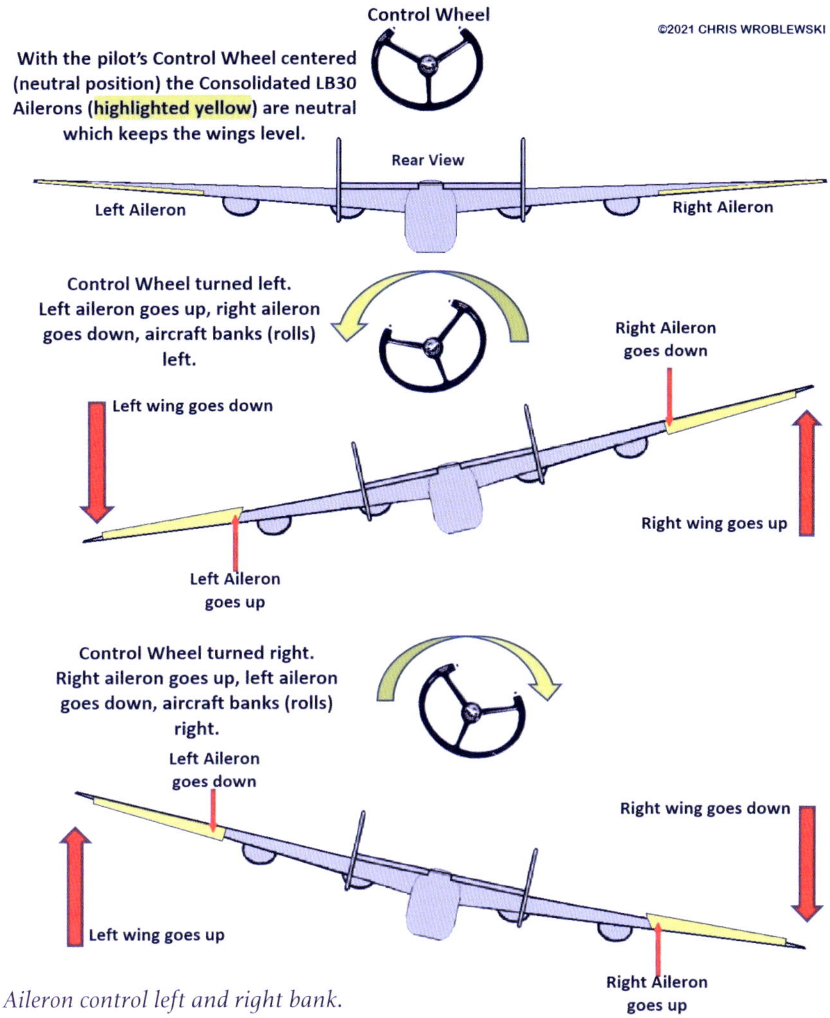

Aileron control left and right bank.

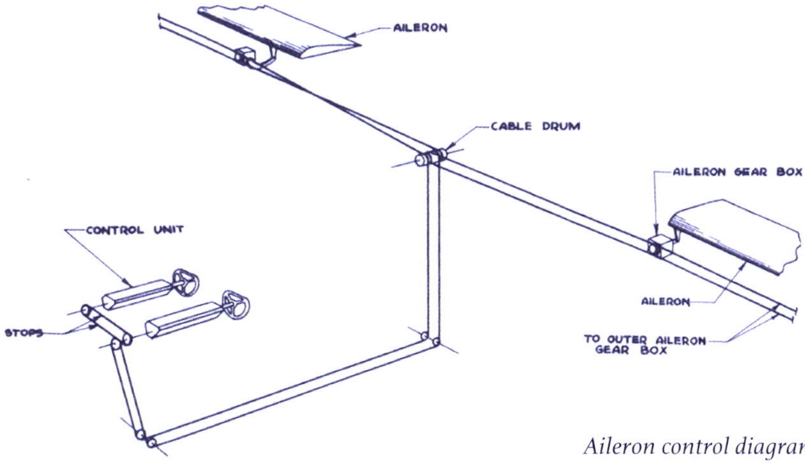

Aileron control diagram.

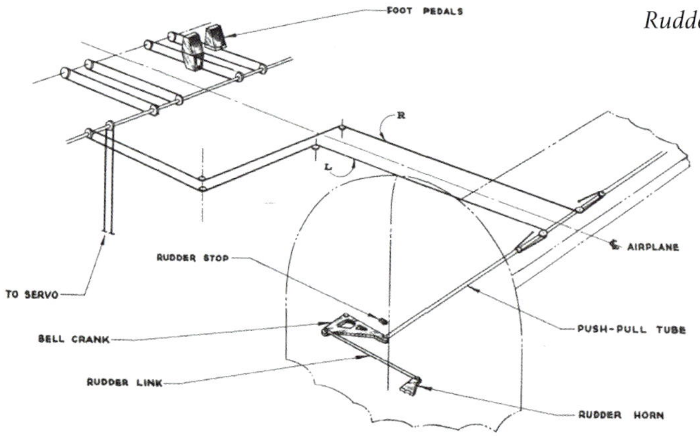

Rudder Control Diagram

With the pilot's Rudder Pedals centered (neutral position) the Consolidated LB30 Twin Rudders keep the aircraft flying straight.

Rudder Pedals Left and Right

Rudder control, neutral rudder position.

Top view

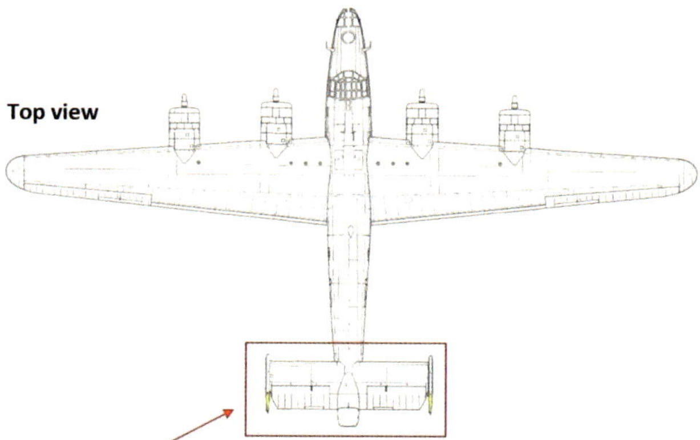

Side View

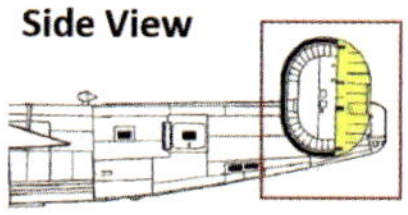

With Rudder Pedals centered the Consolidated LB30 Twin Rudders (highlighted Yellow) are centered (neutral position). Aircraft flies straight.

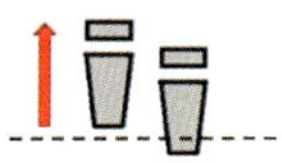

Pilot pushes left Rudder Pedal forward with their left foot. Twin Rudders (highlighted yellow) move left, aircraft nose moves left, aircraft slides (yaws) left.

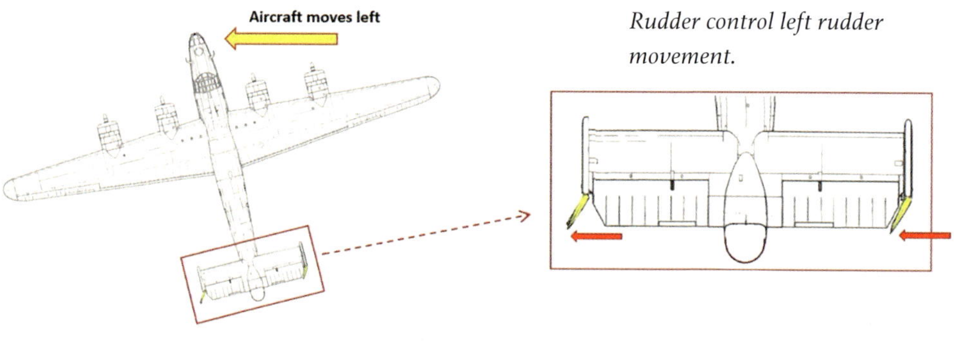

Rudder control left rudder movement.

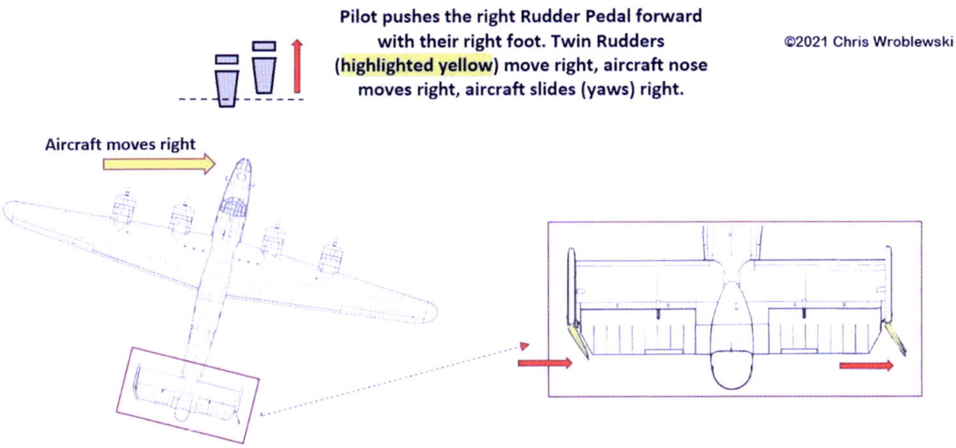

Rudder control, right rudder movement.

> movement of the control column backwards, and secondly, although I cannot actually remember operating the aileron or rudders in the air, I am certain I should have known if they had not been free.

Prchal's last statement implies that 'had' the rudder and ailerons been locked he would have also emphasized this in his testimony which he never did because they were not, only his elevators were. The possible cause was previously outlined in Part One. To give further clarity to Prchal's testimony it should be noted that when an aircraft takes off, as airspeed increases, the pilot applies inputs of rudder and aileron to counter crosswinds and engine torque which tends to induce a swing (yaw) of the aircraft left or right as well as a left or right roll. A better sense of this can be observed in a five-minute video titled 'What it's like to fly a B-24 Liberator' by AOPALive taken during take-off starting at time stamp 2:14 minutes. Flight controls are inherently heavy on all versions of the Liberator. The use of aileron and elevator in the video is obvious as are rudder inputs seen at the pilot's knees as he pushes the rudder pedals with his feet. The following images explain the basics of aileron and rudder movement.

PART THREE: FLIGHT CONTROL LOCK NOT ENGAGED

During the court of inquiry it was suggested by Prchal, and theorized by investigators, that the crash was possibly due to the aircraft's flight control lock being reengaged during take-off. Testimony by crash investigator Flight Lieutenant John Buck on 5 August 1943 made it clear that this was not the case given the undamaged condition of the locking pins:

> BUCK: An examination of the control locking mechanism showed that all locking pins were disengaged. There was no evidence to show that the locks had been engaged at the moment of impact.
> QUESTION 1: If the locking pins had been engaged at the moment of impact, what would you expect to find?
> BUCK: Signs of shearing or bending of the locking pins.

This put to rest the theory of the flight control lock having somehow caused the crash and lends further weight to an external cause outlined in Part One. An overview is provided of the flight control lock system in the image below. The system was a series of pulleys and steel cables, and though complicated in appearance it worked much like an old pulley-style clothesline. Locking flight controls prevents damage to their surfaces from wind and weather. This was accomplished by lifting the locking lever in the cockpit which overcame an unlocking spring. Three spring-loaded pins (highlighted in red) were then inserted through two rack and pinion actuators into the aileron control drum, rudder and elevator control tubes. The use of springs ensured that the pins withdrew when the controls were unlocked or if the system failed. Such a system is nowadays termed 'fail safe'. A more detailed description of the flight control lock system is covered later in the book.

Liberator flight control lock system. (Chris Wroblewski)

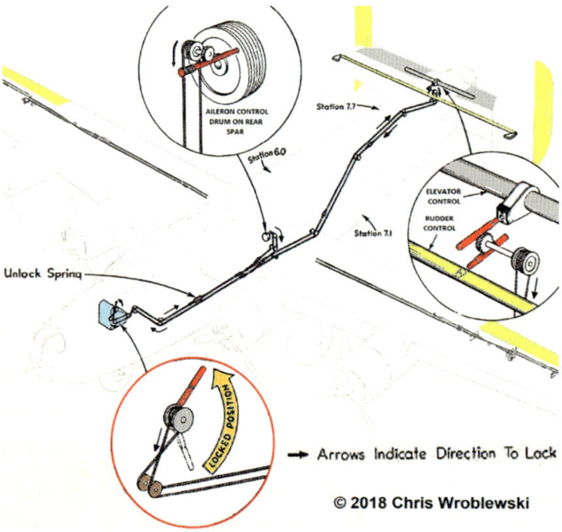

Putting Theory into Practice

Though the idea of a cotton rag locking AL523's elevator seemed a reasonable theory at this point it was little more than an educated guess described through a half dozen drawings. The real concern was the unknowns, could a cloth remain trapped within the U-channel's narrowing cavity, would it be pushed or drawn out of the finger-width gap as airspeed and airflow increased? Once the cloth's travel stopped at the narrow end would it lock the elevator to the stationary fairing? How big would the rag need to be? It seemed the only logical way to prove these unknowns would be to gain access to a Liberator, climb a ladder up to the sabotage location, tuck a cotton rag into it, unlock the flight controls and pull on the control column. Unfortunately, the prospect of gaining access to a Liberator was very unlikely considering there are few left in the world, most are on static display with only two airworthy examples flying in the United States at present. The only option was to construct a full-scale working cross-sectional replica of the elevator and stationary fairing. Detailed dimensional drawings of the tail assembly proved difficult to locate, none could be found among Liberator technical literature but eventually a 1:72 scale three-view drawing with cross-section illustrations was located. Using a 1:72 scale of 1 inch to 6 feet, an elevator airfoil cross-section measuring 47¼ inch long by 7¼ inch wide, and a stationary fairing 47½ inch long by 9¾ inch wide, was drawn out and cut from ¾-inch plywood. The last 5⅜ inch of their lengths were removed as they were too thin and narrow to support hardware.

Determining the exact width and gap of the U-channel cavity proved to be another challenge which involved examining rivet patterns in close-up images of Liberator tail planes. From a close-up image of B-24A/LB-30 registration N24927 tail assembly the stationary fairing and elevator end ribs showed them to be fastened together with ⅛-inch rivets. Using a standard edge or setback distance of two rivet diameters from the centre of a ⅛-inch rivet hole[51] gave an ¼-inch setback distance to the skin and rib edges, and ¼-inch distance to the rib vertical walls for a total width of ½ inch. With these dimensions it was possible to determine the gap between the elevator and stationary fairing to be a ½ inch for a total U-channel cavity width of 1½ inch. To replicate the U-channels, galvanized steel flash strips 1¼-inch wide and 0.015-inch thick were secured in place along the replica edges with framing screws. For additional strength a second piece of right-angled 0.015-inch galvanized steel flash was fabricated and fastened with framing screws at four locations along the last 23 inches of the replica's top and bottom portions. Two right-angle strips were fabricated from a ⅜ x ½ x 20-inch aluminium angle. The strips and both angles were secured together with ⅛-inch pop rivets. The elevator and fixed fairing are separated by a section of a black four-inch ABS Permanent Plug cut down to a thickness of 1½ inches. The plug width diameter[52] replicates the control tube that passes through the fixed fairing connecting the left and right elevators, and also maintains the double U-channel cavity width and gap formed by the elevator and stationary fairing.[53]

The replica pivots on a hinge made from short lengths of ¾ inch and 1-inch iron pipe machined to fit within one another that pass through the black 4-inch plug and 1⅛-inch holes bored through both plywood sections. The pipes are supported by ½ and ¾-inch iron floor flanges fastened to both plywood sections and black plug with eight ¼-20 inch steel bolts, nuts, and washers. The replica halves are held together with a ⅝-inch by 12-inch threaded rod and nuts. A captive spring held between two jar caps and four 1¾-inch washers maintains a light tension and friction on the replica hinge. The replica is held in place by two cradles made of ¾-inch plywood, the forward cradle supports the replica's hinge while the rear channel-shaped cradle supports the stationary fairing but only allows up and down movement of the elevator. The rear cradle's narrow channel shape simulates the horizontal rigidity of the elevator and stationary fairing by preventing their cross sections from spreading apart. Graduations from 0 to 8 degrees measured from the horizontal with a digital inclinometer were penned onto the rear cradle.

TRIALS 1 THROUGH 6

With the replica complete six videotaped trials were conducted with a 16-inch x 32-inch cotton rag inserted within its U-channel cavity.[1]

Trial 1. The replica was flipped over to expose its lower side to demonstrate how the saboteur might have inserted a cotton rag.

Trial 2. In this trial a smooth and steady forceful pull on the replica lever with a 16-inch x 32-inch cotton rag inserted within the double U-channel of the elevator and fixed fuselage fairing locked the elevator at approximately 14 inches from the end of its tapered structure when deflected up. The harder the lever was pulled above the hinge point the more solid was the jam as the rag compacted in shear with the elevator deflecting up to 6.0 degrees (replica rear mount marked in 0- to-8-degree

1. The trial videos can be viewed on Garth's website at www.aviationresearch.co.uk/sabotage.

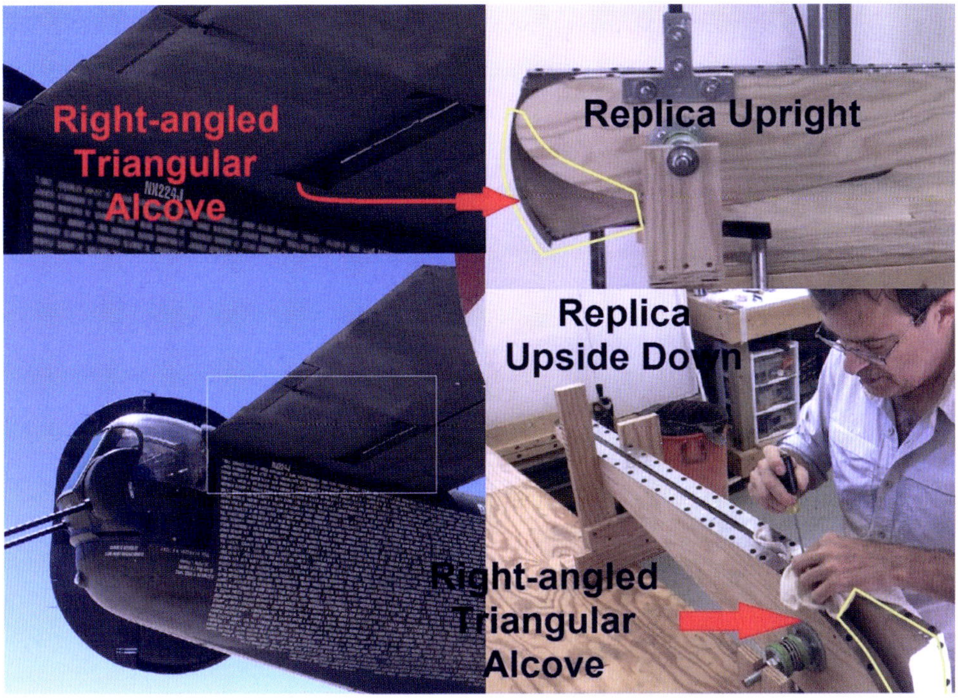

Left: Images of B-24 'Witchcraft' tail section used by permission. Right: Images by Chris Wroblewski.

gradients). Pull on the lever was stopped after 20 seconds as AL523 only flew for approximately 16 seconds and would have already struck the water.

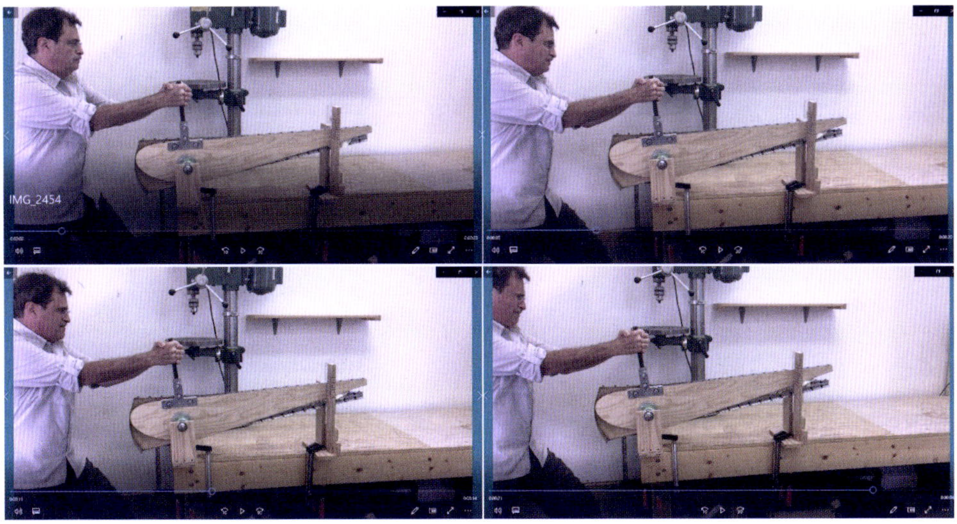

Trial 2 (Chris Wroblewski)

Trial 3. In this trial a sudden abrupt forceful pull resulted in the elevator immediately breaking free due to the elevator's shearing motion that rolled the cotton rag out from the U-channel.

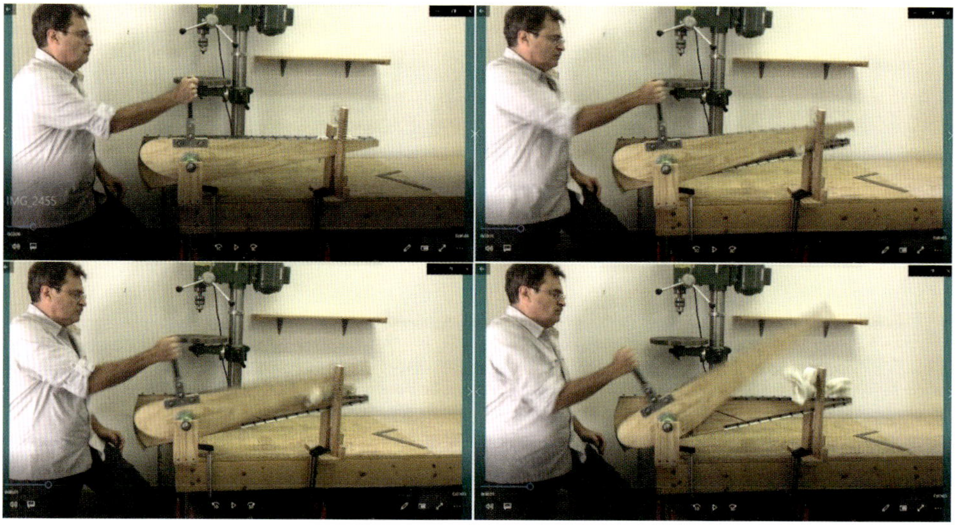

Trial 3 (Chris Wroblewski)

Trial 4. In this trial forcefully jerking the lever to impart an up and down movement to the elevator gave the same result as in Trial 3 taking approximately two seconds for the elevator to break free.

Trial 4 (Chris Wroblewski)

Trial 5. Elevator travel 30 degrees up, 20 degrees down with the cotton rag set within the U-channel just aft of the hinge point. The rag does not affect elevator travel.

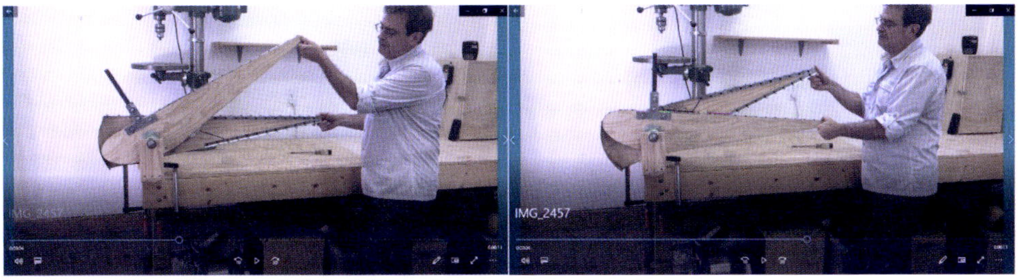

Trial 5 (Chris Wroblewski)

Trial 6. Elevator travel with cotton rag moved further aft along the U-channel. The rag has no effect on elevator travel.

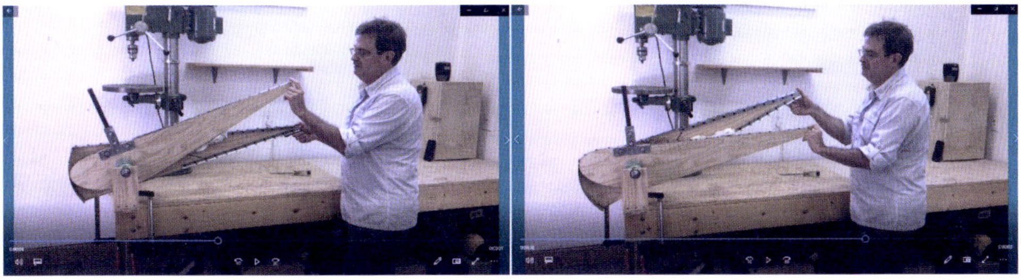

Trial 6 (Chris Wroblewski)

For each trial the following points provide context to the results

In Trial 1, the actual sabotage location on the aircraft would have been above the saboteur who would have required a ladder. As gaining access to a Consolidated Liberator is not practical the replica was turned over to expose the lower right-angled triangular-shaped alcove to demonstrate how sufficient space allowed the saboteur to easily insert a cotton rag through the ½-inch gap between the elevator and fixed fairing and into the U-channel they form.

In Trials 2, 3 and 4 it should be remembered that an aircraft's flight controls are generally not operated to their extreme limits of travel while in flight unless doing a control travel test during a pre-flight check. Also, pilot input to the control column and rudder pedals are generally smooth and controlled as seen at the beginning of Trial 2. Further to this, flight controls are generally not operated abruptly and forcefully as seen in Trial 3. In addition, pushing the control column forward to impart a jerking motion to free the elevator as seen in Trial 4 would be counter-intuitive to a pilot struggling to control a rapidly descending aircraft approaching the ground or water surface; they would not push the control column forward in an uncontrolled descent. During the court of inquiry when Flight Lieutenant Prchal was asked if the control column felt like it might go forward he replied he could not say, but if he had been higher he would have tried it.[54]

In Trial 5, with the rag inserted beneath the elevator's hinge point, a control travel check from 30 degrees up to 20 degrees down of the Consolidated Liberator's elevator travel limits would not restrict its movement. The rag remains trapped within the U-channel and would not be felt in the pilot's control column as it was moved.

In Trial 6, with the cotton rag moved further aft along the U-channel elevator travel remains unrestricted and the rag remains trapped within the U-channel and would not be felt in the pilot's control column as it was moved.

It should be noted that during Prchal's nose-down descent to gain airspeed he would be maintaining forward pressure on his control column which would deflect the elevator surface a few degrees down. This would appear to contradict results from Trial 2 showing the elevator deflected up six degrees as it binds against the cotton rag suggesting several degrees of upward travel prior to lock up. Prchal could not recall whether the column was rigid or had any play but did confirm that he could not pull it back and that it was immovable or locked, unlike during take-off where he had pulled back the column considerably which resulted in a large upward deflection of the elevator. That he could not pull the column back sufficiently to arrest his descent and raise the nose suggests a foreign object such as a pinched cotton rag was trapped in narrow U-channels of the elevator and fairing. As to how far rearward the rag would be pushed by 130 to 165 mph airflow it is uncertain. It can only be speculated that the rag was possibly pushed a little further and restricted the elevator up travel to less than six degrees. A wind tunnel test on a mock-up elevator would confirm the rag's final position. It should also be noted that with the elevator deflected slightly upward the nose would begin to rise. Unfortunately Prchal did not have sufficient altitude or time, and the nose-up trim may have also counteracted the elevator's small upward deflection restricted in place by a compacted rag.

AL523'S SIXTEEN-SECOND FLIGHT

It has been recorded that AL523's flight after take-off lasted approximately sixteen seconds. Though it is unknown as to exactly when the pilot noticed his locked elevators; if you consider that this event occurred in the last one-third of the flight then Prchal had only approximately five to seven seconds to pull hard enough on his control column to expel the rag from the U-channels. It is important to consider that even if Prchal had freed the elevators in those last seconds AL523 was already at a dangerously low altitude, pitched down approximately 15 degrees and approaching the water at 165 mph with all four engines switched off and throttles closed. A crash would have been inevitable thus rendering the sabotage effective. Further details of this flight time are discussed later in the chapter.

CHAPTER THREE

THE CRASH SEEN THROUGH COMPONENTS

This chapter examines multiple recovered aircraft components associated with AL523 including those referred to during the court of inquiry. The recovery and examination of these parts served as valuable evidence throughout the crash investigation and inquiry. Their condition attested to aircraft condition and the pilot's actions up to the accident moment. Unfortunately, none of the recovered components remain today so cannot be examined. Fortunately post-crash photos still exist as well as many documents in the form of court of inquiry records, Liberator flight, maintenance, parts, and component manuals, performance reports, service bulletins, accident reports, air force journals, government reports, and published accounts. In addition, there are surviving Liberators both flyable and on static display throughout the world. As each component is examined through these sources a new picture of AL523's crash emerges. Each is described in the context of its function and how its operation was relevant or irrelevant to AL523's performance, its pilot, and investigator perceptions. It is appreciated that many components and systems described in this chapter may be difficult to understand for some readers. So some component descriptions and functions have been pared down to their basics while others have been simplified and summarized as best as possible. Pictures and illustrations are also included to further help in comprehending descriptions and locations. In several examples alternative theories including known flight and technical anomalies were included in the interest of transparency. Not content to simply agree with the inquiry findings an effort was made to satisfy both the authors and discerning readers that all known alternative technical hypotheses, no matter how remote, were reasonably examined as best as possible, ruled out, or considered a potential contributing factor.

THE QUESTION OF TAKE-OFF WEIGHT

Though not an airframe component, weight affects aircraft flight performance and is a factor that cannot be overlooked in the crash of AL523. There is no disputing that AL523 was likely heavier than the 53,313 lbs quoted in the court of inquiry records. How much heavier remains unknown. There is also no disputing the relevancy of Liberator flight performance tests conducted by the Aircraft and Armament Experimental Establishment (A&AEE) at Boscombe Down which documented results for various weights, centres of gravity, power settings, airspeeds, take-off distances, and distances to achieve 50 feet of altitude. In short Liberators could take off at greater weights than what Prchal had on AL523.

As first stated in the introduction no attempt in the writing of this book was made to calculate the weight and take-off performance of a Consolidated Liberator II, there was no need as past researchers have already studied this in detail. It has also been sufficiently documented by witnesses that a successful take-off was accomplished by Prchal despite AL523's weight. The technique used by Prchal of hauling a heavy Liberator off by pulling the control column back smartly at 130 mph was not considered unusual by the court of inquiry. This take-off style was acknowledged as a known technique by two fellow Liberator pilots who knew and had flown with Prchal. The technique was also familiar to air accidents investigator Flight Lieutenant John W Buck.

Fellow No. 511 Squadron pilot and former wing commander Algernon Llewellyn told Carlos Thompson that he considered Prchal's Gibraltar take-off normal. He also described having "once [taken] off with a 57,000 lbs load in a Liberator, and Prchal's load sheet only indicated 54,313 [lbs]".[55] Llewellyn also said he had: "never taken off [from Gibraltar] with a Liberator loaded to the hilt. But once, with a seven-eighths load and a mild, ten-mile-per-hour breeze, I only used up about 950 yards." Thompson then asked how dangerous it was to take off with a full load. Llewellyn replied:

"With the Liberator, the only real weight danger, except from gross overall weight, comes when you overload the tail section. This, as a pilot, you would notice already when taxiing, because it was a tricycle landing gear aircraft and you could not fail to feel the tail tending to hug the ground. This is something which a first-class pilot as Prchal was, could not have failed to notice. As for the take-off behaviour of the Liberators: when you lifted the nosewheel to become airborne, the Liberator did not fly itself off the ground under the medium to heavy load – you had to pull it off. As it became airborne, it had a special characteristic: for a second or two, it would tend to raise its nose and although airborne, not to gain altitude, but this did not demand corrective action from the pilot, you simply let her find herself."[56]

Captain Josef Klesnil had flown as co-pilot with Prchal at Czech Airlines post-war, during the war he had flown Liberators with No. 311 (Czechoslovak) Squadron. Carlos Thompson asked Klesnil about Prchal's Liberator being overweight and if it was "possible that just as Prchal reached the levelling-out point, the aircraft went into a stalled configuration and was held aloft only by the sheer great power of its four engines, while travelling downwards until it hit the water." Klesnil replied:

"If she was heavy enough to stall like that, Prchal would never have been able to climb at all. And about this overweight business, you have told me that his load was an odd 54,000 lbs – I remember that later, in Coastal Command we had rockets installed in the bomb bay and we flew those Liberators without a problem, much heavier than they had ever been flown before. We went well over 2,500 pounds above the maximum allowable for the aircraft."

Thompson then asked if Prchal should have made a longer take-off run, that he should not have left about 800 feet of runway unused. Klesnil replied:

"As soon as you have the right take-off speed, you get her off the ground, for the simple reason that you have your friction to consider the sooner you are airborne, the faster you can build up speed. Even if Prchal was on top weight, he did the right thing yanking her off the ground when she indicated 130 mph. I'll say more: if he had been that *much* overweight, Prchal would never have reached his take-off speed on the runway in the first place."

When Thompson mentioned there had been a suggestion that the Liberator was "lazy on take-off" Klesnil offered that:

> "The Liberator was 'lazy' on take-off need not mean that the cause was overweight. A totally unpredictable set of circumstances could give you that effect – ground temperature, for one."[57]

Flight Lieutenant John Buck who had been an air accidents investigator assigned to the Sikorski crash was also familiar with the technique for getting a heavy Liberator off the ground. During his interview with Thompson he spoke of an identical technique told to him by an RAF pilot. Thompson paraphrased the pilot's story:

> "'I am a Liberator pilot and I took my aircraft off in the normal way one does with a heavily laden Liberator.' He went on to explain to me that the drill was to get up as many knots as you could along the runway and then hoik it into the air. He distinctly said that you do not fly it off the deck, but you just hoik it off. I think he added that it would not fly itself off. Having become airborne you then put the control forward and build up speed. On the occasion he was speaking of he did exactly this, but when some 200 or 300 feet up the aircraft dropped its tail and went into a stalled condition. I think he said that he went through the gate and on full boost the engines were powerful enough to drag the aircraft through the air in this attitude and maintain height."[58]

In summary, though pilots were initially trained to apply gentle back pressure on the control column to assist in lifting the aircraft on the undercarriage, it will easily leave the ground with a full load at 130 mph; this take-off technique soon evolved to a more aggressive style most probably as a result of operational experience and necessity. Put simply Prchal was able to take off and gain altitude because the excess weight was not sufficient enough to limit AL523's take-off performance as operational experience had dictated.

The Crash of AL503 in San Diego Bay

In the 2015 episode of *WW2 Air Crash Detectives* the possibility of a design flaw within AL523's elevator-control system was considered due to a 1941 crash in San Diego Bay California of an early production LB30 Liberator. This aircraft, AL503, was part of a British contract order for 139 LB30s. On 2 June 1941, AL503 crashed on its acceptance flight killing the five-man crew including Consolidated Aircraft Corporation's chief test pilot William Wheatley. A news report by the Associated Press of the accident stated:

> "Witnesses said the huge plane left the airport on what appeared to be a normal take-off, but that the bomber pulled up steep into a vertical climb instead of levelling off. At about 500 feet the plane apparently was in a stall. The bomber then fell off to the left, and nosed down and the pilot, using the throttle appeared to have recovered. This difficulty was experienced over the airport, but by the time the pilot apparently had regained control of the craft it was flying over the water at an altitude of about 100 feet, the bomber again fell off to the left and the wing struck the water. A Consolidated spokesman said the crash had 'evidence of sabotage'. The spokesman said the $250,000, 25-ton land bomber had been 'thoroughly tested, and things like that just don't happen'."[59]

Sabotage was finally ruled out after investigators determined that AL503's crash was due to a small machine screw having caught in the chain and sprocket of the pilot's

Recovered wreckage of AL523's pilot and co-pilot Type I control columns. The assembly is upside down with its broken control wheels facing away from the camera. (After the Battle *No. 20)*

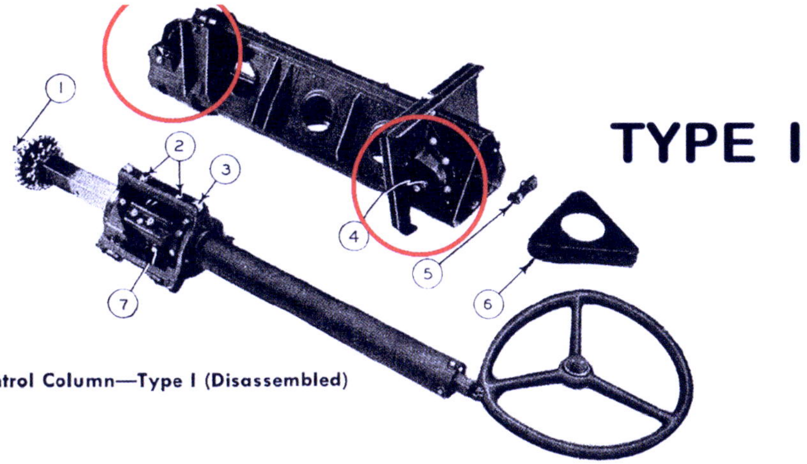

Figure 22. Control Column—Type I (Disassembled)

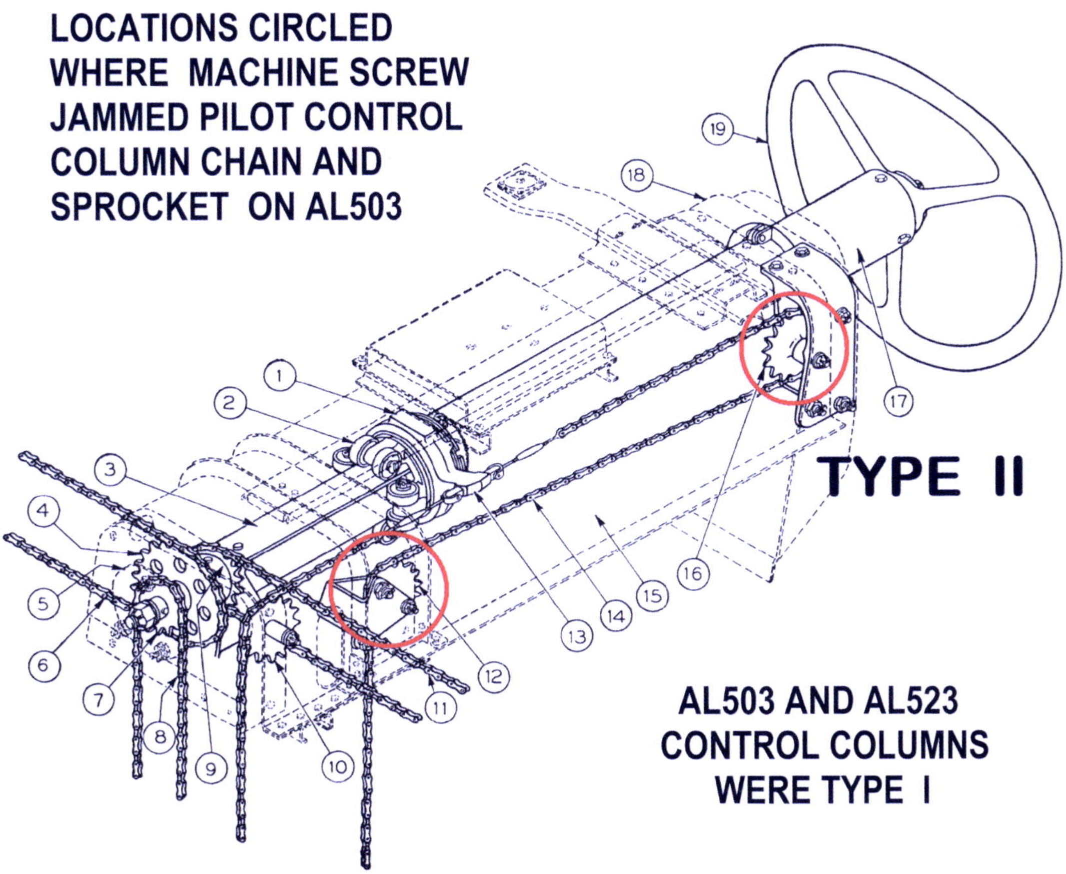

Figure 23. Pilot's Control Wheel Unit—Type II

Annotated pilot control column illustration. (Consolidated Vultee Aircraft Corp [1944], p. 24)

Type I control column (see illustration for possible locations). The hardware had wedged itself in such a manner that it locked the column mechanism causing the aircraft to climb at a steep angle.[60] AL523's control columns were also Type I. If there was any flaw it was carelessness on the part of Consolidated production staff.

Above: *Consolidated Model LB-30, Liberator B Mk II, AL503, photographed 2 June 1941. (US Army Air Forces, T.O. No. 01-5ED-2)*

Left: *The broken Type I control wheel of Prchal's control column.* (After the Battle *No. 20)*

CHAINS, SPROCKETS, MAILBAGS AND THE LLEWELLYN INCIDENT

As seen in the court of inquiry testimony, investigators had considered a similar scenario to that of AL503 having possibly caused AL523's accident. A detailed examination by Flight Lieutenant Buck of the elevator control column chains and sprockets had found no evidence of a foreign object like a machine screw having jammed them. Another consideration was the possibility of the nosewheel having somehow jammed the elevator control tube and cable chains of the pilot control columns. These chain runs were located beneath the cockpit floor which was also the ceiling of the nose undercarriage compartment. At RAF Lyneham a Liberator Mk II, similar to AL523, was put on jacks and its undercarriage retracted several times while the nosewheel mechanism was carefully examined. These tests demonstrated that such jamming of the elevator control chains was unlikely and was eliminated as a possible cause of the accident.[61]

The notion that the retracted nosewheel could have caused AL523's elevators to jam was resurrected in the early part of 1969 during an exchange of correspondence between then Marshal of the Royal Air Force, Sir John Slessor who had been president of the 1943 court of inquiry; former Wing Commander Algernon Llewellyn who had been CO of No. 511 Squadron's Liberator Flight up to May 1943; Squadron Leader Roland Falk former chief test pilot at RAE Farnborough; and publisher William Kimber of William Kimber & Co. Limited concerning historian David Irving's controversial second printing of *Accident* written in German. In this revision he alleged that the crash of AL523 was the result of "deliberate sabotage on the orders of Winston Churchill" and had removed all reference of suggestion that a mailbag had been the cause.[62 63] While internal deliberations within the British Ministry of Defence sought to formulate a measured reply to these allegations Llewellyn, now retired, had recalled an incident where he experienced fouling of his flight controls by unsecured freight caught up with his retracted nosewheel during a Liberator test flight. This incident he felt could potentially explain the crash of AL523. Falk who had been an expert witness during the 1943 inquiry had not agreed with the court's conclusion that the nose undercarriage could not have jammed AL523's elevator controls during examination of the Liberator at RAF Lyneham. Llewellyn's incident confirmed to Falk that the court may have been wrong in its conclusion

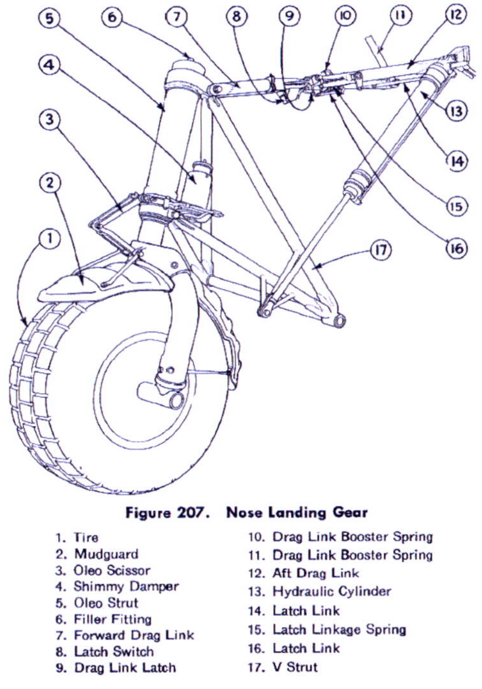

Liberator nose undercarriage component diagram.

and that an unsecured mailbag in the nose compartment was the likely culprit.[64] When Slessor became aware of Llewellyn and Falk's joint theory he concurred with their conclusions as it made complete sense essentially debunking any suggestion

Llewellyn letter to Falk, 8 January 1969. (AIR 2/15113, The National Archives)

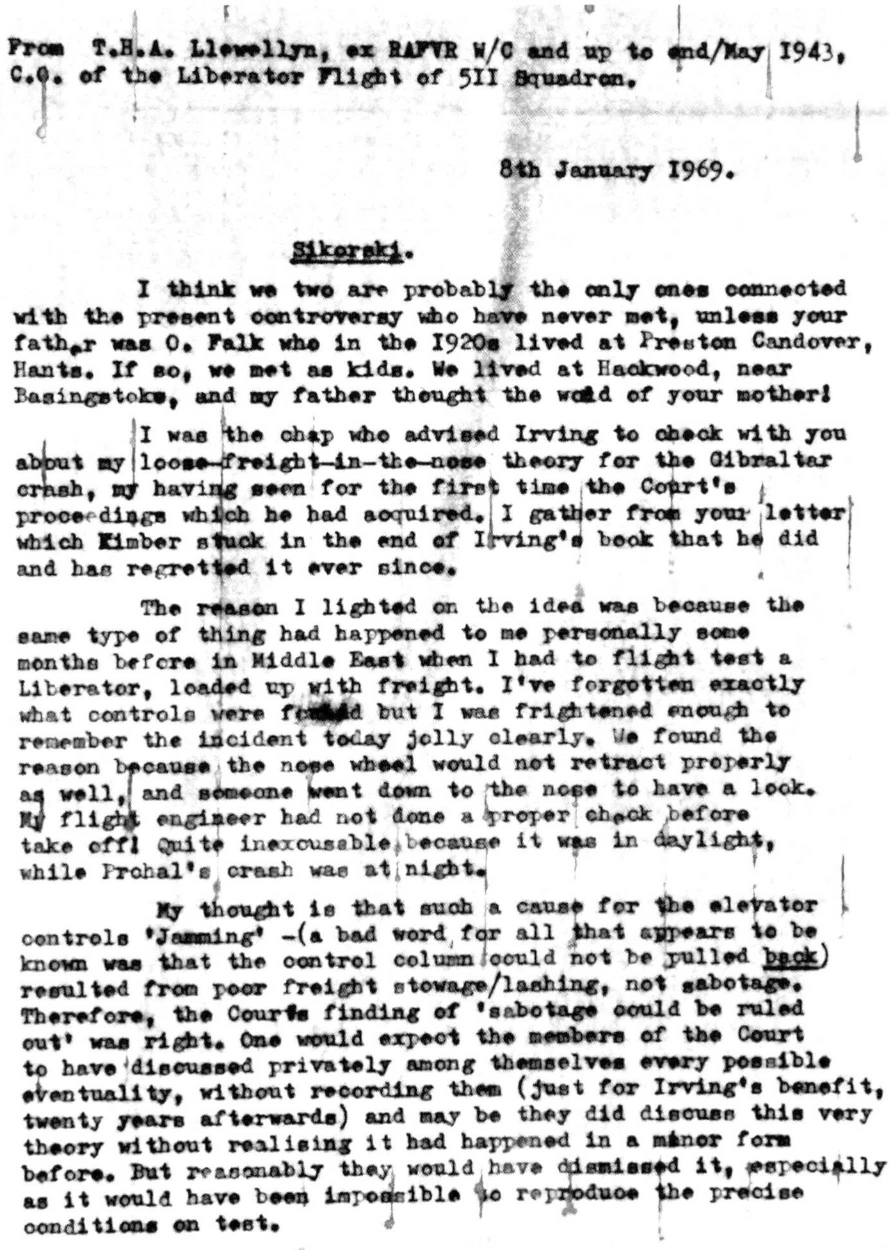

From T.H.A. Llewellyn, ex RAFVR W/C and up to end/May 1943, C.O. of the Liberator Flight of 5II Squadron.

8th January I969.

Sikorski.

I think we two are probably the only ones connected with the present controversy who have never met, unless your father was O. Falk who in the I920s lived at Preston Candover, Hants. If so, we met as kids. We lived at Hackwood, near Basingstoke, and my father thought the world of your mother!

I was the chap who advised Irving to check with you about my loose-freight-in-the-nose theory for the Gibraltar crash, my having seen for the first time the Court's proceedings which he had acquired. I gather from your letter which Kimber stuck in the end of Irving's book that he did and has regretted it ever since.

The reason I lighted on the idea was because the same type of thing had happened to me personally some months before in Middle East when I had to flight test a Liberator, loaded up with freight. I've forgotten exactly what controls were fouled but I was frightened enough to remember the incident today jolly clearly. We found the reason because the nose wheel would not retract properly as well, and someone went down to the nose to have a look. My flight engineer had not done a proper check before take off! Quite inexcusable because it was in daylight, while Prchal's crash was at night.

My thought is that such a cause for the elevator controls 'Jamming' -(a bad word for all that appears to be known was that the control column could not be pulled back) resulted from poor freight stowage/lashing, not sabotage. Therefore, the Court's finding of 'sabotage could be ruled out' was right. One would expect the members of the Court to have discussed privately among themselves every possible eventuality, without recording them (just for Irving's benefit, twenty years afterwards) and may be they did discuss this very theory without realising it had happened in a minor form before. But reasonably they would have dismissed it, especially as it would have been impossible to reproduce the precise conditions on test.

of sabotage and reinforced the court's original conclusion that sabotage was not a factor in AL523's crash. Slessor then sent letters to Irving's former publisher William Kimber & Co. detailing the new theory,[65] and also sent a similar letter to *The Times*.[66]

To appreciate how Llewellyn's flight controls may have become fouled an understanding of how various control cables and components are routed in the Liberator's nose undercarriage compartment is required. An examination of images and diagrams detailing the nose undercarriage compartment directly beneath the cockpit floor show three control cable groupings that could potentially be fouled by cargo caught in the nose strut and wheel assembly on retraction. One grouping is for flight controls, the second are engine controls, and third are for the Sperry automatic pilot. In the provided illustrations it is significant to note the location of the green pulley bracket in the floor structure relative to the elevator control and the retracted nosewheel when the images are merged together. The reader will see that the elevator control is well protected.

The most significant of the three groupings are sets of three multiple cable runs for engine mixtures (red), throttles (black), and superchargers (orange) that exit vertically from the ceiling of the undercarriage compartment and are turned left by three banks of pulleys housed within a large bracket protruding from the ceiling (see image on page 68). The cables are then turned rearward by three more banks of pulleys that direct them along the upper-left side of the ceiling. When the nose undercarriage retracts it is hinged upward by a hydraulic actuator. At the completion of its retraction the tyre assembly sits between two floor joists within a scalloped ceiling panel alcove. During retraction the nosewheel moves upward and passes directly behind the large, unprotected pulley bracket assembly housing the three control cable groupings for the engines. The orientation of the retracted wheel assembly and engine control bracket assembly is illustrated on pages 71 to 73. If during take-off a large piece of cargo like a mailbag, box, or irregular-shaped cargo were to fall across the undercarriage opening in the floor as the strut retracts, that object could potentially become entangled and carried upward. The entangled cargo would soon be wedged against the ceiling structure stalling nose undercarriage movement and potentially damaging the bracket and engine control cable grouping. This damage could result in cable jamming or abrupt cable displacement causing multiple changes in engine power settings. If one, several, or all engines abruptly lost power the aircraft would suddenly lose height and be difficult to fly if not uncontrollable during the critical phase of take-off.

The second grouping are flight control cables, chains, and torque tubes for aileron, elevator, and rudder that run along the undercarriage ceiling. All of these components are well protected by lengthwise and crosswise structural beams as seen in the opposite diagram. Like the first scenario, if during take-off a large piece of cargo were to fall across the undercarriage opening in the floor as the strut retracts that object could potentially become caught, carried upward and wedged against the ceiling. From the illustrations it can be seen that the elevator control cables (grey) run next to coves between the ceiling and fuselage sides, they are also far from the

Below: *Engine control cable routing beneath cockpit floor structure.*

Opposite: *Flight control routing beneath cockpit floor structure.*

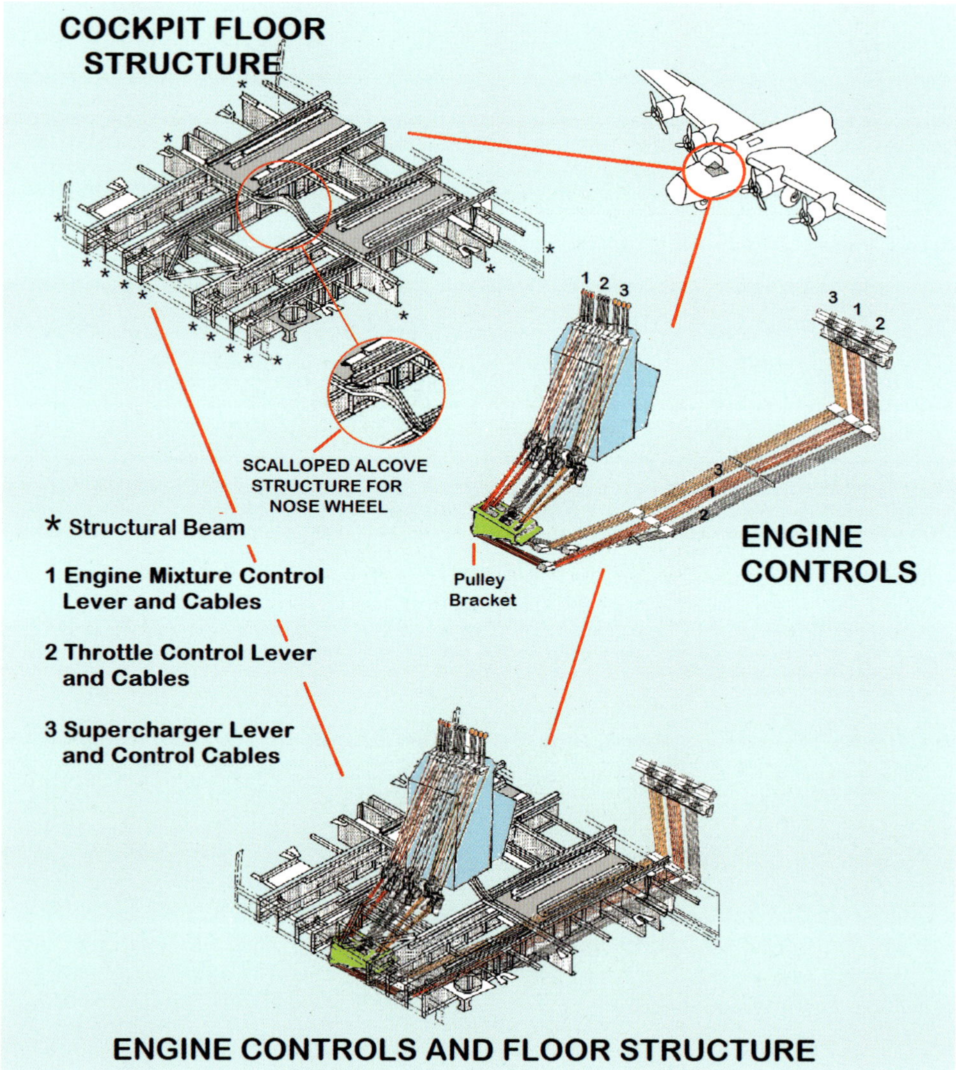

wheel alcove and protected by beams. The elevator torque and sprocket tube (grey) is well protected by a beam and pulley bracket. The aileron controls (red) sit well above the cockpit floor, are turned down and run along the far left ceiling next to the elevator cables (grey). The rudder controls (yellow) are similarly protected by beams. Given how well these controls are protected by structure the only system that could possibly be fouled by cargo would be the cable chain pairs for pilot and co-pilot rudder pedals that sit closest to the ceiling centre on either side of the wheel alcove. An irregular-shaped piece of cargo, despite the structural beams, could potentially be wedged against a chain to render the rudders stiff and difficult to move.

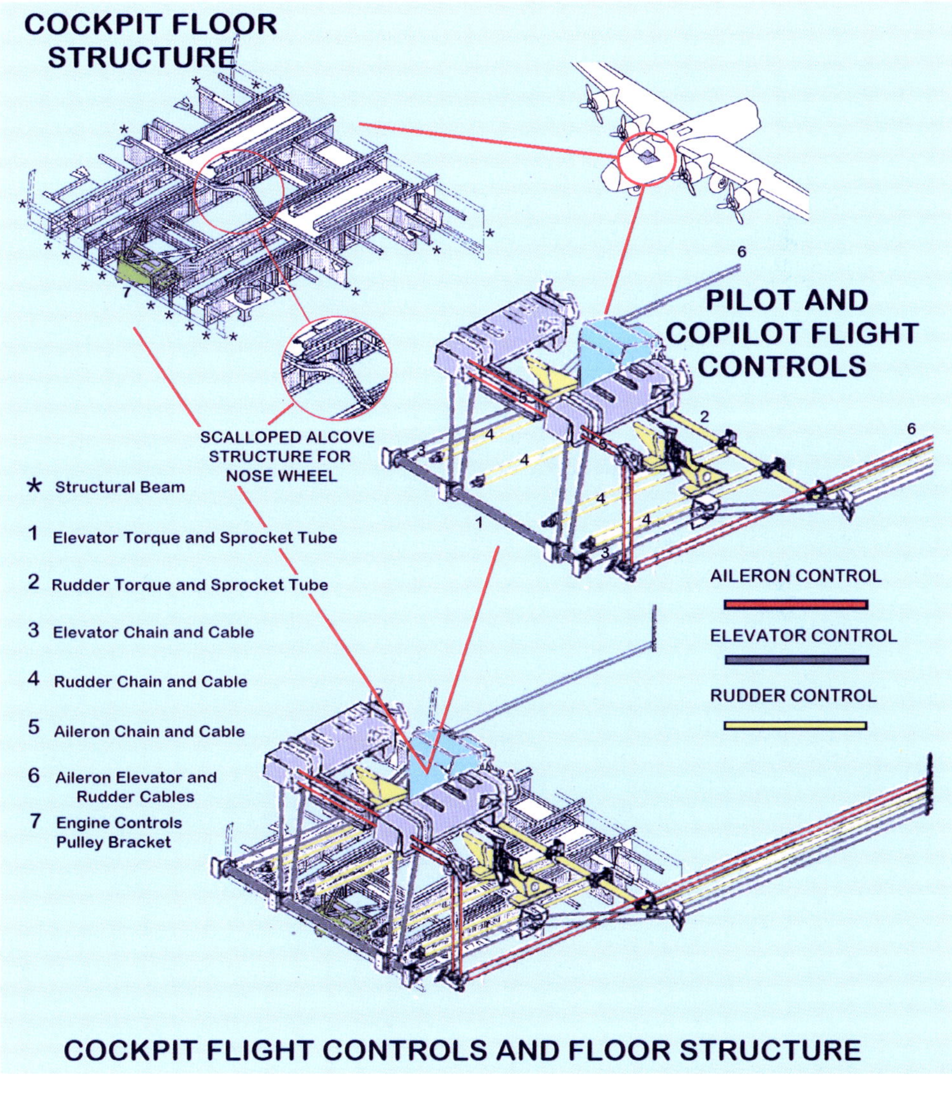

The third grouping are the cable chains and follow-up cables of the Sperry automatic pilot servo actuators mounted in the left ceiling. This assembly is supported with its own structural brackets between two beams beneath the pilot. In the automatic pilot the aileron controls (red), elevator controls (grey) and rudder controls (yellow) all operate within close proximity to each other (see opposite). The three servos sit next to the wheel alcove. Each of the servo actuators is connected in tandem by cable chains to a separate flight control system which it operates when the automatic pilot is turned on. A follow-up cable is also attached to each servo actuator to provide feedback from its respective flight control to the automatic pilot in the cockpit. When the automatic pilot is turned off the servo actuators remain connected in tandem but travel freely with the flight controls when they are moved. As in the previous scenario if an irregular-shaped piece of cargo, despite the structural beams, were to be wedged with sufficient force against the servo actuators beneath the pilot, particularly against their chains and cables there is a potential to inhibit their movement which directly affects the flight controls. It is significant to note that the elevator servo and cable chains are furthest from the wheel alcove.

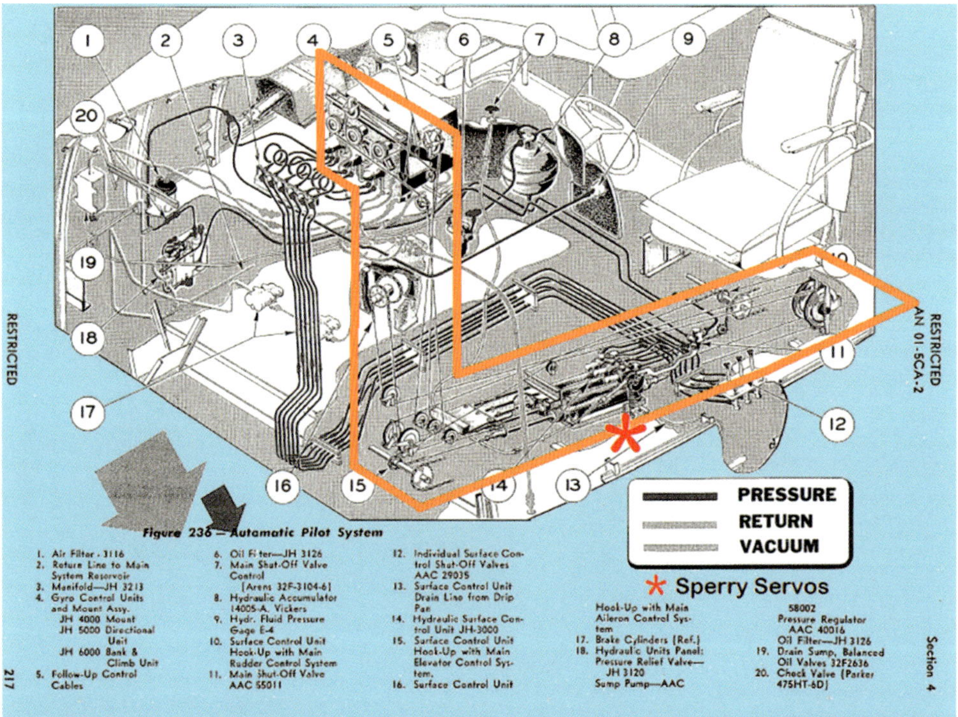

SPERRY AUTOMATIC PILOT SYSTEM COCKPIT LAYOUT SCHEMATIC

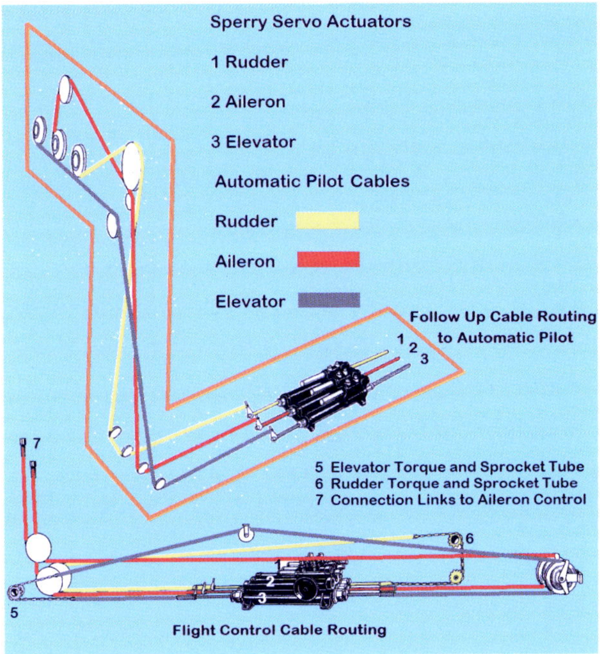

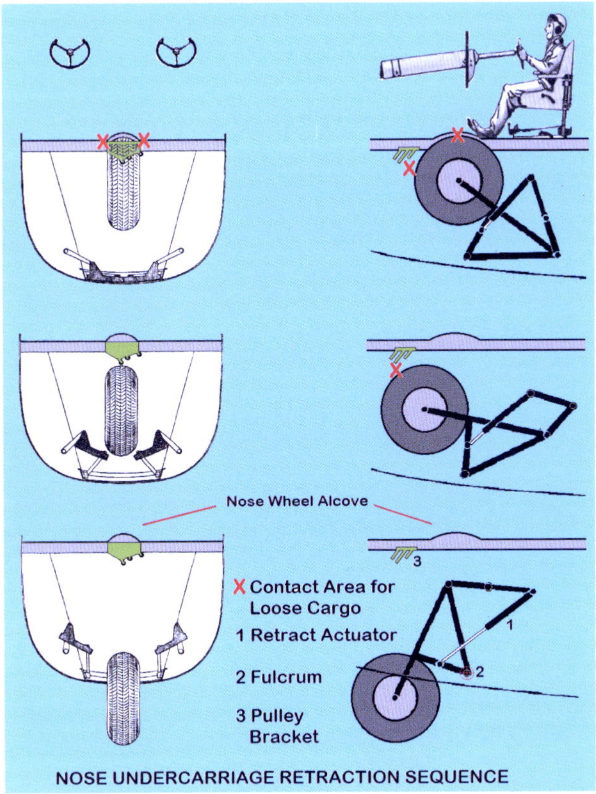

Looking at the retraction sequence diagram below the configuration of the Liberator nose undercarriage is in the style of a Class 3 lever; the hydraulic actuator's exerted force is closer to the fulcrum, further out along the arm where the wheel sits the exerted force would be much less. Put simply the 1,000-psi actuator force applied above the bottom undercarriage hinge point would be greater while the force felt at the upper portion of the tyre nearest the ceiling structure of the compartment would be far less. It should also be kept in mind that the Liberator's 1,000-psi hydraulic system which retracts and extends the undercarriage would not result in the crushing and

Previous page: *Sperry automatic pilot servo actuators and cable routing beneath and above cockpit floor.*

Top: *Sperry servo actuators and flight control cable and follow up cable routing.*

Left: *Nose undercarriage retractions sequence. Note orientation of wheel relative to pulley bracket.*

distortion of the aluminium ceiling structure if an object is caught between it and the nosewheel. In addition the engine-driven 1,000-psi pump pressure will drop as it tries to lift the combined 2,774-lb weight of all three undercarriages into their compartments further reducing any force the retracting nose undercarriage might impart to surrounding structure while pinning an object against it. A situation where an object is trapped between a wheel and ceiling of such construction would cause actuator movement to stall and the hydraulic system relief valve to open and bypass pressurized fluid through a return line to the reservoir. The nose undercarriage would remain in this stalled condition until the undercarriage selector was moved to the down position. For example it is not unheard of, during undercarriage retraction or extension, for wheels to get hung up on doors that did not fully open. The undercarriage does not go smashing through the doors or push them out of the way, it just hangs there.

As Llewellyn was unable to recall which of his controls were affected it can only be presumed, given the orientation of the retracted nosewheel and strut to the surrounding engine and flight controls, that whatever difficulties he experienced

B-24J Liberator No. 44-44052 Witchcraft nosewheel compartment perspectives of structure and control components. Note: This aircraft is not fitted with a Sperry automatic pilot and cable group number 8 controls turbochargers on this specific B-24J model. (vintagetin.net).

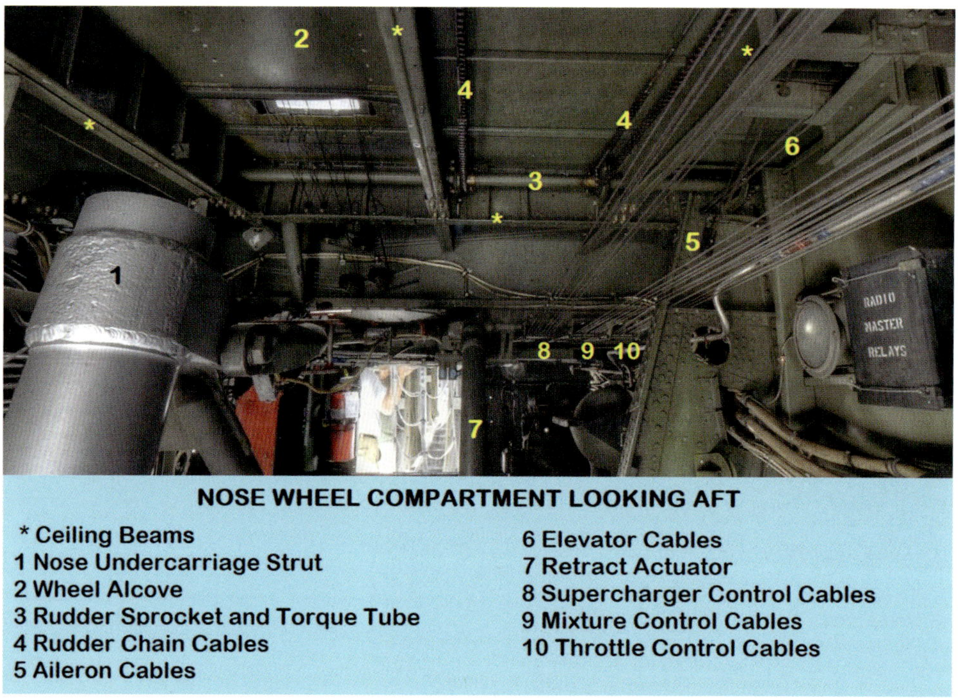

from unsecured cargo in his Liberator's nose undercarriage compartment were likely related to engine control, possibly rudder control, or possibly the Sperry servo actuators. Unfortunately this analysis is limited to images and maintenance data from military and manufacturer manuals. Given that there are few Liberators left flying in the world a more comprehensive investigation is currently not practical. Readers will also note use of the term 'irregular-shaped cargo' as there is no way to know what type or form of unsecured freight caused Llewellyn's incident. Was this freight solid like a box or soft like a large mailbag containing packages with hard protruding contours that could be pushed between beams or frames to press against a cable or chain? Lastly this freight would have to be of sufficient bulk and weight to not be thrust away by the spinning tyre, stop its rotation, and remain entangled with the strut assembly as it retracted.

Llewellyn was able to retain control of the Liberator, investigate the problem in flight, and return to the airfield. Prchal on the other hand experienced a hard locking of his elevator controls in a time frame of less than ten seconds to which Llewellyn's incident and theory cannot account for. Lastly there is one photo of AL523's wreckage that offers a hint as to the condition of flight and engine controls in the nose undercarriage compartment at the time of impact (see page 74). In the photo the Sperry servo actuators, pulley bracket assembly for engine control cables, and nosewheel alcove can be clearly seen. Despite damage to the cockpit floor structure the pulley bracket appears intact as are the three Sperry servo actuators covered by a panel. Also of interest are the individual pushrods for each servo which do not appear bent or damaged given the violence of the crash suggesting that the retracted nosewheel had not wedged an object against them, or the pulley bracket.

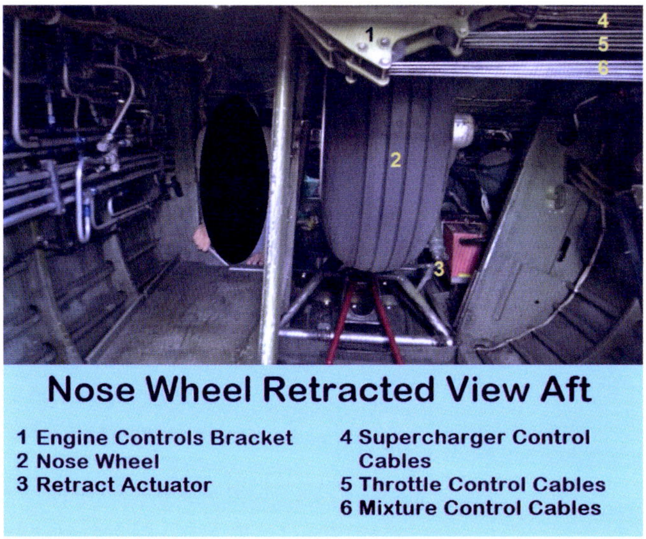

Nosewheel retracted, note how close the wheel is to the engine control bracket and pulleys. B-24J serial no. 44-44052. Image used with permission.

Nosewheel compartment overhead view, note the close proximity of the wheel alcove to the engine controls bracket. B-24J Serial No. 44-44052. (vintagetin.net)

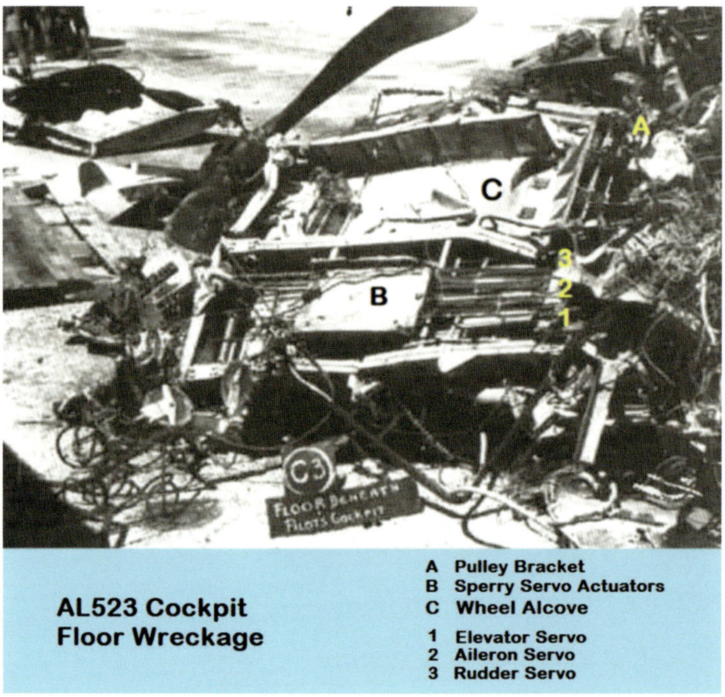

Recovered wreckage of AL523 cockpit floor. (After the Battle *No. 20)*

FLIGHT CONTROL LOCKS

The notion that AL523's flight control lock had possibly been engaged after take-off was a question put to Flight Lieutenant Prchal during the inquiry, Prchal had also considered it himself. Throughout the inquiry he maintained that his elevators had been locked when attempting to climb after descending to increase his airspeed. Investigators Wing Commander Stevens and Flight Lieutenant Buck's examination of the flight control lock's sliding pinions, also referred to as locking pins, could find no evidence that they had been engaged when the accident occurred. The only damage found was the rudder-elevator lock drum spindle sheared due to torsional stress. The excessive force applied by its cables during the tail and fuselage break up likely resulted in the lock drum rotating beyond its limit of travel. They further added that had the locking pins been engaged at the time of impact they would have been bent or showed evidence of shearing.

Flight control lock system, locking pins and locking handle are highlighted in red.

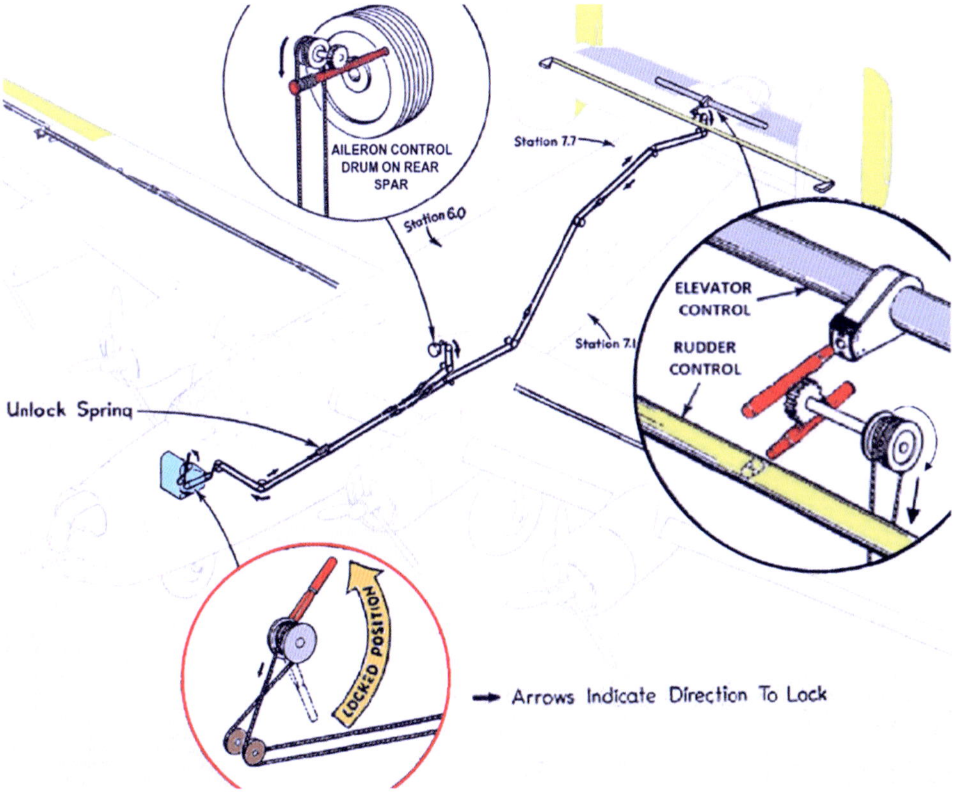

Further context and perspective of Stevens' and Buck's observations is gained through a detailed examination of the Liberator II flight control lock system. The locking procedure for all models of Liberator was identical. From Liberator II Pilot Notes we have this description:

"Move all controls to neutral. Pull up slowly on controls locking lever, while moving rudder pedals back and forth slightly until rudder locking pin seats. Continue pulling up on lock lever and turn aileron control wheels from side to side slightly until aileron locking pin seats. Continue pulling up on

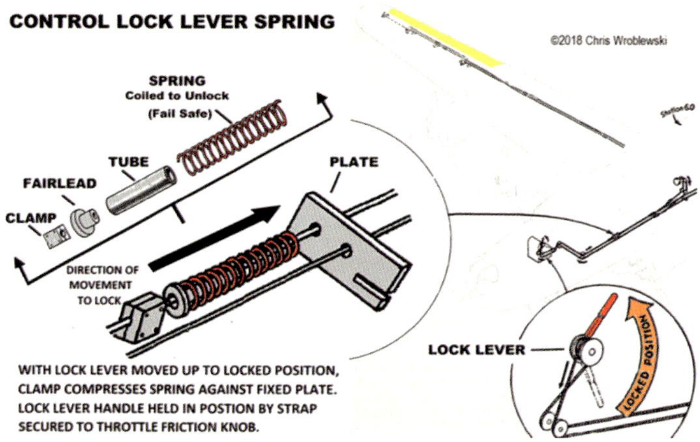

Left: *Flight control lock lever spring coiled to unlock (fail safe).*

Below: *Aileron control lock assembly mounted to the wing rear spar.*

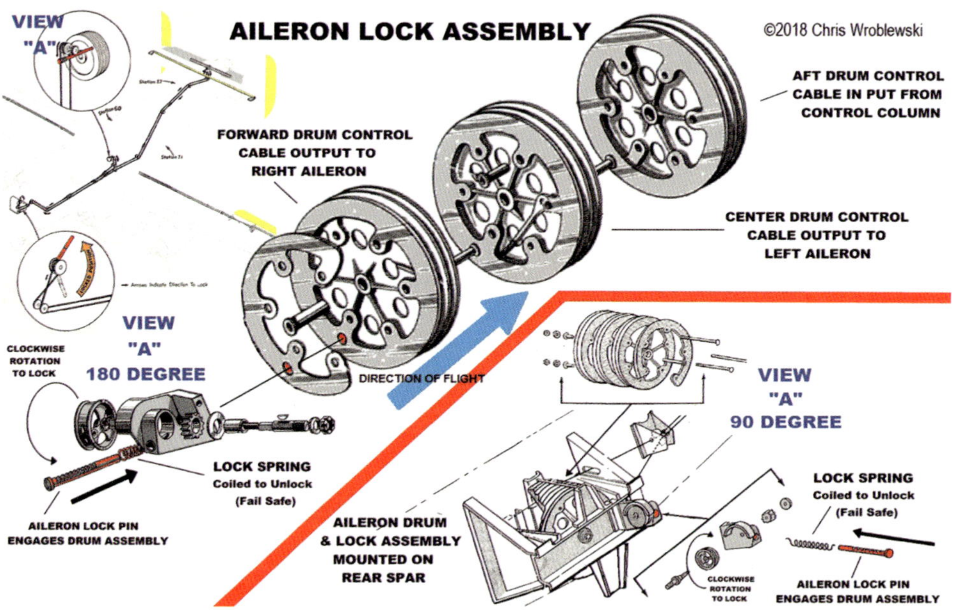

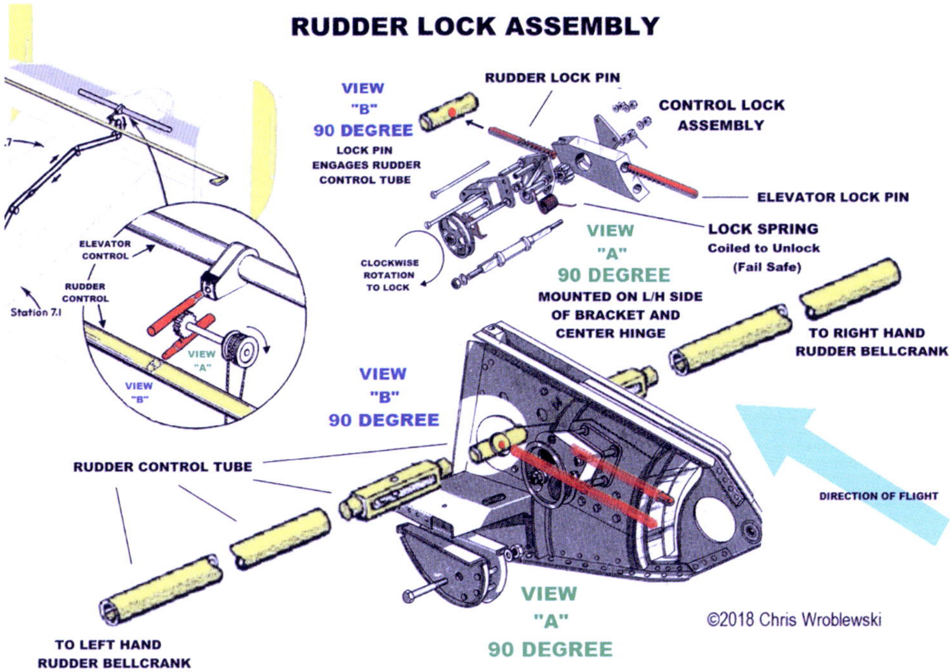

Above: Rudder lock control.

Below: Elevator lock control.

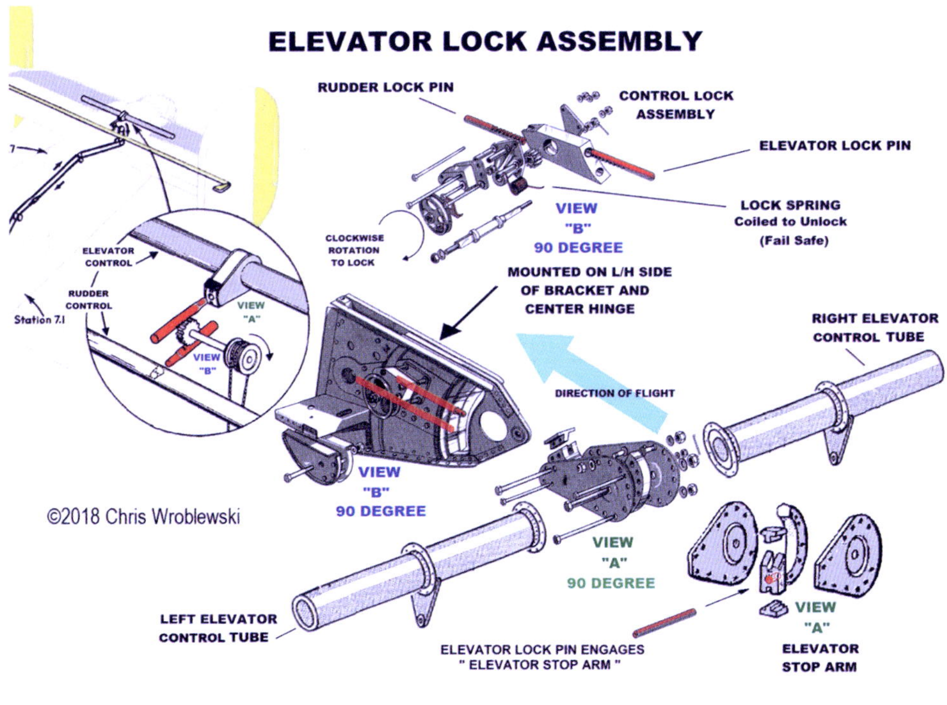

locking lever while moving elevator controls back and forth slightly until elevator lock pin seats."[67]

The spring-loaded control lock handle was then held in the lock position by a strap secured to the throttles. Liberator pilot and maintenance manuals describe the same locking sequence. For technically minded readers simplified drawings of the aileron, rudder, and rudder control locks are provided in the four illustrations on pages 76–77.

Though it was concluded that AL523's crash was not caused by engagement of its flight control locks, an examination of all Liberator maintenance and factory manuals describe a specific and similarly complicated rigging procedure that was critical to their safe operation.

1. Loosen the stake and slip the cable from the drum. With control lever pulled backward so that the top of the handle is 2½" from the pedestal, set the control cable so that the rudder lock is just starting in hole. Since the elevator and rudder lock pins are operated by the same gear, the elevator lock is adjusted with the setting of the rudder lock. Move the operating handle to the full unlock position and adjust aileron drum so that the rear end of the locking pin is 1¾" from the housing. If lock should bind or fail to return to unlocked position check spring at station 4.1.
2. Wrap cable around drum in stabilizer 3½ turns.
3. Wrap cable around drum aft of aileron control drum 3½ turns.
4. Wrap cable around drum in pedestal 1½ turns. Locking handle must be in locked position when drum is wrapped.
5. Stagger all turnbuckles on cables to prevent them passing each other when cables are moved.
6. The forward face of fairlead is 8⅝" forward of station 4.1. Tighten clamp forward of fairlead with the handle in unlocked position.
7. Rudder lock pin should just be starting to engage when the control handle is 2½" from pedestal. Adjustments can be made by cable lock stake and by slipping the cable on the drum. Aileron locking pin must clear aileron control drum by a minimum of ⅛" when the locking handle is in full unlocked position.
8. With handle in locked position locking pins should enter locking holes approximately ⅜". If pins do not engage sufficiently an inspection of system should be made and the trouble corrected.[68]

Liberator maintenance manuals revised in July 1944 go on to caution that:

"All lockpins should enter the locking holes approximately ⅜ inch in the locked position, and if they fail to do so, a check of the system should be made to determine cause of failure. However, clearance between pin, and hole must never be sacrificed to provide more secure locking, as clearance is necessary to prevent inadvertent locking of control surfaces at high altitudes, when cables may become a little slack."[69]

This revision was the result of *Consolidated Vultee Field Service Bulletin MCR 454-1* issued 15 March 1944 which described the incorporation of a safety device to the aileron and rudder-elevator lock gear boxes to prevent inadvertent locking of the controls while the aircraft was in flight. The service bulletin explained that "[in] low temperature, the control lock cables become slack and tend to release the lock plungers which during flight are normally held in a disengaged position." It further added that "[the] safety device is installed to engage the locking plunger, when the controls are unlocked, by means of the retainer ball which falls into the notch on the locking plunger."[70]

Erection and maintenance instructions. Flight control lock system schematic. (T.O. No.01-5EC-2)

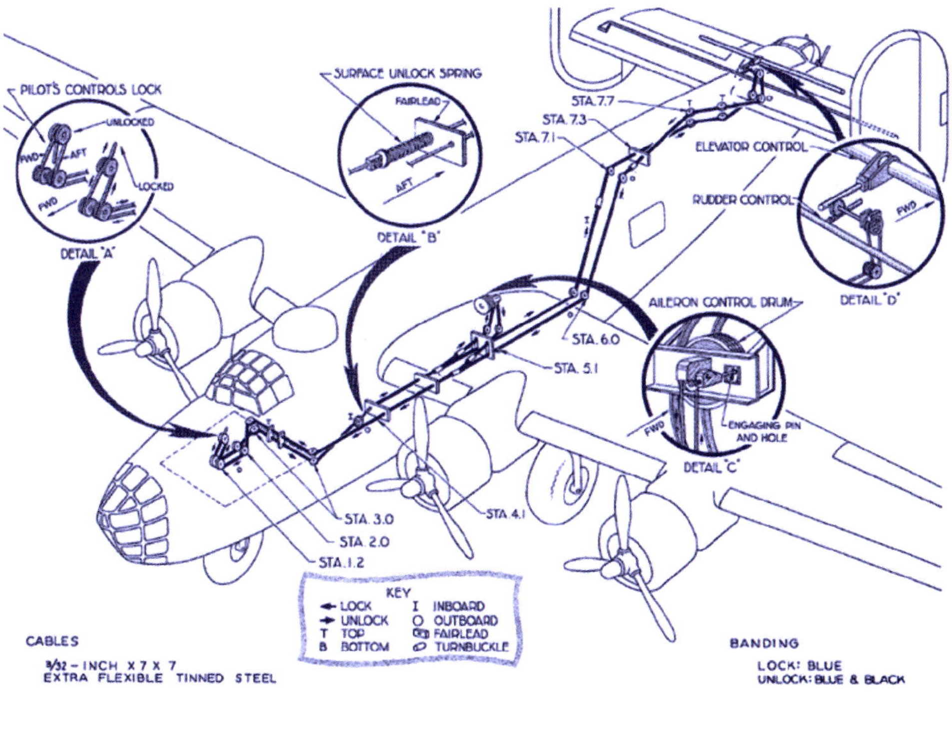

The service bulletin was the result of extreme cold weather trials conducted by the engineering division of the Air Technical Service Command at Ladd Field Alaska in the winter of 1944–45. Eleven Army Air Force aircraft which included two B-24s had taken part in the trials. It was not surprising that among many findings was a reduction of control cable tension and stiffness of flight control movement in extreme cold on all aircraft, most notably on the B-24.[71] Through these findings Field Service Bulletin MCR 327 was issued on 15 May 1944 for the installation of tension regulators in the cable systems of the B-24 flight control system. The tension regulators were designed to maintain a rigging load on the control cables over a temperature range of -65°F to +160°F. Nine tension regulators were installed, three in the aileron, four in the elevator, and four in the rudder cable systems.[72]

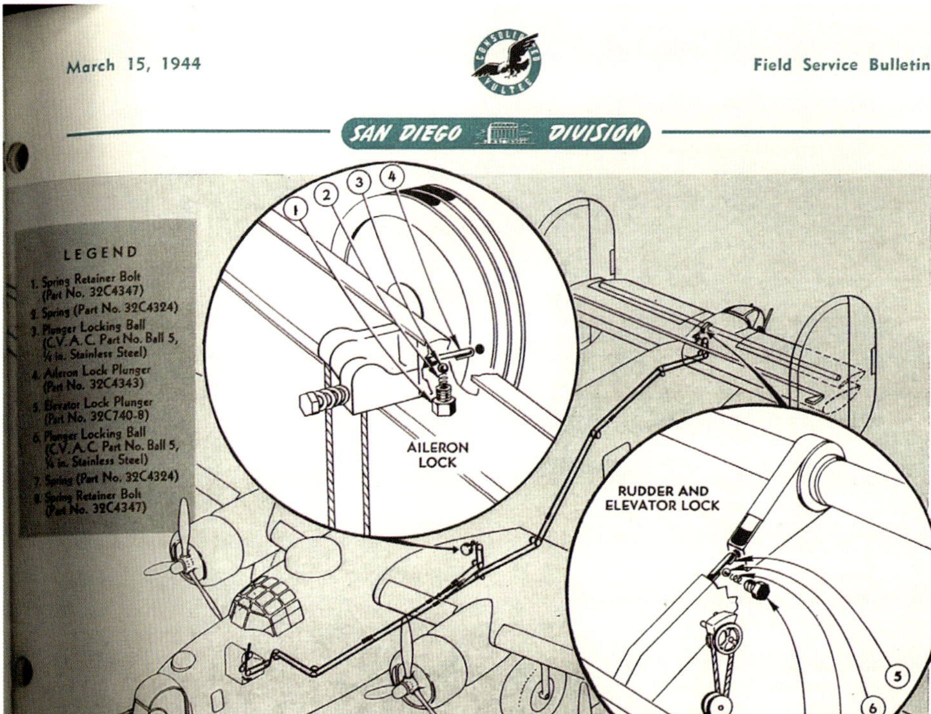
March 15, 1944

Field Service Bulletin

SAN DIEGO DIVISION

Figure 1. Lock System with Safety Device Installed

Consolidated Vultee Field Service Bulletin MCR 454-1. *(San Diego Air & Space Museum)*

When reading the control lock rigging procedure, one is left with the impression that it was a very tedious and complicated job. Though the cables were staked to the drums they might rotate slightly and change the lock pin measurements as cables were adjusted to meet the required tension values for temperature. In many modern aircraft rig pins are inserted into quadrants at either end of a cable circuit to lock them in place and tension cables evenly, the rig pins should pull out easily if tensions are equal. It is unclear in the service bulletin and the Ladd Field reports as to why the control lock pins would migrate toward the locked position in cold temperatures. A probable explanation lays with the aircraft's aluminium structure and the control lock's loop of steel control cables having different coefficients of expansion; aluminium shrinks more than steel at low temperatures. In addition, the rigged tension values for the aileron, and elevator-rudder lock cables were 21 lbs, while the cables for the lock handle were 40 lbs. These differences in combination with lowering tensions of the steel cables and the shrinking aluminium structure likely caused incremental rotation of the cable drums and lock pins towards their lock positions. Though AL523's accident occurred in a warm climate, temperature would have had a negligible effect on cable tensions with no influence on the position of flight control lock pins.

Engaging the Flight Control Lock after Take-off

During the court of inquiry the chief test pilot at RAE Farnborough, Squadron Leader Roland Falk, was asked if it was possible for a Liberator with an all-up weight of 54,600 lbs to leave the ground with its flight controls locked. Falk testified it was possible but that its airspeed would need to be somewhere near 180 mph, that a take-off under these conditions was only theoretical. He was further asked if it was possible to dispose the load in a manner that a Liberator with locked controls could take off in approximately 1,100 yards under calm conditions. Falk replied it was possible but, in his opinion:

> "If the [centre of gravity] was aft to this extent, the aircraft would be unmanageable in any case. If it took off in this condition with the controls locked it would immediately assume a steep climbing attitude and stall. In [his] opinion this [was] not a practical possibility."

Falk was further asked if it was possible for a Liberator to take off with only the rudders locked. He answered:

"Yes, that steering on the initial stage of the run is done by manipulation of the throttle, and it is quite possible to meet conditions in which there would be no subsequent swing, and therefore there would be no need for rudder correction." [73]

The possibility of the control lock having been somehow engaged after AL523's take-off, though theoretical, was unlikely given that all three flight controls, aileron, rudder, and elevator must be in a precise neutral position in order for the control lock pins to engage. This is particularly true of the rudder and elevator as they share a common control lock assembly. What is unique about this assembly is that the elevator cannot be locked until the rudder is first locked. This specific locking sequence is due to the assembly's design in that the elevator and rudder lock pins are operated by the same pinion gear; the elevator pin will only start to enter the elevator lock arm after the rudder lock pin has engaged the rudder push-pull tube. "The lock pin for the rudder is also longer than the lock pin for the elevator."[74] When the gear and spindle are rotated in the locking direction "the rudder lock pin leaves the casting a ¼ inch ahead of the elevator lock pin."[75] The control lock cables are rigged to lock the flight controls in the following sequence: rudder, elevator, and aileron.[76] The locking procedure for all models of Liberator was identical.[77]

With this in mind it will be remembered Prchal testified experiencing a locked rudder in a previous take-off incident which speaks to this unique locking sequence. He further testified that prior to the 4th July take-off he had set his rudder trim four divisions to the right,[78] this trim adjustment corrects for propeller torque during take-off which pulls the aircraft left. He further stated that during his take-off run he first used engines then a very slight amount of rudder to keep AL523 straight. This small amount of rudder deflection made it impossible for the lock pin to engage the offset rudder push-pull tube's locking receptacle as it was out of alignment with the lock pin. In this offset condition had the cockpit control lock lever been lifted, the lock pin, being a ¼ inch longer, would have only pushed against the side of the displaced push-pull tube leaving the elevator free to move. It should also be considered that as AL523 climbed its elevators were deflected slightly upward, and out of alignment for locking, with Prchal applying just enough back pressure to his control column to establish a shallow positive climb and steady airspeed. When he pushed his control column forward the rudder was still displaced leaving elevator movement unrestricted by its locking pin had the lock lever been lifted. The

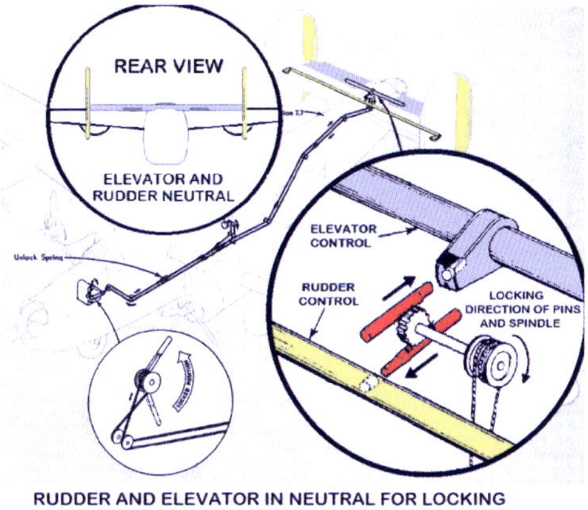

following images provide context to rudder and elevator control movement, lock pin engagement, and rudder trim input. The push-pull tube of the yellow rudder control moves from side-to-side imparting movement to rudders through a bell crank at either end. Cables from the pilot's rudder pedals move the push-pull tube, when the tube is shifted left the rudders move

Above: *The yellow rudder control tube and grey elevator control torque tube are in neutral position with their respective locking receptacles in alignment with the two red locking pins of the gear and spindle locking assembly.*

Below left: *With the yellow push-pull tube of the rudder control shifted left for right rudder input, and the grey elevator control torque tube rotated counterclockwise deflecting the elevator up, their respective locking receptacles are out of alignment with the gear and spindle locking assembly's red locking pins.*

Below right: *With the yellow push-pull tube of the rudder control shifted left for right rudder input, and the grey elevator control torque tube rotated clockwise deflecting the elevator down, their respective locking receptacles are out of alignment with the gear and spindle locking assembly's red locking pins.*

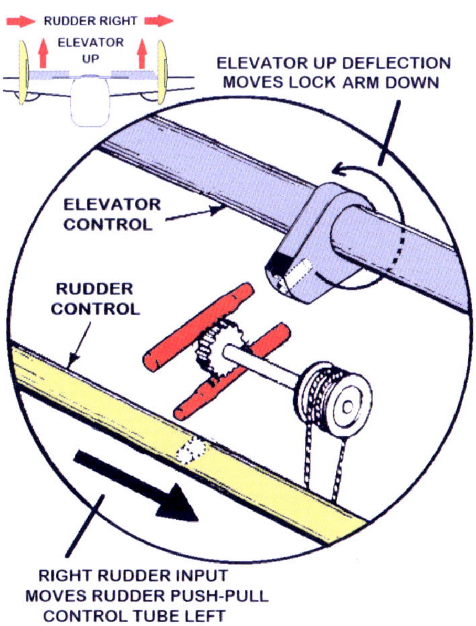

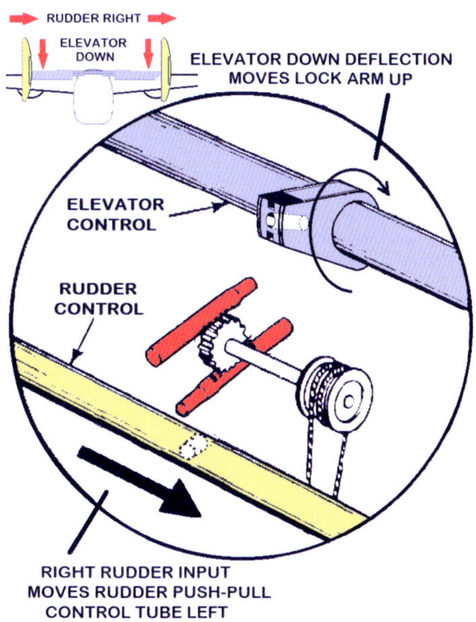

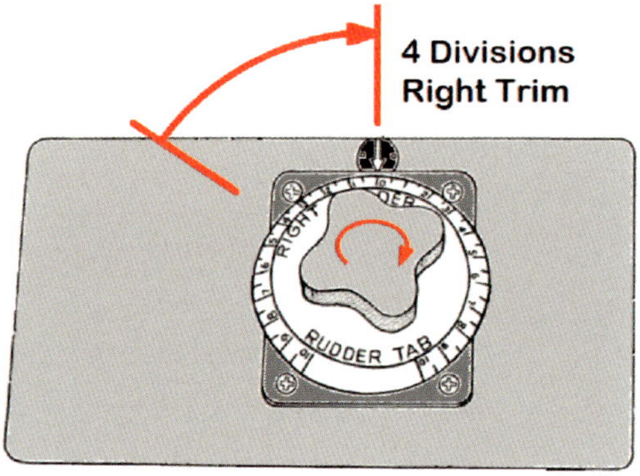

Left image Rudder Trim panel outlined in yellow. Rudder Tab Knob Rotated Clockwise for Right Trim, Counter Clockwise for Left Trim.

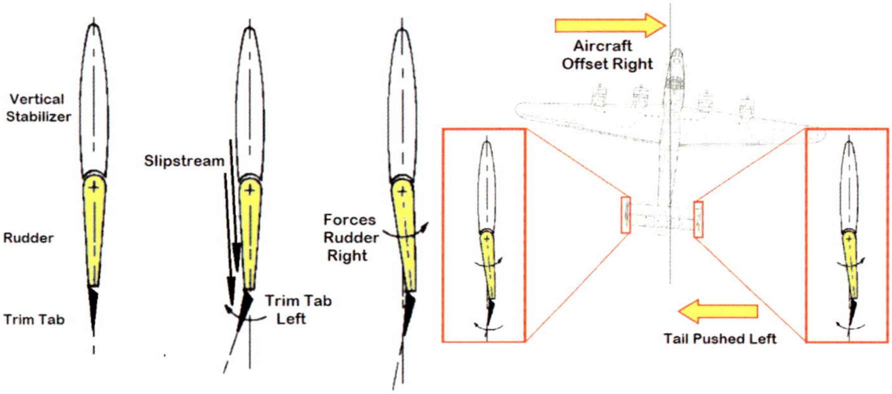

Right Rudder Trim moves Trim Tab left. Slipstream pushes against Trim Tab forcing Rudder right. Aircraft Tail is pushed left which offsets Aircraft Nose to the right.

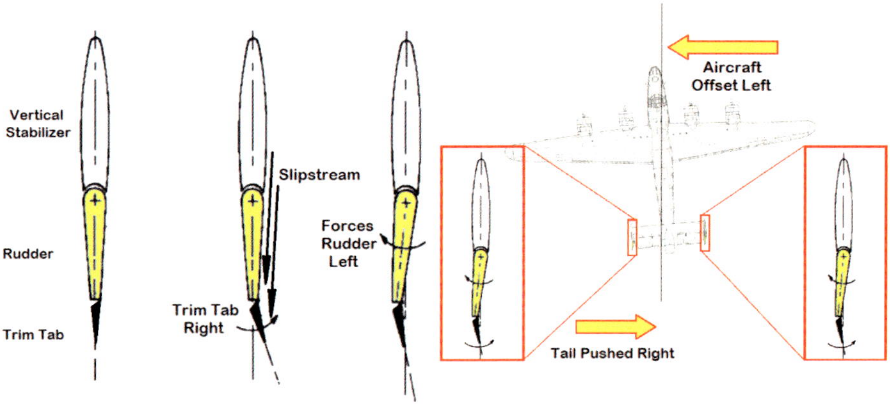

Left Rudder Trim moves Trim Tab right. Slipstream pushes against Trim Tab forcing Rudder left. Aircraft Tail is pushed right which offsets Aircraft Nose to the left.

Rudder trim control panel location. Rudder trim control input effect on trim tab and rudder movement. Trim tab illustration from Experimental Aircraft Association/Tony Bingelis. Used with permission from EAA.

right and vice versa. Movement of the grey elevator control is imparted to its torque tube from a pushrod – when the tube rotates counterclockwise the elevator moves up, clockwise moves it down.

Sixteen Seconds and Undercarriage Side Brace Damage

During the inquiry Wing Commander Stevens testified, "From an examination of the undercarriage it would appear that it was well up at the time of the impact with the water as the locks, both up and down positions, are undamaged as are the tyres and wheel fairings."[79] It is difficult to determine from this statement with any certainty what type of damage the undercarriage locks may have suffered had the up lock been engaged during the crash. That being said two issues stand out. The first, though Stevens did not elaborate on what type of damage the locks would have suffered his emphasis of the tyres and fairings being undamaged speaks to the likelihood that the undercarriage was almost, if not completely, retracted. Secondly, it also speaks to the amount of time it took for the undercarriage to retract which reflects AL523's flight time.

It is recorded that AL523 took off at 23:07 and crashed at 23:07, sixteen seconds having been quoted as the total flight time.[80] With this in mind a review of YouTube videos of Liberator take-offs revealed the main undercarriage fully retracting within twenty-four to twenty-six seconds for a B-24 while the LB30 retracts within sixteen to nineteen seconds when timed with an iPhone. Given Prchal's adherence to procedures, his accepted take-off technique and AL523's narrow flight time (wheels off the ground) of sixteen seconds it would not be unreasonable to conclude that the undercarriage was nearly retracted but not up and locked prior to impact. The combined overall average times for both Liberator types for slowest and fastest undercarriage retraction times work out to:

Fastest = 20.00 seconds.

Slowest = 22.50 seconds.

Average = 21.25 seconds.

A basic description and overview of the main undercarriage retraction and locking sequence is outlined overleaf in the annotated illustrations numbered 175 to 177 taken from the *Service and Instruction Manual. Airplane General B-24 Bombardment Airplane. Second Edition. 1944.*[81]

The dynamics of any air crash such as wreckage pattern, eyewitness accounts, impact loads and stresses help investigators in the determination of a probable cause. The last two characteristics of load and stress come into play when an undercarriage that is almost retracted is abruptly and violently subjected to a 165-mph impact. (Impact forces are explained in the next section titled AL523 Overturning on Impact.) For the sake of argument let us assume that AL523's undercarriage was partially retracted, say three quarters of the way. In this position its door fairings at impact would have a degree of shelter due to the aircraft nose, belly and engines creating a trough as they struck the water. It should also be remembered that moments before the crash Prchal had closed the throttles and that the ignition switches were found in the off position by investigators. With all four engines shut down the hydraulic pump driven by No. 3 engine would no longer supply 1000 psi to the Liberator's hydraulic system,[82] hydraulic pressure would suddenly decrease and stall undercarriage movement. The undercarriage might start to lower from its weight with the loss of pressure. Further, Stevens did not elaborate as to what damage the tyre might have suffered, one can only guess that given its size the damage would be minimal to none with brake hoses possibly broken away or displaced from the strut.

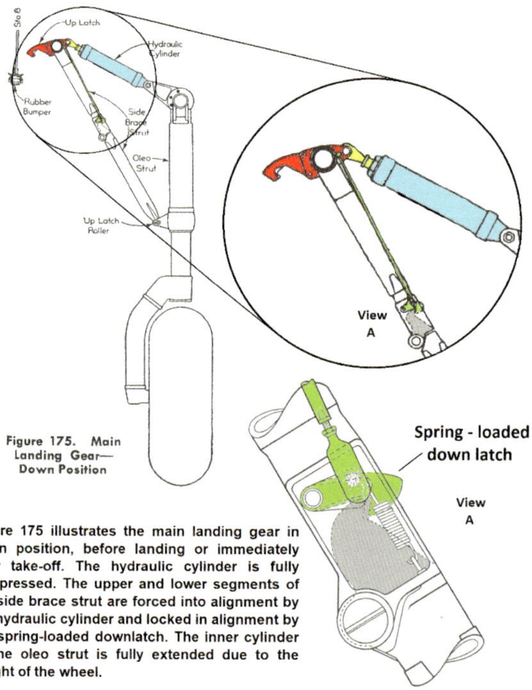

Figure 175. Main Landing Gear—Down Position

Figure 175 illustrates the main landing gear in down position, before landing or immediately after take-off. The hydraulic cylinder is fully compressed. The upper and lower segments of the side brace strut are forced into alignment by the hydraulic cylinder and locked in alignment by the spring-loaded downlatch. The inner cylinder of the oleo strut is fully extended due to the weight of the wheel.

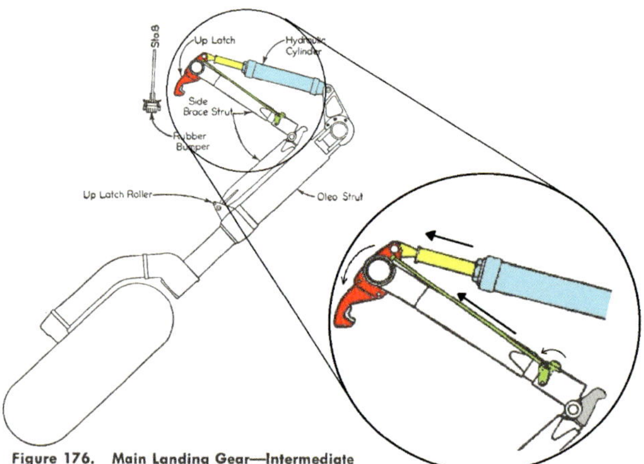

Figure 176. Main Landing Gear—Intermediate Position

Figure 176 illustrates an intermediate position in raising or lowering of the gear. To raise the gear from down position the hydraulic actuating piston extends. The first movement of the actuating section unlatches the side brace, then the upper side brace strut is forced to rotate upward, causing the knuckle to break and move inboard.

Only a single post-crash photo of each undercarriage exists.[83] [84] In both photos

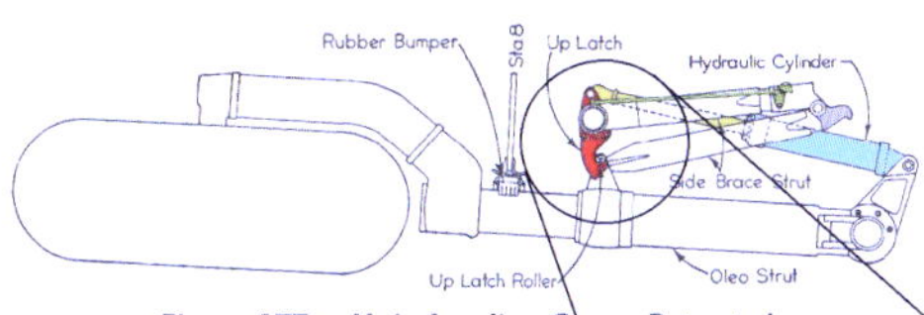

Figure 177. Main Landing Gear—Retracted

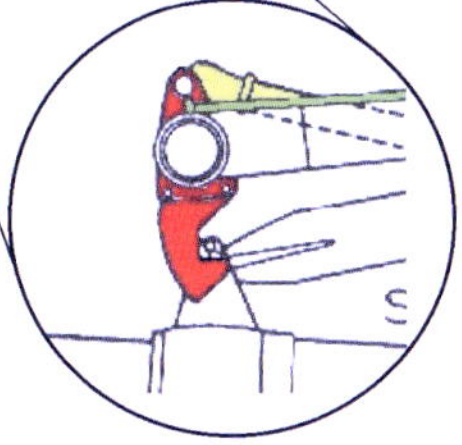

Figure 177 illustrates the up and locked position. When the oleo cylinder contacts the rubber bumper mounted on the bulkhead at wing station 8, the rubber bumper compresses, while the uplatch rotates into position to engage the uplatch roller. Hydraulic pressure increases as the rubber bumper compresses; when hydraulic pressure has increased to 1100 p.s.i. the landing gear selector valve returns to neutral and allows the gear to drop back on the uplatch.

Below: *Left undercarriage. (Taken from* The Assassination of Winston Churchill*)*

Overleaf: *Right undercarriage.* (After The Battle *No. 20)*

LEFT UNDERCARRIAGE

MAGNIFIED AREA IN YELLOW OF SIDE BRACE FISH - MOUTH WELD SEPARATION. FISH - MOUTH JOINT LOCATION CIRCLED IN RED.

RIGHT UNDERCARRIAGE
MAGNIFIED AREA IN YELLOW OF SIDE BRACE FISH - MOUTH WELD SEPARATION. FISH - MOUTH JOINT LOCATION CIRCLED IN RED.

the fairings are clearly missing, presumably lost, or removed during salvage. What is of significance in each photo is that the lower side brace has broken cleanly away from beneath the side brace knuckle. Of particular interest is that the welded V-notch, or fish-mouth joint used to increase weld surface area to the knuckle at manufacture, is cleanly broken along the entirety of its weld locations on the side strut pipe. Such a clean break could not have been the result of attempts to hoist the wing section by HMS *Moorhill* or by a salvager's cutting wheel or torch.

The Liberator's undercarriage strut was manufactured by Bendix[85] and constructed of SAE 4130 chrome-molybdenum, American-produced steel that contained 0.33 per cent carbon. Undercarriage components manufactured in the 1940s from this grade of steel, after welding and heat treatment, could achieve a strength of 150,000 psi. The welded strength of these components was dependent upon suitable high tensile welding electrodes that could achieve a 120,000-psi weld strength with proper pre- or post-heating to delay cooling and the formation of cracks. A weld strength of 150,000 psi could also be achieved with automatic Heliarc or Argon-arc welding. Reliable welding technique was needed as high carbon welds were susceptible to cracks due to hydrogen embrittlement.[86] The side-braced style undercarriage of a Liberator, like any side-brace type, would

Liberator undercarriage hydraulic system. Note the cluster of piping in the nose and cockpit areas. (Erection And Maintenance Instructions T.O. No. 01-5EC-2)

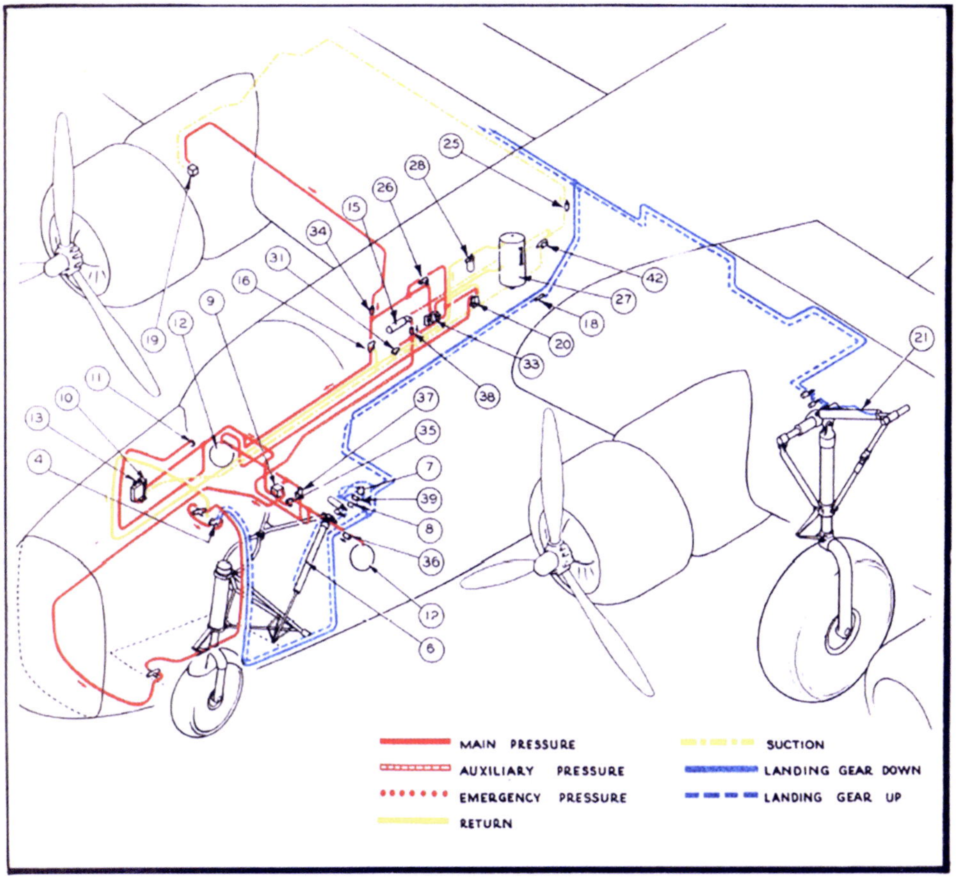

4. Landing Gear Control Valves
6. Nose Wheel Cylinder
7. Nose Wheel Dump Valve
8. Nose Wheel Restrictor
9. Unloading Valve
10. Hand Pump
11. Hydro-Pressure Gage
12. Accumulators
13. Emergency Flap Valves
15. Electric Pump
16. Relief Valve
18. Main Landing Gear Restrictor
19. Engine Driven Pump
20. Pressure Switch
21. Landing Gear Cylinder
25. Suction Line Check Valve
26. Emergency Shut-Off Valve
27. Fluid Reservoir
28. Filter
31. Relief Valve
33. Test Stand
34. Engine Pump Check Valve
35. Check Valve (Unloader)
36. Left Accumulator Check Valve
37. Right Accumulator Check Valve
38. Auxiliary Pump Check Valve
39. Nose Wheel Cylinder Check Valve
42. Suction Valve

experience vertical, drag and torsion loads through all cycles of take-off, landing and taxiing. This cyclic loading fatigues the undercarriage over time and can induce cracks; any welded undercarriage joint with hydrogen embrittlement would eventually suffer weld fractures.[87] Among inspection items listed in later model Liberator maintenance manuals are visual inspections of the main undercarriage for cracks every 25 hours.[88] Of significance within the *Aircraft Inspection And Maintenance Guide For B-24D, RB-24E, B-24G, B-24H and B24J aircraft,* dated 1 May 1944, is main landing gear inspection item No. 236 which states: "Side Brace Upper Strut, Oleo Collars: Inspect for cracks." The interval for this item was every pre-flight inspection. Curiously, it was not incorporated in 25, 50, or 100-hour inspections given its importance.[89]

One possible scenario that could account for the lack of damage Stevens described, with resultant breakage of the lower side brace welds, was that the undercarriage was forcibly extended on impact. It is logical to assume AL523's undercarriage was selected up shortly after becoming airborne and nearly retracted moments before impact. After approximately sixteen seconds of flight AL523 impacted the water at 165 mph at a shallow nose-down angle of approximately -15 to -20 degrees with its undercarriage nearly up but not locked. As forward and downward momentum abruptly stopped, the nose section was crushed and the tail broken off as the remaining fuselage and wing overturned onto its back. In that instant, hydraulic lines in the destroyed nose section supplying what little pressure was left to the main undercarriage actuators were broken which resulted in immediate fluid loss. With the actuators depleted of pressure and their fluid displacement unrestricted each 1,281-lb[90] steel undercarriage was free to move. The kinetic energy of impact aided by the centrifugal force of wings and fuselage flipping onto its back forcefully threw the heavy undercarriage toward its extended position. These forces were so great that peripheral and V-notch, or fish-mouth, welds of the side braces cracked as they rapidly reached their locked position and limit of travel. AL523's undercarriage remained extended as the inverted Liberator sank and remained extended underwater due to the additional buoyancy of the tyres. Further credence to AL523 having overturned on impact is given with the arrival of the rescue launch HSL 181 several minutes later where eyewitnesses onboard reported finding the aircraft floating upside-down.[91] Given that the nose section and bomb bay had been torn away at impact the only possible way eyewitnesses could know the Liberator was upside-down was the sight of the extended undercarriage sticking out of the water pointed upward.[92]

The wing section was lifted twice by HMS *Moorhill* on 5 and 6 July slung by its undercarriage which likely separated the already cracked V-notch joints. During the third lift on 7 July it was slung by its propeller bosses as the wing section had overturned during the second lift.[93] The side brace separation seen in the photos was due to the truck hoist lifting the struts by their towing eyelets. It is unknown as to what condition AL523's undercarriage side braces were in on the day of the accident. Whether their lower-side brace welds failed because of crash forces, normal fatigue, hydrogen embrittlement or a combination of these factors is uncertain. That being said consideration should be given to the force required to break the side-brace welds as it would have had to equal or exceed the 120,000 to 150,000 psi weld strength value of SAE 4130 steel. Whether inspection of undercarriage side braces was incorporated into the inspection forms that airmen used the day before in Gibraltar to carry out the daily inspection is again unknown. Whether any weld cracking would have been visible is also unknown.

AL523 Overturning on Impact

To give some perspective as to how AL523 overturned, in a typical crash scenario involving fuselage break-up the impact force of a nose-down shallow crash is not imparted at the aircraft's centre of gravity. Impact force is instead offset by its distance from the aircraft's centre of gravity. This offset force accelerates the aircraft upward rotating it about its centre of gravity (Figure 1, page 92). Due to this rotation, every piece of fuselage mass is accelerating differently depending on its distance from the fuselage's centre of gravity. An aircraft typically moves downward with a constant sink rate, the impact force violently brings it to a stop creating an impact acceleration and G loads on its structure and occupants. Since rotational speed is zero at the centre of gravity, the G loads along the fuselage will also vary in a similar manner increasing further out from the centre of gravity (Figure 2). Fuselage breaks can occur at the front or back depending on where the first impact occurs. If a second break occurs, it is usually from a secondary impact. Beyond this simple pattern the process becomes less predictable. Tumbling can occur for several reasons such as off-centre impact, sloping ground, or ploughing of the nose. Spinning a heavy aircraft like AL523 about its centre of gravity takes considerable force and speaks to Liberator tail sections breaking off during water impacts. With the tail being the furthest from the centre of gravity inertial loading would increase the weight of its structure. Inertial loading acts like a virtual uniformly distributed weight load. Eventually, there will be a value of upwards acceleration that will break the tail off.[94] As for the wing and fuselage overturning on impact this was not uncommon during Liberator water impacts. Such was the case of a B-24D Liberator belonging to the USAAF's 343rd Squadron, 98th Bombardment Group. On 6 May 1943, aircraft No. 112 U, serial number 42-40112 ditched with its undercarriage extended and no flaps while attempting to reach Malta for an emergency landing. Flaring 20 feet above the water at 120 mph the aircraft struck tail first breaking the tail off. It then overturned and floated upside-down for five minutes. Interestingly nine of the ten crew members survived due to being at their crash positions.[95] In another instance on 28 July 1943 a USAAF 13th Air Force Liberator in the Pacific also overturned while ditching. Three other instances are also recorded of Liberators floating with their tails vertical after ditching.[96] Six video stills from a digital simulation illustrate how AL523 likely overturned (see opposite).[97]

AL523's crash meets the category of a low velocity, low angle impact. In this classification "the aircraft hits the ground at a fairly low angle, bounces, hits again and perhaps a third and fourth time. In the process, it may have shed wings and engines, but it still looks pretty much like an airplane. There is none of the mass destruction seen in high velocity impacts. Impacting water is no different and is primarily a function of velocity, if the aircraft is going fast enough, water is a solid object as far as the aircraft is concerned."[98] When an aircraft impacts water it comes apart the same as if it had crashed on land. What made water impacts particularly

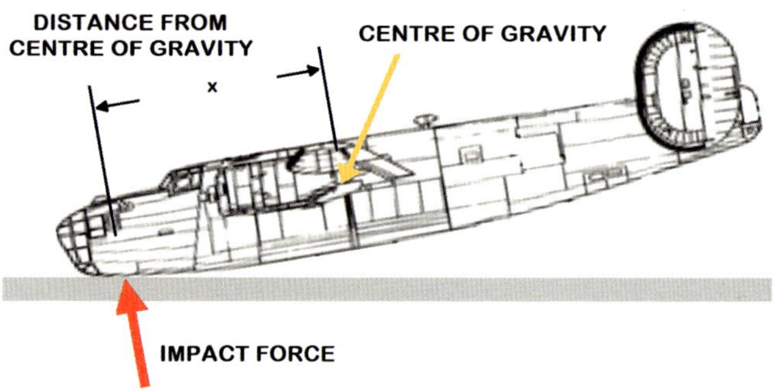

Left: *Figure 1: Impact force rotates the aircraft about its centre of gravity. Aircraft rotational inertia resists this rotation resulting in inertial loads.*

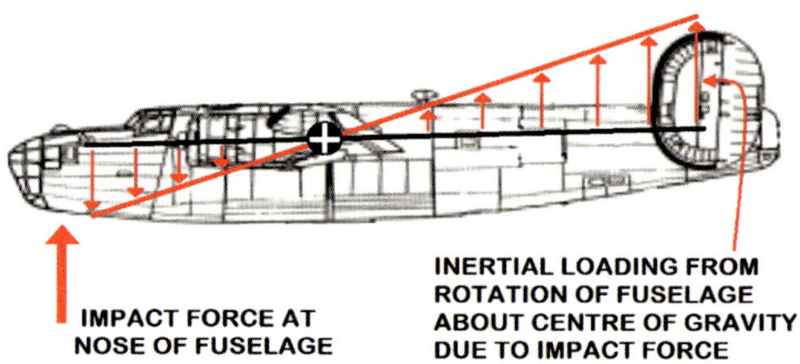

Right: *Figure 2: An impact force not through the aircraft's centre of gravity will cause up acceleration and rotational acceleration (clockwise rotation for impact on nose as shown).*

severe on the Liberator was collapse of its bomb-bay doors which caused the aircraft to dive.[99] Reports from AAF and RAF pilots indicated:

> "That the ditchings of the B-24 [were] very severe. There is a great loss of life in the ditchings of this aircraft. In a number of instances the airplanes have broken into two or three parts when ditched. Because of a general collapse of the bottom of the fuselage, there is always a great inrush of water and the airplane sinks almost immediately to wing level."[100]

NACA ditching investigations carried out in 1943 confirmed that a 1:16 scale model Liberator with a damaged bomb bay dived violently and stopped abruptly in a nose-down attitude with most of the model submerged. Results were at landing attitudes of +1-degree attitude, 40^0 flap, 104 mph; +5-degree attitude, 40^0 flap, 87 mph; and +9-degree attitude, 40^0 flap, 87 mph[101]. (See overleaf, Table 4 of NACA B-24 model-ditching investigation. Note damaged results beneath table.)

Six video stills illustrate the crash sequence of B-24J, 42-51430 The Tulsamerican. It is believed the crash of AL523 was nearly identical. (GBH Archives)

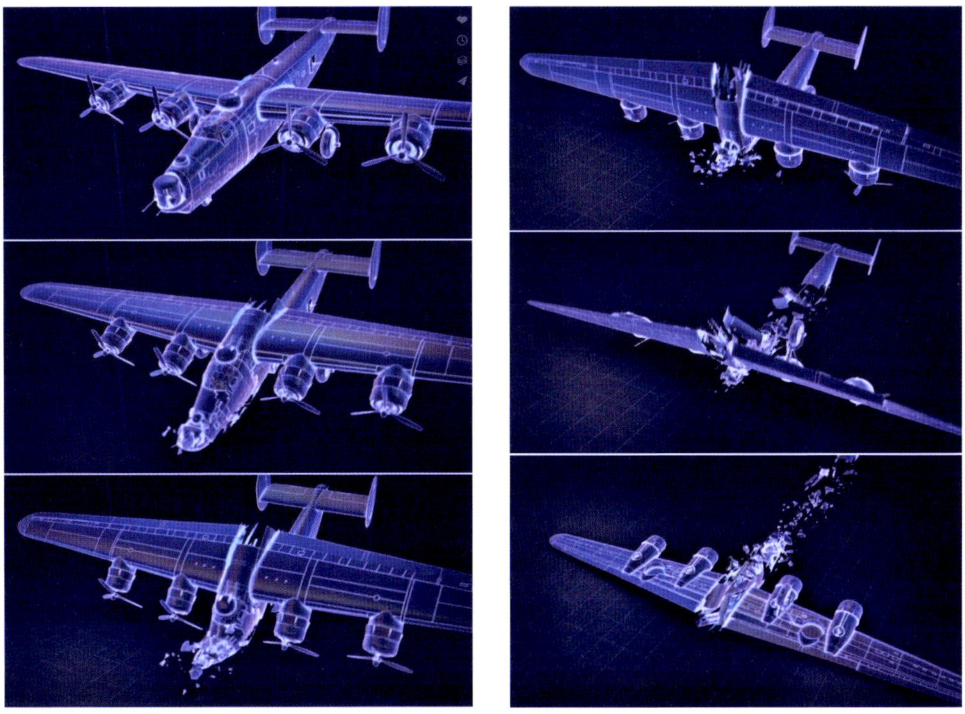

TABLE 4

SUMMARY OF MODEL-DITCHING INVESTIGATION OF BOMBER D

[Model scale, $\frac{1}{16}$; gross weight, 48,500 lb; center-of-gravity location, 30 percent M.A.C.; all values full scale]

(a) Without hydroflap.

Damage simulated by removal of parts (crosshatched areas)

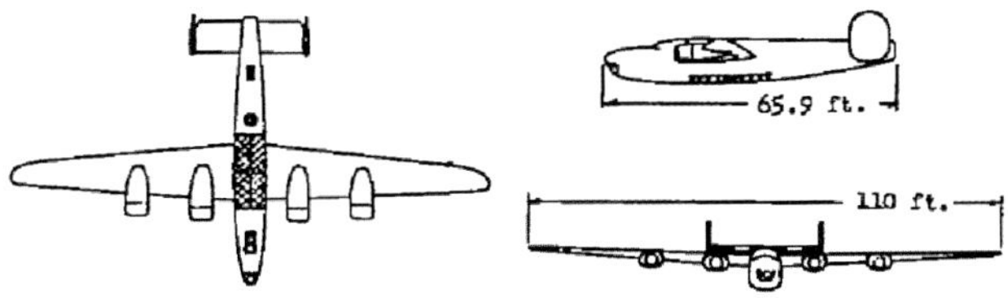

Landing attitude, deg	Flap setting, deg	Langing speed, knots	Length of run, ft	Maximum longitudinal deceleration, g units	Average longitudinal deceleration, g units	Motions of model (*)
			Undamaged model			
1	40	104	550	$1\frac{1}{2}$	1	h
			900	$2\frac{1}{2}$	$\frac{1}{2}$	s
5	0	104	950	1	$\frac{1}{2}$	s
			800	1	$\frac{1}{2}$	p
5	40	87	600	$1\frac{1}{2}$	$\frac{1}{2}$	h
			550	$1\frac{1}{2}$	$\frac{1}{2}$	p
9	0	87	300	3	1	h
9	40	87	250	$3\frac{1}{2}$	$1\frac{1}{2}$	h
			550	--	$\frac{1}{2}$	p
			Damaged model			
1	40	104	200	--	$2\frac{1}{2}$	d_1
			300	--	$1\frac{1}{2}$	s
†5	40	87	250	--	$1\frac{1}{2}$	p d_1
9	40	87	150	--	2	d_1

*In this column, the letters indicate the following motions:

d_1 dived violently - the model stopped abruptly in a nose-down attitude with most of the model submerged
h ran smoothly - the model made a very stable run
p porpoised - the model undulated about the transverse axis with some part of the model always in contact with water
s skipped - the model rebounded from the water

†Recommended ditching attitude and flap setting.

Remarks: The bomb-bay doors on this airplane are exceptionally weak and will probably fail in a ditching. The tests of models indicated that failure of the bomb-bay doors caused a diving moment. The amount of damage to the bulkhead aft of the bomb bay determined the severity of the behavior of the airplane.

FLIGHT INSTRUMENTS

Three flight parameters were quoted during the inquiry. They were airspeed, altitude, and pitch attitude. Instruments providing these parameters to AL523's pilot were (as illustrated below and on page 95): a (1) pioneer altimeter[102 103], a (2) Bendix airspeed indicator[104 105], a (3) Sperry gyro horizon[106], a (4) pioneer vertical speed indicator[107], and a Kollsman pitot static tube[108 109]. Their types were confirmed through an examination of period Consolidated LB30 cockpit photos, LB30 parts and service manuals, and online research. Though these four components did not contribute to the accident their inclusion in this section serves to provide the reader with an appreciation of the parameters Flight Lieutenant Prchal observed and those quoted by witnesses. A brief description of each component's operation is provided in the following paragraphs along with their significance to the crash.

LB-30 pilot instrument panel layout. (Image from T.O. No. 01-5ED-1. Preliminary Operation and Flight Instructions. LB-30 "Liberator II")

Altimeter, Airspeed and Position Error

Airspeed, altimeter, and vertical speed indicators rely on air pressure measured outside the aircraft by a pitot tube and static port referred to as a pitot-static system. The pitot-static system is a combined system that utilizes static air pressure and dynamic air pressure due to motion of the aircraft through the air. These pressures are utilized for the operation of the airspeed indicator, altimeter, and vertical speed indicator. Altimeter position error is caused by the airflow around the static ports that supply air pressure to the airspeed indicator and altimeter. Prchal testified he did not take off by instruments stating he had set his altimeter to zero, that there was good visibility, a good horizon, and only glanced at his airspeed indicator and altimeter from time to time.[110]

The Liberator pitot–static system consisted of two airspeed heads, one on each side of the fuselage mounted on masts with static pressure openings twenty-nine inches out from the fuselage and 4½ inches forward of the nose and fuselage intersection line.[111] The left airspeed head supplies pitot–static pressure to pilot instruments, the right supplies pitot–static pressure to the bombardier and navigator instruments. As the air flows past an aircraft in flight, the speed of the air relative to the aircraft is different at different positions on the aircraft's outer surface. It is this difference that causes altimeter position error due to the location of a static port or hole. The ideal position for a static port is a position where the local air pressure in flight is always equal to the pressure that is remote from the aircraft.[112] Altimeter position error can be different between similar aircraft and varied with airspeed and altitude. Flight Lieutenant Prchal testified the position error of the Liberator II he normally flew, AL616, as being +20 feet.[113] Prchal added that he "never allowed for it, because it is so

Altimeter, airspeed, gyro horizon and vertical speed. (AirCorps Library)

small, except when doing blind landings". Squadron Leader Falk on the other hand testified that the Liberator II position error was -33 feet at 140 mph at ground level. [114] [115] * Performance evaluations by American and British test establishments issued reports on various Liberator models that included altitude error charts attesting to those differences.

An airspeed indicator is a sensitive pressure gauge that measures the difference between pitot and static pressure. This difference is displayed as airspeed. Pitot

* Squadron Leader Falk's position error matches the Liberator III.

CONFIDENTIAL Page 5

Flight Section
MEMORANDUM REPORT NO. PHQ-M-19-1401-A
May 22, 1942

4. Take-off tests, concrete runway.

Weight	Flap Setting	No. of Trials	Total Distance required to Clear 50 ft. Obstacle	Length of T.O. Roll
41,000	1/2 (18°)	Best 3 out of 5	1770	1253
48,000	1/2 (18°)	Best 4 out of 4	2320	1630
56,000	1/2 (18°)	Best 2 out of 4	3240	2265

5. Determination of airspeed and altimeter errors with two type D-1 airspeed heads, one on each side of fuselage with static openings 2? inches out from fuselage and 4-1/2 inches forward of line of intersection of nose and fuselage.

Indicated Airspeed MPH	Indicator vs. Water Col. MPH	Calibrated Airspeed MPH	Airspeed Installation Error MPH	Altimeter Error
[illegible]	[illegible]9.5	229.5	0	+ 20'
210	210	209.5	+ .5	+ 20
190	190	189.5	+ .5	+ 20
170	170.5	169.5	+1.0	+20
150	150.5	149.5	+1.0	+ 20
130	130	129.5	+ .5	+ 20

Top right: War Department Air Corps, Material Division. Consolidated B-24D No. 40-696. Acceptance Performance Tests. May 22, 1942. Note the altimeter error correction in the far-right column. (WWIIaircraftperformance.org)

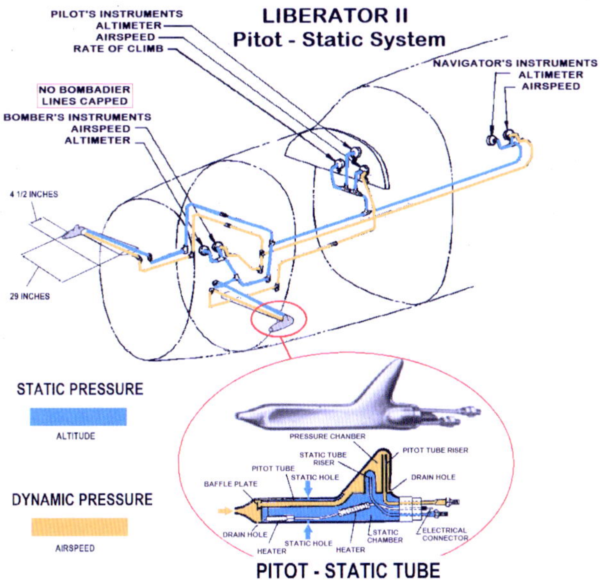

Bottom right: Liberator II and B-24 D pitot–static system schematic. Note the pilot and navigator altimeters have independent static pressure lines. Pitot–static tube cross section, EA-AC 65-15A. (Pitot-Static Tube image, AirCorps Library)

Below: Pitot–static system simplified schematic. (EA-AC 65-15A)

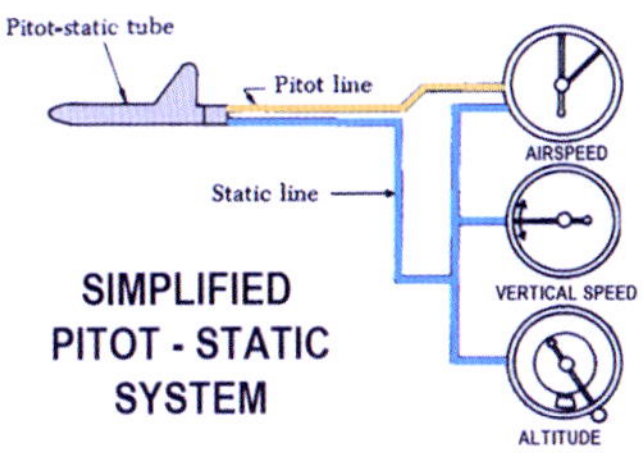

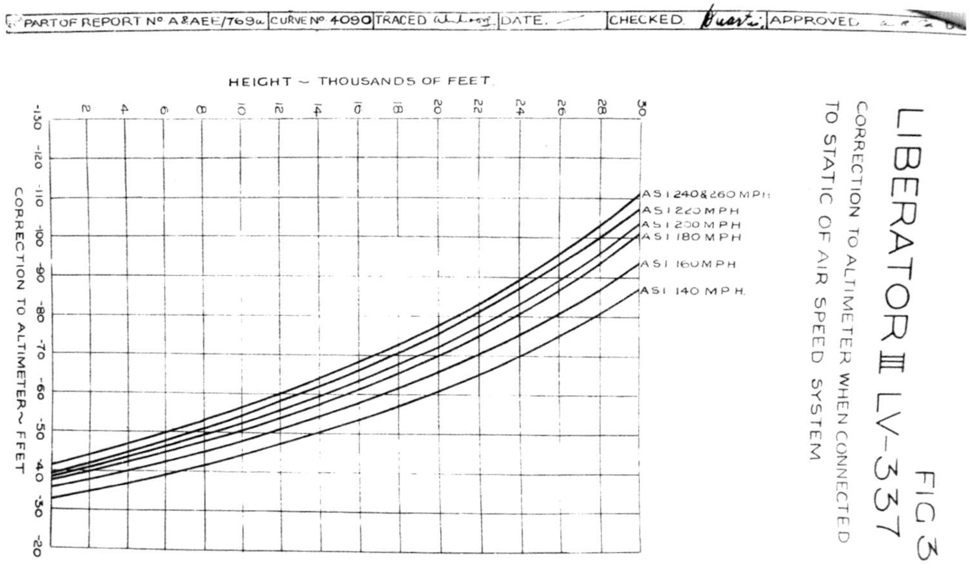

Liberator III. LV 337. Performance and tail buffet tests. AA&EE Boscombe Down. July 31, 1942. Squadron Leader Falk's position error matches Liberator III graph. (wwiiaircraftperformance.org, AVIA 18/720)

pressure enters a capsule surrounded by static pressure within the instrument case. Expansion and contraction of the capsule moves the airspeed needle. An altimeter displays altitude by sensing the atmospheric pressure outside the aircraft from an external static pressure port through a line connected to the back of its instrument case. A sealed capsule expands and contracts with the changing pressure and is displayed by mechanical pointer movement. A vertical speed indicator (VSI) displays the rate of climb or descent in thousands of feet per minute at 100-foot increments and operates similarly to an altimeter. When an aircraft is in level flight neither descending nor climbing the VSI needle sits at zero. During the inquiry Prchal testified that at about 130 mph he was airborne and that after reaching 150 feet of altitude he eased the control column forward to pick up airspeed. Upon reaching 165 mph he found his control column locked. The airspeeds and altitudes Prchal described are illustrated in the images opposite.

Witnesses testified to AL523 reaching altitudes of 30 and 100 feet.[116] Prchal's altimeter reading of 150 feet would have been displayed as seen in the proceeding illustrations. The question of AL523's different altitudes was first examined in detail by Franciszek Grabowski in his 2017 book titled *Liberator AL523*. Through use of flight simulator software and aerodynamic formula, seventeen Liberator take-off simulations at a weight of 56,400 lbs[117] were conducted under different parameters

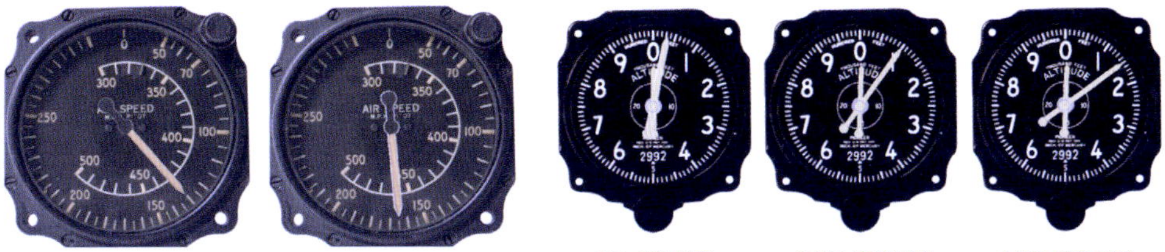

130 MPH 165 MPH 30 FEET 100 FEET 150 FEET

and scenarios. Of that number one was conducted using an altitude of 33 feet, two at 66 feet, and one at 164 feet.[118] Simulation values and results were converted from metric with both 66-foot altitudes representing corrections for Liberator altimeter error. In all four simulations the flight ended at approximately the same location where AL523 crashed.*

1. 33 feet, impact pitch attitude + 2.1 degree, rate of descent 413 ft/min, airspeed 179 mph
2. 66 feet, impact pitch attitude -0.8 degree, rate of descent 1,417 ft/min, airspeed 179 mph
3. 66 feet, impact pitch attitude -0.7 degree, rate of descent 1,299 ft/min, airspeed 181 mph
4. 164 feet, impact pitch attitude -5.0 degree, rate of descent 2,598 ft/min, airspeed 188 mph

Rate of descent conversion from feet per minute to feet per second give the following values.

413 ft/min = 6.8 ft/sec
1,417 ft/min = 23.6 ft/sec
1,299 ft/min = 21.6 ft/sec
2,598 ft/min = 43.3 ft/sec

"A sink rate, or rate of descent, of greater than 25 ft/sec is more or less a demarcation line for significantly increased injury potential. In a set of forty-six crashes with identifiable sink rates studied by McDonnell Douglas and Lockheed, sixteen had sink rates of 25 ft/sec or higher. Of those sixteen crashes, 75% involved fatalities. Of the remaining crashes, all with a sink rate less than 25 ft/min, 50% had fatalities."[119] A 1996 report by the US Federal Aviation Administration of eleven high-energy water accidents saw a 40.6% fatality rate out of 507 occupants. Fuselage breaks occurred in six of the eight high-energy water impact accidents, leading to a fatality rate of 36.8%.[120] Prior to these studies the American Eighth Air Force compiled statistics

* Simulation height and weight value results converted from metric to imperial.

for 1943 where B-24 crew who ditched or bailed out over water showed only a 10.3% survival rate compared to 35.2% of surviving B-17 crew.[121] In addition, there is also a marked difference between Prchal's testimony of -15 to -20 degrees nose-down attitude when AL523 struck the water and those of simulation pitch attitudes. The accepted ditching technique for Liberators in 1943 was to maintain a low forward speed and rate of descent with a tail-down attitude. Flight manuals further warned of severe deceleration upon alighting that could result in the tail breaking off behind the bomb bay.[122] NACA ditching behaviour tests in 1943 using 1:16 dynamic scale models supported the Liberator's poor ditching qualities. The recommended ditching altitude of +5 deg. and flap setting of 40 degrees at 100 mph resulted in the model porpoising and diving violently as it decelerated in the water.[123][124]

AL523's nose-down attitude was less than ideal for ditching. Given the seconds Prchal had prior to impact, ditching cannot be considered his intention, at this point he was along for the ride. In his interview with Carlos Thompson, Flight Lieutenant Buck did not consider AL523 having been ditched given the aircraft's severe damage. "The evidence of the body being ripped off clearly indicates that the aircraft struck the water at considerable speed and this is in no way consistent with standard ditching technique."[125] It should be remembered that, in an unsuccessful effort to gain height, Prchal testified to applying elevator nose-up trim when unable to pull back on his frozen control column.[126]

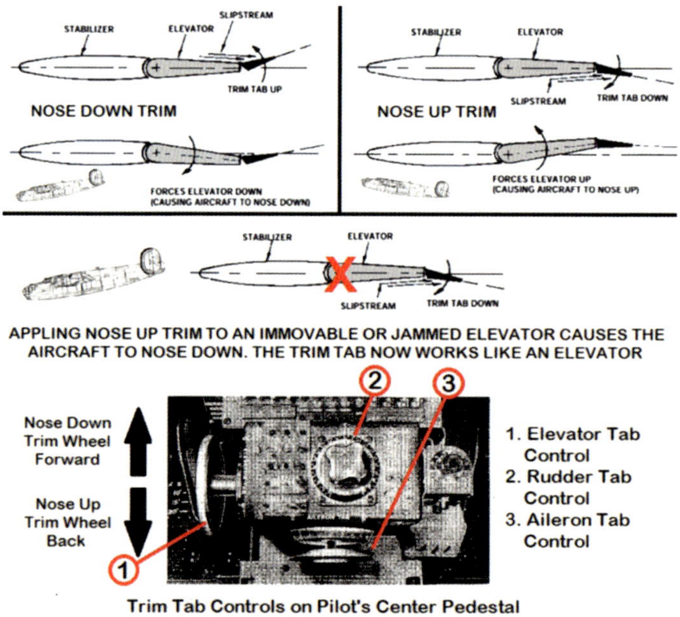

The use of elevator trim frees the pilot from exerting constant force on elevator controls. To nose the airplane down the trim wheel is turned counter-clockwise (moved forward); to nose the airplane up, the trim wheel is turned clockwise (moved back). (Trim tab illustration from Experimental Aircraft Association/ Tony Bingelis. Used with permission from EAA.)

Unfortunately, because AL523's elevator was locked in a neutral position the application of nose-up trim by Prchal resulted in the trim tab acting like a small elevator which pushed the Liberator's nose down further.

The Altitude Discrepancy

The discrepancy between Prchal's testimony of reaching an altitude of 150 feet and Flight Lieutenant Capes' testimony of AL523 passing him at approximately 30 feet from his tower vantage was never reconciled during the court of inquiry.[127] It was briefly alluded to but not pursued when Prchal and Squadron Leader Falk were asked what the Liberator's altimeter position error was. Prchal quoted +20 feet while Falk quoted -33 feet; Prchal's value was correct for the Mark II Liberator[128] while Falk's was correct for the Mark III.[129] It should be noted that it is difficult for a person to accurately judge altitude from a ground perspective particularly at night, altimeter accuracy at very low altitudes is not reliable and over time in-service can vary plus or minus 20 feet or more. The desert environment of North Africa and Egypt had similarly adverse effects on altimeter accuracy, the fine sand finding its way into the instrument's sensitive mechanism further contributing to faulty readings.[130] In retrospect this altitude discrepancy of 150 feet verses 30 feet might lastly have also been due to a static-pressure line leak within the fuselage. Static-pressure lines provide atmospheric pressure to the pilot's altimeter, airspeed indicator, and vertical speed indicator.

To recap, an altimeter displays altitude by sensing the atmospheric pressure outside the aircraft from an external static pressure port through a line connected to the back of its instrument case. A sealed capsule expands and contracts with the changing pressure and is displayed by mechanical pointer movement. Atmospheric pressure within the fuselage of an unpressurized aircraft in flight is slightly lower than the atmospheric pressure outside the fuselage. This difference is due to the venturi effect of the air flowing around the fuselage which lowers the static pressure inside it. This lower pressure equates to a higher altitude. If there is a leak in the static line within the fuselage the altimeter will indicate a higher altitude than indicated and the airspeed indicator will display a slightly higher than actual airspeed.

30 FEET 150 FEET

An example of this change in altitude and airspeed is seen in the North American B-25 Mitchell, or Mitchell III, which utilized static pressure in the cockpit as an emergency alternate static source. On some aircraft an alternate static source is provided should the external static pressure port become clogged or iced over causing erratic altitude, airspeed, and vertical speed readings. The Mitchell III flight manual warned, "should the normal source fail, the switch should be set to ALTERNATE SOURCE when the static pressure is drawn from the interior of the cabin. In this event the instruments will continue to function but they will not be so accurate."[131] A correction chart in the flight manual listed the changing airspeeds and altitudes.[132] An example of a higher reading altitude is illustrated in the chart below.

North American Mitchell III position error corrections chart
When the static source selector switch is set to ALTERNATE SOURCE the ASI and altimeter readings are affected as follows:

AT AIR SPEED TUBE READINGS	110	120	140	160	180	200	220	240	mph IAS
THE ALTERNATE SOURCE READINGS ARE	115	125	149	170	190	220	240	260	mph IAS
AND THE ALTIMETER OVERREADS BY	20	50	100	125	200	300	330	400	feet

With alternate source selected and static pressure sensed from the cabin, an air speed tube reading of 140 mph will display 149 mph and the altimeter overreads by 100 feet. Though early model Liberators did not have an alternate static source[133] the maintenance manual states that a high-reading altimeter should have its static pressure lines inspected for leaks.[134] An alternate static source was incorporated in the modified US Navy Liberator version designated PB4Y-2 Privateer with the cargo and passenger transport version designated RY-3. Both aircraft were designed with a single vertical fin and rudder. On the PB4Y-2 only the pilot had an alternate static source selector[135] while each pilot on the RY-3 had a selector for his respective instruments.[136] The RY-3 flight manual states that altimeter error when using alternate static will always indicate higher than the true altitude and may be as high as 800 feet.[137] To put this result into perspective the atmospheric pressure at sea level is 29.92 in.Hg (inches of mercury), at 1,000 feet above sea level it is 28.86 in.Hg which equates to approximately 100 feet per 10th inch of mercury. AL523's take-off was at sea level with the altimeter set to zero, Prchal testified he reached an altitude of 150 feet while Capes witnessed AL523 passing him at around 30 feet. A static pressure leak from a line, hose, fitting or instrument glass seal equating to approximately 100 feet, or one 10th of an inch of mercury, easily explains the discrepancy between Prchal and Capes.

Standard atmosphere chart up to 15,000 feet

ALTITUDE (FT)	PRESSURE (IN. HG)	TEMPERATURE (°C)	TEMPERATURE (°F)
0	29.92	15.0	59.0
1,000	28.86	13.0	55.4
2,000	27.82	11.0	51.9
3,000	26.82	9.1	48.3
4,000	25.84	7.1	44.7
5,000	24.89	5.1	41.2
6,000	23.98	3.1	37.6
7,000	23.09	1.1	34.0
8,000	22.22	-0.9	30.5
9,000	21.38	-2.8	26.9
10,000	20.57	-4.8	23.3
11,000	19.79	-6.8	19.8
12,000	19.02	-8.8	16.2
13,000	18.29	-10.8	12.6
14,000	17.57	-12.7	9.1
15,000	16.88	-14.7	5.5

An argument can be made that the open nose undercarriage doors allowed a slight pressurization of the fuselage interior by the 130-mph airstream when the nose lifted during take-off. Unfortunately this slight pressurization due to ram effect of the open doors is incalculable as the Liberator interior is inherently draughty regardless of undercarriage position. It would require a direct altitude measurement taken within the aircraft interior during take-off and climb. Results from this effect can only be guessed, instead of a 100-feet altimeter reading due to a static pressure leak a slightly lower altimeter reading might likely be indicated.

This altimeter reading would be brief as it would steadily rise in consort with the retracting nose undercarriage gradually blocking and reducing the 130-mph airflow until the closing doors stopped it completely resulting in the altimeter climbing past 100 feet as the venturi effect increased. The Liberator's nose undercarriage retracted quicker than the mains taking approximately six to seven seconds, the mains taking thirteen to fifteen seconds longer. If this indeed was the reason for

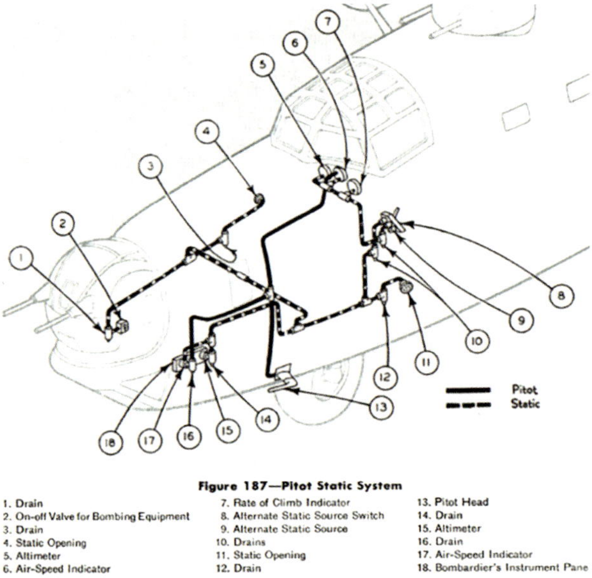

Consolidated Vultee Aircraft Corporation. Service and Instruction Manual. PB4Y-2 Bombardment Airplane. Item 8 and 9 Alternate static switch and source.

the altitude discrepancy then testimonies of Prchal and Capes were honest and reasonably accurate from their points of view. An altimeter needle not moving much past 30 feet during AL523's take-off would have been very disconcerting to Prchal and something he might have recalled. The sensation of AL523 climbing was likely reassuring to Prchal and further confirmed by his altimeter needle steadily moving toward 150 feet. The increased altimeter difference at higher altitudes would be unnoticeable and might only be perceived if another aircraft flew alongside and altitudes compared between flight crews.

Map from the inquiry with Flight Lieutenant Capes and AL523's positions indicated in red.

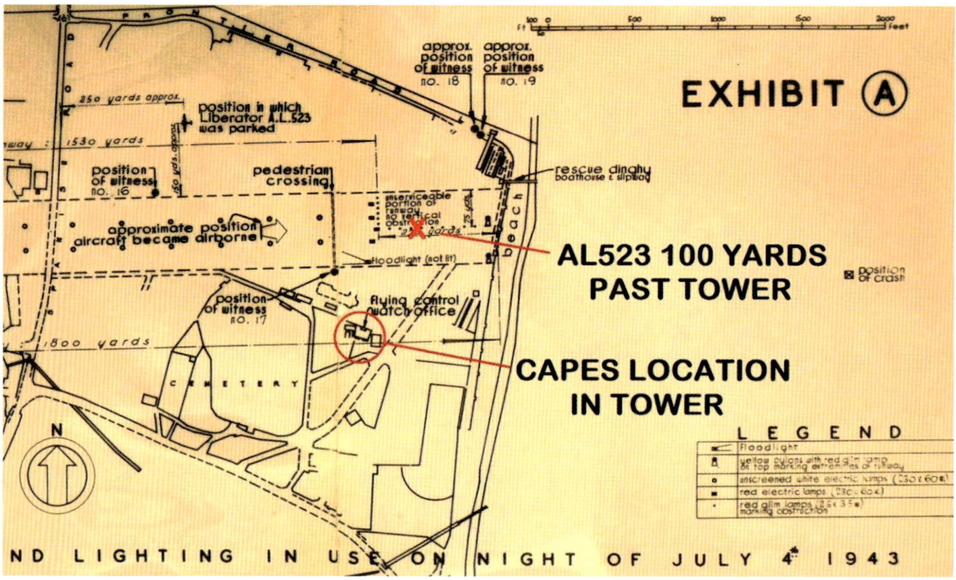

North Front's three-storey control tower identified by a red arrow, the building on the right is the flying control watch office. Both were located on the airfield's south-east end. A close-up of the tower is shown above. (Imperial War Museum)

Gyro Horizon

The Sperry operation and service instruction manual gives the following description of a gyro horizon:

> "A gyro horizon indicator is an aircraft flight instrument that provides the pilot with a constant visual indication of the aircraft's attitude relative to the earth. The air-driven gyro rotor rotates with its spin axis in an upright position. Due to gyroscopic inertia, the gyro maintains the vertical position as the aircraft rolls or pitches. This produces relative motion between the gyro and the instrument case which is shown on the face of the instrument by displacement between the miniature airplane and the horizon bar. The relation of the miniature airplane to the horizon bar furnishes an indication of the attitude of the aircraft in roll and pitch. Thus the pilot's 'sensing' of the gyro horizon's indications is the same as the interpretation of the relation between the wings of the airplane and the natural horizon during contact flight; level flight is maintained by keeping the miniature airplane aligned with the horizon bar."[138]

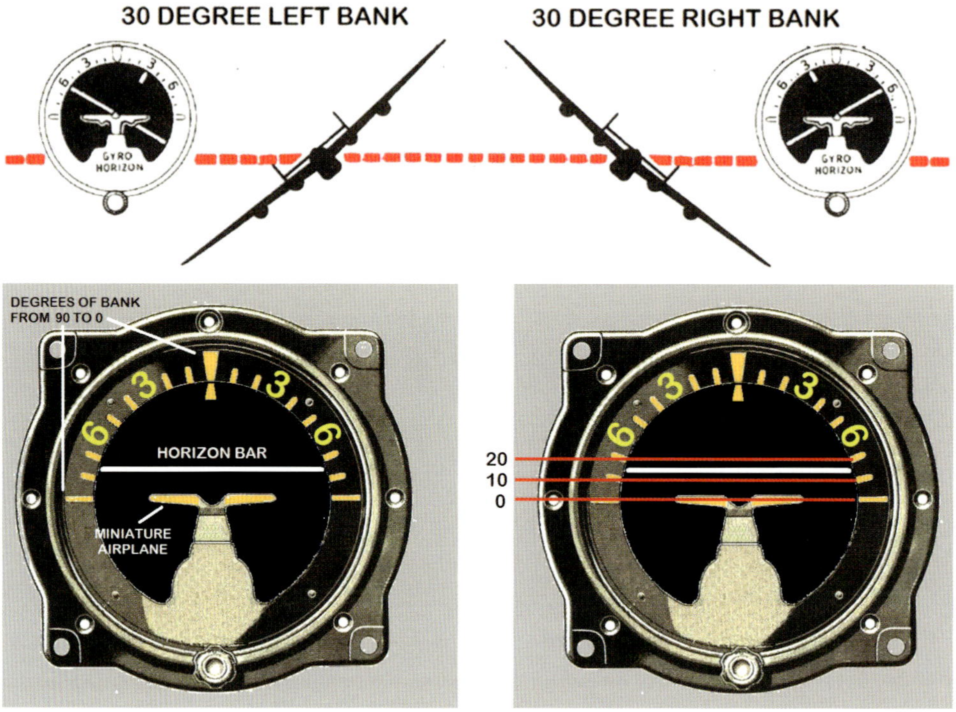

The Sperry gyro horizon. The illustration on the right shows the miniature airplane in level flight approximately -15 degrees pitch down beneath the horizon bar. (AirCorpsLibrary.com)

During the inquiry Prchal was asked, "In what attitude was the aircraft when it struck the sea?" Prchal replied, "Laterally level, about 15 degrees–20 degrees nose down." How could Prchal know this, what visual clue gave him that impression at night despite stating that he had not done an instrument take-off? The only instrument that could possibly give him this information was the vacuum-driven Sperry gyro horizon P/N 643710 on his instrument panel. But, unlike modern horizon displays it only has degrees of bank and no markings for pitch, or does it? Actually, because it is a gyro, and because its display is in ten-degree increments of bank there is no mystery. In the illustration three red lines have been added to the gyro horizon image illustrating how ten-degree pitch increments might be discerned with the miniature airplane beneath the white horizon bar. One reference from a B-24 pilot training manual states that best climb attitude is achieved by "keeping the miniature airplane approximately ⅛th inch above the horizon bar".[139] Curiously ⅛th of an inch measured against the roll degree arc markings is in the area of approximately four to five degrees. How Prchal determined his pitch angle is uncertain. Was it simply an intuitive guess based on experience, or an instinctual rule of thumb observed of gyro horizons, or a combination of both?

ELEVATOR BUNGEE SPRING

Though this component was not part of AL523's elevator-control system it is included to address statements made by Prchal in later years regarding circumstances of the crash. A 1944 Consolidated service letter, MCR 523, described a modification which incorporated a bungee-tension spring for aerodynamic balance in the Liberator's elevator-control system. The load applied by this tension spring prevented automatic deflection of the elevators to the up position during certain speed and loading conditions of the airplane.[140] As earlier stated all early model Liberators including AL523 did not have this modification in 1943. Two statements by Prchal give perspective to conditions this modification addressed. In a 1953 interview Prchal gave to the *Polish Daily* in London where he recalled that, "after trimming the elevator I suddenly felt a mighty shudder and found that the controls were entirely blocked."[141] In the book *The Assassination of Winston Churchill* published in 1969 the author Carlos Thompson asked Prchal to recall how the elevator jamming occurred. Prchal answered:

> "It was something I had never experienced before. The control stick went slightly forward, with a sudden jerk, about an inch, enough to put the aircraft in a shallow-angle gliding-path. [...] It felt as if the whole system had broken down. It became paralyzed." [142]

The Consolidated service letter described that when:

> "The centre of gravity is aft of the normal specified limitations, the airplane will fly tail low. This attitude applies an up-load on the empennage; the elevators, being movable, are deflected up. Automatic deflection occurs when the airplane is climbing at a speed below 140 mph."

The service letter goes on to say: "As a result of the elevator-up automatic deflection, the airplane is placed in a steep climb or stall attitude." Lastly the service letter emphasized conditions that tended to vary the point at which the elevator-up automatic deflection occurred. These were centre of gravity, airspeed, degree of climb or turn, power, and cable tension.[143] There is no disputing that AL523 was heavy, possibly tail heavy, when it took off. Prchal's statement that the control stick went slightly forward with a sudden jerk about an inch, suggests that his elevators, whether he was aware or not, may have been in the 'up automatic deflection' and the 'jerk forward' was an unloading or loosening, and beginnings of a stall. This condition where the controls suddenly loosen is described in the B-24 flight manual where it states that "usually there is clear warning of an approaching stall. Controls will loosen somewhat, and airspeed will be falling off. You will observe a shuddering of the tail and a slight pitching action."[144][145] A stall is an aerodynamic condition which occurs when smooth airflow over an airplane's wing is disrupted, resulting in loss of lift.

Further credence is given to the service letter's automatic deflection, or up-load, condition by Mr Algernon Llewellyn a former wing commander and CO of No. 511 Squadron's Liberator Flight. Mr Llewellyn described a Liberator flight characteristic to Carlos Thompson where "very often [...] after you left the ground, the tail of the Liberator would drop suddenly – this could worry the neophyte pilot, he said, but the way out was to let her ride it, until she found her way."[146] This same condition was also described by Flight Lieutenant Buck to Thompson. The former investigator recalled learning of a fundamental instability the Liberator had which at the time of the accident was unknown to pilots and himself. He asserted that it "leads me to believe that the accident was perhaps due to a heavily laden aircraft being taken off with an inherent vice". Buck related to Thompson of an RAF Liberator pilot's story he had investigated which shared similarities to the Sikorski crash (see page 61).

Prchal's recollections, if viewed within the context of the service letter, suggest he may have been unaware that his elevators were deflected slightly up due to an aft centre of gravity as he climbed. If so, then the shudder he felt was AL523 entering a stall which suddenly relieved the 'up-load' on the elevators and empennage. This allowed the control column to abruptly jerk forward, or loosen, as the B-24 flight manual describes. If a cotton rag were present at this critical point its migration aft along the narrowing U-channels between the elevator and fixed fairing would soon lock both surfaces together. Though similarities exist between the service bulletin, Buck's Liberator pilot, and Prchal's recollections they are not intended to cast doubt on Prchal or that a cotton rag locked AL523's

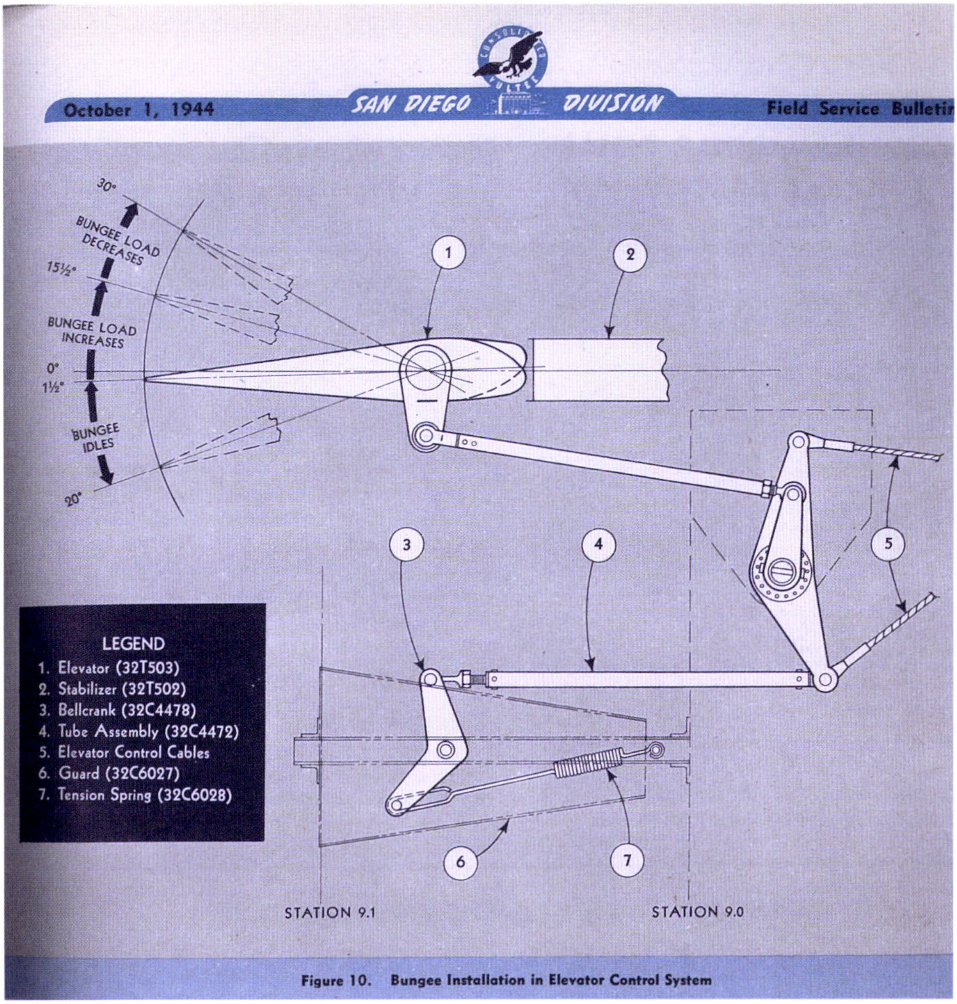

Figure 10. Bungee Installation in Elevator Control System

Consolidated service letter MCR 523 elevator bungee spring modification. (San Diego Air & Space Museum)

elevators. They are presented in the interest of unbiased transparency and that all potential scenarios were considered and researched as best as possible.

TRIM TAB SPROCKETS

Prchal testified that moments before AL523 struck the sea he applied elevator nose-up trim. Contrary to this statement Wing Commander Stevens testified finding the elevator trim tabs "to be almost in the neutral position"[147] when he inspected the largely intact tail section. Further to Stevens' findings Carlos Thompson interviewed Leading Aircraftman J P Hammond in the late 1960s who, as a fitter, had assisted Stevens in examining the wreckage. Hammond described his findings after opening an inspection panel in the tail section:

> "I came upon this chain and sprocket. The metal wheel on which the chain rested was clearly cracked across, and I thought the chain, which had become loose, could have interfered with the elevator control mechanism, since it was part of the trim-tab control."[148 149]

There is no way to know the precise crash dynamics that caused the condition Hammond described. The damage was likely due from extreme force on the tail as it was violently wrenched and broken from the fuselage. What can be concluded is that the amount of force required to break the elevator trim 3/32 inch 7 x 7 flexible tinned steel cables[150] exceeded its rated breaking strength of 920 lbs.[151] The elevator trim cables broke from their chains as they were pulled during the fuselage breakup resulting in fracture of the sprocket and rotation of the trim tabs towards neutral. The sprocket damage was a consequence of the crash and not its cause.

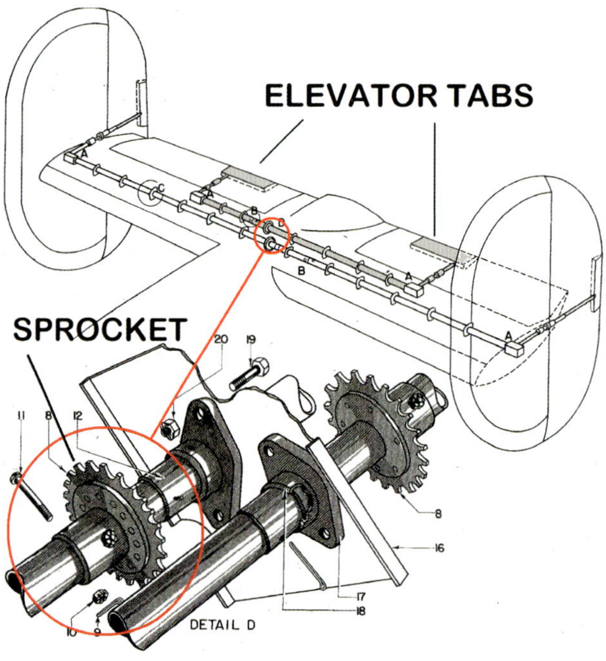

Elevator tabs and sprocket location.

SHEARED CONTROL LOCK SPINDLE

The rudder and elevator control lock retrieved from the tail section wreckage and examined by Wing Commander Stevens is of particular interest in that, like the cracked elevator trim sprocket discovered by Leading Aircraftman Hammond, it had also suffered damage but not to its lock pinions as he had confirmed. Stevens testified that the locking control pulley spindle had been found sheared, so he immediately sent it to Farnborough for a detailed examination. It was later determined that the spindle had sheared due to torsional stress likely as result of the crash.[152] The cables of the control lock system were, like the elevator trim, 3/32 inch 7 x 7 flexible tinned steel cables[153] which had a rated breaking strength of 920 lbs.[154] Shearing of the spindle occurred when the tail violently broke from the fuselage upon water impact. As the two sections separated a sudden and excessive cable load rotated the pulley beyond its limit of travel twisting the pulley off its spindle. As with the cracked elevator trim sprocket this damage was a consequence of the crash and not related to its cause.

Rudder and elevator control lock. The pulley was secured to the spindle by a nut within the assembly which was secured with bolts to the horizontal stabilizer's centre hinge bracket.

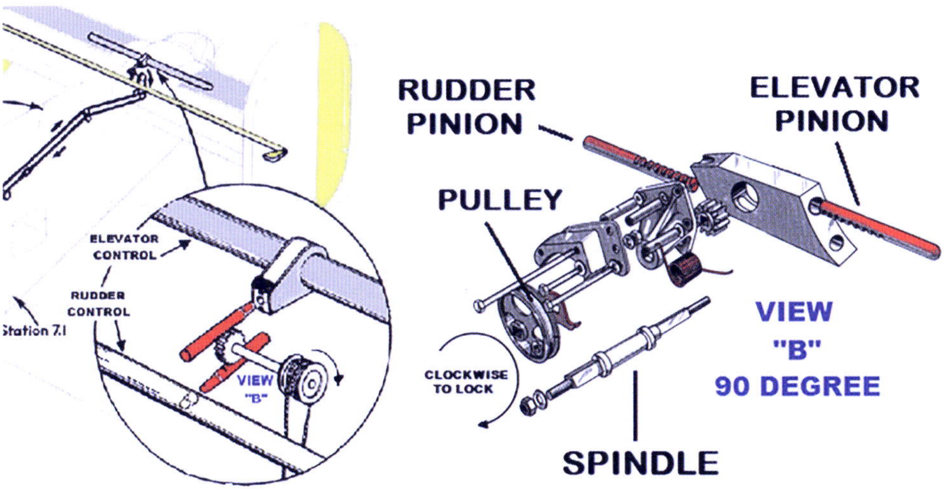

ENGINE OVERHEAT

Among Garth Barnard's new eyewitness accounts found in Chapter Four is Jack Waterfield an RAF AC2 mechanic who described events on the night of AL523's departure. Jack recalled AL523 parked on North Front's apron with its engines running. He was joined by an Indian serviceman who commented that the aircraft would never take off with all that weight and the engines getting hot the longer they idled.[155] Garth wondered if AL523's engines could have overheated and what would happen if they did. Idling a radial engine for a long period of time would more likely cause spark plug fouling than overheating. Leaning the mixture during high power pre-take-off checks easily clears the fouled plugs which is what Prchal most likely did. Overheating is usually associated with higher power settings during take-off and cruise flight. High cylinder head temperatures can result in power loss or engine failure due to preignition and detonation of fuel air mixture which causes extremely high temperatures that burn valves, pistons, and rings. Detonation is a combustion phenomenon that results in abnormal and spontaneous burning of the unburned portion of the fuel-air mixture within a combustion chamber after normal ignition has occurred, setting in motion pressure waves within the cylinder that travel at high velocities. Put simply detonation occurs when the fuel-air mixture explodes rather than burning evenly in a controlled manner. Detonation and preignition can cause cylinder head failure and produce severe forces on pistons and connecting rods. Management of cylinder head temperatures was accomplished by the opening and closing of

LB-30 Liberator II Erection and Maintenance Instructions. (T.O. No. 01-5ED-2)

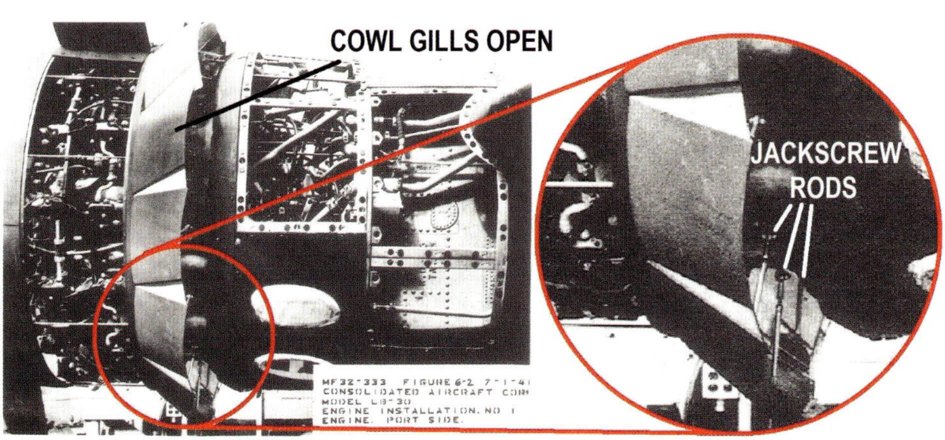

Above left: *Consolidated Liberator Mark II. (Imperial War Museum)*

Above right: *LB-30 Liberator II Erection and Maintenance Instructions. (T.O. No. 01-5ED-2)*

cooling gills at the rear of each engine cowling. Cowl gill control switches on early model LB30s and Liberator IIs were located on the lower right-hand corner of co-pilot's instrument panel. The cowl flap system consisted of a twenty-four-volt electric motor mounted on top of each engine accessory bay which drove individual jackscrews for each cowl flap through interconnected rotary flex cables.[156] Cowl flap movement was accomplished by toggling the control switches toward open or closed. Stevens testified that all cooling gills were closed which suggests all engine cowl flap jackscrew actuators were found retracted and their associated gills flush with the engine cowlings.

Two things speak to Stevens' findings. First, that AL523's cylinder head temperatures were likely within limits at take-off; the Liberator II cylinder head temperatures should be below 232°C prior to take-off. And second, that Prchal adhered to warnings to set cowl flaps to ½ or as required.[157] Air Commodore Simpson testified that AL523's exhaust flames were a steady blue and that there was no change in the note of the engines.[158] A steady blue exhaust flame meant the engines were running well at an optimum mixture and power setting. This observation speaks to Prchal handling his engines competently and conscientiously to get their temperatures within limits and achieve maximum performance prior to and during take-off.

FLAP POSITION

Prchal testified that prior to take-off he had set AL523's flaps to ½ which was a setting of 20 degrees. The Liberator used Fowler-type flaps which slid rearward while hinging down when deployed. The settings were 0 through 40 degrees. A setting of ½ or 20 degrees flap is illustrated. Flaps enhance lift-drag characteristics of the wing and are used to reduce take-off distance. Examination of the wreckage by Wing Commander Stevens confirmed the flap position to be approximately ⅜ths down.[159] The ¼ difference of flap position was likely due to the crash and wreckage recovery. Most Liberator take-offs were made with 10 or 20 degrees of flap. Flap controls were

Below: *Liberator flap cross section deployed to 40 degrees with 20 and 0 degree increments. (Service and Instruction Manual, Airplane General B-24 Bombardment Airplane, Second Edition, 1944)*

Bottom: *Parts Catalogue for Army Models C-87, C-87A and AT-22 Navy Models RY-1 and RY-2 British Model Liberator C VII Airplanes. (T.O. No. 01-5-4)*

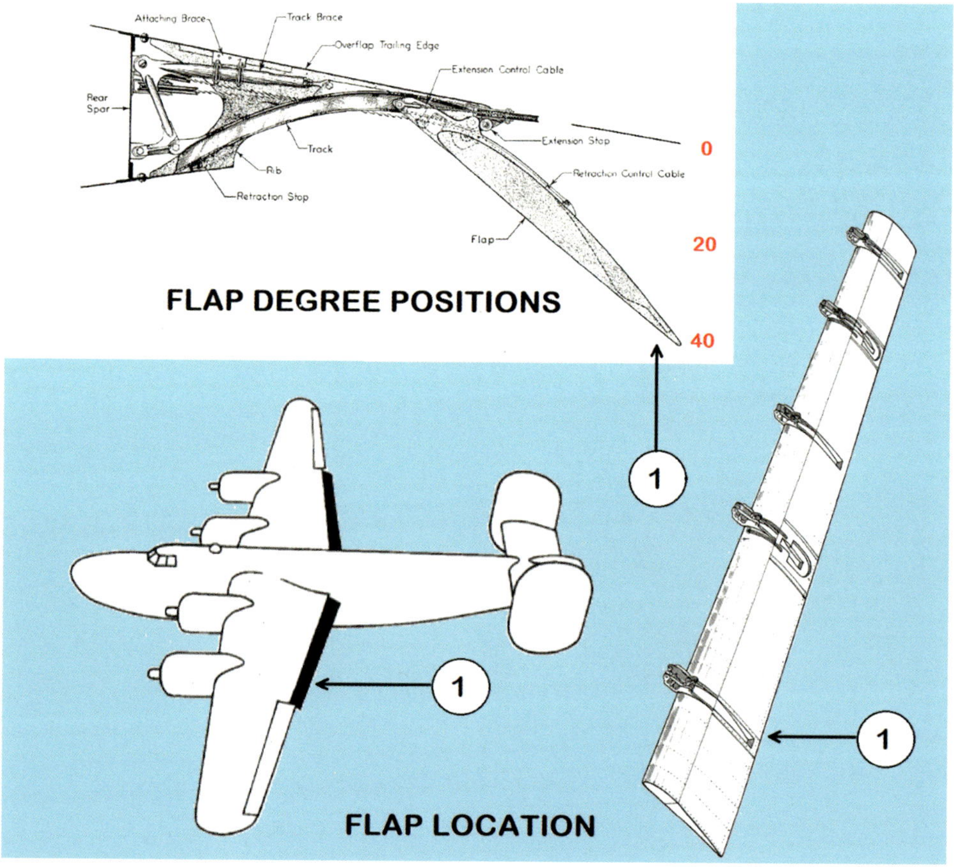

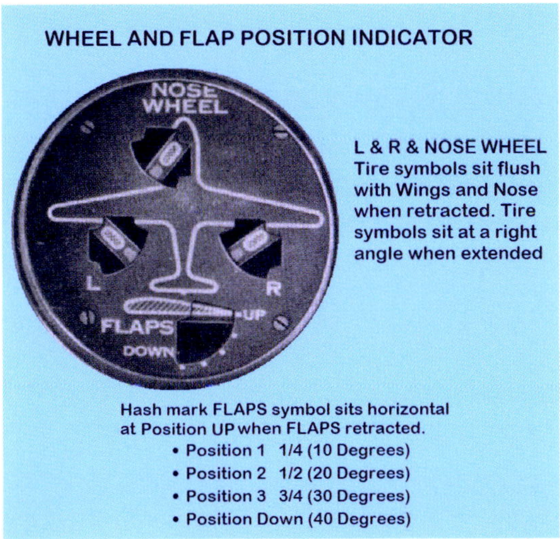

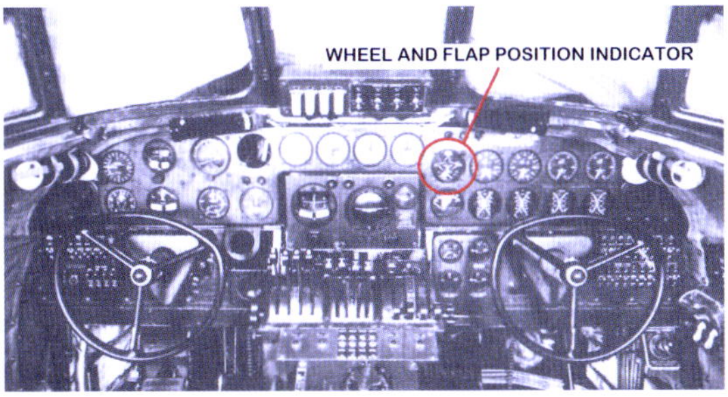

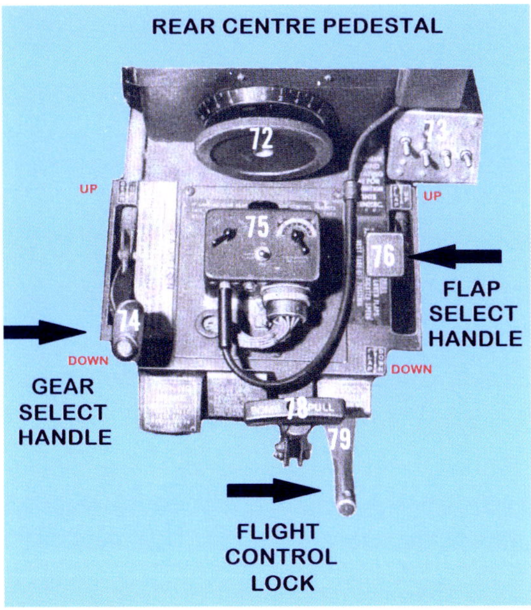

comprised of a selector lever located on the centre console's right-hand side and was operated through a cable system driven by a hydraulic actuator energized by pressure from the aircraft hydraulic system.[160]

AUTOMATIC PILOT

During the inquiry Prchal was asked what type of automatic pilot was fitted to AL523, and replied it was a Sperry. A search of LB30 and Liberator II equipment confirmed it to be a Sperry Type A-3 automatic pilot which was hydraulically powered. He was then asked, "when you carried out your cockpit drill on the runway prior to taking off on this occasion, what exactly did you do?" When Prchal described the

***Top:** General Electric wheel and flap position indicator P/N 8DJ4PXC4 used on the Liberator II. (TO No. 01-5ED-4 via AirCorpsLibrary.com)*

***Middle:** Location of wheel and flap position indicator on LB30/Liberator II instrument panel.*

***Bottom:** Centre Pedestal displaying typical location of undercarriage select handle, flight control lock handle and flap control handle found on all Liberator models.*

automatic pilot he testified that, “the three oil cut-off valves were off, and the main switch was off [...] I uncaged directional gyro and artificial horizon of the automatic pilot.”[161] Prchal had ensured that his automatic pilot was off and that all three flight control selection valves, rudder, aileron, and elevator were selected off. The three flight control selection valves (surface control shut-off valves) and main switch selections ensured his autopilot was off.[162] They were located left of the pilot’s seat by the side wall near the floor.

In his book *Liberator AL523* Franciszek Grabowski’s research revealed that a Polish Liberator pilot named Bolesław Korpowski had considered AL523’s crash the result of the automatic pilot being left selected on. His theory was based on an incident in August 1944 where he had neglected to switch off his automatic pilot. Korpowski had fought for control and crashed on take-off with the automatic pilot engaged. This theory was dismissed when research revealed that Korpowski in August 1944 was flying later model Liberators equipped with Minnesota-Honeywell Type C-1 automatic pilots which were electrically operated.[163] Late-model B-24 Liberator pilot manuals warned, “If you attempt a take-off with this unit connected, it is extremely difficult to overpower it.”[164] The B-24 D flight manual contained this warning in its

LB30 - Liberator II cockpit showing Sperry automatic pilot location.

1. Rudder Control Knob
2. Aileron Control Knob
3. Dual Illumination Lamp
4. Bank Index
5. Aileron Follow-Up Index
6. Elevator Control Knob
7. Suction Gauge
8. Banking Scale
9. Horizon Bar
10. Elevator Follow-Up Index
11. Elevator Alignment Index
12. Miniature Airplane
13. Miniature Airplane Adjusting Knob
14. Caging Knob
15. Knobs For Valve Adjustment
16. Valve Adjustment Reference Dials
17. Ball Bank Indicator
18. Directional Gyro Card
19. Rudder Follow-Up Card
20. Dual Illumination Lamp
21. Autopilot On-Off Select Knob

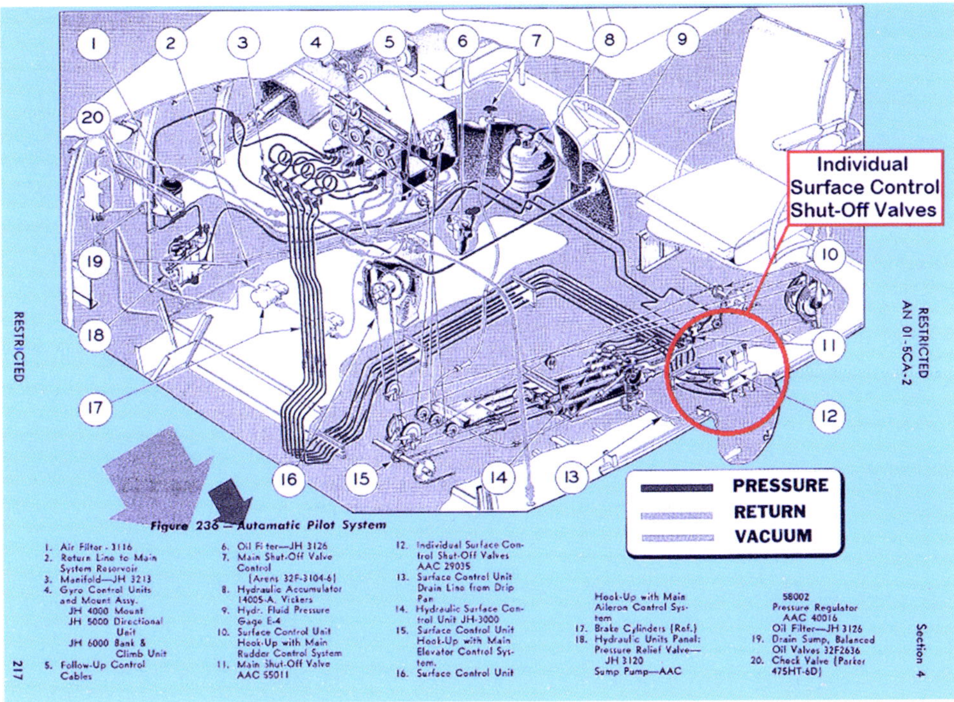

checklist, "Automatic flight control must be OFF. If take-off attempted with unit connected, free operation of the controls is impossible."[165]

The Sperry Type A-3 automatic pilot installed in AL523 was gyro-controlled, vacuum-operated, and hydraulically powered by a 200-psi system regulated to 150 psi.[166] The three oil cut-off valves, main on-off knob (push-pull style), and artificial horizon of the automatic pilot described by Prchal are illustrated above. Unlike the Minnesota-Honeywell system the Sperry system could be easily overpowered by the pilot. This is emphasized in Sperry's operation and instruction manual for the Type A-3, "Do NOT forget that if necessary the automatic pilot can be overpowered by applying about twice the normal force on the controls."[167] [168] The ability for the pilot to overpower the Sperry system was through two overpower valves located in each hydraulic surface control servo actuator, connected in parallel to each flight control cable system.[169] The overpower valve essentially acted as a pressure relief valve when a pilot overpowers an engaged automatic pilot. Given the amount of force Prchal applied to his control column his Sperry automatic pilot could not have been engaged otherwise he would have easily overcome it.

A basic operational description of automatic pilot components outlined in the previous pages is provided in the following paragraphs. This description was

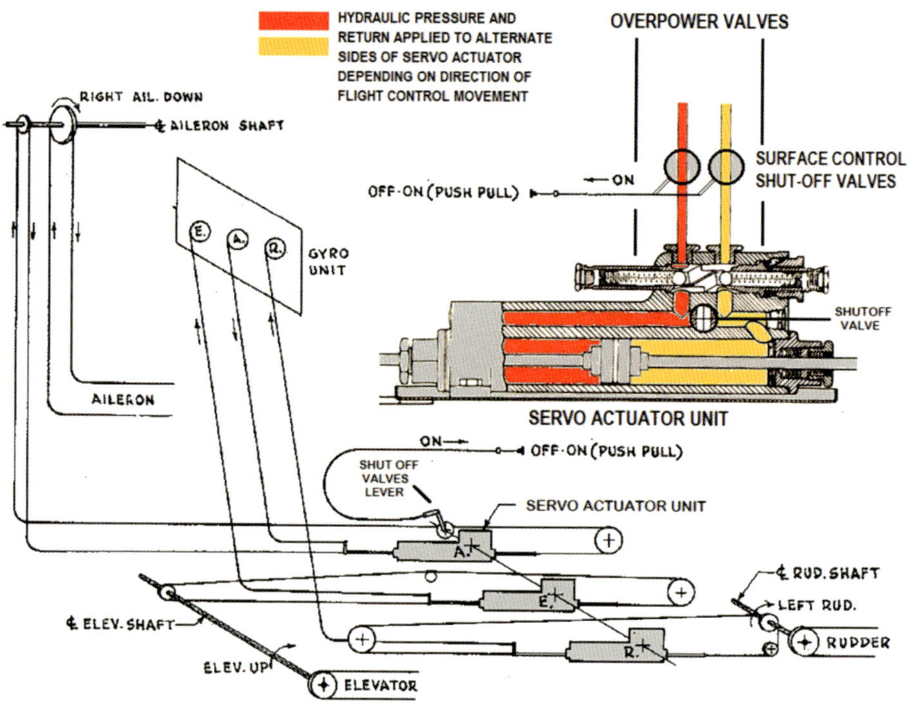

Three servo actuator units. A - Aileron, E – Elevator, R – Rudder operating in parallel with flight control system. Upper right, servo actuator unit cross section cutaway illustrating overpower valves and surface control shut-off valves. (T.O. No. 05-45AB-1, T.O. No. 05-45AB-2 via aircorpslibrary.com)

extracted from the Sperry Type A-3 Automatic Pilot Handbook of Operations and Service Instructions manual and applied to the elevator-control system illustrated on pages 119 and 120. The aileron and rudder system operation are identical with the rudder system having its own gyro.

> A gyroscope is a spinning wheel, universally mounted. Such a wheel exhibits a characteristic called "rigidity"; that is, it tends to remain in what-ever position it is set. This property of rigidity is the basic principle in the operation of the automatic pilot.
>
> The automatic pilot's bank-and-climb gyro spins with its axis vertical in exactly the same manner as the pilot's instrument panel-mounted horizon gyro. It is erected by the action of pendulous vanes. With the airplane flying level, the horizon bar on the face of the bank-and-climb unit is level and the miniature airplane is parallel to it. Due to "rigidity", the gyro remains fixed as the airplane climbs or descends.

The gyro rotor is supported in a gimbal ring which has a knife-edge disc (nozzle plate) attached to it. These parts, which comprise the sensitive element including the gyro rotor, rotor housing, and gimbal ring, are shown in the case in images 1 and 2.

The air pick-offs (A-A'), composed of the knife-edge nozzle plate and the air nozzles, surrounding the sensitive element, are also enclosed within the box. Air is drawn in through the air filter (V') into the bottom of the case by the suction pump (B) and directed to the gyro rotor to spin it. Air is also drawn in through the air filter and through the air relay (C) past the air pick-offs (A-A').

The air relay (C) has two inlet ports (D and E), one on either side of the diaphragm (F). The diaphragm is connected by the rod (G) to the core of the balanced oil valve (H), in which a constant oil pressure is maintained by the oil pump (J).

Movement of the core of the balanced oil valve to left or right permits oil to flow to the hydraulic surface control (K) where it moves the piston rod (L-L') one way or the other. The piston rod is connected to the control cables which operate the elevators (M-M').[170]

In image 1 the airplane is assumed to be level laterally, and the automatic pilot system is therefore neutral. The gyro is upright and the knife-edges of the disc intercept equal amounts of the air being drawn in from the air relay (C). An equal suction is maintained at both sides of the diaphragm

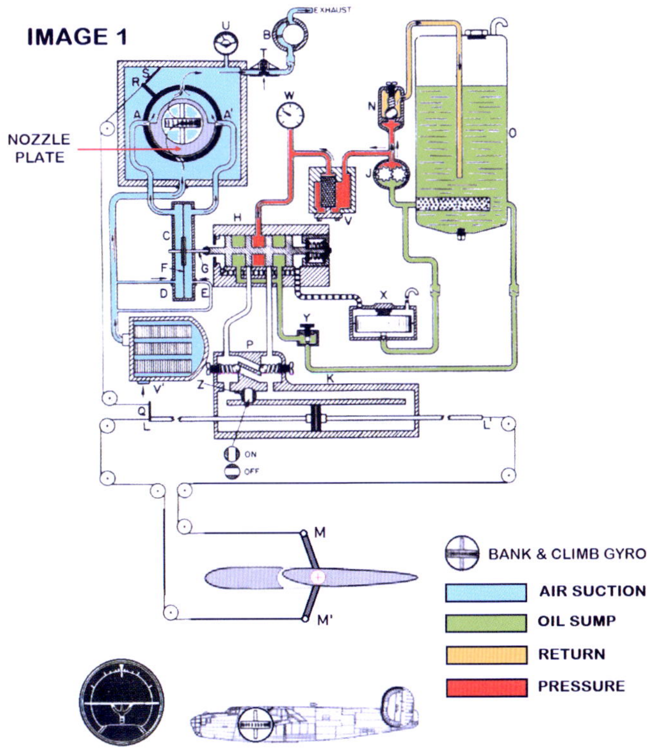

BANK-and-CLIMB GYRO, AIRCRAFT FLYING LEVEL

T.O. No. 05-45AB-1. (via aircorpslibrary.com)

IMAGE 2

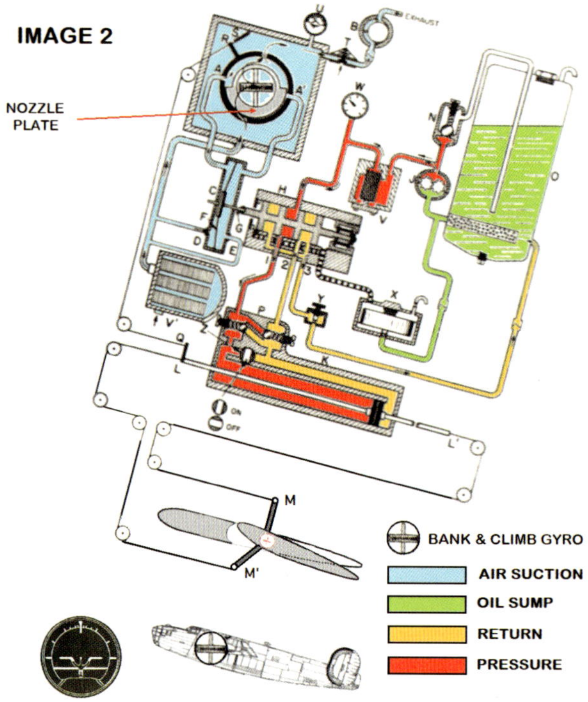

BANK-and-CLIMB GYRO, AIRCRAFT NOSE UP

T.O. No. 05-45AB-1. (via aircorpslibrary.com)

(F), the balanced oil valve core is centralized, and no oil can flow to the hydraulic surface control. The pressure regulator (N) relieves the oil pressure at the balanced oil valve and permits the oil to flow back to the sump (O).

In image 2 the airplane is assumed to have been displaced horizontally (to an exaggerated degree) so that the nose is up. Because of its characteristic of "rigidity," the gyro maintains its vertical axis, and port (A') of the air pick-off system is closed. Since port (A) is open, the suction on the left-hand side of the diaphragm (F) is increased, and the diaphragm moves to the left. The corresponding movement of the balanced oil valve core permits oil to flow through pipe No. 1 to the hydraulic surface control, where it passes around the overpower valve (P) and enters the hydraulic surface control cylinder, moving the piston to the right and applying the necessary elevator control movement to restore the airplane horizontally to level flight. The oil from the other side of the piston returns to the balanced oil valve through pipe No. 2 and flows back to the sump through pipe No. 3.[171]

STRUCTURAL FAILURE OF TAIL SECTION

Suggestions of AL523 having suffered structural failure were never brought up during the crash inquiry. It is also not known if it was ever considered in later years by authors and researchers. This catastrophic phenomenon is presented in the interest of transparency to address and acknowledge a well-documented flaw with the Liberator that may, or may not, have been associated with the Gibraltar accident.

NACA Test Aircraft Consolidated B-24D. Langley Field Virginia

NACA three- component accelerometer located at center of Horizontal Stabilizer of B-24D. Fairing Removed.

Images from NACA Wartime Report L-583.

In the summer of 1943, several Liberators were mysteriously lost due to tail failure. Their twin fins and rudders would unexpectedly vibrate and break off during normal conditions where flight manoeuvres where not considered severe. Some accidents had even occurred during landing. That same year the army approached the National Advisory Committee for Aeronautics (NACA) to investigate why Liberators were experiencing catastrophic tail failures. [172]

Making use of a B-24, the engineers attached an accelerometer, strain gauges and cameras to record undue flexing of the tail in flight. [...] In the course of the tests during which the B-24 was put through various manoeuvres, a deliberate effort was made to create turbulence. Changes were made in the setting of cowl flaps, wing flaps, and power conditions, to induce buffeting. But in flight tests at various speeds the Liberator came through all conditions favourably. [...] The instrumentation failed to show excess stress on the aircraft. Since some of the aircraft experienced their tails falling off upon landing, the engineers turned their attention to that phase of the flight. The findings were amazing and conclusive. As the Liberator's two main wheels hit the runway, they had to immediately spin up as the B-24 rolled out at about 100 miles per hour. As this was happening, the long main landing gear legs set up an alarming fore and aft oscillation. Concurrently the engineers saw the tail begin to shake to the same frequency as the landing-gear vibrations. Transmitted through the structure to the tail, the vibrations were fatiguing the horizontal tail structure to the point where failure of the metal could occur later under normal flight stresses.[173] [174] The Liberator was subsequently modified to eliminate this structural tail stress.[175]

Considering that AL523's underwater wreckage pattern shares marked similarities to recent discoveries of submerged Liberator wrecks lost in combat conditions such as No. 112 U B-24 D, No. 42-40112, Lady Luck B-24 H, No. 42-52774, and Tulsamerican B-24 J-1, No. 42-51430, the notion that Prchal's Liberator crashed due to structural failure appears questionable. In addition, given the short duration of AL523's flight and even shorter duration in which its elevators were locked, it is difficult to assign structural failure as a contributing factor.

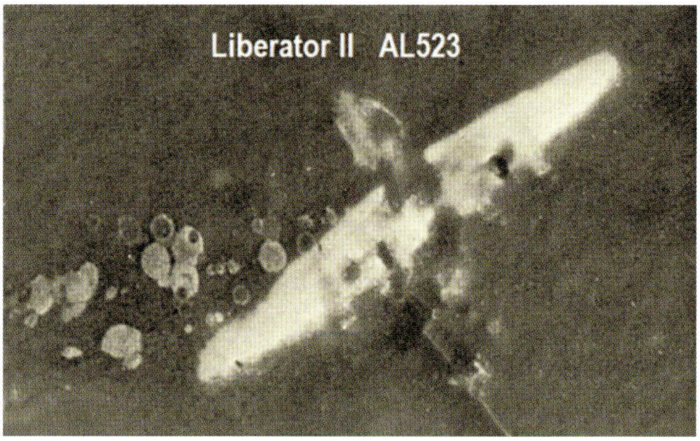

Above left: *Left main wheel of B-24 D showing wheel markings and reference target.*
Above right: *Underwater wreckage of Liberator II AL523 Gibraltar 5 July 1943. Overturned on impact. Sixteen of the seventeen passengers were fatalities. (James D Oughton via Richard Forder)*
Below: *Ditched attempting to reach Malta for an emergency landing 6 May 1943. Overturned on impact with nine of the ten crew members surviving. (Steven Galicia)*

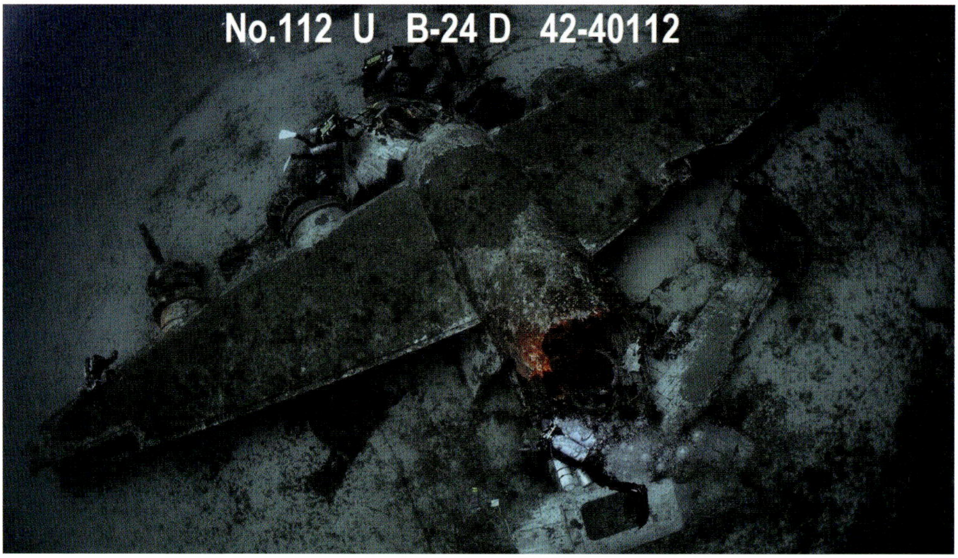

Ran out of fuel attempting to land on Vis in the Adriatic 17 December 1944. Possibly overturned on impact. Seven of the ten crewmen survived. (National Parks Service)

Ditched in Adriatic 5-10 miles NW of Biševo 17 November 1944. Aircraft broke in two, rear-half from bomb bay sank immediately. One of the ten crew survived. (B-24 Diving Center www.diving-croatia.hr)

HAVERSACK FOULING ELEVATOR CONTROLS

In 25 October 2006 online academic journal *Intelligence and National Security* published an article authored by M R D Foot titled *The Death of General Sikorski* recounted the contents of a missing appendix from AIR 2/9234 RAF Inquiry into the Gibraltar crash. This missing appendix described how:

> "An RAF corporal and three airmen were inside [AL523], cleaning and polishing everything they could reach in the passenger area, till the last minute. As the corporal fell them in on the apron, one of them cried that he had forgotten his haversack. Too late now, said the corporal, and marched them away."

Foot postulated,

> "The inference is irresistible. The pilot did all his cockpit checks, finding everything in perfect order, taxied down to the end of the runway, and took off. With the sudden acceleration of take-off, the haversack slid aft along that perfectly polished floor, and jammed the elevators; from which it was thrown clear by the shock of hitting water at 165 miles an hour."[176]

The idea that a haversack somehow jammed AL523's elevators from within the aircraft interior is illogical. Wing Commander Stevens had testified that he found it impossible to jam or impinge any accessible elevator control cable or pulley within a Liberator's interior. A haversack left on the floor crowded with passengers and luggage would have nowhere to slide. Also, the elevator control cables ran along either side of the fuselage walls well above the floor line. A more logical conclusion would be that the haversack was found by the flight crew or passengers, given to ground staff, or stowed with the rest of the luggage.

ELEVATOR JAMMED BY MAILBAG

In the 2001 publication titled *Disasters in the Air: Mysterious Air Disasters Explained*, Jan Bartelski attributes a mailbag having jammed AL523's elevator causing its crash. His theory was based on testimony given by Gunner Joseph Miller who found a 15-lb mailbag in the early morning of 5 July at 01:40 hours across from his anti-aircraft gun position adjacent to the north side of the runway 400 yards from its western end.[177] Bartelski hypothesized that the recovered one-quarter full, 15-lb mailbag was one of two that were swept out of the forward bomb bay by a forceful 130-mph draft from the open nose undercarriage doors. This air surge carried the mailbags from the rear bomb bay, through the Liberator's fuselage length, and out the unsecured starboard side hatch which swung open when AL523's nose raised during take-off rotation. One bag fell to the runway while the second caught between the narrow gap separating the deflected elevator leading edge and horizontal stabilizer. The jammed elevator began to vibrate due to the bag fluttering violently against its lower surface.[178] Bartelski's theory is interesting but highly improbable given that a 15-lb mailbag would immediately fall away from the aircraft due to its weight let alone being blown aft along the fuselage interior length. This effect is easily demonstrated during flour-bombing competitions where a flour bag falls away immediately when dropped from an aircraft. It should also be noted that these bags contain two cups of flour, weigh little more than a ½ lb and fall like a brick. Even if a 15-lb mailbag could have miraculously risen and contacted the elevator it is implausible that a slender fold of its heavy cloth and blunt shape could have neatly slipped into the narrow gap separating the downward deflected elevator leading edge and horizontal stabilizer at 130 mph. Bartelski cited photographic proof by stuffing a shirt between the right-hand elevator leading edge and horizontal stabilizer of a B-24 displayed at Cosford Aerospace Museum.[179]

Within Bartelski's research are performance calculations of AL523's take-off distance and altitude. These calculations based on a weight of 56,400 lbs corrected for temperature, density, wind direction, and runway surface show a calculated take-off distance of 1,166 yards which was remarkably close to the actual distance of 1,150 yards witnessed by Air Commodore Simpson and Flight Lieutenant Capes. Through take-off graphs it was determined that AL523 passed Capes at approximately 37 feet which nearly matches his testimony of 30 feet from the control tower. In addition Bartelski calculated a 225 ft/min rate of descent, which equals 3.75 ft/sec, at a glide path of approximately 1 degree.[180] These results compliment Franciszek Grabowski's detailed flight simulator research and performance calculation results. From this flat trajectory Bartelski further concluded that this was an attempt to ditch. In fact Prchal had no elevator control as it was locked in neutral with the nose pitched down, he was essentially at the mercy of the Liberator.

WALKER'S SIKORSKI ACCOUNT

Charles Walker, a leading aircraftsman attached to No. 172 Squadron in Gibraltar, wrote an account of examining AL523's interior and later witnessing its crash.[181] He recalled looking through the cargo door at control rods about one inch in diameter along the starboard side, their long lengths coupled together by universal knuckle joints to allow for fuselage curvature. He described the tubes being held by three rollers, the upper rod for the rudders, the lower rod for the elevators. Walker theorized unbalanced luggage had shifted during take-off and jammed these control tubes. Unfortunately, there are no flight control tubes in the fuselage of the Liberator, only flight control cables. This is easily proven when examining Liberator flight and maintenance manuals as well as Wing Commander Stevens' testimony, or any Liberator fuselage interior image. An examination of a Liberator illustrated parts catalogue reveals that only the rudder control rods have three, three-bearing, girdle assemblies which are only found inside the horizontal stabilizer that match Walker's description. Walker's son David Walker, to his credit, later acknowledged the oversight and pointed out several discrepancies within his father's account. In addition David conducted some definitive research on sky conditions for the date and time of AL523's crash. The results were very compelling and raise questions as to the validity of some crash accounts. David's findings are discussed in Chapter Four.

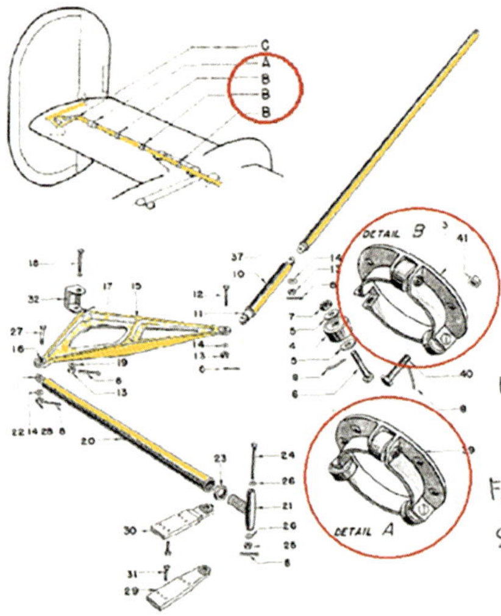

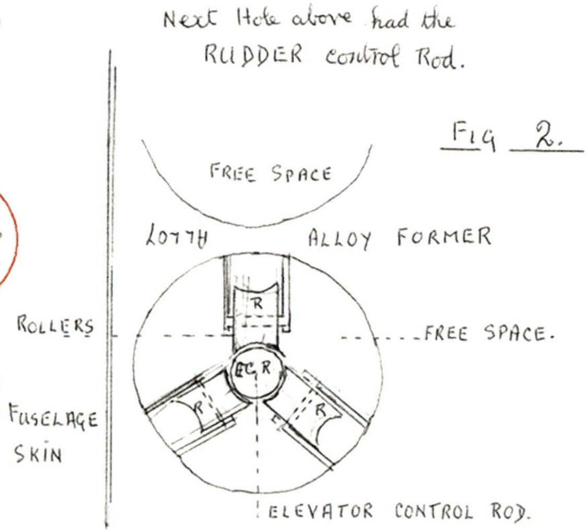

Liberator Parts Catalogue T.O. NO. 01-5-4. Drawing from Walker's Sikorski accident account.

KIM PHILBY: CROSSED ELEVATOR CABLES

It has been speculated that British intelligence officer and Soviet double agent Kim Philby had been responsible for the death of General Sikorski and is alleged to have been present in Gibraltar at the time of the accident.[182] During this period Philby had been head of the British secret intelligence service's counter-intelligence for the Iberian peninsula since 1941. It is claimed Philby had arranged for AL523's control cables to be switched prior to its departure. It is worthy of note that Philby could not have performed the sabotage himself, or advised anyone on such a method for that matter, as he had no technical skills or knowledge of aircraft.[183] The suggestion that accomplices had 'switched' the elevator controls, which essentially implies they were somehow reversed, is a far-fetched notion. First off, even if the elevator controls had somehow been reversed as this statement suggests then AL523 would have never left the ground. Pulling back the column to climb would just push the nose down. AL523 would have never become airborne and instead gone off the end of the runway with Prchal pulling the control column all the way back wondering why he was unable to lift off. Secondly, the reversed elevator controls would have been noticed by the flight and maintenance crew during pre-flight control travel checks. Thirdly, the only possible way to reverse the elevator controls would be to cross their cables. Such work is not a simple quick tweak with a wrench but labour intensive and noisy requiring access to specific elevator control cables and associated turnbuckles in an attempt to cross them. Fourth, in July 1943 Philby was posted in London. Lastly the NKVD had grown distrustful of Philby since December 1941 because, and despite repeated requests, he had been unable to provide them names of British secret intelligence service agents operating in the Soviet Union. It was inconceivable to the Soviets that Britain did not have agents in the USSR during this period and suspected Philby of latent British loyalties.[184] The last thing the NKVD would do is assign a high-level political assassination to an agent they did not trust.

Illustration of fuselage station locations for cable and chain turnbuckle pairs.

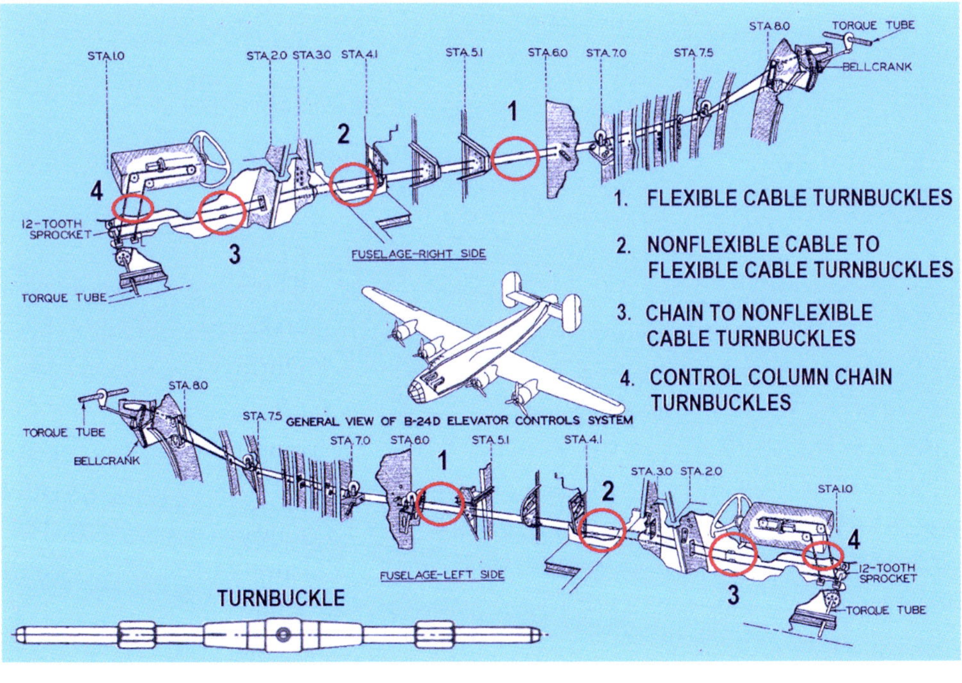

There were only four locations on AL523 where elevator controls could possibly be crossed and all were in locations that were difficult to access.[185] The primary location to adjust flexible cable tensions is through use of turnbuckle pairs on the left and right side of the fuselage located in the bomb bay between STA (Station) 5.1 and 6.0. On AL523 there was no quick access to these cables due to a semi-circular metal shield running the length of the bomb bay as testified by Wing Commander Stevens.[186] A second location had turnbuckle pairs connecting flexible to non-flexible cables located between STA 3.0 and 4.1, these ran parallel to the floor on the left and right sidewalls of the compartment behind the cockpit. Access to these cable turnbuckles would also be difficult as you have to reach them either from the floor of that compartment or beneath the floor in the rear section of the nose-landing gear compartment among all the piping, electric wiring, and equipment etc. The third location is where turnbuckle pairs connect non-flexible cables to the elevator chains between STA 1.0 and 2.0 beneath the flight compartment floor in the nose-landing gear compartment.

The first problem with this alleged sabotage method is that in all three locations the turnbuckles are staggered, which was intentional to prevent incorrect installation. The second problem is that the flight controls were locked, our saboteur would only be able to connect one cable as it would be too long and not the other because it would be too short. In order to connect them you would need to release the control lock so as to move the cables closer to each other, if that is at all possible. Our saboteur would also have to cross both left and right elevator systems simultaneously. The fourth location is the elevator chain turnbuckle pairs located forward and beneath the pilot's control columns forward of the rudder pedals. Though accessible from

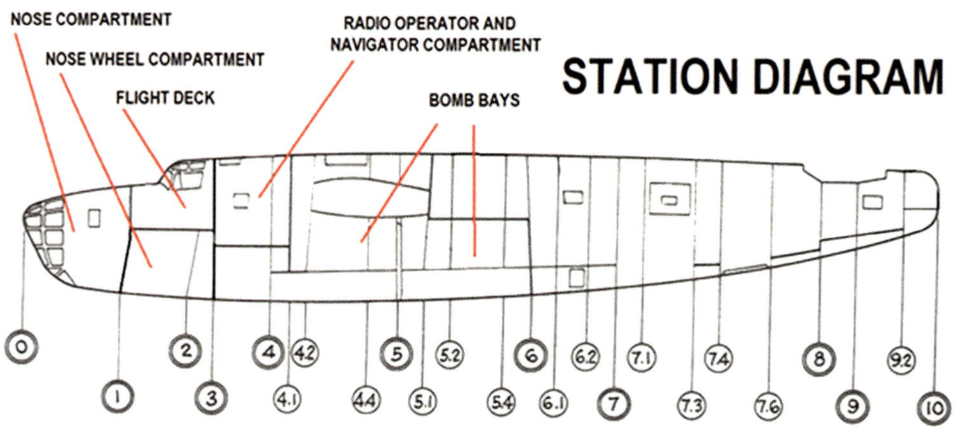

Illustration of fuselage station (STA) locations numbered 0 through 10 (circled)

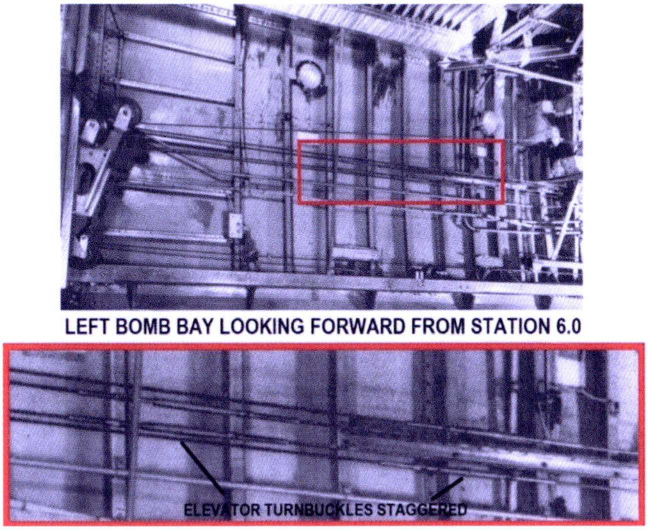

LB-30 Liberator II Erection and Maintenance Instructions. (T.O. No. 01-5ED-2)

the nose compartment it is doubtful the chains would be long enough to cross and reconnect to opposite turnbuckles. Another problem is that chains have limited side-to-side movement; if they were crossed, they would rub and catch against one another when moved, the turnbuckles would also catch on each other. The pilot would feel a ratcheting and binding in his column as he moved it forward and back. The potential difficulties and time constraints associated with such difficult and absurd sabotage methods are innumerable. The whole notion that Kim Philby had arranged the sabotage of AL523 is implausible and should be ignored.

PRE-FLIGHT AND DAILY INSPECTIONS

One issue that has not been considered is why Flight Lieutenant Prchal did not see the saboteur's green cotton rag during his pre-flight inspection. Also, how did No. 511 Squadron maintenance personnel miss the rag during their daily inspection of AL523 on 3 July, or during their pre-flight inspection the following day? In order to appreciate how this was possible it is important to understand the differences between a pilot pre-flight inspection, maintenance pre-flight inspection, and a maintenance daily inspection. A pilot's pre-flight inspection walk around on the Liberator was a visual exterior inspection of the aircraft's general condition and was intended as a final check of its airworthiness. The inspection was continued inside the aircraft from a checklist of over fifty-two items with the co-pilot and flight engineer prior to take-off.[187] The pre-flight inspection carried out by Prchal prior to departure was a general inspection from the ground that took approximately five

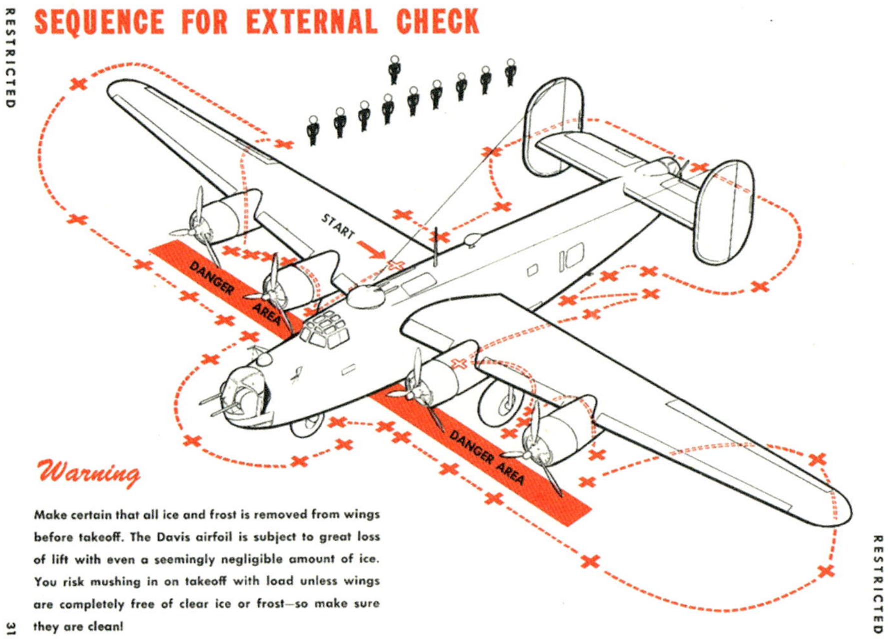

External check sequence. Pilot Training Manual for the Liberator B-24. (AAF Manual No. 50-12)

minutes or so as he walked around AL523. A training manual example of a pilot's pre-flight inspection sequence around a Liberator is illustrated above. Among items visually inspected by Prchal was the general condition of flight-control surfaces and their fabric covering. [188]

The daily maintenance inspection, or DI, on the Liberator was much longer with over 100 detailed inspection items. The DI carried out on AL523 in the late afternoon of 3 July by No. 511 Squadron's airmen included items on the engines and propellers. In addition there were ailerons, elevators, flaps, and rudders to be inspected for obvious signs of damage as well as inspections from within the cockpit of all flight controls for full range of movement.[189] Given the Liberator's size an airman standing outside would confirm control surface position to the airman moving the control column. This daily inspection could have potentially exposed the cotton rag for which our saboteur presumably was aware of. He likely acted only after the daily inspection was completed on the evening of 3 July.

The Liberator's maintenance pre-flight inspection, or PF, carried out on 4 July was slightly shorter. Over ninety inspection items covered everything from fuel and oil, tyres and brakes, to running engines. Among those items were visual inspections of wings, flaps, ailerons and trim tabs for obvious signs of damage. Further inspections carried out in the cockpit ensured all flight controls were checked for full range of movement.[190] Presumably an airman standing outside would confirm the control-surface position. From the Liberator inspection schedule below it can be seen that several inspection items for the PF and DI are repeated including those for flight controls. This repetition was a designated time interval between inspections that assured certain critical items such as flight controls were serviceable and safe for flight. A USAAF training film titled 'Crew Chief Pre-flight Inspection of the B-24 Bomber – 1943' illustrated the control travel check. The RAF presumably followed a similar pattern of work tasks and delegation.

The reason Prchal and maintenance personnel did not find the cotton rag was possibly due to how it was placed in the elevator. Going back to our elevator cross-

Liberator Inspection Schedule, pages 12–13. Empennage – Fixed And Movable Surfaces. Inspection Item 189 is repeated at PF and D (Pre-flight and Daily Inspection). (Aircraft Inspection and Maintenance Guide No. 00-20A-2-B-24 via aircorpslibrary.com)

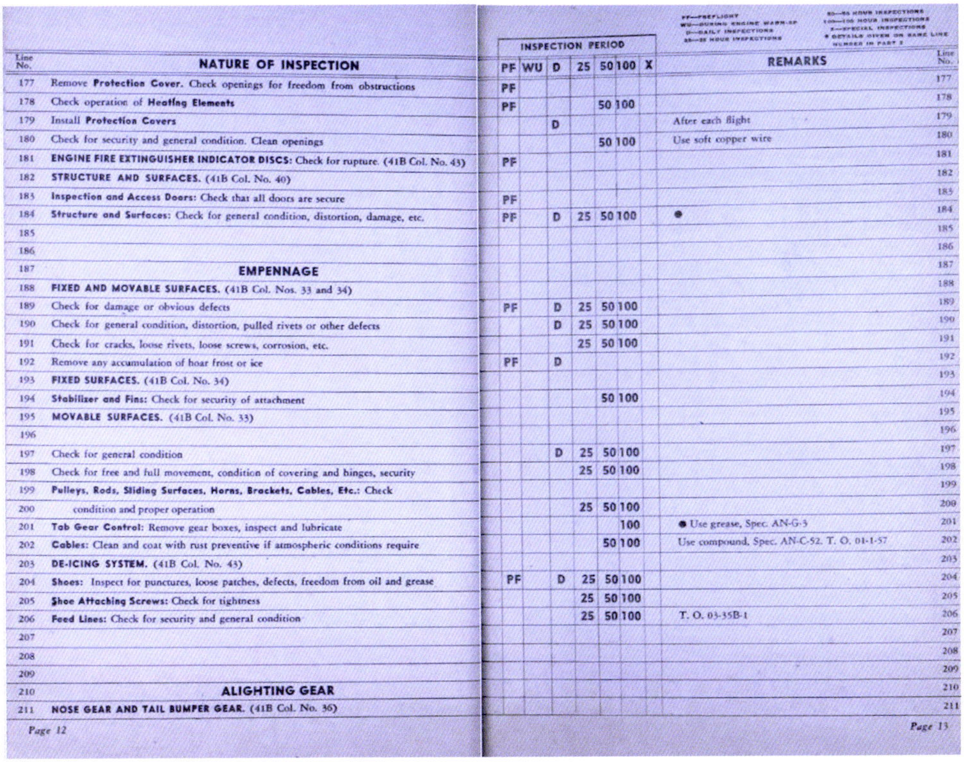

Line No.	NATURE OF INSPECTION	PF	WU	D	25	50	100	X	REMARKS	Line No.
177	Remove **Protection Cover.** Check openings for freedom from obstructions	PF								177
178	Check operation of **Heating Elements**	PF				50	100			178
179	Install **Protection Covers**			D					After each flight	179
180	Check for security and general condition. Clean openings					50	100		Use soft copper wire	180
181	**ENGINE FIRE EXTINGUISHER INDICATOR DISCS:** Check for rupture. (41B Col. No. 43)	PF								181
182	**STRUCTURE AND SURFACES.** (41B Col. No. 40)									182
183	**Inspection and Access Doors:** Check that all doors are secure	PF								183
184	**Structure and Surfaces:** Check for general condition, distortion, damage, etc.	PF		D	25	50	100		●	184
185										185
186										186
187	**EMPENNAGE**									187
188	**FIXED AND MOVABLE SURFACES.** (41B Col. Nos. 33 and 34)									188
189	Check for damage or obvious defects	PF		D	25	50	100			189
190	Check for general condition, distortion, pulled rivets or other defects			D	25	50	100			190
191	Check for cracks, loose rivets, loose screws, corrosion, etc.				25	50	100			191
192	Remove any accumulation of hoar frost or ice	PF		D						192
193	**FIXED SURFACES.** (41B Col. No. 34)									193
194	**Stabilizer and Fins:** Check for security of attachment					50	100			194
195	**MOVABLE SURFACES.** (41B Col. No. 33)									195
196										196
197	Check for general condition			D	25	50	100			197
198	Check for free and full movement, condition of covering and hinges, security				25	50	100			198
199	**Pulleys, Rods, Sliding Surfaces, Horns, Brackets, Cables, Etc.:** Check									199
200	condition and proper operation				25	50	100			200
201	**Tab Gear Control:** Remove gear boxes, inspect and lubricate						100		● Use grease, Spec. AN-G-3	201
202	**Cables:** Clean and coat with rust preventive if atmospheric conditions require					50	100		Use compound, Spec. AN-C-52. T. O. 01-1-57	202
203	**DE-ICING SYSTEM.** (41B Col. No. 43)									203
204	**Shoes:** Inspect for punctures, loose patches, defects, freedom from oil and grease	PF		D	25	50	100			204
205	**Shoe Attaching Screws:** Check for tightness				25	50	100			205
206	**Feed Lines:** Check for security and general condition				25	50	100		T. O. 03-35B-1	206
207										207
208										208
209										209
210	**ALIGHTING GEAR**									210
211	**NOSE GEAR AND TAIL BUMPER GEAR.** (41B Col. No. 36)									211

Page 12 Page 13

section replica trials (on pages 51–56), a portion of the cotton rag could be seen during the full up travel. When returned to neutral portions were exposed from the lower gap. In these instances, the cloth had been stuffed loose and jumbled into the U-channel space next to the alcove. In further trials it was found that if the cloth was folded like a napkin upon itself three times into a square, and then tucked firmly up into the U-channel against the aft side of the torque tube, there was a notable difference in how it sat during elevator movement. A travel check done several times from 30 degrees up, to 20 degrees down, and back to neutral saw only a small cloth section exposed during up travel but little or none from the bottom ½-inch gap in neutral. If our saboteur folded his cloth similarly it may be the reason why it was never spotted with the elevator in neutral, even after being carried within the U-channel during travel checks. It should be considered that Prchal conducted his pre-flight walk around sometime at or near dusk under floodlights.[191] The sweep

Liberator Inspection Schedule, pages 16–17. Flight controls: Check for freedom and full range of operation. Inspection Item 270 is repeated at PF and D (Pre-flight and Daily Inspection). (Aircraft Inspection and Maintenance Guide No. 00-20A-2-B-24 via aircorpslibrary.com)

PF—PREFLIGHT
WU—DURING ENGINE WARM-UP
D—DAILY INSPECTIONS
25—25 HOUR INSPECTIONS
50—50 HOUR INSPECTIONS
100—100 HOUR INSPECTIONS
X—SPECIAL INSPECTIONS
• DETAILS GIVEN ON SAME LINE NUMBER IN PART 2

Line No.	NATURE OF INSPECTION	INSPECTION PERIOD PF	WU	D	25	50	100	X	REMARKS	Line No.
248										248
249	**ELECTRICAL (Fuselage)**									249
250	**BATTERIES.** (41B Col. No. 46)									250
251	Check specific gravity readings of two cells of each battery			D					Use temperature corrected hydrometer. Replace bat-	251
252	Check specific gravity readings of all cells of each battery				25	50	100		tery if any cell reads below 1.240 or above 1.310	252
253	Check for general condition, corrosion, leakage, security, etc.				25	50	100		• T. O. 03-5B-1	253
254	Check felt pad in battery sump for proper saturation. Resaturate if necessary				25	50	100		Use solution of sodium bicarbonate and water	254
255	Replace with service tested batteries							X	200 hours or every 30 days, which ever comes first	255
256	**ELECTRICAL.** (41B Col. No. 22)									256
257	**Battery Circuit Solenoid Switch:** Check operation			D	25	50	100			257
258	**Voltage Regulators:** Inspect for proper condition, security, proper voltage, etc.				25	50	100		• Carbon pile type every 25 hours, others 50 hours	258
259	**Lighting:** Check lighting of all lamps	PF		D	25	50	100			259
260	**Fuses:** Check and replace if necessary			D	25	50	100			260
261	**Inverters:** Check for proper operating condition							X	• 500 and 1000 Hours	261
262	**AUXILIARY POWER PLANT.** (41B Col. No. 45)									262
263	Check unshielded **Spark Plugs** for proper gap and cleanliness				25	50	100		T. O. 19-45-11	263
264	Check **Brushes** for wear and tension of brush springs							X	300 Hours. Replace brushes if within 1/16 inch of holder	264
265	Check for general condition, proper operation, etc.							X	Annual	265
266										266
267										267
268	**FLIGHT CONTROLS**									268
269	(41B Col. No. 32)									269
270	**Cockpit Controls:** Check for freedom and full range of operation	PF		D	25	50	100			270
271	**Flaps Controls:** Check for proper operation	PF		D	25	50	100			271
272	**Control Wheel:** Check for condition, proper functioning, lost motion, binding, etc.				25	50	100			272
273	**Rudder Pedal Assembly:** Check for proper functioning and setting with rudders				25	50	100		See that rudders do not interfere with elevators in extreme positions	273
274	**Tab Control Mechanisms:** Check for proper functioning				25	50	100			274
275	**Control Cables:** Check tensions						100	X	First 25 and subsequent hour periods	275
276	**Control Cables:** Check for fraying, particularly at pulleys, guides, etc.					50	100		Not more than 6 broken wires per inch	276
277	**Control Cables:** Clean and coat with rust preventive if atmospheric conditions require					50	100		Use compound, Spec. AN-C-52. T. O. 01-1-57	277
278	**Pulleys, Rods, Guides, Brackets:** Check for alignment, condition, security, proper operation				25	50	100			278
279	**Control Chains, Sprockets and Cables:** Check tensions and general condition						100			279
280	**Lubricate** flight control mechanisms and flap controls				25	50	100		See lubrication charts, Part 7	280
281	**AUTOMATIC PILOTS, TYPE A-5.** (41B Col. No. 32)									281
282	**Ground Check** for proper operation		WU						• T. O. 05-45AD-2	282
283	**Servos:** Check for security, proper oil level				25	50	100			283

Page 16 Page 17

of a flashlight beam, if he used a flashlight at all, across a flight-control surface at night would not have exposed a dark-coloured well-hidden cloth in the narrow gap between the elevator and empennage. In addition, AL523 had been guarded throughout the previous night giving Prchal little reason to suspect he would find anything unusual. As departure time drew near everyone was focused on loading baggage and freight, seeing off Sikorski and preparing to depart AL523. The last place anyone would be looking at was some dark shadowed corner of the Liberator's tail. Prchal testified that he did a control travel check just before take-off after the flight control lock was released[192] as required in the Liberator's checklist.[193]

Why the cotton cloth rag was not detected will never be determined with any absolute certainty. We can never know whether Urbański folded his into a square before inserting it into the elevator, or just quickly stuffed it inside crumpled up in a desperate act of sabotage. Was this specific method of sabotage taught to him, or was it something he came up with on the spur of the moment? There is also no certainty as to how close airmen stood from the tail section while observing elevator movement during control travel checks. Did they only observe elevator movement from a distance, were they complacent given the frequency of the check and only concerned that they moved correctly? If they had watched closely would the rag have been seen, did its dark colour conceal it? Did a small portion become exposed, and no one noticed? Was the sabotage so covert that it remained unseen, or was Urbański just lucky? What is certain is that Prchal took AL523, its passengers and crew, into the air that evening suggesting that at the very least he was satisfied with the Liberator's mechanical condition and serviceability.

PART III

REVELATIONS AND PERSPECTIVES

CHAPTER FOUR

NEW EYEWITNESSES, OLD ALLEGATIONS AND MYTHS

In Chapter One we saw how Sikorski and AL523's departure did not appear out of sorts or unusual to those present. Court of inquiry testimonies also gave no hint of any difficulties prior to take-off as well. The Polish liaison officer on Gibraltar Lieutenant Ludwik Łubieński recalled how Sikorski before boarding turned toward him and smiled saying: "Captain Łubieński we will meet soon in London. Do not delay your departure from Gibraltar."[194] After what seemed a normal take-off AL523's sudden crash and Sikorski's death was shocking and unexpected. A month-long court of inquiry could not determine a reason for the crash and absolved Prchal of any blame for the accident.

What is lesser known and recently brought to light are revelations that smuggling was not uncommon which speaks to accounts surrounding the loading of AL523 in the hour prior to departure. Another account tells of recovering General Sikorski from the water and his death shortly afterward. Lastly there is an eyewitness recollection of the accident by a wireless operator that touched off an unfounded myth. Several of these accounts belie the congenial farewell and routine departure from North Front's apron described in Chapter One. Curiously none of the individuals associated with these accounts were approached to testify at the court of inquiry in 1943. What is remarkable is that nearly all these narratives align with each other and other allegations, some of which were once considered unsubstantiated. Several individuals came forward after the airing of Garth Barnard's 2015 episode of *WW2 Air Crash Detectives* titled *Sikorski's Last Flight*. In the following pages through interviews, letters, emails, published accounts and allegations these sources present the reader with a narrative that was never documented nor was part of the official record.

FLIGHT LIEUTENANT ALAN BEAUMONT

Alan Beaumont. (Richard Beaumont)

In an email dated 3 February 2018 to Garth Barnard, Mr Richard Beaumont wrote about his late father Alan Beaumont's recollection of AL523's crash and poignant account of having pulled General Sikorski from the water only to have him die in his arms moments later. Flight Lieutenant Beaumont's story is a curious omission to the official record. He was one of several men aboard the RAF rescue launch HSL 181 commanded by Albert M Postage dispatched to the crash site.[195] It was Ludwik Łubieński, a Polish army lieutenant and liaison officer on Gibraltar, who first recounted that only Brigadier Whiteley had been recovered barely clinging to life but had died shortly afterwards. It was also Łubieński that later officially identified Sikorski. He later described the general having a deep wound that started above the left ear, on the temple that went over the cheek and down to his mouth.[196] RAF medical officer Peter Sutton who had carried out an examination on Sikorski recalled removing a long wood-splinter from a wound above the eye "at least as long as a pencil, which went clear through practically the whole length of the brain".[197] In 2008 during a forensic examination of Sikorski's exhumed remains a small wood fragment identified as Douglas fir was found wedged within fractures of the left orbital region. Examiners concluded that "most likely, this fragment inflicted all the cranial injuries".[198]

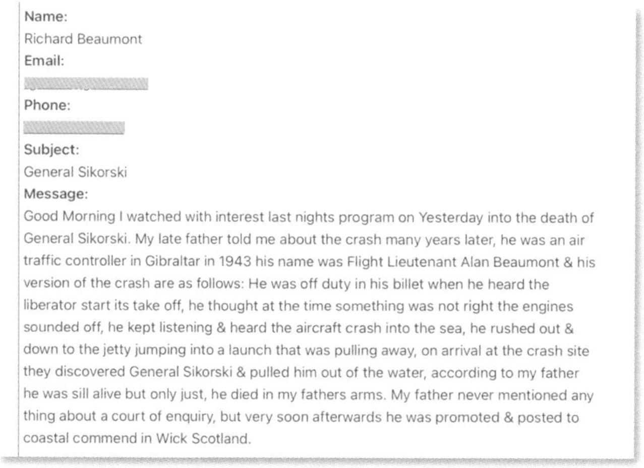

Name:
Richard Beaumont
Email:

Phone:

Subject:
General Sikorski
Message:
Good Morning I watched with interest last nights program on Yesterday into the death of General Sikorski. My late father told me about the crash many years later, he was an air traffic controller in Gibraltar in 1943 his name was Flight Lieutenant Alan Beaumont & his version of the crash are as follows: He was off duty in his billet when he heard the liberator start its take off, he thought at the time something was not right the engines sounded off, he kept listening & heard the aircraft crash into the sea, he rushed out & down to the jetty jumping into a launch that was pulling away, on arrival at the crash site they discovered General Sikorski & pulled him out of the water, according to my father he was sill alive but only just, he died in my fathers arms. My father never mentioned any thing about a court of enquiry, but very soon afterwards he was promoted & posted to coastal commend in Wick Scotland.

Richard Beaumont message sent to Garth Barnard through his aviation research website, 3 February 2018.

LIEUTENANT COLONEL ADRIAN SCROPE

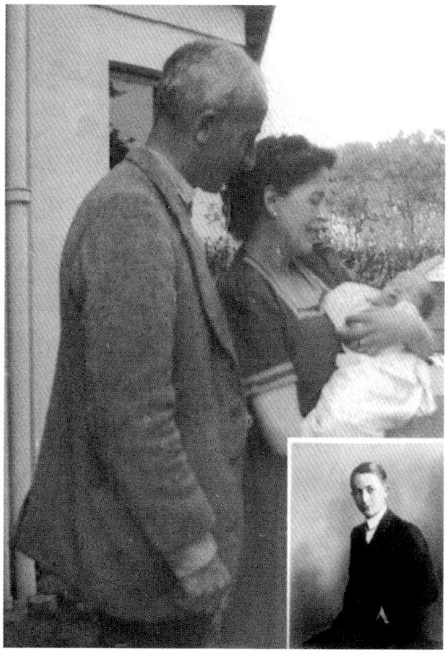

***Above:** Adrian Scrope with wife and infant daughter early July 1943.*
***Inset:** 1927 photo age 21.*
(Adrian Scrope)

Of all the messages Garth received after his documentary an email from Mr Adrian Scrope on 16 January 2015 proved to be of considerable significance. Mr Scrope's father Lieutenant Colonel Adrian Scrope, who was a British army officer, had been a passenger onboard a USAAF B-17 Fortress conveying him and General Walter Clutterbuck, GOC 1st Infantry Division, and also Sir James Grigg, Britain's Secretary of State for War to England during a stopover at Gibraltar on 4 July 1943. The men had been offered a ride home at the invitation of General Carl Spaatz of the Allied North-West African Air Force who had put the B-17 at their disposal.[199] [200] Their take-off had been delayed due to General Sikorski's departure running late. When Lieutenant Colonel Scrope and a crewman went to inquire as to when General Sikorski's aircraft was expected to leave a ground crewman told them the delay was due to loading of many boxes of liquor and that there had been an altercation between the flight crew

Mrs. Barbara Tuge - Erecińska
Ambassador
Embassy of the Republic of Poland
47 Portland Place
London
W1B 1JH

30th November 2008

Your Excellency,

Exhumation of General Wladyslaw Sikorski

My family has read with interest the recent press coverage of the exhumation of Gen. Sikorski, including the revival of the stories of the various supposed plots to kill the General. The following information should be of interest to those concerned in reaching the truth about the General's death. The information that follows suggests that the General's death resulted from nothing more than a tragic accident resulting from his aircraft being unfit to fly.

During June and early July 1943, our father, Lt. Col. Adrian Scrope, was Assistant Quarter Master General to General Clutterbuck, serving with the 1st Division, Eighth Army in North Africa. He was involved in logistics co-ordination during the latter stages of the North African campaign, and particularly in the preparations for Operation Corkscrew, the taking of Pantelleria, which had just been successfully completed.

On the day of Gen. Sikorski's death, General Clutterbuck and Lt. Col. Scrope were passengers on an American aircraft bound for England. They were on the aircraft at the invitation of General Carl Spaatz, Commander-in-Chief of the North West African Air Force, and with whom our father had been working closely in Allied Command. This trip had been cleared by General Eisenhower. Their USAAF aircraft had arrived at Gibraltar from North Africa (Tunis, I believe) for refuelling on its way to England. Thus, Lt. Col. Scrope was on the apron at Gibraltar Airfield as Gen. Sikorski's aircraft was being prepared for departure just prior to the fatal accident.

Our father recounted that there was a lengthy delay to his aircraft departing from Gibraltar, caused by the priority given to Gen. Sikorski's aircraft. General Sikorski's aircraft was behind schedule and was being loaded with wooden boxes. There was an altercation on the tarmac between the Gibraltar ground crew and General Sikorski's aircrew. My father and one of the crew of the aircraft on which he was a passenger disembarked and went to ask when General Sikorski's aircraft might be expected to leave, thus enabling them to continue their journey to England.

A ground crewman responded that the aircraft ahead was indeed that of General Sikorski and that the delay was being caused by the loading of the many boxes which contained sherry and port. The ground crewman also told them that the aircraft was so seriously overloaded that it was very unlikely to take off at all. Despite being told this, Gen. Sikorski's entourage had refused to heed the warning and had insisted on all the boxes being loaded.

The remaining passengers arrived late after the loading, embarked, and the aircraft finally took off. Unable to gain height, it crashed into the sea.

We have every reason to believe that my father gave a truthful account of what he witnessed. His mother was Polish, and one of his cousins was Jan Ciechanowski, later Polish Ambassador in Washington. Thus, Lt. Col. Scrope would have had no interest in fabricating a story and he was, in any event, a man of principle to whom the truth meant everything. Indeed, he rarely spoke about the incident before his death in 1992. One of the reasons he gave for not telling people what he knew was that he felt it could cause trouble for the surviving pilot of Gen. Sikorski's aircraft and the RAF crew at Gibraltar whose Commanding Officer was still alive at that time.

We trust that this information will be useful to those who seek to ascertain for once and for all the truth about the tragic and untimely death of Gen. Sikorski.

Yours faithfully,

Adrian Scrope

c.c. Andrzej Drogon – National Remembrance Institute

Mr. Andrzej Drogon
Institute of National Remembrance
ul. Towarowa 28
00-839 Warszawa
POLAND

Adrian Scrope Jr's letter to Polish ambassador Mrs Barbara Tuge-Ericińska, 30 November 2008.

and Sikorski's entourage over this excessive cargo. In 2008 Adrian had written to Mrs Barbara Tuge-Ericińska, the Polish ambassador to Britain, about the incident recalled by his father. Scrope's account is significant in that it confirms the loading of crates of port and sherry but is also the first to mention an altercation having taken place between AL523's flight crew and a member of Sikorski's entourage. In a later email Adrian told Garth that his father had also "said that one of the Polish forces was waving a pistol around and threatening to shoot somebody if the aircraft was

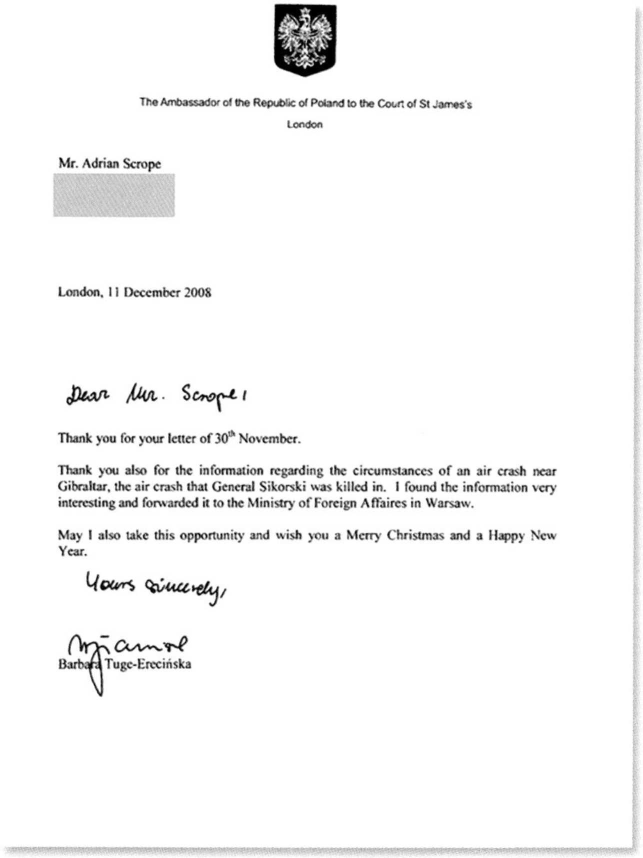
The Ambassador of the Republic of Poland to the Court of St James's

London

Mr. Adrian Scrope

London, 11 December 2008

Dear Mr. Scrope,

Thank you for your letter of 30th November.

Thank you also for the information regarding the circumstances of an air crash near Gibraltar, the air crash that General Sikorski was killed in. I found the information very interesting and forwarded it to the Ministry of Foreign Affaires in Warsaw.

May I also take this opportunity and wish you a Merry Christmas and a Happy New Year.

Yours sincerely,

Barbara Tuge-Erecińska

Polish ambassador Mrs Barbara Tuge-Ericińska's reply to Adrian Scrope, 11 December 2008.

not loaded up".[201] Adrian had not included this part of his father's recollection in his letter to the Polish ambassador. That a weapon was drawn during this altercation suggests Prchal's reluctance was extreme enough to compel a Polish official to threaten him and his crew at gunpoint.

The loading of crates containing port and sherry is a recurring theme that has always been alluded to but never confirmed until Sydney Knowles in a 2009 autobiography about his career as a Royal Navy diver alleged seeing crates of brandy and whisky inside the wreckage of AL523.[202] Scrope's account lends some credence to Knowles' description and is further evidence that crates of alcohol were loaded onto AL523. Curiously historian David Irving alleged and cited Flight Lieutenant Perry telling him of passengers making large purchases of alcohol.[203] Carlos Thompson interviewed Perry and asked about the excessive load and liquor crates. Perry replied that he only learned of this story years later from David Irving.[204] Thompson's research revealed that Irving's allegation was so convoluted that he cited Anthony Quayle's remarks about AL523's jam-packed and untidy interior to infer that it was stacked with crates of sherry, and then inexplicably attributed those remarks to Perry.[205] [206]

LEADING AIRCRAFTMAN CHARLES WALKER

LAC Charles Walker. (David Walker)

Garth's documentary bore more results when on 12 January 2015 he received an email from Mr David Walker describing his father Charles Walker having witnessed the unsupervised loading of a large quantity of luggage and freight aboard AL523 on the day of the Sikorski crash. Charles Walker was an AC1 airframe mechanic posted to Gibraltar with No. 172 Squadron RAF Coastal Command. Mr Walker in his later years had penned a written account[207] of the crash and had also recorded an oral account with the Imperial War Museum.[208] Though Charles described with certainty of Sikorski and his entourage being present during the Liberator's unsupervised loading[209] many other details he provided unfortunately did not fit or were unrelated to circumstances of the crash. For example an insistence that the crash occurred in daylight, that the Liberator was painted white,[210] [211] that he saw elevator control tubes with universal knuckle joints inside the fuselage,[212] that the three-ton or 15 CWT truck tailgate was level with the aircraft side door despite the Liberator only having side hatches,[213] that he saw the aircraft floating on the water and could hear people inside as it sank and all that stuck out afterwards was the tail, and that only the co-pilot survived. [214] AL523 was painted in a temperate camouflage sea scheme of dark sea grey and dark slate upper surfaces with azure under surfaces,[215] and had no side door incorporated for cargo.[216] All versions of Liberator had elevator controls that were cable operated. His recollection of seeing the aircraft in daylight and floating with people inside may have been a No. 24 Squadron Dakota III that overshot its landing and crashed into the sea off the western runway end on 8 July 1943 with no fatalities. [217] Claims of the co-pilot Squadron Leader Herring surviving were the result of unsubstantiated tabloid stories published in 1968. [218]

EARLY EVENING ON JULY 4th

Roughly 1.5 hours before the accident I left the N.A.A.F.I. about 9pm local time. Crossing the airfield to go to my Billet-hut, I noticed a crowd of uniformed people behind a 3-ton covered lorry. The lorry was tucked close to the fuselage of the Liberator with the tailgate down. Men within the lorry were bringing all sorts of boxes and crates to be transferred forward into the dark forward hold.

COMMENT This loading concerned me as there was no Aircrew or worthy Ground-crew to supervise distribution and securing the additional cargo. Are the boxes secured properly and not interfering with controls? Anything loose becomes 'floating cargo' during a flight.

While watching I noticed under the port wing an open personnel-door to give access to the lower floor. Is that where these passengers go?

Seeing an RAF chap stood near the tail-plane, I went over to him and enquired 'What's going on?'. His reply was that the passengers have been here since 8 o'clock and the Aircrew have not arrived yet. My next question was 'Who is supervising the loading?'. The answer was 'They are.', but he didn't seem to be concerned.

As I left the scene, my thought was; I hope they know what they are doing.

***Above:** Excerpt of Charles Walker's written account page 3.*

***Below:** David Walker's email to Garth Barnard, 15 January 2015.*

On 15 January 2015 at 20:13, David Walker <[redacted]> wrote:

Hello Garth

I've greatly enjoyed your recent TV series on the Yesterday channel on WWII crash investigations. The recent one on the Sikorski crash was of particular interest as it has a family connection. My father now 92 was an eyewitness of the aftermath of the crash and also was a witness to unsupervised extra heavy baggage loading by the Gibraltar passengers rather than ground staff before take off. His billet as an RAF LAC was nearby.

He wrote up his observations on the crash for the family history and was keen to put these in the public domain so these are linked to as a pdf file on the web page below if of interest. Also a link his audio recollections of the crash for the War Museum.

http://www.microscopy-uk.org.uk/dww/sikorski/sikorski.html

He was concerned about the unsupervised loading of considerable extra baggage at Gibraltar. He was of the opinion that it could be related to the controls jamming if load shifted.

with regards

David Walker

The Imperial War Museum's oral history recordings of Charles Walker's time in the RAF are rich and vivid in their detail, particularly those descriptions of life on Gibraltar. Like Prchal he also smuggled home oranges on Wellingtons scheduled for extensive repair and servicing in the UK.[219] Their value to present and future researchers are immeasurable. It is not the intention of the authors to discredit Mr Walker or be unkind but to merely offer clarification of select statements and provide context. Bearing this in mind the most likely explanation for these inconsistencies is that Mr Walker simply misremembered events or confused them with others during his time on Gibraltar. David Walker to his credit recognized and appreciated the inconsistencies in his father's account, particularly the lighting conditions at the time of the incident. As a result, he took an unusual step in researching the twilight conditions in the minutes before and during Prchal's take-off. David had noted the differing published accounts by witnesses of how dark it was at 23:07 hours local time (GMT + 2 hours British Double Summer Time)[220] of the crash. Witnesses reported it being pitch dark while Prchal reported good visibility and a good horizon. David's father described the lighting condition as 'dusk' and stated he could clearly see the last moments of the aircraft after ditching, despite being well after a calculated sunset of 21:42 hours and a moonless night.[221]

A Stellarium sky simulation of the view east from Gibraltar out to sea on 4 July 1943, 21:07 hours GMT (23:07 local time) at the time of the crash showing best case conditions for a clear night and no manmade light. The horizon line passes through the red 'E'. The Stellarium planetarium freeware is reported to be one of the best to accurately recreate sky brightness levels for clear skies.

Same Stellarium sky location and time except it shows the sky view eighteen minutes before the crash at 20:49 hours GMT (22:49 local time) which almanac software calculates to be the official end of 'nautical twilight'.

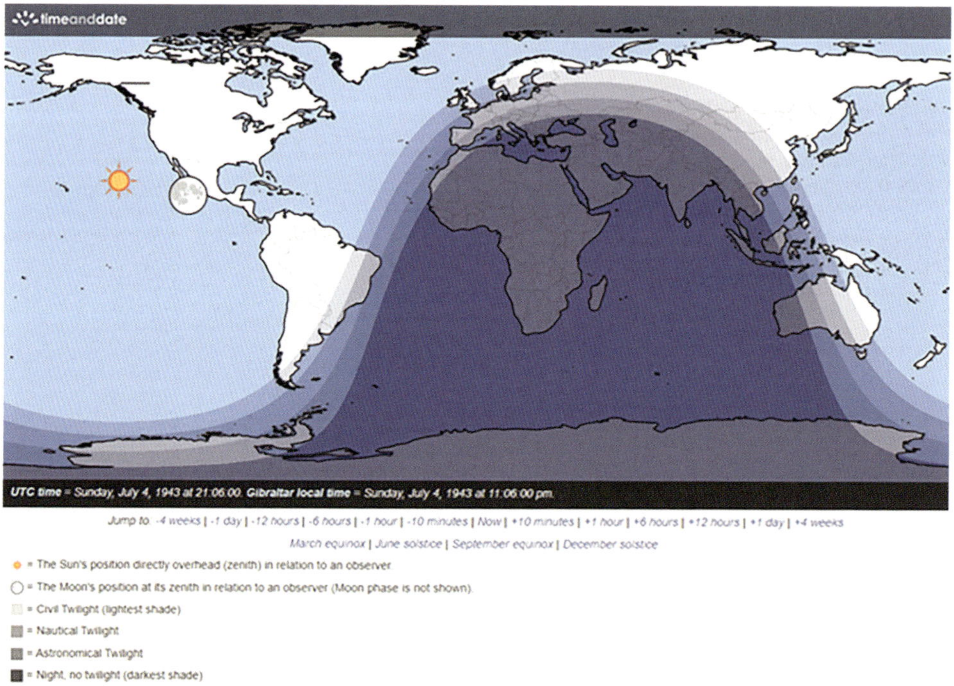

Earth shadow arch moving largely across Africa, Middle East, and Southern Asia. Note that the astronomical twilight intersects Gibraltar and its peninsula. (www.timeanddate.com)

At first glance David's twilight simulation results would appear to suggest that the sun was setting in the east. Though the sun sets in the west there is in fact an eastern band of twilight visible due to the curvature of the earth shadow during that time of year as seen in the earth shadow map illustrations above for Sunday 4 July 1943. This is due to the earth's orbit and tilt of the North Pole towards the sun resulting in a very dim band of astronomical twilight in the east prior to full darkness. This phenomenon proves significant as it puts the account of SOE wireless operator Douglas Martin into serious question.

AIRCRAFTMAN JACK WATERFIELD

Jack Waterfield.

In March of 2015 Garth learned of another eyewitness named Jack Waterfield who was an AC2 armaments mechanic in the Royal Air Force stationed at Gibraltar in 1943 and had witnessed the departure, take-off and crash of General Sikorski's aircraft. Mr Waterfield's posting to Gibraltar had come in a roundabout manner during several daring Royal Navy convoy runs from Gibraltar to Malta in 1942 delivering Spitfires to the besieged island from the aircraft carriers HMS *Eagle* and USS *Wasp* during Operation Pedestal. As an AC2 mechanic with extensive Spitfire service experience Jack had sailed on both carriers as part of an RAF maintenance echelon for these aircraft. During one convoy he was among eight RAF mechanics flown off USS *Wasp* in four Fairey Swordfish to their Gibraltar posting with an RAF special erection party in preparation for future convoys.

On 5 November 2021 Garth sat down with Mr Waterfield to talk about and document his time in the RAF including events during the night of 4 July 1943. On the night of the Sikorski crash Jack and other airmen had been assembling Spitfires in a hangar at RAF New Camp and Hurricanes at RAF North Front. RAF New Camp was located south-west of Gibraltar's runway between the seaplane moorings and dockyard. Later that evening after curfew he and another airman were posted to stand a night watch with a fire extinguisher for Spitfires parked on North Front's apron. Walking across the north apron lit by floodlights Jack saw a parked RAF Liberator 50 yards away facing west with its engines ticking over at idle power.[222] An Indian airman, an engine fitter, then came up alongside Jack and commented that "it won't take off [...] it's been ticking over too long"[223] and was getting hot. Garth asked if there had been an argument between the flight crew and ground crew, and were any Poles among the ground crew. Jack did not see anything that appeared to be an argument or altercation between the aircrew and ground crew, and that there were no Poles present as ground crew, nor was he aware of any Polish airmen posted at North Front. This detail is noteworthy as Adrian Scrope had been told that there had been an altercation between the Gibraltar ground crew and the Sikorski aircrew over the excess cargo, and that Sikorski's entourage had been insistent on their boxes of alcohol being loaded. It can only be speculated that perhaps Jack arrived after the altercation. During an interview on 24 February 2022 Jack related how anything could be brought in Gibraltar during the war:

> "It was to impress the Spaniards that Britain was not for want of anything.... [Gibraltar's] shops were well stocked, you could buy clothing, chocolate, cameras, watches, anything. [...] [servicemen] could go into town to buy things for their wives and girlfriends, things you could not get in England."

Jack said whisky could be purchased, that it was common for pilots to buy whisky and hide it in their aircraft, that Spitfire pilots often put their bottles in the aircraft

RAF Hillman van.

gun wells. [224] Jack added that the RAF had three Hillman vans that were used to bring out stores to departing VIP aircraft.[225]

Jack's mention of three Hillman vans utilized for transporting stores to departing aircraft speaks to similar details provided by Flight Lieutenant Capes in an article about the crash and Sikorski's death published by the London-based Polish magazine *Dziennik Polski I Dziennik Żołnierza* (*The Polish Daily and Soldier's Daily*) on 20 April 1946. From his vantage point in the control tower Capes described a number of vehicles pulling up to AL523 prior to taxi departure from the airfield's northern tarmac.

> "Indeed, at the other end of the asphalt road, one could see a huge machine throwing dust clouds from under its tail. One could also see three black cars gliding towards it. The first one approaches the very hull of the machine. A group of people disembarking from it stop for a short conversation, and then some of the arrivals enter the plane. The other cars approach the plane one by one. Travellers also get out from these. All are devoured by the huge plane. Another pause. Now the volume of the motor's drone increases as the machine rolls along the runway. The plane contacts the control tower: 'May I taxi to the start of the runway?' The request is in an accent that is clearly not English, but the controllers are already used to this and do not pay it much attention. When cleared, the machine makes a deep turn and rolls slowly towards the western part of the runway ... the furthest from the traffic control officer's station, whose watchtower is in the vicinity of the lift-off line. Now the machine turns and approaches the starting line, with engines facing east."[226]

Jack went on to describe to Garth that as the aircraft left North Front's tarmac and taxied past he noticed a woman looking from one of the windows. It continued to the end of the runway, did a run-up and then received a green light from the tower. Jack said the Liberator did not use the entire runway. "It took off, climbed, done a dip, then climbed again, then done a dip and into the sea."[227] Jack estimated the Liberator rose approximately 60 ft, he likened the height to that of two houses. As it descended the engines quit just before hitting the water. Jack added that Gibraltar's search lights were on and that they lowered to a horizontal position just before the tower flashed a green light for take-off. He also said that judging height was always difficult because of light pollution from searchlights and because Gibraltar did not have blackouts. Jack was not aware until the following day that Sikorski had been on board.

SOE WIRELESS OPERATOR DOUGLAS MARTIN

Though Douglas Martin is not a new eyewitness his story has endured for almost fifty-five years and perpetuated a myth surrounding the crash of AL523. On the night of 4 July 1943, deep within an enclosure amid Gibraltar's high cliffs, SOE wireless operator Douglas Martin took a break from his wireless equipment and walked down a tunnel path to an opening 500 feet above the eastern end of North Front's runway. Looking out from the rock-hewn balcony an aircraft suddenly came into view beneath him:

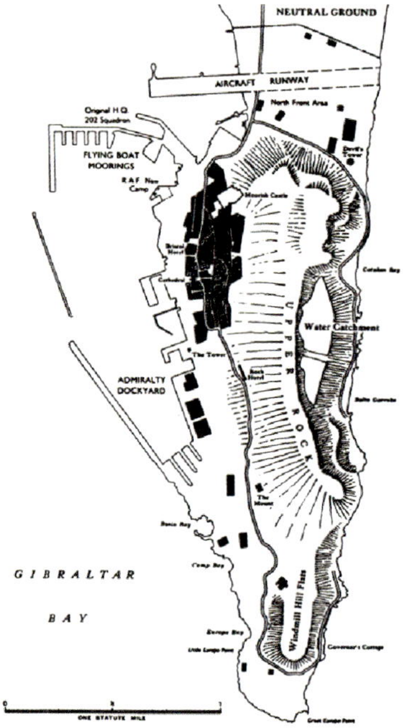

Left: *1943–1944 period map of Gibraltar identifying RAF New Camp and RAF North Front. The Royal Air Force Medical Services. (Crown Copyright public domain)*

Below: *Jack Waterfield's location on RAF North Front marked with an X on the night of 4 July 1943.*

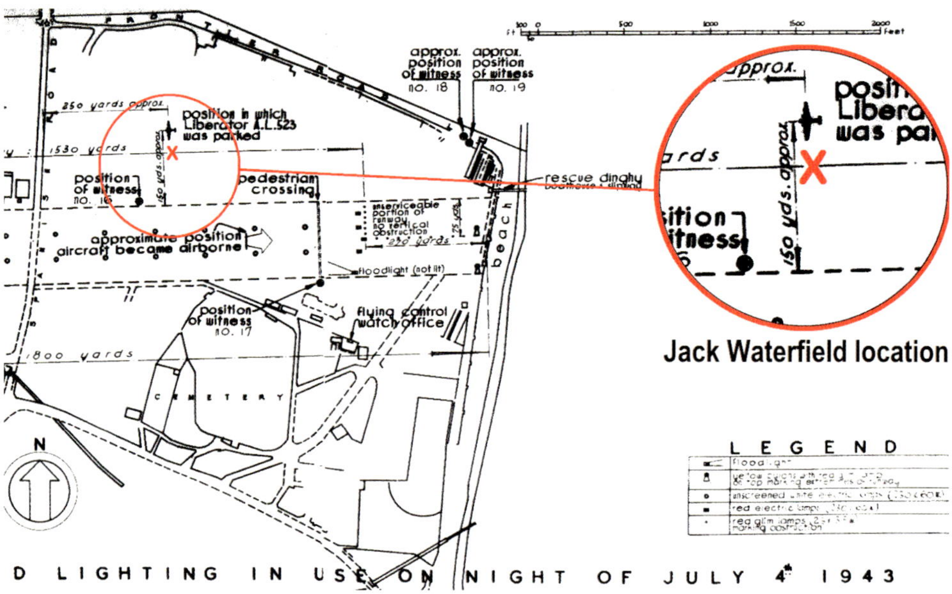

"It was a very clear evening; it wasn't really dark. It was more than dusk and less than night. I saw it appear, already airborne, climbing though it was not a steep climb. Then it changed attitude, but not violently. It was below me, I'd say, itself, no more than 200 feet above the ground. It went into a normal descent path and pancaked into the water."[228]

Shortly afterwards Martin noticed a man standing on the right wing of the floating aircraft.

In 1967 Carlos Thompson interviewed Douglas Martin about his account of AL523's crash; upon hearing the term 'pancake' he pressed Martin to clarify his statement.

Thompson: "When you say 'pancake', do you mean that you saw it fly towards the water, then, just before contact lift its nose and settle down first with its tail, in the emergency-routine to put down a land plane on the water?"

Martin: "Oh, no. It just went straight in. It's only that since the descent-path was not steep, it did not go nose-down, as in a dive."

Thompson: "There was no change in flight attitude?"

Martin: "None. I remember that the sea was very calm. There was no tremendous impact, that I could see. It didn't sink in fact, I don't remember the wings disappearing under the water, really – it just floated on."

Thompson: "Did the man whom you saw on the wing walk along the right or the left one?"

Martin: "It was the wing on my side, the right one."

Thompson: "Could you see from that distance, and in that light, whether the man was wearing a military tunic or civilian clothes or a flying overall? Did he give you the impression that he was dazed, moving about in a state of shock, or rather that he knew what he was doing?"

Martin: "The lighter part of the sky was away from me, so that any object between me and the sky became a silhouette. I saw him for the first time when he was a yard or so along the wing; I did not see in detail, but I'd say that the man was in command of his senses, as he walked along the wing, towards its tip I watched him as he walked about three fourths of the wing's length. He did nothing hasty, he never attempted to jump into the water or walk back to the body of the plane. I cannot remember exactly how much time passed, but I do remember that it was very little, before the plane began to sink. The man did not move, he just stood there. When the water was already up to his knees, I left the balcony to call the airport."

Thompson: "You saw no heads bobbing on the water?"

Martin: "Nothing at all."

Thompson: "Do you remember seeing an orange glow about the body of the man on the wing, something to indicate that he was wearing a Mae West life jacket?"

Martin: "I remember that I assumed that he must be a member of the crew, or somebody wearing some sort of flying clothes, because he made a bulky figure, something like the commercial-ad 'Michelin Man'. But this does not mean that I saw he was wearing a Mae West."

Thompson: "Were you able to distinguish whether the man was tall or small?"

Martin: "He was smallish, bulky."

Thompson: "Did you keep a diary in those days?"

Martin: "No. But the reason I tell you of that commercial-ad is because ever since then, every time I've seen that 'Michelin Man' in posters, I've always thought of that man on the wing. The strange thing is that the next day, when I had a chat with our chaps at our HQ and told them about what I'd seen, they didn't seem to attach any importance to it."

Thompson: "Did you already know that Sikorski had been on that plane?"

Martin: "No. I only found out later. And I have never really thought about it all again, that is, I never gave any importance to what I'd seen, until I saw what was published in *The Observer* about the crash and this play by Hochhuth. When I wrote that letter to *The Observer*, it didn't for a moment occur to me to hint that the man on the wing had been the pilot, or that he had been wearing a Mae West. I wrote it on the spur of the moment, without ever thinking that I was revealing anything sensational."

Thompson: "Were you ever, at that time, called to testify, by the court of inquiry?"

Martin: "No. Up to this day, I have never had anything whatsoever to do in connection with the Sikorski crash."[229]

Thompson was dumbfounded with Martin's descriptions of AL523 striking the water, floating for several minutes, and a figure walking along its right wing before sinking. What was confounding was all of this was witnessed at night without mention of searchlights, Martin claiming that the aircraft was silhouetted against the horizon. Thompson wondered how he was able to distinguish the aircraft so clearly while witnesses testified to only being able to follow AL523's descent by its navigation lights.[230] Douglas Martin's account is well known and was first published in the November 20th 1967 issue of *Der Spiegel*, the story coming to light after a telephone interview with David Irving.[231] There is also a plaque at Gibraltar's tunnel entrance citing Martin's story. Irving and Hochhuth concluded his story as conclusive proof that Prchal had deliberately ditched AL523 and was part of a larger plot to kill Sikorski.

During the 2015 episode of *WW2 Air Crash Detectives* Garth Barnard explored Gibraltar's tunnels in an effort to validate Douglas Martin's account. After locating the balcony from which Martin witnessed the crash Garth took several pictures. It quickly became apparent from this 500-foot vantage that figures walking in the streets below near the eastern runway's threshold were barely discernible. It did not take long to conclude that if people in the streets below were difficult to discern during the day then an individual standing atop the wing of a sinking aircraft in water at night, at a distance of 2100 feet (700 yards) off the runway's eastern end, would be impossible to perceive even with help of searchlights.[232] On pages 154–156, seven annotated images produced by Garth illustrate comparative distances from Martin's vantage point and key reference points related to AL523's crash position. Within the first three images (page 154), it is difficult to discern the individual circled in yellow walking along a street near Runway 27's eastern threshold until magnified. In the next two images, the angular directions from the runway and Martin's cliff face view, illustrated by intersecting yellow lines, provide the reader additional perspectives of distance. It is also significant to note the distant yellow-coloured air navigation buoy located 3,000 feet (914 metres) from the seawall of Runway 27 below a haze-shrouded horizon off the bows of two ships.[233] To further corroborate the crash site Garth referenced the salvage location where a propeller then believed from AL523 was recovered off the end of Runway 27 through sponsoring by *After The Battle* magazine in November 1977.[234] [235] On page 155 the salvage map from the magazine's 1978 article on the recovery which provides distance perspective from the shoreline and Gibraltar's cliffs. In the next image intersecting yellow degree lines from the salvage map overlay on a satellite view to identify the salvage and crash location. The air navigation buoy circled in red is illustrated in the final image (page 156).

When comparing these views against David Walker's twilight and darkness simulations Martin's account appears very suspect and extremely unlikely. The eastern horizon that he claims silhouetted the wing walking figure was only an obscure afterglow at 22:49 hours when viewed at sea level before the crash, by 23:07 hours it was gone. With Martin's vantage point, 500 feet above sea level, he may have had an extra minute of this indiscernible horizon but it was well above and beyond the crash site making it impossible to produce a silhouette. It is also unlikely that Prchal could have walked immediately after the crash considering he had two broken legs given the violence of the crash.[236] Also, as outlined in Chapter Three, AL523 very likely overturned on impact ejecting Prchal from the wrecked cockpit. Keeping in mind that Prchal had been described as only having suffered "shock, lacerations of the face, and fracture of the right ankle",[237] it is curious that on the first page of the inquiry sheaf titled 'Proceedings Court Of Inquiry Or Investigation', under Prchal's extent injured column, is the word 'seriously'.[238] A British internal government document from 3 May 1972 cites Prchal having suffered a broken leg in the crash.[239] Three cypher telegrams sent to the Air Ministry and other RAF recipients in England during the morning hours of 5 July described Prchal's condition as badly injured and seriously injured.[240] This medical evaluation term appears to have been overlooked or ignored by researchers who were quick to jump on Irving's version of Martin's story instead of taking a more objective look at Martin's account and Prchal's medical condition before condemning him. Still puzzled with Martin's story Thompson sought clarification by meeting with Prchal's ex-flight commander, Mr T H A Llewellyn. Thompson

Page 1 of RAF Form 412. Proceeding Of Court of Inquiry Or Investigation, Section 2. Description of Occupants. Prchal's condition under 'Extent injured (f)' is classified as 'Seriously'.

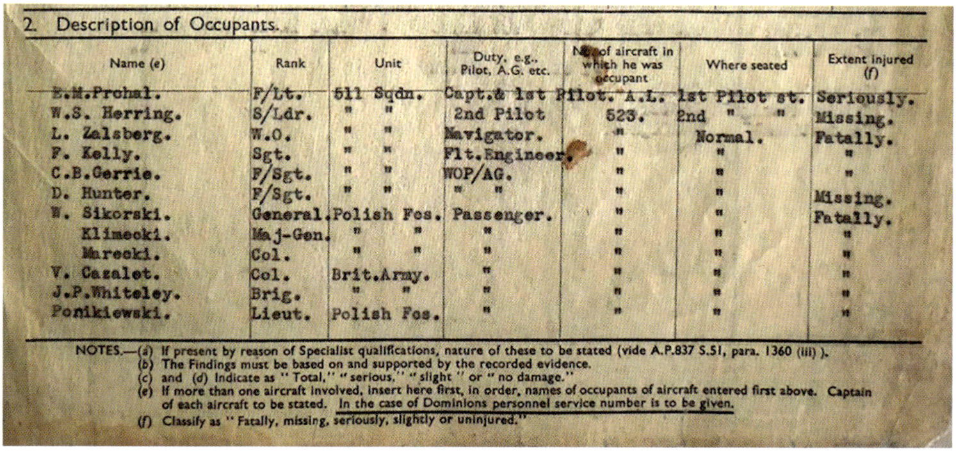

2. Description of Occupants.

Name (e)	Rank	Unit	Duty, e.g., Pilot, A.G. etc.	No. of aircraft in which he was occupant	Where seated	Extent injured (f)
E.M.Prchal.	F/Lt.	511 Sqdn.	Capt.& 1st Pilot.	A.L.	1st Pilot st.	Seriously.
W.S. Herring.	S/Ldr.	" "	2nd Pilot	523.	2nd " "	Missing.
L. Zalsberg.	W.O.	" "	Navigator.	"	Normal.	Fatally.
F. Kelly.	Sgt.	" "	Flt.Engineer.	"	"	"
C.B.Gerrie.	F/Sgt.	" "	WOP/AG.	"	"	"
D. Hunter.	F/Sgt.	" "	" "	"	"	Missing.
W. Sikorski.	General.	Polish Fos.	Passenger.	"	"	Fatally.
Klimecki.	Maj-Gen.	" "	"	"	"	"
Marecki.	Col.	" "	"	"	"	"
V. Cazalet.	Col.	Brit.Army.	"	"	"	"
J.P.Whiteley.	Brig.	" "	"	"	"	"
Ponikiewski.	Lieut.	Polish Fos.	"	"	"	"

NOTES.—(a) If present by reason of Specialist qualifications, nature of these to be stated (vide A.P.837 S.51, para. 1360 (iii)).
(b) The Findings must be based on and supported by the recorded evidence.
(c) and (d) Indicate as "Total," "serious," "slight" or "no damage."
(e) If more than one aircraft involved, insert here first, in order, names of occupants of aircraft entered first above. Captain of each aircraft to be stated. In the case of Dominions personnel service number is to be given.
(f) Classify as "Fatally, missing, seriously, slightly or uninjured."

related Martin's account to which Llewellyn replied: "I just do not understand how Martin could have seen a silhouette perspective against the horizon. Anyone standing 400 feet up, looking down on what happened would have the dark surface of the sea as background."[241] Carlos Thompson for his part in 1967, without help of celestial software and digital illustrations, quickly concluded that Douglas Martin had seen a plane crash that was not Sikorski's. Given the many air crashes at Gibraltar during the war, whatever crash Douglas Martin witnessed it was likely a different accident confounded by time and memory and not AL523.

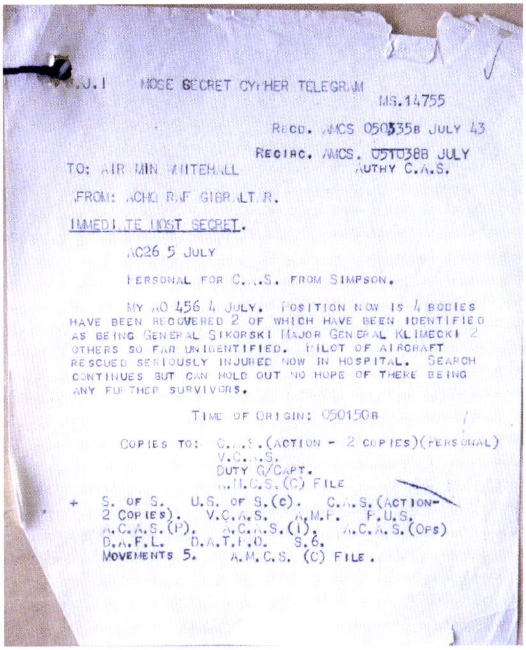

.J.I MOSE SECRET CYPHER TELEGRAM

MS.14755

RECD. AMCS 050535B JULY 43

RECIRC. AMCS. 051038B JULY

AUTHY C.A.S.

TO: AIR MIN WHITEHALL

FROM: ACHQ RAF GIBRALTAR.

IMMEDIATE MOST SECRET.

AC26 5 JULY

PERSONAL FOR C.A.S. FROM SIMPSON.

MY AO 456 4 JULY. POSITION NOW IS 4 BODIES HAVE BEEN RECOVERED 2 OF WHICH HAVE BEEN IDENTIFIED AS BEING GENERAL SIKORSKI MAJOR GENERAL KLIMECKI 2 OTHERS SO FAR UNIDENTIFIED. PILOT OF AIRCRAFT RESCUED SERIOUSLY INJURED NOW IN HOSPITAL. SEARCH CONTINUES BUT CAN HOLD OUT NO HOPE OF THERE BEING ANY FURTHER SURVIVORS.

TIME OF ORIGIN: 050150B

COPIES TO: C.A.S.(ACTION - 2 COPIES)(PERSONAL)
V.C.A.S.
DUTY G/CAPT.
A.M.C.S.(C) FILE

\+ S. OF S. U.S. OF S.(C). C.A.S.(ACTION- 2 COPIES). V.C.A.S. A.M.P. P.U.S. A.C.A.S.(P). A.C.A.S.(I). A.C.A.S.(OPS) D.A.F.L. D.A.T.P.O. S.6. MOVEMENTS 5. A.M.C.S. (C) FILE.

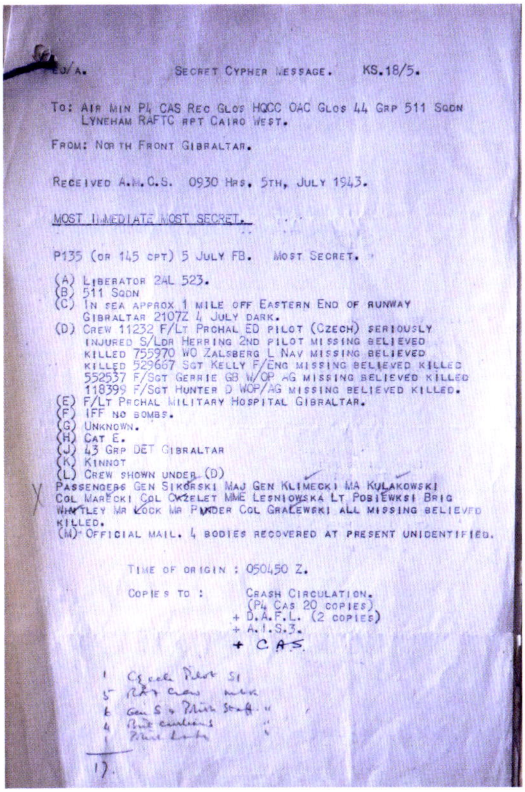

EJ/A. SECRET CYPHER MESSAGE. KS.18/5.

TO: AIR MIN P4 CAS REC GLOS HQCC OAC GLOS 44 GRP 511 SQDN LYNEHAM RAFTC RPT CAIRO WEST.

FROM: NORTH FRONT GIBRALTAR.

RECEIVED A.M.C.S. 0930 HRS. 5TH, JULY 1943.

MOST IMMEDIATE MOST SECRET.

P135 (OR 145 CPT) 5 JULY FB. MOST SECRET.

(A) LIBERATOR 2AL 523.
(B) 511 SQDN
(C) IN SEA APPROX 1 MILE OFF EASTERN END OF RUNWAY GIBRALTAR 2107Z 4 JULY DARK.
(D) CREW 11232 F/LT PRCHAL ED PILOT (CZECH) SERIOUSLY INJURED S/LDR HERRING 2ND PILOT MISSING BELIEVED KILLED 755970 WO ZALSBERG L NAV MISSING BELIEVED KILLED 529667 SGT KELLY F/ENG MISSING BELIEVED KILLED 552537 F/SGT GERRIE GB W/OP AG MISSING BELIEVED KILLED 118399 F/SGT HUNTER D WOP/AG MISSING BELIEVED KILLED.
(E) F/LT PRCHAL MILITARY HOSPITAL GIBRALTAR.
(F) IFF NO BOMBS.
(G) UNKNOWN.
(H) CAT E.
(J) 43 GRP DET GIBRALTAR
(K) KINNOT
(L) CREW SHOWN UNDER (D)
PASSENGERS GEN SIKORSKI MAJ GEN KLIMECKI MA KULAKOWSKI COL MARECKI COL CAZELET MME LESNIOWSKA LT POBIEWKSI BRIG WHITLEY MR LOCK MR PINDER COL GRALEWSKI ALL MISSING BELIEVED KILLED.
(M) OFFICIAL MAIL. 4 BODIES RECOVERED AT PRESENT UNIDENTIFIED.

TIME OF ORIGIN : 050450 Z.

COPIES TO : CRASH CIRCULATION.
(P4 CAS 20 COPIES)
\+ D.A.F.L. (2 COPIES)
\+ A.I.S.3.
\+ C.A.S.

Top and left: *Pages from the cypher telegram sent the morning of 5 July to the Air Ministry with news of General Sikorski's death and mention of the surviving pilot being seriously injured. (AIR 8/779)*

Top left: *A street corner circled in yellow near North Front's Runway 27 threshold viewed from Douglas Martin's balcony. Figures within the circle are indiscernible. (Garth Barnard)*

Top right: *The same street corner formally circled in yellow now magnified. A figure walking behind the white vehicle is just discernible. (Garth Barnard)*

Left: *The same magnified street corner with the figure walking behind the white vehicle circled in yellow. (Garth Barnard)*

Above, left: *Note the yellow-coloured inner air navigation buoy located 3,000 feet (914 metres) from the seawall end of Runway 27. The buoy sits below the haze-shrouded horizon left of two stationary ships. The intersecting yellow lines indicate AL523's crash site. (Garth Barnard)*

Left: *Inner air navigation buoy circled in yellow located 3,000 feet (914 metres) from the seawall of Runway 27. (Garth Barnard)*

Above: The first day. The Fantasia anchored in the approximate crash position off the eastern end of the Gibraltar runway. Devil's Tower RAF Camp and the Admiralty radio-transmitting masts in the foreground.

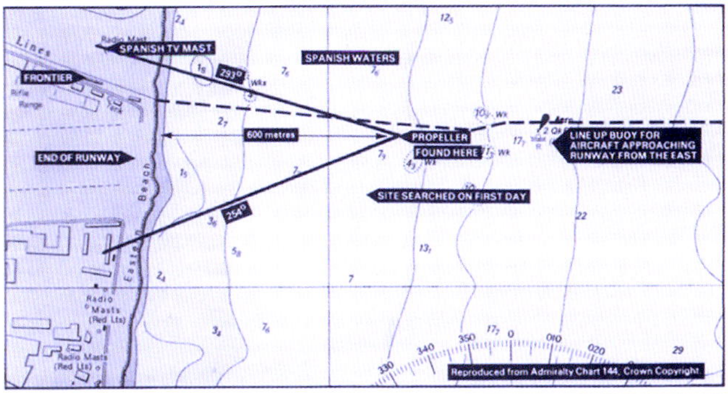

Bearings taken to re-orient the search on the second day — the end windows on a block of flats and the Spanish TV mast.

Left: After The Battle. *Sikorski Sequel: Seabed Site Investigation. Number 24, page 44.*

Below: *Intersecting 293° and 254° yellow degree lines overlayed on a satellite view pinpointing the salvage and crash location. (Garth Barnard)*

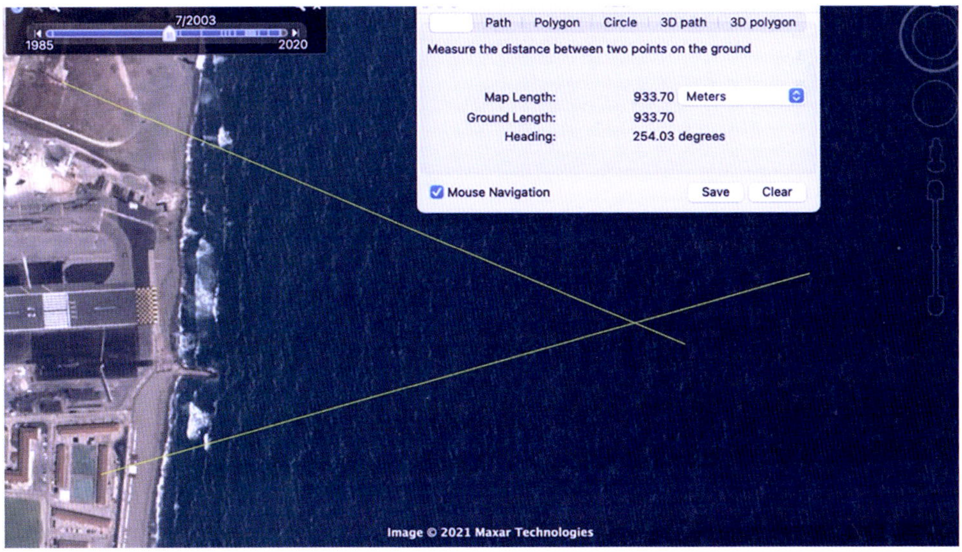

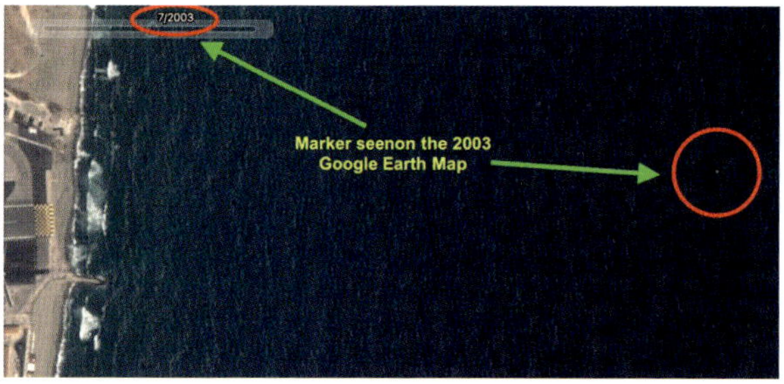

Left: The air navigation buoy circled in red located 3,000 feet (914 metres) from the seawall of Runway 27. (Garth Barnard)

Below: HMS Moorhill *and RAF rescue launch HSL 181 tied alongside at location of crash site. Note that there is no recovered wreckage or debris visible on the deck suggesting this picture was taken during the start of recovery operations on the afternoon of 5 July. In the background is the eastern end of Gibraltar's runway, which is approximately 700 yards from the shoreline. (NAC)*

Left: *Western view of the east runway end. Picture taken from RAF rescue launch HSL 181 tied alongside HMS* Moorhill. *From this vantage point figures on the beach or runway would be difficult to discern with any detail which speaks to the difficulty of seeing anything at this distance from the shore or Gibraltar's cliffs. (NAC)*

Above: *HMS* Moorhill *anchored at the crash site, moored in front is a small lighter with a Royal Navy diving party on board. Looking north toward the Mediterranean coast of Spain. (NAC)*

Below: *View east of the Royal Navy diving party working from a lighter. Note the ocean surface has a petrol sheen drifting away from behind the vessel. (NAC)*

SMUGGLING AND FICTITIOUS CONFESSIONS

Jaroslav Prokop

Over the years several unsubstantiated myths of smuggling and post-crash confessions clouded the 1943 court of inquiry's findings and conclusions on the crash of AL523. These myths were perpetuated by David Irving in a lengthy 1969 letter posted to then Prime Minister Harold Wilson. The letter was an attempt to sway the government to reopen the crash inquiry through what Irving deemed new evidence. Part of this new evidence came in the form of two eyewitness accounts which alleged Prchal had covered up and lied to the court of inquiry about the real cause of the crash. The first was a Czech navigator named Jaroslav Prokop whom Prchal had flown with in 1946.[242] Prchal allegedly told Prokop:

> "He had lied to the RAF court of inquiry, because – as he said – after the crash he could only assume that it was his crew's smuggling activities (which have been very extensively proven from other sources) which had caused the crash, and he had covered up for them, honourably, as they were all killed in the crash or missing."[243]

Alternately Carlos Thompson in 1968, having read Irving's book *Accident* published in 1967, sought to find out who the (then unnamed) mysterious Czech navigator was that recounted a similar story confided to him by Prchal. In this earlier 1967 version Prchal allegedly told this Czech navigator:

> "That he could only assume that the plane had crashed because of its load. When he took off, he did not have enough speed and he tried to gain speed by climbing and diving. As he was so heavily laden the control surfaces had little effect and the plane had just crashed into the sea."[244]

In September 1968 Thompson identified and traced Mr Prokop to London England where he agreed to be interviewed regarding statements attributed to him by Irving.

> Thompson: "Irving has written in his book that you flew with Prchal as his navigator."
>
> Prokop: "Well, as radio operator/navigator."

Thompson "Irving also writes that you flew 'regularly' with Prchal. Is this so, were you part of his steady crew?"

Prokop: "No. I only flew with him occasionally."

Thompson: "But still, were you and Prchal particularly close friends?"

Prokop: "You know how it was in those aircrews we were all friendly, it was like a brotherhood."

Thompson: "To Prchal, in Toronto, Irving said that he had it from you that Prchal had invented the jamming of the controls story."

Prokop: "Prchal never said that to me."

Thompson: "What did Prchal tell you, exactly?"

Prokop: "He said that she was a bit lazy on take-off, and that this must have been because of overloading."

Thompson: "Did Prchal say to you that he knew she was overloaded, or that maybe she was? To what degree did he affirm this suspicion or knowledge to you?"

Prokop: "He only said that: 'She was lazy on take-off that was a sign of overloading'."

Thompson: "But you do realize that this need not have been the cause of the crash. Even 'lazy', once a plane reaches take-off speed, it'll fly off successfully and, properly handled, it'll stay airborne. I repeat my question, did Prchal tell you that he knew for certain that they had exceeded the pay-load dangerously?"

Prokop: "No, he didn't. You see, in those secret flights, all the VIPs carried all sorts of things, extra luggage, etc. which the pilot did not weigh himself. All he could do was to estimate roughly; all pilots simply guessed the weight and wrote it down; it was the duty of the ground people to weigh what went into the plane."[245]

Thompson: "Are you sure that when you talked about this with Prchal in Prague there was no mention of the jamming of the controls?"

Prokop: "Never. It wasn't mentioned at all."[246]

Leslie Swabey

The second example of Irving's new evidence was an account given by Flight Lieutenant Leslie Swabey.[247] This officer alleged that shortly after returning to No. 511 Squadron in September 1943 Prchal admitted to fellow pilots and Swabey that he "[invented] the story of elevator controls jamming" for the inquiry, but added he had had to do so because he felt controls go "all soggy" on take-off, and he had attributed this to an error by his co-pilot who had perhaps selected the flap control lever by mistake instead of undercarriage. He had fabricated the other story, he said, in order to cover up for his co-pilot (with whom he had never flown before), whose body was never found."[248] Mr Swabey's account was never verified as he refused to answer publicly to the story's validity.[249]

Josef Klesnil

Though Carlos Thompson was unable to contact Leslie Swabey he continued to pursue the question of Prchal discussing the accident with fellow pilots and of smuggling. Following his visit with Prokop he traced Captain Josef Klesnil, a close friend of Prchal and his regular co-pilot during their time at Czech Airlines. Thompson visited Klesnil in London on 11 September 1968 where he related his experience flying Liberators with the Czechoslovakian air force.

> Klesnil: "I was also with 311 Squadron. I was also flying Liberators. One thing I do remember definitely: about one month to forty days after Prchal's accident, an important modification was introduced in the controls-locking system, thanks to which you could no more lock your controls accidentally, inadvertently; with the new device you had to go through more thorough, complicated action to effect the unlocking."
>
> Thompson: "When you and Prchal were flying regularly together back in Prague, did you ever discuss the crash?"
>
> Klesnil: "Of course we discussed it."
>
> Thompson: "When you discussed the crash, what did Prchal say to you about it?"
>
> Klesnil: "What we already knew from the RAF."
>
> Thompson: "I have been told that Prchal had no way of knowing exactly what his all-up weight was."
>
> Klesnil: "True. Particularly in those VIP flights, a pilot could only roughly estimate his weight, he had no way of accurately checking it."
>
> Thompson: "I take it that you and Prchal not only flew together back in Prague but were truly close friends: do you think it likely that he would have made some 'confession' to someone not as close to him as, say, yourself?"
>
> Klesnil: "It certainly doesn't sound like Ed. To me, certainly, he never said anything 'secret'." Captain Klesnil chuckled: "Anyone who goes around saying that in the war days you needed to ditch a plane to kill a political

figure, should have his head examined. A pilot, no matter how experienced, who is not scared every time he lands a big plane, is a fool. To imagine that you would find a pilot willing to crash a Liberator in the hope of surviving, is sheer idiocy."[250]

Josef Rechka

At the suggestion of Klesnil the next person Thompson interviewed was Captain Josef Rechka another close wartime friend of Prchal who had also flown with No. 310 Czechoslovak Squadron during the Battle of Britain. Rechka was later posted to No. 24 Squadron, a VIP transport squadron flying Lockheed Hudsons based at Hendon in December 1942 and later to No. 512 Squadron in August 1943 flying Douglas C-47 Dakotas also based out of Hendon. Rechka was at Gibraltar the night of the crash and was the first to visit Prchal in hospital. The two later flew with Czech Airlines and both escaped to the west in September 1950 flying a DC-3 to Manston England.[251] After Rechka related his recollections of the crash Thompson finally asked:

Thompson: "Did Prchal ever talk again about the crash? Did he discuss it, let us say, trying to rationalize it, to understand it?"

Rechka: "Yes, many times, at our club, he discussed it with anyone who'd be interested in discussing its possible causes."

Thompson: "Did you fly back to Czechoslovakia together with Prchal?"

Rechka: "No. We were in different squadrons. I flew back taking Jan Masaryk."

Thompson: "Did Prchal, in the many talks you must have had back in Prague, ever tell you that he thought he had taken off at Gibraltar with an excessive load?"

Rechka: "Never."[252]

Eduard Prchal

In late 1967 Carlos Thompson travelled to Los Altos California where he contacted Eduard Prchal and interviewed him at his home. Prchal was amicable with Thompson and answered many questions regarding the 1943 crash and court of inquiry including allegations made by David Irving about smuggling.

Thompson. "In his book, David Irving writes that in London he interviewed an anonymous 'friend' of yours, someone who was your regular navigator back in Czechoslovakia after the war, who claims that you confessed to him that you felt that the true reason for the crash was that you had taken off with an excessive load. Allow me the audacity of this question: if this is so, where does it leave your testimony to the court of inquiry that your controls jammed after take-off? Do you agree that this is as good as saying that you invented the locked-controls testimony, when interrogated?"

Prchal took no exception and answered calmly:

"Mr. Thompson, if you were inside my skin, if you had caused such a terrible tragedy through irresponsibility, would you have gone about telling it to others? And how dare Mr. Irving quote a man who is alive and able to speak, but does not seem ready to confront me?"

Thompson. "David Irving has also said that you were smuggling half-a-ton of oranges."

Prchal. "What nonsense. I would have needed a lorry to get them to the plane."

Thompson. "Did you never smuggle anything?"

Prchal. "I would lie if I didn't tell you that, like the rest, I often took back to England oranges or cigarettes, or any of the things of which there was a shortage, as indeed everyone else did petty, domestic smuggling, you could call it; but I would never have considered sizeable smuggling for the simple reason that I cared too much about my work and my future, and the various cases of court-martialled people were enough to give one pause.

"Except for the bodies which drifted away, all that was in the plane was lifted to the surface, together with the Liberator's wreckage. Has anybody been able to produce the great quantities of smuggled goods? Where were the crates of spirits? And the half-a-ton of oranges? And the famous furs? Even if there were furs in some suitcases, why must they have been mine, just because I was the only survivor?"[253]

Jack Sach, Anthony Quayle, Ludwik Łubieński, William Bailey, John Buck

Though the subject of smuggling was never brought up during the court of inquiry it was indirectly alluded to when Squadron Leader Jack Sach was asked if he had noticed any tendency to relax regulations when carrying very important passengers.

Sach replied: "[yes], there have been occasions within my experience when VIPs have refused to conform with regulations."[254] During earlier discussions Thompson had with Anthony Quayle, Ludwik Łubieński, William Bailey, and John Buck, each had mentioned smuggling as prevalent and not necessarily unusual among pilots passing through Gibraltar. Major Anthony Quayle, who along with Flight Lieutenant Arthur Perry served as aide-de-camp to Gibraltar's governor General Mason-MacFarlane, recounted:

> "I knew very few airmen who did not smuggle in those days. I knew a lot of pilots then – they all smuggled. Now, these pilots, they knew they might die any minute, so if they got a chance to put a few silk stockings or a dozen bottles of perfume or a sack of oranges in their empty bomb bay, why, they did it. I said to Irving, 'You don't surprise me if you tell me that Prchal, too, did a bit of smuggling'."[255]

Ludwik Łubieński remarked to Thompson:

> "[I was] not aware of any 'smuggling' especially of cameras, but this is quite understandable, due to the fact that I took care of the Polish passengers and did not pay any attention to the crew or any other British passengers, as it was not any of my business. Sacks of southern fruits could be purchased in Gibraltar, put in a plane, as they had been very scarce at that time in the United Kingdom. One item which I remember well, was that the divers fished out of the sea three suitcases of fur coats and we have been rather astonished, as it was summer."[256]

Łubieński had also written that rules prohibiting transport of contraband on VIP aircraft "were not so rigorously applied". [257]

During discussions with William Bailey, one of the wreck recovery divers at the crash site, Thompson asked:

> "As you know, there are many theories about the reasons for the crash. One of them speaks of overloading of the plane; that it was carrying a large amount of smuggled goods; that the pilot, alone, was smuggling half a ton of oranges and that between him and the Polish party, a considerable number of crates of spirits were being brought back to London. Did you find all this cargo at the bottom?"

Bailey: "Not at all. We only found personal things. Presents, boxes of Turkish Delight, etc. I remember that the sun was streaming through the water and we could see quite clearly. Neither I nor any of my chaps found anything but personal luggage; there were quite a lot of zip-bags and regular suitcases, but it is to be remembered that there were at least fifteen people in that plane. [...] I myself, for example, found lying undisturbed on the sand a cigarette case which I have been told General Sikorski had presented to the pilot."

Thompson: "But Irving has received precise information about many cases of Leica cameras."

Bailey: "One case, about the size of a six-bottle case of wine. I sent it up to the surface and I was present when it was opened; it contained twelve cameras at the most."[258]

John Buck who had been the air accidents investigator for the British Air Ministry had also dived on the wreckage. When Thompson asked about smuggled cargo, cases of Leica cameras, and a half ton of oranges Buck replied:

> "I can assure you that only one case of Leica cameras was found. I speak advisedly in this instance because I was on the sea bed when it was found and personally assisted in bringing it to the surface. [...] Bear in mind that the plane's tanks had been topped, and that in it sat something like fifteen people, the retinue of a Head of State, who always claim certain secret privileges for themselves – it was certainly not unusual for a certain amount of smuggling to take place in VIP aircraft! But I think it is very wide of the mark to talk in terms of 'crates' of spirits. I certainly did not see them on the sea bed or on the diving barge."[259]

The British government of the day, after an extensive review of Irving's new evidence and allegations, concluded there was nothing within his claims that was new or worthy of reopening the court of inquiry. Of those claims the government noted that his two star witnesses, Prokop and Swabey, refused to answer in public for their statements.[260] The government recognized that much of Irving's information was an "imaginative attempt to make a few facts and a great many assumptions fit a predetermined theory. Most of [which had] already been set out in [his book] *Accident*."[261] It was further recognized that he and playwright Rolf Hochhuth had drawn on arguments made by Jerzy Klimkowski in a book he wrote in Poland in 1965 suggesting the crash was engineered by the British with Churchill's approval as part of British support for General Anders' opposition to Sikorski.[262] Klimkowski had been General Anders' aide-de-camp but was imprisoned in 1943 for conspiracies against Sikorski.

Among the people tasked with assessing Irving's new evidence against the court of inquiry's findings in February 1969 was Foreign Affairs Deputy Secretary Sir Robin Hooper, a former wartime RAF pilot. Hooper also acknowledged:

> "There was a certain amount of smuggling by Transport Command crews during the war – enough to lend some colour to a theory of this kind. But
>
> (a) The take-off was a normal one. An aircraft overloaded to the extent that Irving alleges (62,000 lbs) would have staggered into the air, after a much longer run than was the case, in a semi-stalled attitude. It is inconceivable that, e.g. the flying control officers, one of whom had 7,000 hours as a pilot, would not have noticed something wrong.
> (b) Prchal was an experienced and careful pilot. To take off from a 1,500-yard runway ending in the sea, in a light wind, at 62,000 lbs would have been an excessively dicey proceeding – too such so to be acceptable in an aircraft carrying VIPs.
> (c) Irving's allegations that the all-up weight was in reality 62,000 lbs and that there were "30 or 40 cases of liquor aboard" are unsupported."[263]

The presumption of smuggling was again challenged in 2009 when Mr Sydney Knowles published a biography about his time as a Royal Navy clearance diver during and after the Second World War. Much of his wartime diving had been with the Underwater Working Party (UWWP) in Gibraltar under the command of Lionel Crabb. Knowles had dived on the wreck of AL523 recovering victims and salvaging sensitive material both outside and inside the wreckage. He wrote about entering the overturned interior:

> "[The visibility] inside the plane was very difficult, due to the fact that it had been carrying many cases of cigarettes and cigars, which had burst open on impact and badly stained the water. We also came across cases of brandy, whisky, etc. and many rolls of silk. During my search inside the aircraft, I recall seeing a small packing case with a badly-stained address label reading either Ribbens or Ruben's Hotel London."[264]

It is curious that while Knowles recalled seeing cases of alcohol in the wreckage; Bailey and Buck claim to have seen none. The reason for this discrepancy is unclear, perhaps Bailey and Buck simply did not see cases of liquor on the seabed or salvage barge. Though both men recalled luggage, Leica cameras and personal items being recovered there is no mention of liquor bottles or crates. One answer to this discrepancy is that Sydney Knowles enjoyed embellishing his stories.

This propensity for story telling came to light in 1957 when a headless corpse was recovered in Chichester Harbour and later identified as Lionel Crabb who had disappeared under mysterious circumstances fourteen months earlier in Portsmouth during Nikita Khrushchev's visit to Britain in April 1956. Though Knowles had known Crabb he relished publicity and often chatted with reporters for a few pounds claiming that he could identify the body if only he were allowed to see it. Days later he told reporters that he had seen the corpse, but it was still in its wetsuit. He later claimed the chief inspector of police put pressure on him to say it was the body of Crabb.

Sydney Knowles in fact had never seen the corpse nor been asked to identify it, his wild stories leading police to consider him unreliable. What was believed to be Crabb's remains were in fact identified by the chief pathologist in Chichester through known physical features and condition of the body.[265]

A more plausible reason for this discrepancy might lay in the unspoken acceptance that VIPs passing through Gibraltar took liberties smuggling contraband, that they were the exception rather than the rule. Perhaps it was easier for Bailey, Buck and other senior officers to tacitly acknowledge that VIPs frequently smuggled rather than reveal recovering large quantities of spirits that could humiliate the respected Polish leader's memory causing further political embarrassment to Britain and Poland. With that said, these new revelations detailing the loading of contraband and their subsequent discovery on the seabed should not be considered proof that Prchal was their sole owner or that he was some kind of master smuggler. They in fact reveal that Prchal likely and reluctantly acquiesced to the whims of a high-ranking dignitary and his entourage, nothing more. Had a different pilot been assigned to fly Sikorski on that fateful night the outcome would have likely been similar.

SIKORSKI'S EARLIER FLIGHTS: A PERSPECTIVE

During General Sikorski's tenure as prime minister and commander-in-chief there were several noteworthy flights that proved hazardous and unsettling for all involved including the general. In some instances Sikorski's relationship with pilots was strained wavering between blind trust in their skill and resentment when they refused, or were unable to comply with his requests. In other instances politics, weather, personal motives, technical faults and bombs left the aircraft and all aboard to the mercy of those circumstances. Given that these flights were missions of diplomatic urgency where the future of Poland's people and its military hung in the balance, it is understandable that Sikorski would have been extremely concerned about delays and schedule setbacks. It is noteworthy that myth makers saw some of these events as assassination attempts when in fact they were not and had no association with each other. It is further noteworthy of references made to contraband goods carried during one of Sikorski's diplomatic trips.

The first known record of General Sikorski having travelled by plane was on 14 November 1939 when he flew with his Foreign Affairs Minister August Zaleski from France to England onboard an Air France Dewoitine D.338.[266] The next occurred on 18 May 1940 during the Battle of France when he was flown from Bordeaux on a Lockheed Hudson to Britain.[267] On 20 June 1940 Sikorski returned aboard a BOAC Short S30 flying boat G-AFKZ to collect senior members of the Polish General Staff and bring them back to Britain ahead of over 25,000 Polish troops soon to be evacuated from French ports. [268] [269] Escorting Sikorski on this flight departing from Poole was Captain Peter Wilkinson of the British No. 4 Military Mission liaising with the Polish government and military administration in France. Wilkinson described the following incident.

> "The engines were on, and we took off absolutely straight away. Then a very curious incident happened. Just when we were taxiing to take off, Sikorski summoned me – he and [his aid Lieutenant] Tyszkiewicz were sitting right in the rear of the aircraft and I had withdrawn to a discreet distance and was reading a book quietly by myself, but he called me. I went down and he said to me words to the effect: '*Dites au pilote que j'ai toute confiance en lui.*' [Tell the pilot that I have complete confidence in him]. Frankly, this was a bit of a flummox, because the chap was just about to take off. It was a strange message in any case. It was very, what you might call a very, un-English sort of a message. So I

signified obviously that the order had been received and made my way gently forward and kept out of sight until we were airborne, and then I went up to the bridge, which on those boats was a great sort of deck above the passenger deck, and I said to the pilot that the general had complete confidence in him."[270]

Landing late morning on Lake Biscarrosse south-west of Bordeaux in southern France the aircraft anchored offshore to await transport for Sikorski's party. While waiting the captain of the aircraft asked Wilkinson up to the flight deck to explain "that his orders were, that if there was the slightest risk to his aircraft, he was to take off. And that perhaps [he] ought to explain this to the general before he left."

"So I did explain this to the general, and it was not at all well received. The general said: 'But I order him to stay.' This, being translated to the captain of the aircraft, was not at all well received either. He said that he had received his orders from the Air Ministry and therefore was in no position to receive orders from General Sikorski. So, hoping to calm the waters a little bit, I said rather self-importantly that, in any case, I would be there. Whereupon General Sikorski said rather tartly that he did not care very much whether I was there or not, the important thing was to have the aircraft there. So anyhow, I said, he will obviously come back and fetch you, and I will know the signs, and signals, and all this sort of thing, and that I should be here, and there it is. I must say, it would be unfair to say he took it with not too good a grace, but he was certainly not in the best of temper ... although Sikorski was always absolutely courteous. He was an incredibly self-controlled and courteous man. So it would be quite wrong to suggest that he would show that he was ruffled, but it was perfectly clear to me that he was."[271]

Later that morning Sikorski departed by car to Bordeaux with French officials and would not return until the next morning to depart for Poole; Major Wilkinson remained with the aircraft. At 14:10 there was an air raid warning prompting the flying boat's captain to taxi the aircraft for fifteen to twenty minutes to avoid damage from a possible dive-bomber attack.[272]

While in England Sikorski would travel in No. 24 VIP Transport Squadron aircraft. The first recorded instance was on 9 August 1940 when he flew in a de Havilland DH-95 Flamingo to inspect No. 300 and No. 301 Polish bomber squadrons at RAF Bramcote.[273] Fourteen months later Sikorski set out on his first trip to the Middle East and Russia which took place 31 October 1941 through to 6 January 1942. During this period he flew to Gibraltar, Malta, Cairo, Lydda, Baghdad, Tehran then onto Russia to Baku and Moscow. During a flight from Cairo to Lydda on 12 November his British liaison officer Major Victor Cazalet wrote:

> "As usual we had much too much luggage. This time the extra weight consisted of every conceivable commodity which we had bought for the Poles in Russia. From cigarettes and Oxo cubes to dates and peanuts which I got specially for Cripps. From wristwatches, blotting paper and fountain pens to anti-scurvy pills, all of which are quite unobtainable in Russia, our luggage was a very miscellaneous collection of articles."[274]

This admission of contraband smuggling, though understandable given the plight of Poles recently released from Soviet labour camps, would later speak to future acknowledgements that VIPs frequently smuggled despite strict rules to the contrary. In an interesting side note to Sikorski's Middle East trip he was permitted to sail aboard the destroyer HMS *Kipling* on 13/14 November transporting 300 British reinforcements to besieged Tobruk in Libya. Here he inspected troops of the Polish 'Carpathian' Rifle Brigade defending Tobruk's western perimeter. As their ship pulled into harbour in the early morning darkness Major Cazalet recorded:

> "In the harbour itself there are twenty-eight known wrecks of ships of every size. On none of these was there any light whatsoever. There is no proper quay or landing stage so we crept up to one of the wrecks, put a plank down from the destroyer to the wreck, and walked over the wreck on to the land. [...] We finally got ashore and unloaded the most precious cargo of all, namely, twenty-five cases of whisky. I must admit some of it disappeared in the night, but quite a fair proportion eventually found its way to the Polish troops."[275]

As to where this whisky was obtained Cazalet does not say though he did offer that, "Cairo is best described as a city of 'Total Peace', with unlimited petrol, sugar and liquor. Polo, tennis, hockey, football, racing, all in full swing. Day life and nightlife to please all kinds and ranks." One can only speculate as to whether this generous and noble gesture by Sikorski was an early pattern of freewheeling that would fuel future controversy surrounding his death in 1943.[276]

On 25 November 1941 during a flight from Cairo to Moscow with stops at Baghdad, and Tehran, Sikorski's Liberator made an unscheduled landing at an airfield near

Hamadan Iran after turning back due to deteriorating weather. [277] This event was related to Carlos Thompson by Michal Protasewicz who was then a colonel in the Polish army and member of Sikorski's entourage on this trip.

> "We left England for Cairo on a four-engine aircraft. The ultimate destination was Russia.
>
> "The pilot was Lieutenant Colonel Forbes, of the British Air Force. We had five crewmen in all. With us travelled General Klimecki, Sikorski's Chief of Staff; Major Victor Cazalet, the British liaison officer; Colonel Tyszkiewicz, who was also General Sikorski's ADC, and myself. The first leg of the flight was Cairo–Baghdad, with an in-between re-fuelling stop. We arrived in Baghdad about one p.m., spent the rest of the day there and the next day we took off for Teheran, at nine a.m. The weather was particularly beautiful that morning, as we left Baghdad. As we climbed, we began to fly towards a mountain range and I remember that we all greatly admired the splendid view.
>
> "During the flight, I jotted down my impressions, for my diary. I wrote down that the view of the snow-clad mountains, in that most pure air, reminded me of the Carpathos of my native Poland. But as we flew on, [...] about eleven o'clock, the weather began to change, the sun was no more visible and fog began to envelop us. After a while, the pilot, Lord Forbes, came back to the cabin and said to General Sikorski, 'I'm sorry, sir, but the weather has deteriorated completely ahead of us, we must return to Baghdad'. This rather upset the general, who was always keen on keeping his precise schedule, but Lord Forbes made it plain that there was no choice and the plane turned back.
>
> "After an hour, we began to leave the storm behind us and eventually the air cleared and we could see that we were again flying over the plains. A short while later, Forbes' voice came over the intercom, telling us to fasten our seat belts and prepare for landing. A few minutes later, the machine did a perfectly safe landing in an open field. When the plane's door was opened, we found ourselves next to a road and about ten kilometres away, we could see a town. It was Hamadan."[278]

Protasewicz went on to describe a safe arrival and that Forbes had made a "splendid landing, with no more than the bump or two".[279] In time fuel was arranged and it was decided between Sikorski and Forbes that it would be best to return to Tehran, Protasewicz describing their mutual decision in the following terms:

> "I do not have here in my notes whether it was the general who expressed his wish first, or whether Forbes, knowing how displeased he had been by the delay, suggested it, but I'd be inclined to think that the two things happened simultaneously – the fact is that it was agreed to take off and try to reach Teheran [sic] again. We left the ground at 14:20 and at 16:45[280] we landed in Teheran [sic]. Nobody was expecting us at that time, so we phoned the Polish and the British embassies and shortly after, we were installed in Teheran [sic]."[281]

Sikorski remained in Tehran for a week holding talks with General Anders and British military authorities on how to best evacuate Polish soldiers in Russia to Persia where they would be incorporated in the British army and trained for future deployments. At the conclusion of these discussions Sikorski flew to the Russian city of Baku. From Baku Russian authorities insisted that the general fly on a Russian aircraft with a Russian crew. Protasewicz went on to describe Sikorski's reaction.

> "At first the general refused, because he said he felt happier flying on with Forbes, but the Russians insisted and Forbes flew back and Sikorski continued with a Soviet machine. In all his flights within Russian territory, he flew with Russians. Only when he came out again, at Baku, Forbes was waiting for him and they continued flying together.
>
> "There is something else which might interest you to show to you General Sikorski's true feelings about the Russians. When it was decided that the general would continue from Baku to Moscow in a Russian plane, General Klimecki and he decided that the vast quantity of secret documents we had with us ought not be entrusted to a Soviet crew. (We had various cases of such material.) The general decided to entrust all this to Lt Col Forbes. After the general left, Forbes had all this baggage taken to a hotel room and placed three RAF men in charge, with the orders that one man must be at all times in the room. On the return of the general, we flew back to Cairo, with Forbes."[282]

On 3 January 1942 at the end of Sikorski's trip, as his Short Empire flying boat G-AFCT[283] prepared for take-off from Malta harbour on its midnight departure to Gibraltar it was caught in an air raid. As the aircraft raced across the water a stick of bombs struck within 300 feet of the aircraft, Cazalet writing "[owing] to the noise of the engine we did not hear much, but the plane shook somewhat mysteriously".[284]

General Sikorski travelled three times to Canada and the United States. The first trip was by sea on 24 March 1941 onboard the battleship HMS *Revenge*[285], the remaining journeys were by airplane.[286] One of the most bizarre events to plague Sikorski's flight travels occurred over the Atlantic during 21 March 1942 on his second trip while flying in BOAC Liberator AM262 from Prestwick to Montreal for a meeting with President Roosevelt in Washington, D.C. Escorting the general were Colonel Mitkiewicz; deputy Chief of the General Staff, Lieutenant Colonel Protasewicz, aide-de-camp to Sikorski;[287] Wing Commander Kleczyński, Polish military attaché to Washington; Doctor Retinger, Sikorski's physician; with Monsignor Kaczyński, priest and including seven British passengers. The flight left Prestwick at approximately 02:20 local time, two hours later the Liberator was cruising at 30,000 feet. Passengers wore oxygen masks and bulky flight suits due to extreme cold and were trying to sleep. Approximately eight hours into the flight several people observed Kleczyński make his way to the back of the plane. The incident was described by Colonel Mitkiewicz:

> "From the bottom of the plane comes Lieutenant Colonel Kleczyński and, keeping one hand in his suit pocket, walks past us to the back of the plane, where, behind a not very discreet and tight tarpaulin, [is the] toilet. As he passes by, I have the impression that he is sick, that he suffers from air sickness (vomiting), he was pale as linen cloth. After a few minutes I wanted to go to him, but I wouldn't risk without an oxygen mask to turn off; I'm not used to flying at high altitudes, I'm afraid I won't [reach him]. Kleczyński sat in the toilet for about three quarters of an hour. I was very worried about him, but since there were no sudden noises, I just thought he was relieving himself of the effects of air sickness. Finally, Kleczyński left the toilet and returned to his

Short Empire flying boat G-AFCT 'Champion'.

old place. He seemed to have a better face. The plane, meanwhile, descends gently to 15,000 feet. In beautiful sunny weather, we fly to Newfoundland. We should be landing there in the twelfth or fourteenth hour of flight. At 2 p.m. (Prestwick time) we are informed by the commander of the plane that there is a snowstorm over Newfoundland, landing there is impossible and that we are going straight to Montreal. After a further five hours of flight, flying at a completely low altitude, without oxygen masks, we land very deftly at the airport in Montreal. After eighteen and a half hours of sitting."[288]

After being greeted by Canadian dignitaries Sikorski and his entourage were driven to the Ritz-Carlton Hotel to rest and recuperate for the remainder of the day. Shortly afterwards Wing Commander Kleczyński telephoned Colonel Mitkiewicz in his room asking if he could see him immediately on a very important matter. Though quite tired Mitkiewicz agreed and shortly afterwards Kleczyński came over carrying a package wrapped in newspaper. The wing commander calmly opened the package to reveal a black-lacquered metal tin around 4.5 inches in length and handed over the object explaining he had found it on the aircraft. Mitkiewicz asked why he was only informing him now and had not said anything during the flight.

Kleczyński explained that around eight hours into the trip the flight engineer came through the bomb bay asking if anyone could smell something burning. He and Doctor Retinger could smell the strong odour of burning rubber and both began looking around to find the source. Kleczyński found beneath his mattress an object that was extremely hot, it appeared to be an incendiary bomb, at the end there was a round attachment cap wound with black tape. The cap was so hot the insulating tape was smoking. He broke the wire connected to the cap and made his way to the rear of the aircraft and threw the cap in the lavatory.[289] He had wondered what to do next and initially he thought he would throw it out a window but believed it might affect the aircraft's speed so chose to wait. He sat by the window for more than an hour until the bomb cooled completely. Kleczyński returned to his mattress and chose not to tell anyone until arriving in Montreal.[290]

When he asked what he should do next Mitkiewicz ordered him to keep the matter absolutely secret and not disclose it to anyone until further orders. Colonel Mitkiewicz kept the device and after Kleczyński left he called Lieutenant Colonel Protasewicz to come to his room. Being a sapper and engineering officer Protasewicz quickly recognized the device as an incendiary. Both agreed not to inform Sikorski and to keep the matter secret, after arrival in Washington they would ask the G2 intelligence section of the United States General Staff for a professional analysis of the device. An examination, x-ray, and dismantling of the device by the G2 during their time in Washington from 24 to 26 March confirmed it was an incendiary.[291]

Between 30 and 31 March, Sikorski and his entourage travelled from New York to Ottawa by train. Arriving at 11:00 local time, he was met at the station by Prime Minister Mackenzie King and military representatives. On 1 April he continued to Montreal where Colonel Mitkiewicz had Lieutenant Colonel Protasewicz and Wing Commander Kleczyński go to the district air commander to confidentially notify him of the incident en route from Great Britain and insist on his behalf that protective measures be implemented for their flight back to Great Britain. He also ordered Kleczyński to oversee pre-flight preparations of the aircraft and inspection of its equipment. Protasewicz was tasked with planning departure and arrival arrangements for Montreal and Gander. He was also to deliver in confidentiality to the district air commander the G2 results and testimony of Wing Commander Kleczyński. Protasewicz made it clear that Sikorski was not privy to this matter, that British and Canadian officers were not to speak to the general and to go only through him. While in Montreal Sikorski gave Colonel Mitkiewicz a silver cigarette case with a calligraphic inscription dated 28 March 1942. The general had been grateful for Mitkiewicz's efforts to get a permanent place for the Republic of Poland in the inter-allied staff in Washington which had unfortunately been unsuccessful.[292] On 3 April Sikorski departed Montreal on Liberator AM259 at 13:35 GMT and arrived in Gander Newfoundland at 18:35 GMT. Military guards were posted around the parked Liberator until its departure the next day delayed due to severe weather along the route to Prestwick. AM259 departed Gander the following day at 21:09 GMT and arrived in Prestwick at 07:36 GMT. During the trip's last eastern leg passengers began having breathing difficulties due to oxygen masks freezing up; in the flight's eighth hour General Sikorski fainted. Alarmed, the pilot descended the aircraft to 10,000 feet where Sikorski regained consciousness and passengers could breathe without oxygen masks.[293]

An inquiry led by MI5 official Lord Rothschild saw Wing Commander Kleczyński questioned several times by investigators. Suspicions had been raised after report of a bomb had not been made until nearly a week after its discovery. As the investigation progressed elements of Kleczyński's story were not adding up, investigators finding it difficult to believe this had been a genuine sabotage attempt and that he was perhaps lying. With this in mind investigators considered four possibilities as to how the incendiary might have found its way onto AM262:

1. That it was a genuine assassination attempt on General Sikorski.
2. That it was a faked attempt for any of the following reasons:
    a. Wing Commander Kleczyński wanted to gain kudos for his bravery.
    b. The Poles wished to make protest at the lack of security at Prestwick Airport as there had been several adverse comments over its laxity.
    c. It was the product of internal differences within the Polish forces, either to restore some person's position or to discredit someone else.[294]

Investigators learned the incendiary was a P.R.5 Mark 1 incendiary initiator produced by SOE Section 12.[295] Kleczyński had obtained it in December 1941 from a Polish army officer stationed at Largo House, near Leven. This officer had been in charge of a laboratory that constructed sabotage equipment and instructed officers in their use. Kleczyński had used the pretext of needing an incendiary to destroy his aircraft in event of a forced landing in enemy territory, the officer admitting to investigators supplying him with the incendiary for this reason.[296] Investigators had the incendiary examined by the officer who designed it and the officer who tested it; both confirmed "the bomb had not fired from an incendiary point of view but also had not even flashed (i.e. the match head and quick matches are intact) and failed to pick up". Investigators then asked if there was any other situation where the incendiary might feel hot. The officers explained there had been occasions when this model of device had been sprung and its quick match and primers had initiated and flashed but the main incendiary material had not ignited causing the outside case to heat up and burn through. They further noted that the incendiary's celluloid case was not cold to the touch, that if someone had been lying on it, it might feel warm if handled with cold hands but would certainly not be hot. It was also pointed out that celluloid readily shows signs of heating and there were no blemishes on the incendiary's case that Kleczyński allegedly found.[297]

Liberator I departing Prestwick, Scotland. (Wikimedia, public domain)

They further clarified that it could not be activated by an external attachment as described in Kleczyński's original statement.[298] There was also no reported scorching of mattresses retrieved from the aircraft after its arrival in Montreal.[299] Investigators also learned from AM262's pilot Captain Stewart that a fuse had blown during the flight which accounted for the burning smell. The first officer of Liberator AM259 that flew Sikorski from Montreal via Gander back to Prestwick further explained that blown electrical fuses in the cockpit were frequent and sometimes caused small fires.[300] On 20 July 1942 Wing Commander Kleczyński went before a mixed Polish-British investigating commission in London. When investigators presented their findings Kleczyński finally admitted that he carried the device in his gas mask bag and had forgotten all about it until aboard the aircraft. The bag was lying beside his mattress, that when he smelled burning rubber, it seemed to be coming from near his gas mask. He took the bomb out of the bag and went to the lavatory to throw it in. The bomb was warm and made him think it was about to go off. While in the lavatory he tried to think how best to explain it away. He was afraid Monsignor Kaczyński had seen him with it and having been in the lavatory a long time, long enough for the bomb to get cool, he needed to find some explanation and invented the story of finding the bomb in the plane. This forced him to repeat the story numerous times and insist it was true.

> "I did not know what to do when I found the bomb was warm and was not able to think clearly about anything. I was so worried to think it might go off with the general in the plane, apart from the fact that I thought it would ruin my future. I was afraid to tell the truth after once having lied about it. I want now to tell you how sorry I am I have caused everybody so much trouble, I can only tell you that I do not know why I did it, except that I must have completely lost my head."[301]

At the inquiry's closing Lord Rothschild wrote to Churchill imploring he ask General Sikorski to allow Wing Commander Kleczyński to return to his duties; that he had no ill intent or personal motive; to consider his very gallant and distinguished career; and that as a consequence had been sufficiently punished by the mental anguish of the ordeal. In a follow-up letter to the SOE Rothschild added that Kleczyński had "created a very favourable impression on me and I still think that there is nothing much in the whole business".[302] Kleczyński continued his service as an instructor in Scotland at the Polish War College, *Wyższa Szkoła Wojenna*, until

1944.[303] Over the investigation's course it was also learned that Kleczyński suffered acute psychological strain due to wounds and injuries suffered as a bomber pilot and had become addicted to morphine during his time in hospital. It was reported that he abused cocaine, suffered hallucinations and was a pathological exhibitionist.[304] On 10 March 1944 he was admitted to the Polish Paderewski Hospital in Edinburgh to have a testicular cyst removed. Kleczyński underwent surgery on 13 March and convalesced for three days. On 18 March he began to suffer fever, language impairment, physical spasms and soon lost consciousness. On 19 March he was transferred to the Royal Infirmary in Edinburgh where he died the following day at 15:00. A post-mortem established that cause of death was from acute encephalitis, basal influenza, and bronchopneumonia. Wing Commander Bohdan Kleczyński was buried in Newark, Nottinghamshire on 27 March 1944.[305] The circumstances of Kleczyński death stand in stark contrast to David Irving's claim that he had been killed after stepping in front of a tram in Edinburgh.[306]

On 9 September 1942 General Sikorski was flown from RAF Northolt to RAF Exeter in a Bristol Beaufighter Mk VIF of No. 307 (Polish) Squadron as part of his inspection tour of the unit. Afterwards he was flown back to Northolt in a Beaufighter.[307] In late November 1942 Sikorski would experience another peculiar inflight incident after once again having flown across the Atlantic this time on Liberator AL504[308] for another meeting with President Roosevelt to discuss Polish war and post-war aims.[309] After arrival at Dorval airport in Montreal the general was to fly to Washington aboard an RAF Ferry Command Lockheed Hudson BW409 the same day, the aircraft having been put at the general's disposal at the request of Prime Minister Churchill.[310] On 30 November at 2:15 pm Sikorski's Hudson taxied from Dorval's tarmac to the active runway, ran up its engines to maximum take-off power and was soon racing down the runway. After a take-off run of approximately fifteen

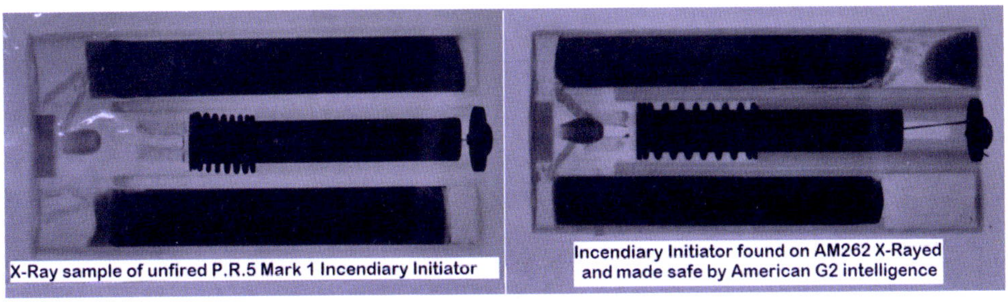

Images from KV 3/274. (The National Archives)

seconds, as the aircraft became airborne the left engine's power abruptly dropped shortly followed by the right at 30 feet of altitude. With rough, uneven fields beyond the runway threshold fast approaching the pilot swung the aircraft left 40 degrees from the runway heading toward level terrain, retracted the landing gear, turned off the magnetos and selected fuel off. The aircraft struck the ground 200 feet from the runway end, bounced twice then came to a stop 400 feet further just 30 yards short of a shallow ditch and stone embankment.[311] Though shaken, Sikorski was uninjured suffering only bumps and bruises as did his entourage and the flight crew. The following day he was taken to Washington aboard a Ferry Command Liberator flown by RCAF Group Captain Taffy Powell.[312] When President Roosevelt saw Sikorski at noon on 2 December, he expressed his indignation about the accident. The Under Secretary of State Sumner Welles offered that their intelligence service considered the accident had been the result of foul play and that the general and his companions had miraculously avoided death. Roosevelt added that providence was watching over Sikorski.[313] In the weeks following rumours spoke of several German Canadians allegedly arrested in connection with the accident.[314]

Though sabotage was suspected with Sikorski's aircraft it is significant to note that there were seventy-three operational losses of Lockheed Hudsons throughout 1942, many from undetermined causes. Some aircraft crashed during or after take-off, many suffered mishaps while being ferried to Britain. These specific losses occurred in the United States, Canada, the Atlantic, Iceland, and Britain. The majority of these Hudson losses were part of a large Lend-Lease effort to Britain that by the end of 1942 had flown 920 various aircraft types across the North Atlantic.[315] The causes of engine failure during take-off are numerous ranging from ignition faults, loss of oil pressure, fuel starvation or mismanagement, water contamination of fuel, and

Lockheed Hudson. (Library and Archives Canada Photo, MIKAN No. 3199074)

carburettor icing. An accident investigation was conducted by RAF Ferry Command in Dorval with components, engines, fuel and oil samples from BW409 sent to the Canadian Wright Company for inspection. Events prior to the accident revealed the pilot of BW409 having had a technical issue with fuel to one of the engines, he had physically checked the fuel quantity and quickly rectified the problem prior to boarding. Concerned at the delay Group Captain Taffy Powell, base flight director, had come out to inquire about the problem. Powell then ran up BW409's engines to his satisfaction ensuring Sikorski's aircraft was safe and ready for flight.[316] The investigation later determined there was no evidence of fuel starvation or indication of sabotage. In the end investigators were unable to determine an exact cause. The Dorval base chief engineering officer suspected an ignition system fault was likely responsible for the accident, it was further noted there was a possibility of ice having formed in the carburettor due to large amounts of fine snow covering the runway.[317]

Double-engine failures were not uncommon as seen on 20 February 1941 when an RAF Hudson III T9449 suffered a double-engine failure and crashed near Musgrave Harbour, Newfoundland.[318] On 16 July 1943 RAF Hudson VI FK571 of a communications flying unit spun into the ground after a double-engine failure at Ashton-under-Hill, Worcestershire, England.[319] It should also be noted that technical faults due to poor workmanship were sometimes attributed to sabotage. Such circumstances occurred on 22 December 1941 in New Zealand when all RNZAF Lockheed Mk III Hudsons were grounded for inspection after an aircraft stalled in a turn at 1,500 feet and crashed. Discrepancies found on several aircraft during inspection of control column aileron chain and cable rigging were initially thought to be factory sabotage. These rigging issues were more likely due to improper assembly at the factory and poor-quality control than sabotage.[320] When considering carburettor icing as a potential cause of the accident the recorded temperature, precipitation and snow accumulations in Montreal for 30 November 1942 were: temperature high -3.3°C (26°F), low -6.7°C (19.9°F). Precipitation 0.03 cm (0.01 in). Snow 0.30 cm (1.18 in). Values recorded the previous day, 29 November 1942, were: temperature high -2.8°C (26.9°F), low -7.2°C (19°F). Precipitation 0.84 cm (0.33 in). Snow 8.40 cm (3.3 in).[321] Though dew point figures were not recorded until 1953 a comparison of temperature values for 30 November 1942 against a carburettor icing chart shows potential for carburettor icing for this day if the relative humidity had been anywhere within 58% to 100% and a dew point of 25°F. The application of carburettor heat during pre-take-off checks usually precludes carburettor icing providing the pilot uses it correctly and judiciously.[322] Given the number of Hudson accidents and possible technical reasons for engine failure it is difficult to attribute sabotage as a singular cause.

It is noteworthy of differences between reports written by Sikorski's accompanying aide-de-camp Flight Lieutenant Glówczynski and Air Marshal Sir Frederick Bowhill head of RAF Ferry Command in Dorval against David Irving's published account of the accident. From PISM document KOL.1/DCNW/40 & 40a two pilots are quoted as having flown BW409 at the time of the accident, RAF Squadron Leader R E Marrow in Glówczynski's report, and American civilian Captain H J Bowen in Air Marshal Bowhill's report. David Irving suggested this pilot discrepancy and inconclusive investigation was subterfuge by Bowhill to downplay the accident's severity and dupe Polish officials into thinking it had not happened as reported. It was in fact normal in Ferry Command to have two pilots assigned to an aircraft. With the aircraft going to Washington it was reasonable that Captain Bowen, being American, would be the logical choice to fly in American airspace with Squadron Leader Marrow serving as second pilot. The Lockheed Hudson had only a single control column and pilot seat with the second pilot in the right jump-seat monitoring instruments. Irving further claimed R E Marrow could not be found in the RAF's 1943 Air Force List. This was because he, or the Poles, confused Marrow with Squadron Leader R E E Morrow, RCAF, who was with Ferry Command for a short period at this time. Morrow had commanded 402 Squadron in Britain prior to a brief sojourn in Canada in the fall of 1942. Like many other pilots needing to get overseas, he volunteered to fly an aircraft over for Ferry Command.

That both are referred as having been pilot flying is of no consequence on the accident and is likely a bureaucratic clerical error. That the investigation found nothing conclusive is not unusual given inherent difficulties in any air crash investigation with similar outcomes seen today despite modern investigative techniques. Irving attempted to portray these inconclusive results as subterfuge by Bowhill to sweep the accident under the rug. Lastly Irving's account neglected to mention that the mysterious unnamed group captain that came from nowhere to run BW409 for unexplained reasons was in fact Group Captain Taffy Powell the base flight director, experienced Hudson pilot and transatlantic aviator. Powell was a hands-on administrator and had likely come out to inquire about Bowen's fuel issue and later ran-up BW409's engines to satisfy himself of its serviceability. Irving suggested Polish officials considered the "unexpected" additional run-up by the mysterious group captain was a ruse to advance engine failure to coincide with

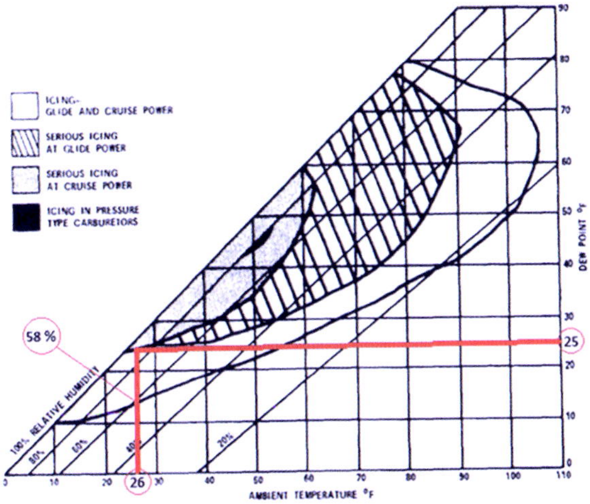

FIGURE 1. CARBURETOR ICING PROBABILITY CHART
MINISTRY OF TRANSPORT - CANADA

DOT/FAA/CT-82/110. Range of temperature and relative humidity which could induce carburettor icing.

take-off insinuating a blatant sabotage attempt. The source of this claim was from Flight Lieutenant Glówczynski who had penned "unexpected" into his typed report in describing Powell's running of BW409. Glówczynski had also speculated that "the accident was most likely caused by a sudden and as yet unexplained stoppage of fuel flow to the engines". He added, "Several trials of the engines prior to take-off resulted in the interruption of fuel flow being accelerated to the moment when the plane was still over the airport and not over the city. Specific investigations of the accident are being conducted by the aviation authorities of the British Ferry Command." [323]

With this said there had been one unusual double-engine failure of a Lockheed Hudson in 1939 that may have lent credence to conclusions drawn by authorities that the accident in Montreal was sabotage. In January 1939 Lockheed had established a reassembly division at Speke in England for 250 B-14 Hudson reconnaissance aircraft ordered by the British Air Ministry and transported to Liverpool by ship. In February during testing of the fifth assembled aircraft Lockheed employees Milo Burcham, test pilot, and Art Kennedy, engineer, experienced a loss of fuel pressure on take-off indicated by fuel warning lights. Burcham cut both engines and applied brakes while Kennedy put the flaps down and a controlled ground loop was executed. Burcham tried again by first running each engine separately to full power – with each check no warning light came on. He next ran up both together with brakes applied with no warning lights illuminating. Finally with brakes still applied he advanced the throttles of both engines to max, at full power he released the brakes and started down the runway and was about to lift off when the fuel warning lights illuminated and stayed on. Burcham cut the power, slowed the aircraft and went back to the ramp.[324]

After a week of troubleshooting a piece of coloured cloth was discovered in a fuel junction fitting where the two fuel tanks came together, fed the wobble pump then separated to supply the left and right engines. The entire assembly was removed and hooked up to a flow test bench exactly as it was on the aircraft with the fuel flow in the same direction from the two sources. The fuel flow was increased to maximum and started to drop after twenty seconds, at twenty-five seconds it dropped sharply to almost no flow. When the fuel junction was disassembled a strip of cloth about a yard long, meticulously accordion-pleated and tamped down into the elbow of the fitting was found. Under pressure of maximum fuel flow it would creep out until the flow was restricted. When the flow dropped it would retract again until the fuel could flow once more. The British secret service had been present during the test and revealed that they had information that one of the Hudsons had been sabotaged during disassembly after being flown from the Lockheed factory to New York. Police in the United States were holding a suspect on a trumped-up charge, a German national who worked for Lockheed as a mechanic. Having no evidence of the sabotage they were awaiting news of the test results from Speke.[325]

Sikorski's Montreal accident, though distressing when viewed in a broader context, appears more an unfortunate operational incident in the midst of a massive effort to move great numbers of aircraft quickly to Britain rather than an act of sabotage or attempted assassination. That being said the similarities between the 1939 and 1942 Lockheed Hudson incidents cannot be ignored. It is also interesting that in both instances sabotage was attributed to German nationals employed at an aircraft servicing facility. That a connection to both might be drawn by American, British and Polish authorities is both understandable and somewhat predictable. As no evidence of sabotage was found during the accident investigation it can only be speculated that such claims were just rumours. Perhaps the circumstance of a German national's involvement in the 1939 Speke incident perpetuated those rumours and were conveniently employed to explain Sikorski's accident as a means to pacify all parties.[326] Colonel Protasewicz, whom Carlos Thompson interviewed regarding his knowledge of both the Atlantic incendiary and Montreal engine failure incident, summarized the Hudson crash circumstances.

"It ended miraculously with a hard shock and minor injuries only but was undoubtedly caused by sabotage of the engines. This was never officially admitted, but it aroused indignation in the White House. There were only rumours of a few Canadian-German workers arrested in connection with this.

"The simplest analysis of the historical picture should convince anyone that Churchill could not possibly have engineered that Montreal accident.

"Qui prederat? [327] Certainly not Churchill. Sikorski's journey was arranged for their discussions of the war strategy and Sikorski had to win over the president for their plan of attacking the German fortress of Europe from the south, through Turkey or Italy."[328]

A 1943 Royal Canadian Mounted Police year-end report to the Canadian Minister of Justice disclosed that over a twelve-month period its special section had investigated a total of 290 cases of suspected sabotage, none of which were due to actions of enemy agents. A large number of investigations had shown that suspicious incidents in many cases were due to carelessness or errors in judgement.[329] The year-end report for 1945 disclosed a total of 128 cases of suspected sabotage, none of which were enemy inspired.[330] The report's summary conclusion stated: "that during the whole war period to date, not one proven case of enemy-inspired sabotage had come to light."[331] This assertion was challenged in 2012 by Professor Grant Grams. Though actual numbers are unknown his research uncovered at least five acts of sabotage committed by German saboteurs against Canadian war industries.[332]

In the late evening of 24 May 1943 General Sikorski and his entourage departed RAF Lyneham for his Middle East tour onboard a Liberator II registration AL616 flown by Flight Lieutenant Eduard Prchal. The aircraft landed in Gibraltar on the morning of 25 May where Sikorski's party was taken to Gibraltar's Government House for breakfast, rest and talks. Arrangements were made for passengers and crew to spend the night before continuing their flight east. In the early morning hours of 26 May they departed for Egypt arriving at Cairo West airfield in mid-afternoon where he was met by General Anders along with Polish and British dignitaries.[333]

Air transport during Sikorski's Middle East tour was provided by No. 173 Squadron RAF equipped with Lockheed Lodestar II passenger transports.[334] Flights within Iraq utilized a DH.98 Dragon Rapide from PaiForce RAF Communication Flight Iraq and Persia (RAF Comm Flight Iraq and Persia). The aircraft registration, flight dates, departures and destinations are listed overleaf.[335]

Lodestar EW987	1 June 1943	Heliopolis, Egypt–Habbaniya, Iraq–Kirkuk, Iraq
Rapide HK862	11 June 1943	Kirkuk–Qizil Ribat, Iraq[336]
Rapide HK862	13 June 1943	Qizil Ribat–Baghdad, Iraq[337]
Lodestar EW994	17 June 1943	Baghdad–Tehran, Iran–Habbaniya–Heliopolis
Lodestar EW989	18 June 1943	Heliopolis–Lydda, Palestine–Beirut, Lebanon[338]
Lodestar EW990	28 June 1943	Beirut–Lydda–Heliopolis[339] [340]

All flights were uneventful though EW989 on its afternoon return flight from Beirut after dropping off Sikorski suffered failure of one of its engines a few minutes after take-off and returned safely to Lydda.[341] EW990 replaced EW987 which had been scheduled to depart on the 27th but returned to Heliopolis due to engine trouble.[342]

Diplomatic travel by plane throughout the Second World War as seen with Sikorski's many trips across the Atlantic, the Middle East and Russia were fraught with dangers. Considering the number of aircraft lost throughout these regions due to weather, navigational trouble, technical faults or operational wear and tear, it is not surprising that a number of Sikorski's flights would experience difficulties all of which were common aviation hazards for this period and not associated with sabotage.[343] Lastly the casual admission by Victor Cazalet of contraband carried during some of Sikorski's trips appears to have been an accepted pattern of behaviour among VIPs.

ACCIDENT CAUSATION AND HUMAN FACTORS

Accident causation and human factors as is understood in its modern-day form was not a concept that was applied during aviation accident investigations in 1943. Given the great number of pilots recruited and trained during the Second World War the human element of pilot performance was focused more on stringent medical and psychological standards, instructional standards, and technical innovation. Though it has been determined that AL523's crash was most likely the result of sabotage, from an accident causation/human factors point of view the confluence of risk elements accumulated in advance of its root cause require examination. The volume of research conducted in the writing of this book would be incomplete without at least a cursory analysis of those factors surrounding the accident and their influence on Prchal.

Though part of Garth's crash hypothesis held an underlying suspicion of sabotage the fact that Prchal was found unconscious wearing his Mae West life jacket had always puzzled him. Prchal had testified that he normally flew with his Mae West hung over the back of his pilot's seat and could not account for why he was found wearing it when pulled from the water. Though Prchal had flown VIPs in the past Garth suspected a degree of stress came with being chosen to fly a high-status military and political figure to the Middle East, it was also a significant highlight in Prchal's flying career. During the return trip to Gibraltar Sikorski had given Prchal the gift of an inscribed cigarette case. Prchal in turn had gone to the rear cabin and had several pleasant chats with Sikorski during their flight across the Mediterranean.[344] This stress was suddenly exacerbated on the evening of departure with the unexpected demand and coercion to load an excessive cargo that could potentially exceed the aircraft's weight capacity and performance.[345] That Prchal reluctantly acquiesced to this demand speaks to the larger issue of quiet acceptance surrounding VIPs sidestepping rules regarding contraband. Within today's transportation safety and crash investigation culture such a mindset is known as 'Normalization of Deviance' which defines a group of people within an organization becoming so "accustomed to a deviation that they don't consider it as deviant, despite the fact that they far exceed their own rules for the elementary safety".[346]

An undated photo of Sikorski at right on board a Liberator sitting in the co-pilot seat wearing leather flight helmet and jacket. (NAC)

All these influences culminated in a cascade of stress that influenced his judgement. Garth strongly suspects Prchal saw these factors potentially weighing against a successful take-off and donned his Mae West out of caution. Put another way, Prchal, though confident in his flying skill and the Liberator's performance capabilities with heavy loads, was anxious and concerned that there was potential for mishap and donned his Mae West life jacket out of wariness prior to take-off. A similar conclusion had been drawn by British diplomat Sir Robin Hooper who sat on a government committee reviewing the Sikorski crash in January 1969. Having served as an RAF pilot during the war he reviewed the court of inquiry report from a pilot's perspective. He wrote:

> "Czech and Polish pilots were apt to be a bit light-hearted about safety regulations imposed on them by the sober British. However Flight Lieutenant Prchal was faced with taking off a heavily loaded aircraft in the dark from a short runway, ending abruptly in the sea, with very little wind to assist him. He easily could have had second thoughts and put on his Mae West. This would have taken some time and could account for the 'considerable pause' observed between taxiing out and take-off."[347]

MAE WEST LIFE JACKET

The RAF used two styles of life jacket during the Second World War, these were the 1932 pattern and 1941 pattern Mae West. Royal Air Force Flying Regulations A.P.1640 stated the following:

> "Life-saving waistcoats of an approved pattern are invariably to be carried for every occupant of an aircraft flying over water. These waistcoats must actually be worn by those occupying open cockpits while flying over water or manoeuvring on water; in other cases they must be kept immediately available, but need not be worn unless so ordered by the first pilot."[348]

A period film of an RAF Lancaster bomber crew preparing for a sortie offers perspective as to how life jackets were donned. The film depicts a crewman standing outside his aircraft in broad daylight leisurely taking in excess of twenty seconds to

Canadian members of an RAF Lancaster crew wearing Mae West life vests. Note the number of straps required to secure the vest. Left is a flight lieutenant the pilot. Both flight sergeants on the right are air gunners. (Library and Archives Canada photo No. 5162416)

put on his Mae West, a far cry from the conditions Prchal faced moments after the crash.[349] That Prchal could have somehow managed to put on his Mae West in the last seconds before impact, or during the violent overturning and submersion of AL523's wrecked nose section while in total darkness seems extremely unlikely. Alternately it is further questionable that Prchal after having swam clear of the aircraft, though badly injured and weighed down by waterlogged flight overalls and boots, could have effectively put on and strapped up a Mae West in darkness without drowning in the effort. It is unknown which version of life jacket Prchal was found wearing.

EPILOGUE

CONJECTURAL NARRATIVE OF A TROUBLED DEPARTURE

Prchal and his crew likely began preparations for the final leg of their journey in the early evening with a visit to North Front's flying control watch office for a weather briefing on the route to England. Prchal's nine-hour flight would involve flying with his navigation lights extinguished outside the twelve-mile limit off the coast of Spain and Portugal, the lights of Lisbon serving as a good navigational landmark. Approaching the Bay of Biscay he would fly below cloud cover or in the clouds at 9,000 feet to avoid any prowling German night fighters.[350] After about six hours he would then adjust his course to go up the Irish Sea between Ireland and the United Kingdom. After two hours he would then steer east and land at RAF Lyneham 93 miles west of London an hour later.

As remnants of ruddy crimson set along the western horizon Prchal and his crew were driven in an RAF Tilly from the watch office to the north apron where AL523 was parked. Pulling up in front of the Liberator illuminated by floodlights they could see mechanics from No. 511 Squadron's maintenance detachment completing the last items of their pre-flight checks. Due to oppressive heat throughout the day all the aircraft's hatches, windows and forward port-side bomb-bay door had been opened for air circulation. As the crew gathered next to the open bomb bay one man climbed inside and began taking flying kits handed to him and setting them on the compartment floor. As the crew set about preparing AL523 Sergeant Moore approached Prchal and handed him the Form 700 certifying the maintenance pre-flight inspection complete for his review and signature. Thanking the sergeant Prchal handed back the signed document and began slowly walking around and examining the Liberator for his pre-flight inspection. Once this was complete, Prchal informed Sergeant Moore of his intention to run and warm up the engines. With Moore standing nearby giving the all-clear, one by one Prchal and his flight engineer, Sergeant Kelly, started each engine letting them idle for a few minutes to allow the oil pressure and temperatures to rise to their required limits before moving the throttles up to 2,000 RPM for several minutes, the four radials throwing up great clouds of dust behind them before finally being shut down.

Shortly afterward an RAF Tilly drove up and two airmen began loading several pieces of luggage through the bomb-bay door. Several minutes later two fuel bowsers drove up and parked in front of the Liberator, two airmen climbed out and began pulling out fuel hoses and setting up ladders to reach the wings.

After a quick chat with the two fuellers to confirm his fuel load Prchal followed the rest of his flight crew up into the bomb bay and began preparing for an 11:00 pm departure. In time he soon made out through his cockpit windscreen vehicles of Sikorski's entourage driving in column across the apron towards AL523. Making his way to the open bomb bay Prchal climbed out to meet the group. As the vehicles pulled up behind the Liberator three Hillman vans drove around and parked on the aircraft's left side. As the entourage stepped from their cars, passengers Lock and Pinder[351] arrived escorted by an ARDU embarkation officer. As Sikorski exchanged farewells with British dignitaries several passengers began climbing up the tail ladder into the Liberator while a group of airmen began removing packages, rolls of cloth, suitcases, and crates of spirits from the back of the Hillmans and hand them up through an open side hatch.

After leaving the local NAAFI AC1 Mechanic Charles Walker crossed North Front to his billet hut and in a far corner of the crowded floodlit apron he noticed activity around a parked Liberator. As he got closer to the aircraft he saw airmen loading boxes and packages from Hillman vans into the Liberator while an entourage of high-ranking dignitaries stood nearby. When Charles asked an armed guard standing nearby who was supervising the loading the man nodded towards the entourage and replied, "they are". Powerless to intervene Charles walked off to his billet troubled by the great quantity of items being loaded.[352]

As Charles Walker left for his billet Prchal and his co-pilot Squadron Leader Herring appeared and began expressing concern about the quantity of items being loaded and ordered the airmen to stop. A Polish NCO overseeing the loading came over to speak with the two pilots, as the three spoke their hand gestures grew animated and voices louder. Finally the NCO produced a pistol and waved it above his head while pointing with the other hand at the vans, the aircraft, and at Prchal and Herring. Airmen stood idle watching as the raucous exchange continued, several within the nearby entourage and dignitaries glanced now and then towards the commotion. An officer standing among Sikorski's entourage came over gesturing for the NCO to put away his pistol, the conversation stopping abruptly as the officer spoke with the three in hushed tones, both pilots silently frowning as they listened. The loading resumed as the officer returned to the gathered entourage, Prchal and Herring cursing under their breath as they boarded the Liberator several minutes later followed by the remaining passengers and General Sikorski. After Sikorski had climbed aboard Major Anthony Quayle, who was part of the British entourage, took a moment to look inside AL523 and noted how awfully untidy and jam-packed the interior was. As cargo and luggage was moved about within the Liberator an ADRU Hillman van drove up. One of Sergeant Moore's mechanics began quickly loading mailbags handed to him by the driver through the bomb-bay door. Minutes later with the loading complete, fuel bowsers gone and the ADRU van departed AL523's engines were started one by one.

As the loading resumed on AL523, across the apron a USAAF B-17 Fortress transport sat waiting to be refuelled so it could depart for England. Curious as to when their aircraft might be refuelled a crew member along with passenger Lieutenant Colonel Adrian Scrope walked over to the British Liberator parked across from them. When they asked a ground crewman if that aircraft was General Sikorski's he responded that it was. He went on to explain that the fuel delay was due to the loading of many boxes which contained sherry and port, and that the aircrew were arguing with the Poles over the excessive load. The ground crewman added that the aircraft was so seriously overloaded that it was very unlikely to take off at all.

While Adrian Scrope was enquiring about fuel for his aircraft AC2 Mechanic Jack Waterfield and another aircraftsman had been standing on North Front's apron and could see the distant Liberator with its engines running. Having spent the early part of their evening assembling Spitfires at New Camp they had been posted to stand a four-hour fireguard and had walked the single mile to North Front's dusty apron. As they got within 50 yards of the Liberator both saw some activity alongside the aircraft where three Hillman vans were parked. An Indian airman then came up and stood next to Jack, being an engine fitter the man commented, "it won't take off, it's been ticking over too long and getting hot". Shortly after the vans drove away, the Liberator started its engines then began to taxi slowly towards the runway. Jack noticed a woman looking out from a window of the lit interior as the aircraft passed him.

Departing the apron around 22:45 Prchal taxied AL523 to the western end of North Front's single runway, turned the heavy Liberator 180 degrees at its threshold until it was pointed down the runway and set the park brake. With his flight engineer Sergeant Kelly in the co-pilot seat Prchal began his pre-take-off checklist by opening up each engine individually to 30 inches of boost and testing the propeller pitch control. He then opened each engine to 48 inches and throttled back to 2,000 rpm in fine pitch, at which Kelly then tested the magneto switches and Prchal tested the two speed superchargers. Upon completion of the engine checks Squadron Leader Herring took his place in the co-pilot seat and completed his cockpit drill releasing control locks and setting the flaps to half. As the two pilots completed the remaining pre-take-off checks Prchal sent Sergeant Kelly back to try and redistribute some of the cargo with another crewman. As the two moved around what cargo they could in the crowded fuselage several mailbags were haphazardly stowed in the nose undercarriage compartment as a last measure.

As Herring completed his final checks and toggled the cowl gills closed, Prchal settled back in his seat and tied the last strap of his Mae West. With the runway's parallel lights narrowing together into the middle distance he checked his flight controls for full travel. In the darkness a distant green light blinked on from the control tower and all of Gibraltar's sweeping searchlight beams abruptly swung to a horizontal position. Releasing the park brake Prchal smoothly advanced the throttles to 40 inches of boost. The engines rose to a dull roar as the Liberator quickly gathered speed and began to vibrate. Herring took over the throttles, moments later Prchal called out for 48 inches of boost. As noise and vibration surging through the fuselage grew to a crescendo, in the compartment beneath mailbags began to slide from where they loosely sat, one falling through open doors of the nose undercarriage. At 130 mph Prchal pulled hard on his control column, to his relief AL523 lifted from the runway and began to climb, as the runway lights disappeared beneath, with his right hand he quickly moved the undercarriage lever forward to its up position. From the dimly lit airspeed indicator and gyro horizon Prchal glimpsed his speed holding steady at 130 mph, the miniature airplane sat just above the horizon bar. He quickly glanced at his altimeter, its needle had passed 50 feet and was moving higher.

From his tower window flying control duty officer, Flight Lieutenant Capes saw AL523's navigation lights slowly rise from the runway as it neared his building, the Liberator's navigation lights nearly level to him as it passed. On the far side of North Front Flight Lieutenant Beaumont was off duty in his billet when he heard the Liberator start its take-off, he frowned as he listened to the engines rising drone, something didn't sound right.

At 150 feet Prchal pushed his control column forward lowering the Liberator's nose to gain airspeed. At 165 mph he pulled back on the control column but it would not move. Over the intercom Prchal shouted for Herring to quickly check the control lock while desperately moving the trim wheel nose up to gain height to no effect. With AL523 rapidly approaching the water Prchal shouted crash landing and closed the throttles. Moments later the Liberator was torn apart as it struck the water and overturned.

Seeing the Liberator's navigation lights suddenly descend and hearing its engines stop Capes rushed to his phone and called the area combined headquarters who dispatched two air-sea rescue launches. At that same moment Flight Lieutenant Beaumont, hearing the engines abruptly stop, rushed down to the jetty and jumped on to motor launch HSL 181 that was pulling away. Minutes later searchlights atop Gibraltar's eastern cliffs were sweeping the waters. Around the same time, six airmen launched a small rescue dinghy from the beach near the eastern runway end. The men shouted as they rowed toward the crash site, nearing its location a voice was heard in the darkness, it was that of Flight Lieutenant Prchal wearing an inflated Mae West whom they picked up. A few minutes later they found Brigadier Whiteley and General Sikorski, who were both alive, and General Klimecki who was deceased.[353] Both rescue launches soon arrived with Flight Lieutenant Prchal and Brigadier Whiteley transferred to launch HSL 181. Flight Lieutenant Beaumont helped pull both men from the dinghy, General Klimecki was dead but General Sikorski was alive though barely and soon died in Beaumont's arms. Brigadier Whiteley died shortly afterward. Both air-sea rescue launches continued to search for survivors until 04:20.

Though there was an element of difficulty formulating a precise chronology of events due to slight differences in eyewitness accounts all shared common threads. This allowed construction of an approximate sequence of events based on the collective body of research which is presented in the above paragraphs. Some creative license was taken to provide context to portrayed events.

SUMMARY CONCLUSION

The death of General Sikorski has been mired in controversy for over eighty years, much of it due to outlandish myths perpetuated in the late 1960s. Some involved elaborate assassination scenarios suggesting Prchal was part of a plot, that his smuggling activities had caused the crash, or his co-pilot was an undercover operative. More wild scenarios had assassins boarding the Liberator and killing the passengers just prior to take-off with Prchal then deliberately crashing his aircraft. SOE wireless operator Douglas Martin's improbable account of seeing someone walking along AL523's wing further exacerbated these scenarios lending them a false credence. Incredibly these plots were alleged to have been instigated at the request of Winston Churchill. Sadly the controversy victimized Eduard Prchal throughout his life forcing him to take legal action against these allegations. Unfortunately these myths continue to endure and are often referenced in contemporary publications and documentaries that suggest AL523 had been flown by another pilot for the express purpose of crashing the aircraft, or that the co-pilot had conducted the take-off because Prchal was not instrument rated and therefore not qualified for take-offs in conditions of fog or darkness. In the eighty years prior to this book's writing less than a handful of researchers conducted authentic, independent investigations that ignored these myths and produced a wealth of significant data and information that brought greater understanding to circumstances surrounding AL523's crash. Most notable were Carlos Thompson, Franciszek Grabowski, Garth Barnard, and Mieczysław Różycki.[354]

Through the course of researching and writing this book it did not take long to conclude how illogical, unfounded, and just completely wrong all these myths were. AL523's entire take-off and crash sequence began to fall into place and make sense the moment the cotton rag hypothesis went from theory to verification during trials where it jammed a full-scale Liberator elevator cross-section replica. Prchal's jammed elevator likely occurred during the last third of his sixteen-second flight and could not have been caused by loose freight in the nose compartment as seen in the Llewellyn incident. Neither was the jam caused by the engagement of the control locks as they were not damaged. Nor could the locks have been engaged in flight because the rudder was used by Prchal and offset to the right by four divisions of trim, plus the rudder lock pin is longer and engages first before the elevator pin can engage. Whether AL523 reached an altitude between 30 and 150 feet was of little consequence to the crash. Both Prchal and Flight Lieutenant Capes gave genuine accounts of the Liberator's altitude, Prchal's potentially due to altimeter error or a static leak, Capes because of his vantage point in the tower. AL523 struck the water in a nose-down attitude at 165 mph and overturned. We know this because rescue launch HSL 181 found the aircraft floating upside down, and the main undercarriage side brace welds had fractured likely due to centrifugal force throwing them toward their fully extended position. It is also well documented that Liberators were known to overturn on impacting the water.

How was saboteur Urbański able to gain access to AL523? Despite extensive security measures described by Captain Williams and a list of maintenance personnel allowed aboard AL523 provided by Sergeant Moore, there were clear shortcomings and contradictions of testimony between those guarding AL523 and those that approached the aircraft. Leading Aircraftman Titterington of the ADRU testified approaching and entering AL523 and not encountering a guard. Corporal Hopgood testified that after having spent the night in the aircraft he only observed a handful of guards standing near Mosquitos parked behind the Liberator on the morning of 4 July. Airfield security appeared focused on two areas, the airfield's perimeter and entry points, and keeping unnecessary personnel from entering AL523 presumably to thwart planting of an explosive device. Exactly when Urbański approached the aircraft and committed his act of sabotage without arousing suspicion is unknown and can only be speculated upon. It is highly doubtful he posed as an RAF airman of No. 511 Squadron's maintenance party. Urbański may have acted either before or during the changing of the guard from an unarmed airman to an armed soldier on the evening of 3 July, his presence taken in stride as part of the normal goings on of a busy military airfield; just another eager officer from the local Polish contingent enamoured with his commander-in-chief fussing about the aircraft's exterior and harmlessly wiping at oil stains. It will never be known when Urbański chose his moment or perpetuated such a ruse, was challenged, ignored, or unseen. What is certain is at some point he approached and effectively sabotaged AL523 without consequence.

Was AL523 heavy when it took off? Absolutely. A weight of 54,313 lbs was cited in Exhibit E during the court of inquiry while a theoretical 56,400 lbs take-off weight was asked of Squadron Leader Falk during the court of inquiry. This weight was used by researcher Franciszek Grabowski for his flight calculations and simulations.

Was AL523 overloaded? Probably. To what extent is uncertain as there is no way of knowing how much freight was loaded. If AL523 had been grossly overloaded it would have never been able to get airborne and have run straight off the runway, down the beach and into the surf. What is certain is that AL523, despite its weight, was able to lift off effectively and climb away from the runway.

Had there been smuggling? Absolutely. It was known and quietly accepted that flight crews smuggled goods back to Britain all the time. It was also very well known that VIPs took advantage of their status and smuggled frequently with impunity. This was alluded to by Squadron Leader Jack Sach during the court of inquiry that VIPs refused to conform with regulations. Prchal's friend Jaroslav Prokop had said VIPs carried all sorts of things, extra luggage, etc. Evidence of smuggling was clearly seen with the recovery of a crate containing Leica cameras and boxes of Turkish Delight. Add to this Lieutenant Colonel Adrian Scrope's firm recollection of being told by an airman that crates of spirits were being loaded to excess aboard AL523. Lastly there is the alleged sighting of liquor crates by Sydney Knowles during his recovery dives.

Was Prchal threatened with a pistol and coerced into the loading of an excessive freight load of contraband? According to Lieutenant Colonel Adrian Scrope this is what he had been told when enquiring about fuel for his B-17 transport flight. Curiously no other witnesses recalled an argument or pistol being waved about during the loading of AL523. The simple explanation may be that the incident was brief and occurred either before or after other witnesses had arrived or departed the scene and subsequently never observed by them.

Why did Prchal not exert his authority as pilot in command and stand his ground? It is speculation on the part of the authors but perhaps Prchal acquiesced to the excessive cargo not so much because of a waved pistol but that it may have included warning of disciplinary action from a high-ranking authority if he did not. It may have been easier to just reluctantly follow orders.

Such a mindset is known as 'normalization of deviance' where a group or individual becomes accustomed to a deviation despite far exceeding their own rules for elementary safety. Prchal may have reasoned that the final responsibility would fall upon this higher authority if there were an accident, in that event he and his crew would simply tell investigators they had been threatened and intimidated. The authors are not suggesting Sikorski had directly threatened Prchal but that a member of his entourage or a member of the Polish contingent on Gibraltar had perhaps taken this action upon themselves.

Alternately Prchal might have viewed the pistol incident having no connection to his flight controls becoming immovable and subsequent crash, that unless asked it would have been a very awkward incident to relate before an inquiry and not worth mentioning given its insignificance, that discretion was a better option given Sikorski's status as an Allied war leader. Perhaps he was embarrassed at having given in to external factors in what crash investigators nowadays refer to as 'get-there-itis'. This term is used by the Federal Aviation Administration to describe a pilot's determination to reach a destination even when conditions for flying are very dangerous. Whether Prchal had any such thoughts along these lines will never be known. Why this incident was never mentioned during the court of inquiry is unclear. It may have been a case where if no one asked then no one told. Prchal may have thought that if he brought up the pistol incident during the court of inquiry it might be construed as a shallow attempt by him to shift responsibility or blame for the crash to Sikorski and his dead entourage. Such an accusation might have resulted in his court martial. It is noteworthy that in part 10 (c)(v) of the court's conclusions it was made clear: "that all passengers regardless of importance, should clearly understand that they are entirely under the orders of the captain, at all times whilst carried in the aircraft, who will ensure that applicable regulations are enforced." This is further acknowledgement of VIPs seeing themselves the exception to rules.

Though pressured why did Prchal still decide to fly a potentially overloaded aircraft? Prchal likely chose to fly AL523 because he and other No. 511 Squadron pilots through operational experience understood the capabilities of their Liberators when heavily loaded.

Did senior officials on Gibraltar know about excessive smuggling by Sikorski and his entourage during AL523's departure? Were the senior officers assigned to inquire and investigate the accident aware of this smuggling? Given the number of eyewitness accounts that have surfaced describing excessive quantities of contraband loaded aboard AL523 it is difficult to believe that any senior official or officer could not have known something about it.

If senior officials and officers in fact knew that Sikorski or a member of his entourage had encouraged the loading of a large quantity of smuggled contraband aboard AL523 why was this not considered or investigated during the court of inquiry? The answer to this question might be found with the acknowledgement by Jack Sach, John Buck, and Ludwik Łubieński that VIPs often took advantage of their status and smuggled contraband goods on flights out of Gibraltar with impunity. It is not the belief nor is it the intent of the authors to suggest that this was a deliberate or calculated conspiracy of silence among senior officials but more an unspoken yet accepted principle of the period which again speaks to 'normalization of deviance'. This mindset likely made it convenient within senior authority circles to tacitly accept that VIPs often smuggled rather than reveal the Polish head of state, contrary to regulations, had been conveying large quantities of contraband. Such a revelation could be construed as a factor in Sikorski's death and ran the risk of humiliating his memory along with immeasurable political embarrassment to Britain and Poland on the world stage.

Why did Prchal not come forward after the war or in the late 1960s and admit that he was coerced to take off with an excessive cargo of contraband? It is the opinion of both authors that, if Prchal had suddenly after twenty-five years or so said the Polish head of state had been smuggling, and that a member of his entourage or Polish ground staff had coerced him at gunpoint to load an excessive cargo of contraband, it would likely have been construed by detractors that he was shifting blame away from himself. Such an admission would have stirred even more controversy and unwanted attention upon himself. Prchal was tired of it all and had already faced much controversy and legal battles in previous years, he likely just wanted it to go away and to live in peace.

Why was Prchal found wearing his Mae West life jacket when he normally left it hanging on the back of his seat? Though appreciating the Liberator's weight-carrying capability Prchal likely put on his Mae West in the cockpit just prior to take-off out of caution given the circumstances as outlined earlier in the book. In addition, though Squadron Leader Herring's body was never found there is no reason to believe he did not also don his Mae West. Herring may have been unable to inflate it due to injuries suffered or it was damaged in the crash and un-inflatable. As to why the recovered crewmen were found without their Mae Wests it is uncertain. The authors can only speculate that the crewmen did not don their Mae Wests out of habit, regulations, or possibly out of a misplaced concern that it would needlessly frighten the passengers.

Was AL523 sabotaged with a cotton rag? Yes, though based solely on replica trials. To date no other logical cause has explained how the elevators became jammed. Until such time as access can be granted to a Liberator to perform static tests with a cotton rag on its elevator system while on the ground, or a working replica of a Liberator elevator and horizontal stabilizer can be similarly tested in a wind tunnel, the conclusion that a cotton rag caused AL523's elevator to jam remains the only logical cause. In conclusion it is the opinion therefore of both authors that the crash of AL523 resulting in the death of General Władysław Sikorski was due to an act of sabotage by Bronislaw Urbański. The sole survivor Eduard Prchal was a victim of this sabotage and bore no responsibility for the crash.

Though this conclusion was arrived at logically with the best available evidence and sources at hand it is by no means definitive, we do not have a monopoly on truth.

It is hoped that views the authors have presented will stimulate healthy discussion and bring forth new facts, information and eyewitness accounts that corroborate, challenge, and supplement the accuracy of their research.

WHY BRONISLAW URBAŃSKI'S STORY IS IMPORTANT

A view by Chris Wroblewski

Being a history undergraduate who endeavours to present factual research and primary sources there was an initial degree of scepticism when first learning of Peter Urbański's father and then reading his narrative. But given my interest in Second World War history, Polish military history, Allied and Axis aircraft, and my technical background as an aircraft technician I chose to approach his narrative with an open mind. Curiosity got the best of me while reading his story and I skipped to the part where Peter's father described using a rag to jam AL523's elevator. Though his book was in need of a grammatical edit and citing of sources it was clear that Peter's father had been tasked to commit an act of assassination and had used a very unconventional method. That I was able to successfully replicate an elevator jam with a rag convinced me there was something genuine about Peter and his father's story. With this in mind any scepticism or bias others may hold regarding Peter's story should set this aside and instead try an even-handed perspective of investigation and re-examination rather than derision and ridicule to help bring to light circumstances surrounding Bronislaw Urbański's life of espionage.

I will add that no further research would have been pursued had my attempt at replicating the jamming been unsuccessful. It should be further emphasized that Peter did not know how the rag caused the crash or where it was inserted until my analysis demonstrated its potential to restrict elevator movement. To date no other logical theory has explained how AL523's elevators locked after take-off. That Peter persisted, researched, and refined the story's telling over many years, often enduring ridicule over its plausibility, speaks to his perseverance. Though not an author or an academic he wrote from the heart and in his own voice as many novice writers do. As Peter continued to edit his narrative, I strongly encouraged him to properly cite sources if he wished to be taken seriously. Bearing this in mind, where information came to light that brought his research into question, he amended his father's story to reflect those facts. Within the history community it is understood that it is difficult to research and piece together timelines and circumstances for any researcher be they professional or novice. In short, records and source material are often incomplete or lacking. A 1945 fire at the SOE Baker Street headquarters in London that destroyed a large proportion of records made it impossible to trace any associations Bronislaw Urbański might have had with this organisation. Due to these hindrances there will always be varying degrees of accuracy, inaccuracy, and deficit within any historical narrative. Given the clandestine nature of his job and that many records were either lost, destroyed, or undisclosed at war's end, it is difficult to establish a paper trail.

Peter's story challenged long-established narratives and theories about the Sikorski crash which unlocked a door that few cared to open. Behind this door lay an unexplored avenue of investigation, opening it led Garth Barnard and myself to unearth facts and allegations that challenged myths regarding AL523's crash and Sikorski's death all of which added weight to Peter's story. We hope this avenue has been sufficiently broadened and will encourage others to come forward, explore further, or bring to light information that further corroborates these events.

APPENDIX

AIR 2 9234 ACCIDENT AT GIBRALTAR TO LIBERATOR AIRCRAFT IN WHICH GENERAL SIKORSKI WAS KILLED

Court of Inquiry proceedings, 1943–1946

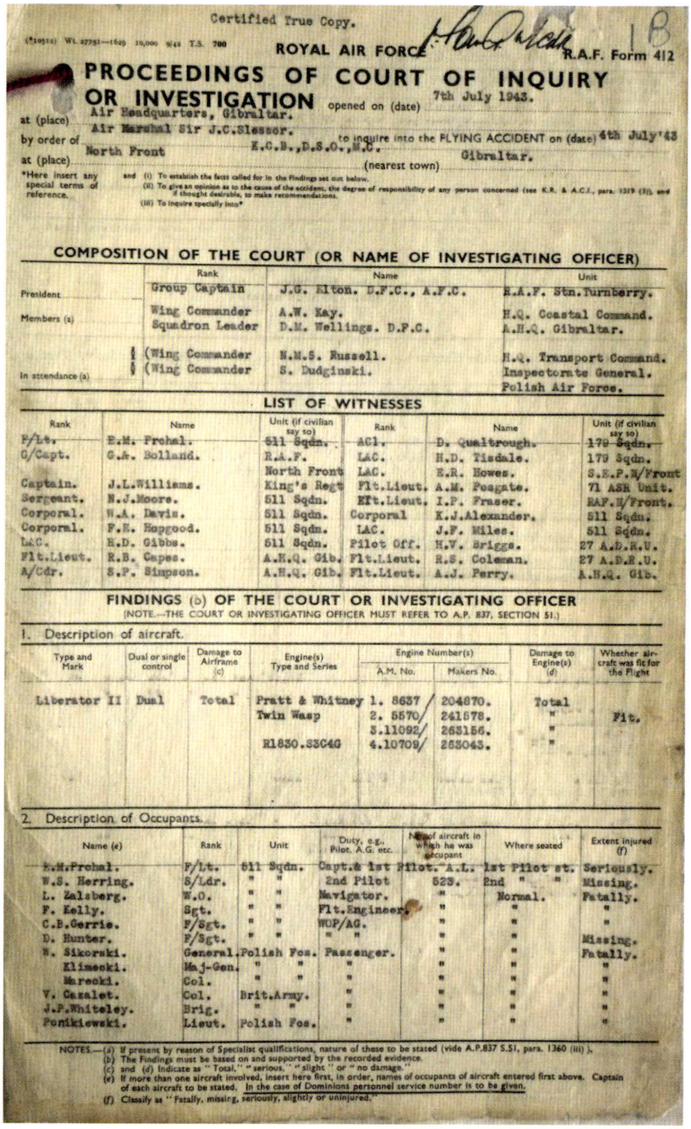

Certified True Copy.

(*10512) Wt. 27751—1629 10,000 9/42 T.S. 700 ROYAL AIR FORCE R.A.F. Form 412

PROCEEDINGS OF COURT OF INQUIRY OR INVESTIGATION opened on (date) 7th July 1943.

at (place) Air Headquarters, Gibraltar.

by order of Air Marshal Sir J.C.Slessor. K.C.B.,D.S.O.,M.C. to inquire into the FLYING ACCIDENT on (date) 4th July'43

at (place) North Front (nearest town) Gibraltar.

*Here insert any special terms of reference. and (i) To establish the facts called for in the Findings set out below.
(ii) To give an opinion as to the cause of the accident, the degree of responsibility of any person concerned (see K.R. & A.C.I., para. 1319 (3)), and if thought desirable, to make recommendations.
(iii) To inquire specially into*

COMPOSITION OF THE COURT (OR NAME OF INVESTIGATING OFFICER)

	Rank	Name	Unit
President	Group Captain	J.G. Elton. D.F.C., A.F.C.	R.A.F. Stn.Turnberry.
Members (a)	Wing Commander	A.W. Kay.	H.Q. Coastal Command.
	Squadron Leader	D.M. Wellings. D.F.C.	A.H.Q. Gibraltar.
	(Wing Commander	N.M.S. Russell.	H.Q. Transport Command.
In attendance (a)	(Wing Commander	S. Dudginski.	Inspectorate General. Polish Air Force.

LIST OF WITNESSES

Rank	Name	Unit (if civilian say so)	Rank	Name	Unit (if civilian say so)
~~F/Lt.~~	~~E.M. Prchal.~~	~~511 Sqdn.~~	~~AC1.~~	~~D. Qualtrough.~~	~~179 Sqdn.~~
G/Capt.	G.A. Bolland.	R.A.F. North Front	LAC.	H.D. Tisdale.	179 Sqdn.
			LAC.	E.R. Howes.	S.E.P.N/Front
Captain.	J.L.Williams.	King's Regt	Flt.Lieut.	A.M. Posgate.	71 ASR Unit.
Sergeant.	N.J.Moore.	511 Sqdn.	Flt.Lieut.	I.P. Fraser.	RAF.N/Front.
Corporal.	W.A. Davis.	511 Sqdn.	Corporal	K.J.Alexander.	511 Sqdn.
Corporal.	F.E. Hopgood.	511 Sqdn.	LAC.	J.F. Miles.	511 Sqdn.
LAC.	H.D. Gibbs.	511 Sqdn.	Pilot Off.	H.V. Briggs.	27 A.D.R.U.
Flt.Lieut.	R.B. Capes.	A.H.Q. Gib.	Flt.Lieut.	R.S. Coleman.	27 A.D.R.U.
A/Cdr.	S.P. Simpson.	A.H.Q. Gib.	Flt.Lieut.	A.J. Perry.	A.H.Q. Gib.

FINDINGS (b) OF THE COURT OR INVESTIGATING OFFICER

(NOTE.—THE COURT OR INVESTIGATING OFFICER MUST REFER TO A.P. 837, SECTION 51.)

1. Description of aircraft.

Type and Mark	Dual or single control	Damage to Airframe (c)	Engine(s) Type and Series	Engine Number(s) A.M. No.	Engine Number(s) Makers No.	Damage to Engine(s) (d)	Whether aircraft was fit for the Flight
Liberator II	Dual	Total	Pratt & Whitney Twin Wasp R1830.S3C4G	1. 8637/ 2. 5570/ 3.11092/ 4.10709/	204870. 241578. 263156. 263043.	Total " " "	Fit.

2. Description of Occupants.

Name (e)	Rank	Unit	Duty, e.g., Pilot, A.G. etc.	No. of aircraft in which he was occupant	Where seated	Extent injured (f)
~~E.M.Prchal.~~	F/Lt.	511 Sqdn.	Capt.& 1st Pilot.	A.L. 523.	1st Pilot st.	Seriously.
W.S. Herring.	S/Ldr.	" "	2nd Pilot		2nd " "	Missing.
L. Zalsberg.	W.O.	" "	Navigator.	"	Normal.	Fatally.
F. Kelly.	Sgt.	" "	Flt.Engineer.	"	"	"
C.B.Gerrie.	F/Sgt.	" "	WOP/AG.	"	"	"
D. Hunter.	F/Sgt.	" "	" "	"	"	Missing.
W. Sikorski.	General.	Polish Fcs.	Passenger.	"	"	Fatally.
Klimecki.	Maj-Gen.	" "	"	"	"	"
Marecki.	Col.	" "	"	"	"	"
V. Cazalet.	Col.	Brit.Army.	"	"	"	"
J.P.Whiteley.	Brig.	" "	"	"	"	"
Ponikiewski.	Lieut.	Polish Fcs.	"	"	"	"

NOTES.—(a) If present by reason of Specialist qualifications, nature of these to be stated (vide A.P.837 S.51, para. 1360 (iii)).
(b) The Findings must be based on and supported by the recorded evidence.
(c) and (d) Indicate as "Total," "serious," "slight" or "no damage."
(e) If more than one aircraft involved, insert here first, in order, names of occupants of aircraft entered first above. Captain of each aircraft to be stated. In the case of Dominions personnel service number is to be given.
(f) Classify as "Fatally, missing, seriously, slightly or uninjured."

Page 1.

LIST OF WITNESSES (CONTINUED)

Rank.	Name.	Unit.	Rank.	Name.	Unit.
W/Cdr.	C. Dunkerley.	Transit Sqdn. North Front.	Lt.Col.	P.E.B.Girling.	Fortress H.Q. Gibraltar.
Gunner.	W.J. Miller.	R.A.	S/Ldr.	J.F. Sach.	511 Sqdn.
LAC.	W.Titterington.	27 ASRU.	S/Ldr.	D. Canning.	R.A.F. N/Front.
Pte.	F.G.Callow.	King's Regt.	W/Cdr.	A.M. Stevens.	A.H.Q. Gibraltar.
Cpl.	T.Tomlinson.	" "			

2. DESCRIPTION OF OCCUPANTS. (CONTINUED)

Name (e)	Rank.	Unit.	Duty.e.g. Pilot etc.	No.of aircraft.	Where Seated.	Extent Injury
Kulakowski.	Mr.	Civilian.	Passenger.	AL.523.	Normal.	Missing
Lock.	Mr.	"	"	" "	"	"
Pinder.	Mr.	"	"	" "	"	Fatally
Lesniowska.	Mme.	"	"	" "	"	Missing
Gralewski.	Col.	Polish Fes.	"	" "	"	Fatally

Addenda to page 1.

2

3. The purpose of and instructions for the flight(s) were as follows :

Aircraft Type and Number	(i) Who authorised the flight(s)? (ii) For what purpose? (iii) Special instructions (if any). (iv) Was instru[ctions] given? If so, by whom?
Liberator A.L. 523.	(i) O.C., 511 Squadron. (ii) Convey important passengers to Middle East and return. via Gibraltar. (iii) No. (iv) No.

4. The aircraft took off as follows :

Aircraft Type and Number	Time	Place (from which)	Weather conditions (including strength and direction of surface wind) at the time and place of take-off.
Liberator A.L. 523.	2307 B	North Front.	Wind easterly. 5 m.p.h. Fine, no cloud. Visibility 10 miles.

5. The accident occurred at the place and on the date set forth on the front page of this Form. Further details are as follows :

Time	Exact location of crash, including height (g) where relevant,	Weather conditions (including strength and direction of surface wind) at the time and place of accident.
2307 B.	Approximately 700 yards due east of eastern end of runway, North Front.	Wind easterly. 5 m.p.h. Fine, no cloud. Visibility 10 miles.

6. The flying experience of the pilot prior to this flight was :

PILOT(S) (h)	Hours flown (quote to nearest hour)										
	Within 6 months prior to accident					Total solo (Day and Night)		Total solo (Night) (k)			
		Day and Night		Night (j)							
Name and where trained.	Type of aircraft including type quoted in para. 1.	Dual	Solo	Dual	Solo	On type quoted in para. 1	On all types	On type quoted in para. 1	On all types	By instruments (l)	Hours on Link Trainer (m)
Prchal.	Hudson	-	11.25	-	-						
Czechoslovakia	Liberator	-	292.10	-	171.20	362.35.	3478.55	205.35	664.15	NK	35.30.
R.A.F. Flying Assessments:- 4"above average" 1"exceptional"											
Herring.	Lancaster	-	86.45	-	14.00					187	NK
No.7 E & R.F.T.S.	Manchester	-	2.25	-	-						
Desford.	Wellington	-	64.00	-	7.15						
No. 6 F.T.S. Netheravon.	Liberator	[illegible].15 2nd Pilot	1.30	15.00 2nd Pilot	-	1.30	1274.50	-	372.20.		
Flying Assessment.	Battle	-	2.45	-	-						
1"above average"	Defiant.	-	1.05	-	-						
2"exceptional"	Beaufighter	-	.40	-	-						
	Proctor	-	1.30	-	-						

27

NOTES.—(g) Give (i) height (above sea level) of ground at scene of accident ; (ii) Height above ground of any obstacle struck by aircraft before impact with the ground, as applicable.
(h) Include all pilots involved in accident except any whose flying hours it would serve no useful purpose to quote.
(j) and (k) Only to be quoted if accident occurred at night.
(l) and (m) To be quoted only if loss of control occurred at night, or in bad visibility necessitating instrument flying, or while flying artificially blind.

Page 2.

1ST WITNESS. Flight Lieutenant Edward Max Prchal, R.A.F. Station, Lyneham, states: -

I am a pilot in No.511 Squadron, and on July 4th 1943 I was captain of Liberator aircraft No. A.L. 523. On 3rd July 1943 I landed at Gibraltar at approximately 1630B hours having flown from Cairo West. The aircraft was in every way serviceable. After landing the aircraft was "D.Ied" by my Flight Engineer, and also by the ground staff of 511 Squadron at Gibraltar. On 4th July 1943, at approximately 2240 I went aboard the aircraft and was satisfied everything was in order. I did not see where the passengers were seated, but before we started, the engines the Flight Engineer reported to me that all the passengers were properly seated. There were eleven passengers, five of whom were in the bomb bay and six in the fuselage. This was one more than when we took off from Cairo, the extra passenger being seated in the bomb bay. The all up weight was approximately 52,000 lbs. I was quite satisfied with the disposal of the load. I started my engines and warmed them up, and then proceeded to the end of the runway where I ran them up and did the normal cockpit check. Everything was satisfactory. I received the "green" signal at 2310 hours and commenced to take off. At about 130 m.p.h. I was airborne. When I was at about 150 feet I eased the control column forward to gather speed. My speed built up to 165 m.p.h. I wanted to climb again so attempted to pull back the control column but I could not do so. The control column was definitely locked. I told my second pilot over the inter-communication to check over the controls quickly. At this time the under-carriage was fully up and the flaps half-down, that is normal take off position. When I found I was unable to move the control column I put on trim in an endeavour to gain height, but nothing happened. All this time I was pulling back on the control column but could not move it backwards. I got no reply from the second pilot over the inter-communication and the aircraft was rapidly approaching the water. I then shouted out "crash landing" to the crew and closed the throttles. The aircraft immediately hit the water and I remember no more.

(Signed) E.M.PRCHAL. F/Lt. 8th July 1943.

Question 1. Roughly how many hours have you flown on Liberators as Captain ?

Answer. Nearly 500 hours.

Question 2. Have you ever experienced controls becoming locked in flight on a Liberator before ?

Answer. Yes, once with Squadron Leader McPhail when taking off from Lyneham. Squadron Leader McPhail was second pilot and had unlocked the controls prior to take off, and when nearly airborne I found I could not move the rudders and realised the controls had been re-locked. I shouted over the inter-communication to him to unlock them; he did so, and I was able to complete the take-off although I had swung off the runway a little as a result. I reported this to my Flight Commander and to the remaining pilots in the Squadron.

Question 3. How long had you known your second pilot, Squadron Leader Herring ?

Answer. Not long. He had been with me as second pilot since leaving England on this trip and he had not flown with me before. On the two take-offs on this trip, at Lyneham and Cairo, one carried out at night and one by day in fog, he had carried out the drill quite normally.

Question 4. Who operates the flap control ?

Answer. The second pilot, but on my instructions only, which I would not give until we had reached 1,000 feet.

Question 5. Did the control column feel that it wanted to go forward ?

Answer. I cannot say, but if I had been higher I would have tried it.

Page 3.

- 2 -

Question 6. Can you remember whether the control column was rigid or whether there was any play at all ?

Answer. I cannot remember.

Question 7. Were you satisfied that the rudders, ailerons and elevators were functioning correctly when the aircraft became airborne ?

Answer. Yes, definitely.

Question 8. What were the weather conditions like at take-off ?

Answer. Perfect, ~~xixm~~,calm, visibility 15-20 miles. I was able to see the horizon clearly.

(Signed) E.M. PRCHAL. F/Lt.

2ND WITNESS. Group Captain Guy Alfred Bolland, R.A.F. Station, North Front, Gibraltar, states :-

I am the Officer Commanding, North Front. The security organisation at my Station is as follows:-
By day all entrances to the camp are guarded by Gibraltar Security Police who check the passes of all civilians. The east and west beaches and also the Spanish frontier fence are patrolled, by British Soldiers. There is also a roving patrol in that part of the aerodrome where freight and passenger aircraft are parked. Between 0530B hours and 2230B hours this day organisation is in force, but this is overlapped by the night organisation which commences at 2130B hours and finishes at sunrise which is now approximately at 0720B hours.
By night the aerodrome is guarded by 6 officers and 100 senior N.C.O's and men with a reserve of 40 for use in any emergency. These soldiers are divided up into various patrols who guard all the entrances to the camp and are assisted by dogs at Eastern Beach and the western extension to the runway.
In the case of Liberator A.L. 523 the following additional precautions were taken. One British sentry was posted to guard the aircraft and was given a list of the names of the airmen who were likely to work on it. He was also instructed that personnel of A.D.R.U. could also board the aircraft. In addition a Corporal of 511 Squadron slept in the aircraft the night of 3rd/4th July. Special guards are only provided for aircraft carrying most important passengers, at the pilot's request because he is carrying special freight, or because the aircraft is fitted with exceptionally secret equipment.
As an additional security measure the entire airfield is flood lit during the hours of darkness except when aircraft are landing or taking off, or when "no lights" is requested by the Navy. It is under the control of Flying Control.

~~(Signed) G.A. BOLLAND. GROUP CAPTAIN.~~

The sea rescue arrangements at Gibraltar are as follows. Three H.S.L's are based on the Flying Boat Station on the western side of the Rock. These craft are controlled by Area Combined Headquarters who are in direct telephonic communication with Flying Control, North Front. In the event of an aircraft crashing into the sea, Flying Control inform A.C.H.Q. by telephone who then give the orders to the launch. The launch is also in R/T communication with Flying Control. In addition there is also a small rowing dinghy kept at instant readiness on a launching cradle at the extreme eastern end of the runway, which is continuously manned by day. The dinghy on this occasion, although the crash occurred by night was launched and reached the scene of the accident within about eight minutes. Further sea rescue facilities can be provided by light naval forces, which are continually patrolling the waters in the vicinity of the Rock, when operational commitments permit. On this occasion one of these craft reached the scene of the crash within a short space of time.

28

(Signed) G.A. BOLLAND. GROUP CAPTAIN.

....../Continued.

Page 4.

- 3 -.

Question 1. In view of the fact that the only road connecting Spain with the Fortress passes across the airfield what precautions are taken to prevent unauthorised persons from deviating from this road ?

Answer. All gaps in the wire fence along this road are guarded by day and night by either Gibraltar Security Police and/or British soldiers.

(Signed) G.A. BOLLAND. Group Captain. 8/7/43.

3RD WITNESS. Captain Jack Llewellyn Williams, Independent Company, King's Regiment, Gibraltar states :-

I am Officer i/c No.2 Platoon, Independent Company, and on 3rd and 4th July I was in charge of the Frontier guards at North Front and of the guard provided for Liberator A.L. 523. The guard mounted duty on the Liberator at 1630B hours on 3rd July and remained on guard until the aircraft left at approximately 2300B hours on 4th July. The sentry consisted of one man who was relieved every two hours by the duty N.C.O. and replaced by another. The following orders were given to the sentry on taking over duty on the aircraft :- "No one excepting personnel in possession of the aerodrome special maintenance pass are to be allowed near the aircraft". The R.A.F. provided a list of personnel to be allowed near the 'plane. The guard was instructed that any other persons approaching would have to be identified by Corporal Alexander of the R.A.F. who was on duty the whole time except when he was relieved for meals. During these periods his relief would identify personnel who wished to approach. During the whole period of the guard no reports were received from the guard commander that any unauthorised person had attempted to approach the aircraft. The guards were inspected from time to time by officers of the Independent Company, who all reported that the aircraft was being properly guarded.

(Signed) J.L.WILLIAMS. Capt. Indept.Coy. 8/7/43.

4TH WITNESS. No.567194 Sergeant Moore, Norman John, Fitter II, R.A.F. Station, Lyneham, States :-

I am a sergeant in 511 Squadron i/c Maintenance detached to R.A.F. Station, North Front, and I am responsible for servicing 511 Sqdn. aircraft at Gibraltar. On July 3rd at 1630 hours Liberator A.L.523 landed at Gibraltar. I was waiting with my personnel, consisting of ten airmen, to service the aircraft. I approached the Flight Engineer, Sgt. Kelly, and asked him about the aircraft's serviceability. He replied that it was perfect. The Pilot also stated to me that the aircraft was serviceable. I then ordered Corporal Davies, senior corporal of my maintenance party, to put a guard on the aircraft immediately. This he did, and this airman remained on guard until relieved by a military armed guard. I then instructed Corporal Davies that an airman must remain on the aircraft throughout the hours of darkness in close proximity to the door, and Corporal Hopgood was the airman detailed. Approximately between 2100B hours and 2130B hours I spoke to the armed military guard enquiring whether he had a list of people permitted aboard the aircraft. His answer was no. I then gave him a list of airmen of my maintenance party and stated that these airmen would vouch for any other persons allowed to board the aircraft. The following morning between 0700B hours and 0800B hours I saw Corporal Davies and asked him who had been on guard. He said Corporal Hopgood and that he had gone off to breakfast. I received no report of any unusual incident from either Cpl. Davies or Cpl. Hopgood, and I concluded that everything was in order. I saw the aircraft from time to time during the day and was present when it left. Throughout this period I received no adverse report either about security or maintenance from any member of my party.

(Signed) N.J. MOORE. Sgt.

............/continued.

Page 5.

- 6 -

4th WITNESS continued. I personally checked the Travelling Form 700 and saw that it was completely signed up for a daily inspection before the aircraft l... I carried out this final check at about 2200B hours and signed as N.C.O. i/c Maintenance Party, and I am absolutely convinced that the aircraft was serviceable.

(Signed) N. J. MOORE. Sergeant.

3rd WITNESS - recalled. Captain Jack Llewelyn Williams questioned by the Court.

Question 1. Who gave the name of the R.A.F. Corporal who was on duty the night of 3rd/4th July?

Answer The N.C.O. i/c of the Military guard on the aircraft. I understood that this was obtained from the list of names provided by the Sergeant in charge of Maintenance.

Question 2. Who told that Corporal Alexander of the R.A.F. was on duty during the whole period, except for meal times, that Liberator A.L.523 was on the airfield?

Answer Sgt. Moore, R.A.F. informed the duty N.C.O. i/c Guard who in turn informed me.

Question 3. What is "the special maintenance pass" to which you refer?

Answer This consisted of a piece of paper on which Sgt. Moore had listed all names of the personnel who were allowed to approach the aircraft, the individuals concerned establishing their identity by producing their identity card.

(Signed) J. L. WILLIAMS. Captain.
Indspt. Coy.
9.7.43.

5th WITNESS. No. 924542 Corporal Davis. William, Arthur, Leonard, Fitter IIE, R.A.F. Station, Lyneham, states:-

I am a corporal in 511 Squadron and the senior corporal of the Maintenance Flight attached to R.A.F. Station, North Front, Gibraltar. On July, 3rd 1943 at approximately 1630B hours just after Liberator A.L.523 had landed from Cairo I was standing by the aircraft when Sergeant Moore gave me the following instructions. He detailed me to have the aircraf guarded continuously by one of our maintenance detachment, and stated further that one of them would have to sleep in the aircraft at night. I drew up a list of the airmen who were to guard the aircraft and told each man how long he was to be on guard, when he was on guard, and who was relieving him. I periodically checked up that the guards were performing their duties. I was withCorporal Hopgood when he mounted guard at about 2200B hours and I was also with him when he came off guard at about 0730B hours on the morning of the 4th July. Neither Corporal Hopgood nor any of the other airmen I detailed for the guard reported any unusualx occurrence to me.

(Signed) L. DAVIS. 9.7.43.

6th WITNESS. No. 918902 Corporal Hopgood. Francis, Edmund. Electrician. R.A.F. Station, Lyneham, states:-

I am a corporal in 511 Squadron and am in maintenance flight att to R.A.F. Station, North Front, Gibraltar. On July 3rd 1943 at about 1700B hours I was instructed by Corporal Davis to act as guard on Liberator A.L.523 during the hours of darkness and was to report for duty at 2230B hours. I was to sleep in the aircraft and to remain on guard until relieved the following morning at 0730B hours. I slept on the floor by the rear hatch and I am convinced no unauthorised entered the aircraft while I was on duty. When I left the aircraft at 0730 hours airmen of my detachment were engaged on servicing the aircraft At approximately 0700B hours an airman whom I recognised as belonging to Air Despatch and Reception Unit took a package from the bomb compartment.

29

(Signed) F. E. HOPGOOD

Page 6.

- 8 -

7th WITNESS. No. 1428808 L.A.C. Gibbs. Harold, David. Fitter IIA, R.A.F. Station, Lyneham, states:-

I am a Fitter IIA in 511 Squadron and am in the maintenance flight attached to R.A.F. Station, North Front, Gibraltar. At about 0930B hours on 4th July 1943 I was instructed by Sergeant Moore to carry out a daily inspection of the airframe of Liberator A.L.523. I had been informed by Sergeant Moore the previous evening that there were no snags with the aircraft. I carried out the inspection in accordance with section 1A, Part 2 of the Maintenance Schedule IX for Liberator II aeroplane, and everything was in order. I signed the Travelling Copy of Form 700 to that effect. When I carried out my inspection I observed that all control cables were free of any obstruction, but I was informed later by L.A.C. Miles that additional baggage had been loaded on the aircraft before departure. As far as I know this was passengers personal baggage being replaced.

(Signed) H. D. GIBBS.

8th WITNESS. No. 646930 Corporal Alexander. Keith, Trelfa. Instrument Repairer I, R.A.F. Station, Lyneham, states:-

I am a corporal in 511 Squadron and am in the maintenance flight attached to R.A.F. Station, North Front Gibraltar. On 4th July 1943 at about 1100B hours I carried out a daily inspection, in accordance with section IC Part 2 of the Maintenance Schedule for Liberator II aeroplane, on Liberator A.L.523, as applicable to this aircraft. No snags had been reported either by the Flight Engineer or Pilot, and after my inspection I was quite satisfied that everything was in order. I signed the Travelling Copy of Form 700 to that effect.

(Signed) K. ALEXANDER. Corporal.

9th WITNESS. No. 1215765 L.A.C. Miles. Jabez, Frank. Fitter IIA, R.A.F. Station, Lyneham, states:-

I am a Fitter IIA in 511 Squadron and am in the Maintenance flight attached to R.A.F. Station, North Front, Gibraltar. On 4th July 1943 at between about 2230B hours and 2245B hours I stowed about twelve pieces of personal luggage in the bomb bay of Liberator A.L.523, on both sides of the forward portion. I am experienced in stowing baggage in Liberator aircraft and am well aware of the importance of ensuring that neither control cables, nor various accessories of the hydraulic system are fouled. In this instance I lashed all the baggage down and was quite satisfied that everything was properly stowed.

(Signed) J. F. MILES. L.A.C.

10th WITNESS. Pilot Officer Harold Vernon Briggs, R.A.F. Station, North Front, Gibraltar states:-

I am an embarkation officer in No. 27 A.D.R.U. and in the morning of 4th July was on duty at North Front. I received a telephone call from Government House asking whether an additional passenger could be carried in Liberator A.L.523 due to depart that evening. I spoke to the captain of the aircraft on the telephone and he agreed that this passenger could be carried and later signed Form 1256 to that effect, which Form I now produce.

(Signed) H. V. BRIGGS. P/O. 9th July, 1943.

Question 1. Can you produce a copy of the manifest for this aircraft Liberator A.L.523?

Answer. No. The only copy available was that retained by the pilot which I saw. As far as I can remember the total pay load on arrival at Gibraltar was 5,840 lbs. We never receive a copy of the manifest on aircraft arriving from Cairo, although it is laid down in the distributions instructions on Form 1256 that we should receive one.

....../Continued.

Page 7.

- 6 -

10th WITNESS continued. Furthermore it is considered essential to have a copy and we have applied for one on several occasions without success.

(Signed) H. V. BRIGGS. P/O. 9th July, 1943

11th WITNESS. Flight Lieutenant Reginald Stanley Coleman, Air Headquarters, Royal Air Force, Gibraltar, states:-

I am an embarkation officer in No. 27 A.D.R.U. On the evening of the 4th July I was on duty at North Front with Pilot Officer Briggs. At about 2200B hours two passengers, Mr. Pinder and Mr. Lock, who were to travel on Liberator A.L.523 reported at the office. Of the eleven passengers due to emplane on Liberator A.L.523 that evening these were the only two passengers whom I checked onto the aircraft, as the remainder were taken direct to the aircraft by the Government House party. I spoke to both Major Quayle and Flight Lieutenant Perry, A.D.C's to the Governor, who stated that all their party was present.

x Exhibit "B" I produce a list x of the eleven passengers who were due to emplane on Liberator A.L.523 that night.

(Signed) R. S. COLEMAN. F/Lt. 9th July, 1943.

Question 1. Can you state, apart from Mr. Lock and Mr. Pinder, whether or not the other passengers on the list which you have produced did in fact emplane on Liberator A.L.523?

Answer. No, because except for Mr. Lock and Mr. Pinder, the remainder were taken direct to the aircraft.

Question 2. Is it customary for passengers to emplane without first reporting to the A.D.R.U.

Answer. No, but certain very important passengers are sometimes taken direct to the aircraft as happened in this instance.

(Signed) R. S. COLEMAN. F/Lt. 9th July, 1943.

12th WITNESS. Flight Lieutenant Arthur John Perry, Air Headquarters, R.A.F. Gibraltar, states:-

I am A.D.C. to H.E. the Governor of Gibraltar and on 4th July, 1943 at about 2215B hours I proceeded to North Front airfield with Col. Cazalet and Lieutenant Ponikiewski. At about 2245B hours I saw all the eleven passengers named on Exhibit "B", shown to me by the Court, emplane on Liberator A.L.523.

(Signed) A. J. PERRY. F/Lt.

13th WITNESS. Wing Commander Claude Dunkerley, R.A.F. Station, North Front, Gibraltar, states:-

I am Officer Commanding, Transit Squadron, North Front, and am responsible for the warning and despatch of communication aircraft. Liberator A.L. 523 was duly warned to Lyneham at 1150B hours on 4th July, 1943 but departure signal was not sent as the aircraft crashed on take-off. A signal was sent to this effect instead.

(Signed) C. DUNKERLEY. W/Cdr.

2nd WITNESS- recalled Group Captain Bolland states:-

On the 5th July the duty officer, Flying Control, reported to me that a gunner on duty at the gun sight on the western end of the runway had picked up a mail bag on the western end of the runway which he handed in to Flying Control. Subsequent enquiries from A.D.R.U. revealed the fact that this mail bag was part of the freight of Liberator A.L.523.

30

(Signed) G. A. BOLLAND. Group Captain.

Question 1. Were you present when Liberator A.L.523 taxied out to take off on the night of the 4th July, 1943?

Page 8.

- 7 -

WITNESS called - continued.

Answer. Yes.

Question 2. Did you notice whether or not the rear hatch was closed?

Answer. No, but I am convinced I should have noticed if it had not been.

(Signed) G. A. BOLLAND. Group Captain.

14th WITNESS. No. 1638146 Gunner Miller, William Joseph, 9th Light A.A.Battery, 3rd Light A.A. Regiment, R.A., states:-

I was on duty at my gun post, which is sited on the north side of the runway about 400 yards from the west end, when at about 0140B hours on 5th July I saw an object lying on the runway close by. On inbestigation I found it to be a mail bag weighing about 15 lbs. As soon as my duty was finished at 0200B hours I took the bag to Flying Control and handed it over to the officer on duty.

(Signed) W. J. MILLER.

15th WITNESS. Flight Lieutenant Renalt Bernard Capes, Air Headquarters, R.A.F. Gibraltar, states:-

I am a Flying Control officer and on the evening of the 4th July 1943 I was on duty in the Watch Tower on North Front airfield. At approximately 2307B hours I saw Liberator A.L.523 taking off. The aircraft became airborne at about No. 12 flare which gave the pilot a take off run of about 1,150 yards. The aircraft appeared to climb normally and had reached a height of about 50 feet when 100 yards past the Watch Tower. The aircraft then appeared to level off, flew for a short distance straight and level and then lost height steadily until it hit the sea. In my opinion all four engines were under full power until the aircraft crashed, and there was no suggestion of a stall.
The flare path at the time of take off of Liberator A.L.523 consisted of a double row of electric flares spaced at 100 yard intervals, the flare path being 50 yards wide. Approximately 100 yards beyond the the last flares a row of red glim lamps indicated the end of the runway.

(Signed) R. BERNARD CAPES. F/Lt.
10th July, 1943.

Question 1. Have youx had any flying experience?

Answer. Yes, about 7,000 hours as a pilot.

Question 2. In view of the fact that there was no moon how were you able to follow the path of the aircraft so clearly?

Answer. By the navigation lights.

(Signed) R. BERNARD CAPES. F/Lt.
10th July, 1943.

16th WITNESS. Air Commodore Sturley Philip Simpson, Air Headquarters, Gibraltar, states,

I am the Air Officer Commanding, R.A.F. Gibraltar. On te evening of the 4th July I proceeded to North Front airfield to say good-bye to General Sikorski. The passengers emplaned and the engines were started normally. Liberator A.L.523 then taxied out to the west end of the runway where, after a considerable pause, it turned into wind and thxx took off. I was standing on the north side of the runway about 200 yards east of the Spanish Road. The aircraft became airborne about 100 yards past where I was standing. The aircraft climbed steadily in a perfectly normal manner and [illegible]

Page 9.

- 8 -

16th WITNESS- continued. all four engines appeared to be functioning properly. I shoul[illegible]ge it was over the east end of the runway at about 100 feet when [illegible] ceased to climb and appeared to sink slowly towards the sea. Owing to the darkness it was not possible to gauge the altitude of the aircraft. Whilst the aircraft was losing height there was no change in the note of the engines and all four were showing the same steady blue exhaust flame that they were showing while climbing. The aircraft disappeared from my view below the sea wall and there was a loud crash.

(Signed) S. P. SIMPSON. Air Commodore.

Question 1. Did you notice whether or not the rear hatch was closed before Liberator A.L.523 taxied out to take off?

Answer. I did not actually see it being closed but I am quite certain I should have noticed it ~~if it~~ had it been left open.

Question 2. Is it customary for very important passengers to emplane at Gibraltar without first passing through A.D.R.U.?

Answer In very special cases this is sometimes done as h appened in this instance.

Question 3. In these cases who ensures that all passengers emplane?

Answer. In this particular case the Governor and myself, but in future I shall ensure that a responsible embarkation officer checks all passengers, v.i.p. or otherwise, into the aircraft.

(Signed) S. P. SIMPSON. Air Commodore.

17th WITNESS. No. 1547087 A.C.1 Qualtrough. Derek. Wireless Mechanic, R.A.F. Station, North Front, Gibraltar, states:-

I am a wireless mechanic in 179 Squadron and on the evening of the 4th July, 1943, at about 2310B hours I was waiting to cross the east end of the runway while an aircraft was taking off. It was just airborne and was climbing when it passed me, and immediately it had gone by I commenced to cross the runway. My attention was suddenly drawn to the aircraft by the fact that the engines had stopped, and it appeared to be about 100 feet high and descending towards the sea. I realised it was going to crash and I started to run to the rescue dinghy boat-house. I am a member of the dinghy crew but I was not on duty at the time. I was accompanied by two other airmen at the time. I did not hear the aircraft crash as I was running. When we arrived at the boat-house other airmen where there and whilst six of us climbed into the dinghy another airman operated the winch and launched us. We arrived at the scene of the crash in about five minutes, and we were hailed by someone in the water whom we at once pulled on board. He was wearing an inflated Mae West and was quite conscious although unable to speak. Searchlights from the Rock began to come on and we started to search amongst the wreckage for more survivors. The aircraft itself had sunk. We next picked up a few minutes later the body of a man who was not wearing a Mae West. He was floating with his head under water and I considered he was dead. About 15 to 20 minutes after we arrived at the scene of the crash a small naval craft appeared. The crew informed us that they had no facilities aboard for dealing with survivors but that the R.A.F. rescue launch was just arriving. We then noticed the launch, hailed it, and transferred the survivor and the body to it. By this time other small craft had appeared and one had recovered a body which we transferred to the rescue launch. We continued to search for about another half an hour amongst the wreckage which by then had drifted about ½ mile south. Finding nothing more we returned to the shore.

31

(Signed) A.C.1 D. QUALTROUGH.
10.7.43.

Question 1. How long elapsed after the crash before the searchlights of the Rock illuminated the wreckage?

....../Continued.

Page 10.

[illegible] WITNESS- continued.

Answer. I should say about ten minutes.

Question 2. Where exactly were you standing on the runway when the aircraft was taking off?

Answer. On the south side of the pedestrian crossing near Flying Control.

(Signed) D. QUALTROUGH. 10.7.43.

18th WITNESS. No. R.101031 L.A.C. Tisdale. Herbert David R.D.F. M/R, R.A.F. Station, North Front, Gibraltar, states:-

I am an airman in 179 Squadron and on the evening of the 4th July, 1943 at about 2300B hours I was proceeding along the Spanish Frontier Road to the ablutions when I heard a Liberator taking off from west to east. When I was at a point about 25yards north of the shooting range the noise suddenly ceased. I stopped and turned around to look for the aircraft. After a couple of glances towards the end of the runway I heard a crash. I immediately ran to the boat-house as I realised that the aircraft must be in the sea. There was an appreciable ~~imp~~ length of time between the stopping of the engine noise and the sound of the crash.

(Signed) H. D. TISDALE. 10.7.43.

19th WITNESS. No. 1235676 L.A.C. Howes. Eric Ronald, R.A.F. Station, North Front. Gibraltar, states:-

I am an electrician in the Special Erection Party. At about 2305B hours on the 4th July I was coming out of my billet, which is situated at the extreme end of the Frontier Road about 100 yards from the eastern end of the runway, when I saw a Liberator taking off from west to east. I turned to go to the lavatory and as I did so I heard the engines cut. A second or two later I heard a loud crash and immediately started to run to the beach to see what had happened. I could see the aircraft floating in the water and immediately ran to the rescue dinghy which I helped to launch. As we were rowing towards the aircraft I saw it sink. I estimate that about six to eight minutes elapsed between the time I heard the crash and the aircraft sank.

(Signed) E. R. HOWES. 11.7.43

20th WITNESS. Flight Lieutenant Albert Morris Posgate, R.A.F. Station, New Camp, Gibraltar, states:-

I am the officer commanding No. 71 Air/Sea Rescue Unit, and I am responsible for the Air/Sea Rescue organisation in the Gibraltar area. My unit consists of three high speed launch es of which, two are always at immediate notice. In day time they a re moored inside the harbour and during the night, from 2000 hours to 0800 hours the next morning, they are moored outside the harbour at Commercial Anchorage. In the event of an aircraft crashing into the sea off the runwaythe officer on duty in the H.S.L. received a message over R/T from t[illegible] Pilot, New Camp. This message has been passed by telephone fro[illegible] to the Controller, New Camp, who in turn has notified the D[illegible] telephone. A.C.H.Q. receives notification of the crash [illegible] Control, North Front, or from any other witness of the c[illegible] receipt of the message by R/T in the duty H.S.L. THE la[illegible] way within 30 seconds. Of the three H.S.L's. two can r[illegible] eastern extremity of the runway, North Front, in approxima[illegible] minutes and the third, a slower launch, takes about nine [illegible] On the night of the 4th July, 1943 on the occasion of [illegible] Liberator A.L.523 the message was received at 2310B h[illegible] launch, being the slow one, took nine minutes to reach [illegible] the crash. The second launch, of which I was in com[illegible] orders to proceed at 2320B hours and reached the sce[illegible] in six minutes. Both launches continued to search f[illegible]

....

Page 11.

FULL TEXT FOR 20TH WITNESS FLIGHT LIEUTENANT POSGATE FROM TORN CORNER OF TRANSCRIPT

20th WITNESS. Flight Lieutenant Albert Morris Posgate, RAF Station, New Camp, Gibraltar, states:

> I am the officer commanding No. 71 Air/Sea Rescue Unit, and I am responsible for the Air/Sea Rescue organisation in the Gibraltar area. My unit consists of three high-speed launches of which, two are kept at immediate notice. In daytime they are moored inside the harbour and during the night, from 2000 hours to 0800 hours the next morning they are moored outside the harbour at Commercial Anchorage. In the event of an aircraft crashing into the sea off the runway the officer on duty in the H.S.L. received a message over R/T from the Duty Pilot, New Camp. This message has been passed by telephone from A.C.H.Q. to the Controller, New Camp, who in turn has notified the Duty Pilot by telephone. A.C.H.Q. receives notification of the crash from Flying Control, North Front, or from any other witness of the crash. On receipt of the message by R/T in the duty H.S.L. the launch is underway within 30 seconds. Of the three H.S.Ls. two can reach the eastern extremity of the runway, North Front, in approximately six minutes and the third, a slower launch, takes about nine minutes. On the night of the 4th July, 1943 on the occasion of the crash of Liberator A.L.523 the message was received at 2310B hrs and the launch, being the slow one, took nine minutes to reach the scene of the crash. The second launch, of which I was in command, received orders to proceed at 2320B hours and reached the scene of the crash in six minutes. Both launches continued to search for survivors until recalled at 0420B hours. During this period the pilot, who was alive, and four bodies were recovered. We also recovered about thirty mail bags, diplomatic papers, money, etc. The pilot was wearing a Mae West but no parachute harness. Three of the four bodies recovered were fully clothed and one, that of Colonel Cazalet, was fully clothed and still strapped to his chair. In my opinion, Colonel Cazalet could not have been wearing a Mae West or parachute harness at the time of the crash. Four watches taken off the bodies had all stopped between 2306 hours and 2307 hours.

(Signed) A. M. POSGATE. F/Lt.

Question 1. Did you subsequently recover any more bodies and how were they clothed?

Answer. Yes. On the morning of the 6th July I recovered two bodies; one was the Navigator and the other the Flight Engineer. Both were fully clothed and neither were wearing a Mae West or parachute harness. On the morning of the 7th July I recovered the body of a W.O.F/A.G. He was fully clothed but not wearing a Mae West or parachute harness. On the 8th July I recovered the body of a Polish officer who was also fully dressed but without a Mae West or parachute harness.

Question 2. Did you observe any Mae Wests floating amongst the wreckage?

Answer. Yes, I picked up three or four in quite good condition.

Question 3. Were you present during the salvage operations?

Answer. Yes, the whole time.

Question 4. How long did they take?

Answer. The Naval Dockyard commenced operations on Tuesday 6th July at about 0830B hours and by 1930B hours on the 9th July, when weather stopped operations, the main planes, centre section, and three engines were in shallow water off eastern beach. The tail unit part of the fuselage and one engine were taken to the dockyard.

Question 5. Do you know the depth of the water where the aircraft crashed?

Answer. Yes, between five and six fathoms.

Question 6. Did you see the aircraft brought to the surface?

Answer. Yes, I saw the main planes, centre section and three engines, brought to the surface three times. The first and second time it was lowered again into the same position and the third time it was lowered into shallow water off eastern beach.

(Signed) A. M. POSGATE. F/Lt.

21st WITNESS. Flight Lieutenant Ian Petrie Fraser, R.A.F. Station, North Front, Gibraltar, states:-

I am a flying control officer at North Front, and was duty officer in the Flying Control Office on the night of the 4th/5th July. Liberator A.L.523 crashed into the sea at 2307B hours on 4th July, 1943.

32

(Signed) IAN P. FRASER. F/Lt.

ITNESS. No. 1203940 L.A.C. Titterington, Walter, R.A.F. Station, North Front, Gibraltar, states:-

I am an equipment assistant in No. 27 A.D.R.U. It is the responsibility of my unit to remove certain diplomatic mail from R.A.F. aircraft arriving from the Middle East for transfer to B.O.A.C. aircraft. On the occasion of the arrival of Liberator A.L.523 at 1630B hours on the 3rd July, 1943 I had been instructed that there were a number of diplomatic mail bags on this aircraft which were to be transferred.

....../Continued.

Page 12.

22nd WITNESS- continued.	At about 1730B hours on the 3rd July I removed five mail bags from the forward bomb bay. And again at about 0700B hours on 4th July I removed a further two bags from the forward bomb bay. On the first occasion I was not challenged by the military guard, nor did I see one. There were a lot of airmen about and it is quite possible I should have missed him. I carried a pass signed by O.C. No. 27 A.D.R.U. On the second occasion, at 0700 hours on the 4th July, when I visited the aircraft I definitely did not see any military guard nor was I challenged. I entered the aircraft by the rear hatch and in doing so woke up Corporal Hopgood who allowed me to pass as he knew who I was. On leaving the aircraft with the bags a minute or two later I still saw no guard nor was I challenged.
	(Signed) W. TITTERINGTON. L.A.C. July 13th 1943.
23rd WITNESS.	No. 3777106 Private Callow, Frederick Christian, Independent Company, King's Regiment, states:-
	I was posted as guard on Liberator A.L.523 at 0600B hours on 4th July. My instructions were to guard the aircraft and to allow no one to approach or enter it unless their name was on the list I had been given by the guard commander. I was relieved from guard at 0800B hours on 4th July and during my guard no one approached, entered, or left the aircraft.
	(Signed) F. C. CALLOW. Pte. July 13th 1943.
Question 1.	Are you quite certain you were guarding Liberator A.L.523?
Answer.	Yes, I saw the number near the tail.
Question 2.	When you stated that no one approached Liberator A.L.523 during your guard from 0600B hours to 0800B hours on the 4th July did you mean that no unauthorised person approached the aircraft?
Answer.	I meant no one at all approached the aircraft.
	(Signed) F. C. CALLOW. Pte. July 13th 1943.
24th WITNESS.	No. 3777849 Corporal Tomlinson, Thomas, Independent Company, King's Regiment, states:-
	On the night of 3rd/4th July, 1943 I was N.C.O. i/c Reliefs for Guards posted on Liberator A.L.523. At 0600B hours on 4th July I posted Private Callow on this aircraft. At 0800B hours on 4th July I posted his relief. During the two hours he was on guard I visited Private Callow three or four times and neither these times nor when I relieved him did he report that anything unusual had happened.
	(Signed) T. TOMLINSON. 13.7.43
6th WITNESS- recalled.	No. 918902 Corporal Hopgood recalled.
Question 1.	Are you quite certain that airmen were working on Liberator A.L. 523 when you left at 0730B hours on the 4th July?
Answer.	No, I am not certain. Another Liberator had landed at about 0710B hours and had parked close to A.L.523 on its port side. I went to meet this aircraft, and other airmen of my detachment arrived shortly after. I cannot therefore remember definitely whether airmen were working on A.L.523 or the newly arrived Liberator.
Question 2.	Where was the military guard for Liberator A.L.523 positioned when you left to meet the newly arrived Liberator?
Answer.	I did not see a military guard and was not aware that one had been

....../Continued.

Page 13.

- 12 -

9th WITNESS - recalled - continued.

been detailed. I did however see two or three military guard the rear of Liberator A.L.523 near some Mosquitos, and I presumed they were guarding the Mosquitos.

(Signed) F. E. HOPGOOD.

25th WITNESS.

Lieutenant Colonel Francis Edward Buller Girling, G.S.O.1 Fortress Headquarters, Gibraltar, states:-

I am, as General Staff Officer, responsible for issuing orders to military formations, regarding the security precautions necessary in Gibralter. I produce a map (Exhibit C) showing the guards and patrols provided by the military to safeguard North Front airfield and R.A.F. installations and aircraft against attempts at sabotage The guards by day are found by the Independent Company and by nigh by the Indepenedent Company plus three officers and eighty of an infantry battalion. In addition to the seguards there are four Gibraltar Special Police posts, two on Devil's Tower Road and two on the road to Spain, in addition to the police posts at Four Corners. Off the western end of the runway there is a motor boat patrol manned by the Independent Company which carries out the inshore patrol and also patrols the commercial anchorage. The following area is a protected area under the defence regulations:- "The area bounded by the south east side of the Caledonian Canal, Devil's Dyke, North Face of the Rock, southern edge of Cross Ditch, thence in a direct line to western beach". The road to Spain is exempt from this order. To the best of my knowledge there have been no cases of sabotage or attempted sabotage of aircraft on the airfield.

(Signed) F. E. B. GIRLING. Lt.Col. G.S.

26th WITNESS.

Squadron Leader Jack Frederick Sach, R.A.F. Station, Lyneham, states

I am "A" Flight Commander in 511 Squadron. Flight Lieutenant Prchal is a pilot in my flight. I have known him personnaly since he was posted to the squadron in November, 1942. His flying ability has always been outstanding and exceptional and he has never been known to leave anything, no matter how slight to chance. He exercises good discipline with his crew and his general bearing has at all times been of a high order. He has always been very interested in his work and I should regard him as being the most valued captain in the Squadron.

(Signed)J.F. SACH. Squadron Leader.

Question 1. What is your experience on Liberators?

Answer. About 800 hours as captain gained over the past 20 months, all in 1425 Flight and 511 Squadron.

Question 2. Is it possible for a mail bag, which had been stowed in the port forward bomb bay, to fall out?

Answer. The port forward bomb door is the only one used for the crew to get into their positions and for loading freight in the bomb bay on Liberator A.L.523, and it is possible, if the bomb door were slightly open as a result of putting on flap or any other reason, that this bag might fall out. This would only occur if the hydraulic system were not properly primed.

33

Question 3. Can you give any reason why a Liberator pilot should want to lock the controls during take off?

Answer. There is no reason whatsoever once the aircraft is into wind.

Question 4. Did you hear of the incident at Lyneham when Squadron Leader McPhail was second pilot to Flight Lieutenant Prchal and locked the controls during take-off.

Answer. No, I did not. (Signed)

....../continued.

Page 14.

26th WITNESS-
continued.

Question 5. What is your opinion of Flight Lieutenant Prchal's ability on instrument flying?

Answer. Flight Lieutenant Prchal's instrument flying ability was exceptional. On one occasion he put a Hudson down at Gibraltar at night in a fog without blind approach facilities.

Question 6. The loading of the aircraft was as follows:- Nose 1545 lbs, forward bomb bay 1793 lbs, rear bomb bay 827 lbs, tail 1161 lbs when the aircraft left Cairo. In addition an extra passenger boarded the aircraft at Gibraltar and was seated in one of the b omb bays. What is your opinion of this distribution of load?

Answer. This load would tend to make the aircraft tail heavy and if half-flap, were used, would most probably cause the pilot to push his control column fairly well forward to prevent the nose from rising too high immediately after take off.

Question 7. Have you noticed any tendency to ~~xxxxxxx~~ relax regulations when carrying very important passengers?

Answer. Yes, there have been occasions within my experience when v.i.p's have refused to conform with regulations.

(Signed) J. F. SACH. Squadron Leader.

27th WITNESS. Squadron Leader Canning, Daniel, R.A.F. Station, North Front, Gibraltar, states:-

I am senior medical officer at R.A.F. Station, North Front. The bodies of the following persons recovered from the crash involving Liberator A.L.523 have been examined by me:- General Sikorski, ~~XXXXXXXXX~~ Maj. Gen. Klimecki, Colonel Marecki, Colonel Cazalet, Lieut. Ponikiewski, Brigadier Whiteley, Mr. Pinder, Colonel Gralewski, Warrant Officer Zalsberg, Sergeant Kelly and F/Sgt. Gerrie. My examination of all these bodies showed head injuries and multiple injuries, the degree of violence in my opinion suggesting that the time of death approximated to the time of the accident. The following bodies have not yet been recovered:- Mr. Kulakowski, Mme. Lesniowska, Mr. Lock, Sqn. Ldr. Herring and Ft/Sgt. Hunter. My examination of Flt. Lt. Prchal after the crash showed him to be suffering from shock, lacerations of the face, and fracture of the right ankle.

(Signed) D. CANNING. S/Ldr.
19.7.43

1st WITNESS. Flight Lieutenant Prchal recalled.

Question 1. Was the bomb door on Liberator A.L. 523 connected to the hydraulic system?

Answer. I don't think so, but I am not certain as this was my first trip on this aircraft.

Question 2. Is the interior of the bomb compartment lighted?

Answer. Yes, all the time.

Question 3. Is it possible that the Flight Engineer would have failed to observe whether either the inside door or the bomb door were not shut?

Answer. No, it is not possible because after running up engines and before taking off he walked up and down the fuselage before reporting to me that everything was all right.

Question 4. Have you ever heard of a mail bag or other article falling out of a Liberator when taxying or during flight?

....../Continued.

Page 15.

- 14 -

1st WITNESS- continued.

Answer. No, but if it were loaded in the nose it is possible for an article to fall out through the nose wheel aperture if not secured.

Question 5. Did you cut your main switches before the crash?

Answer. No, I cannot reach them.

Question 6. Do you think the 2nd Pilot switched them off before you crashed?

Answer. I do not know, but the engines were running perfectly normally until I closed the throttles.

Question 7. What did you mean when you stated in your evidence that you told the 2nd Pilot to "check over the controls"?

Answer. I meant "unlock the controls", and I think that is what I said, because I thought he had locked them with the locking lever.

Question 8. Do you normally push the stick forward to build up speed after take off?

Answer. Yes, always.

Question 9. In this instance do you consider that you would have pushed the control column as far forward as the locking position?

Answer. Yes, I think I did, in fact I might even have pushed it beyond that position.

Question 10. Did you look at your altimeter after you had taken off?

Answer. Yes, I certainly did and it indicated 150 feet. It was set at zero before take off.

Question 11. What is the cock pit drill for your second pilot on take off?

Answer. Before taking off:- $\frac{1}{2}$ flaps down, gills closed, booster pumps on, unlock controls, rich mixture. In taking off:- I open throttles to 40 inches boost, 2nd Pilot takes over throttles opening them on my instructions to 48 inches. At about 200 feet I then give him instructions to switch booster pumps off, but I had not reached that stage in this instance.

(Signed) E. M. PRCHAL. F/Lt.

28TH WITNESS. Wing Commander Arthur Montague Stevens, Air Headquarters, Gibraltar, states:-

I am the Chief Technical Officer at Gibraltar and I was present during the salvage operations of Liberator A.L. 523. The first portion of the aeroplane to be lifted out of the water was the tail unit complete with elevators, fins, and rudders. This had broken off the fuselage just forward of the leading edge of the tail plane. I first inspected the elevator trimming tabs which I found to be almost in the neutral position. The elevators were free to move except for some damage on one end to the skin which prevented total movement up and down. The main planes and centre section complete with all four engines, but severely damaged forward of the navigator's position, was next hoisted up. The fuselage aft of the trailing edge of the main plane was missing as was all the bomb compartment from the navigator's seat back. The flaps were comparatively undamaged and were approximately $\frac{3}{8}$ths down. The starboard plane and aileron were also undamaged, but the port wing and aileron, especially the latter, were damaged.

34

As it was found impossible to lift the mainplane on to the ship, it was decided to move the mainplane in nearer the shore, and drop it

....../continued.

Page 16.

- 15 -

28TH WITNESS. (continued)

pending further investigation of the actual site where the rest of the wreckage lay. The next item to be lifted up was the badly damaged fuselage shell. This consisted of that portion aft of the bomb bay down to just forward of the tail plane. No flooring was left intact, only the roof and sides being recovered. The propellors and reduction gear housings had come off all four engines and only two could be seen in subsequent diving operations, of whice only one has been salvaged. Finally all major wreckage was recovered and taken to the Naval Dockyard, where it was examined by the A.I.B. Inspector. Owing to the dock being urgently required the main plane had to be cut up and removed to the salvage unit where detailed examination occurred.
The tail plane had been examined some time prior to this,however, and the elevator and rudder locking control pulley spindle was found to be sheared. This locking device can be seen in the sketch of the control locking system which I produce herewith, marked exhibit "D". The sliding pinions, which engage respectively in holes in the rudder control tube and a block situated in brackets coming off the ends of the elevator cross shaft, bore no signs of having been subjected to a shear load, which if they had been engaged some signs might have been expected. The whole rudder and elevator locking unit was removed from the tail plane by the A.I.B. Inspector and despatched to U.K. for examination by Farnborough.. Information has recently been received that the operating spindle sheared due to a torsional stress, caused possibly in the crash.
Examination of the throttle pedestal showed the throttle levers to be in the nearly closed positions, the actual throttle positions on the carburettor being as follows:-

No. 1 Engine. - almost closed.
No. 2 " - 1/3rd open.
No. 3 " - wide open.
No. 4 " - half open.

All cooling gills were right closed. The 1st Pilot's control column was badly jammed by sand in the fully forward position, but, on removal of the sand, was found to be perfectly free and in turn this freed the 2nd Pilot's column.
Both main engine ignition switches were found off. The aeroplane was so badly damaged around the pilots cockpit and forward of the centre section that the final positions of any controls operated by cables might be very misleading.
The control column sprockets and chains were found to be in good condition superficially but I have not carried out any minute examination for any signs of foreign bodies having been jammed between the teeth and chain rollers.
The petrol cocks were found to be in the following positions:-

No. 1 Engine. - on.
No. 2 " - partly off due to broken lever.
No. 3 " - on.
No. 4 " - on.

The propeller pitch control switches on the control pedestal were all in the neutral position. Owing to the loss of the reduction gear housings off two engines only two pitch control units are available for inspection. This has revealed that the propellers of Nos. 3 and 4 engines were in fine pitch.
From an examination of the undercarriage it would appear that it was fairly well up at the time of impact with the water as the locks, both up and down positions, are undamaged as are the tyres and wheel fairings.

(Sgd) A.M.STEVENS. W/Cdr.

Question 1. To what extent are the control cables covered in their passage through the fuselage in this mark of Liberator ?

Answer. They are protected by a semi-circular metal shield running longitudinally down the port and starboard sides of the bomb bay, whence they pass through the bulk head under pulleys. Aft of this bulk head they are unprotected for the remainder of their travel to the tail unit.

......../continued.

Page 17.

- 16 -

Question 2. Is it possible for these controls cables to be jammed or obstructed by baggage or passengers in the fuselage ?

Answer. In my opinion, no. I have carried out tests in which I have attempted to restrict all movement of the pilot's control to the elevators. This consisted of clutching the elevator control cables, lying against them and stuffing pieces of rag hard between the cable and its pulleys, all of which had no effect whatsoever. I also attempted by holding the elevator and rudder controls in the neutral position to engage the locking control mechanisms by pulling down on the locking control cables. I was unable to exert sufficient pull on the cable to rotate the actuating pulley.

Question 3. Can you state from examination of the propellers to what extent the engines were under power at the moment of impact ?

Answer. I would not care to give any definite answer as there is only one propeller salvaged which has been examined. From its appearance I would not say it was under much power at impact.

(Sgd) A.M.STEVENS. W/Cdr.

20TH WITNESS. Flight Lieutenant Posgate recalled states :-

Whilst I was engaged in searching for survivors from Liberator A.L. 523. in my H.S.L. I received a message over the R/T stating that aircraft would co-operate and drop flares. I replied that there was a lot of petrol floating on the water. Subsequently a number of flares were dropped over a period of about 20 minutes. They were of little value and all were extinguished before entering the water.

(Sgd) A.M. POSGATE. F/Lt.

35

Page 18.

3

7. We (I) have examined the following aircraft, engine, flight authorization book, and pilot's flying log books and also Form 700 and have ascertained :

Description of book and form	Remarks, including material facts supplementing or confirming evidence of witnesses and whether all necessary inspections were carried out prior to the flight.
Engine) log Airframe) books.	Correct.
Original F.700.	Correct.
Travelling F.700.	Destroyed in crash. All necessary inspections were carried out prior to flight.
Captain's)Flying	Correct and up to date, no endorsements.
2nd Pilot)log bk.	Correct and up to date, no endorsements.
Flight Authorisation Book.	Not available at Gibraltar.

NOTE.—If any of these Documents have not been examined, this must be stated and reason given.

8. We (I) have ~~have not~~ visited the scene of the accident before ~~after~~ aircraft was ~~were~~ removed and have found the following material facts :

Aircraft totally submerged in 5 to 6 fathoms.
Parachutes were not used.

9. We (I) have been unable to obtain the evidence of the following material witnesses :

Name	Rank	Unit	Reasons precluding obtaining of evidence	How concerned with accident

10. **CONCLUSIONS.** Under this Heading the following should always be included :

(a) Brief description of the accident and its attendant circumstances.
(b) Diagnosis of cause or causes including all contributory factors.
(c) Recommendations, if called for.

(a) Liberator AL 523, total all up weight 54,600 lbs, took off from Gibraltar at 2307 B hours on the 4th of July 1943 bound for U.K. The weather was fine, wind light, no cloud, visibility 10 miles.
The aircraft was airborne after a run of approximately 1100 yards, climbed to about 150 feet in a perfectly normal manner and then gradually lost height, striking the sea on an even keel approximately 1200 yards after leaving the ground.
The evidence suggests that the pilot had throttled back a moment before impact and that his engines had been running normally up to that time.
The pilot was recovered by the Station rescue dinghy within six minutes of the crash and was the sole survivor.

(b) The cause of the accident was, in the opinion of the Court, due to the aircraft becoming uncontrollable for reasons which cannot be established. The pilot, having eased the control column forward to build up speed after take-off, found that he was unable to move it back at all, the elevator controls being virtually jammed somewhere in the system. It is impossible, from the evidence available and examination of the wreckage, to offer any concrete reason as to why the elevator system should have become jammed.

(c) It is recommended that all passengers, regardless of their importance, should :-
(i) be checked by the proper authority at the aerodrome of departure prior to emplaning.
(ii) have parachute harness and Mae West, if applicable, fitted by such authority.
(iii) receive instruction in abandonment of aircraft and ditching drill, if applicable, on entering the aircraft.
(iv) be checked by the proper authority at the aerodrome of arrival.
(v) clearly understand that they are entirely under the orders of the Captain, at all times whilst carried in the aircraft, who will ensure that applicable regulations are enforced.

....../continued

Page 19.

4

10. (Continued) (d) It is recommended that the provisions of K.R. & A.C.I. para.704 "Securing of loose articles", should be strictly enforced. The ma[illegible], which was found on the runway after Liberator AL.523 had taken off, had been st[illegible] in the port forward bomb bay according to information received from H.Q. M.E. In view of the evidence of the 1st witness, however, the wooden door in the false floor to the bomb compartment must be presumed to have been closed, and, furthermore, had the bomb door itself been open, this would have been immediately apparent owing to the resulting draught. It is not possible, therefore, from the available evidence to explain how this bag came to be on the runway.

(e) It is recommended that the instructions for the distribution of the aircraft manifest (form 1256) given on that form, should be adhered to. See evidence of 10th witness.

(f) The life of the pilot, F/Lt.Prchal, was undoubtedly saved by the promptness of seven airmen who, although not on duty at the time, were able to launch the small rescue dinghy, kept on a slipway by the east end of the runway, and reached the scene of the accident in a few minutes. It is considered that great credit is due to these airmen for their prompt action and also to the Station Commander who was responsible for initiating the rescue dinghy organisation. It is, however, recommended that a power dinghy be provided to replace the existing rowing dinghy, and also that a duty crew stand by throughout 24 hours. A further recommendation is that the dinghy should be provided with a small searchlight, i.e. Aldis lamp, for searching and signalling purposes. Investigations by the Court have revealed that 15 minutes is the minimum time under the present organisation in which the duty high speed launch can be expected off the east end of the runway after an aircraft has crashed.

......./continued.

11. This accident ~~(is not)~~ is being investigated by the Accidents Investigation Branch.

Signature of President (or Investigating Officer) (Sgd) J. G. ELTON. G/Capt.

" (Member of Court) (Sgd) A.W. Kay. W/Cdr.

" " " (Sgd) D.M. Wellings. S/Ldr.

Date of signing 23/7/43.

REPORT OF COMMANDING OFFICER File Ref. No.

I agree with the conclusions and recommendations of the Court. I am however doubtful of the necessity for a power boat being maintained at the eastern end of the runway in view of the fact that Naval craft are always on patrol in this area and the rapidity with which the high speed launches can reach the spot, moreover, a power boat could only be launched from this beach in very favourable sea conditions.

Signature of C.O. (Sgd) S.P.Simpson. Air Commodore

Date of signing 24/7/43. Commanding R.A.F. ~~Station~~ Gibraltar.

10. (Continued)

(g) The dropping of flares from aircraft to illuminate a crash, as occurred in this instance, is considered very inadvisable in view of the risk of fire. The responsibility for the illumination of crashes in the sea in the vicinity of the Rock should rest with the searchlight posts.

(h) The security organisation for North Front airfield would appear to be comprehensive and thorough. It is considered that there is no question of sabotage involved in the crash of Liberator AL.523. The fact remains, however, that the 22nd witness removed a mail bag from Liberator AL. 523 at approximately 0700 B hours on the 4th July without being observed by the 23rd witness whose duty it was to guard this aircraft from 0600 - 0800 hours that morning. Furthermore, it is considered that this guard should have been able to see whether or not anyone entered the aircraft, despite the large size of a Liberator, if he had kept it under continual observation.

The provisions of K.R. & A.C.I para.1318 sub-para 2 & 4 have been complied with in respect of the 23rd witness.

37 Exhibits A, B, C, and D attached.

Pages 20 and 21.

Certified True Copy H. D. Bailey

1C

Re-opening of the Court of Inquiry on 3rd August, 1943 at Headquarters Coastal Command by order of Air Marshal Sir J.C. Slessor, K.C.B., D.S.O., M.C., to enquire further into the Flying Accident on 4th July, 1943 at North Front, Gibraltar involving Liberator AL.523.

1st Witness — Flight Lieutenant Prchal recalled.

Question 1. — When you entered Liberator AL.523 on the night of the 4th July, 1943 at North Front Gibraltar, prior to starting up, were the flying controls locked ?

Answer. — Yes.

Question 2. — How were they locked.

Answer — By the locking strap, one end of which held the locking control lever up and the other end, the top of the loop formed where the strap divides, being hooked over the throttle friction nut at the mixture control end.

Question 3. — Were they locked when you taxied out to take off ?

Answer — Yes, by the strap in the same way.

Question 4. — Who unlocked the controls when you stopped to carry out your cockpit drill at the end of the runway ?

Answer. — The 2nd Pilot on my instructions.

Question 5. — When you carried out your cockpit drill on the runway prior to taking off on this occasion, what exactly did you do?

Answer. — I ran up my engines; Flight Engineer was sitting in 2nd Pilot' seat looking at the instruments. I opened the engines one at a time up to 30 inches boost, and tested the pitch control. I then opened each engine to 48 inches and throttled back to 2000 r.p.m. in fine pitch, at which figure the Flight Engineer tested the magneto switches and I tested the two speed superchargers. The engines were satisfactory.

(2) I then sent my Flight Engineer to the bomb bay to switch the hydraulic booster pump on, check up the petrol cocks to ensure they were fully open, and to ensure that the bomb doors were closed. The Flight Engineer reported that all was in order.

(3) The 2nd Pilot took up position in the 2nd Pilot's seat and I checked the automatic pilot. The three oil cut-off valves were off, and the main switch off.

(4) I trimmed the aircraft for take off. The elevator trim was zero, rudder trim four divisions to the right, and ailerons one and a half to the right.

(5) I uncaged directional gyro and artificial horizon of the automatic pilot. The directional gyro was set to the compass reading and the artificial horizon assumed a horizontal position. The artificial horizon on the instrument panel was of the free type and this had already assumed a horizontal position. I set altimeter to read zero.

(6) I then instructed the 2nd Pilot to carry out his cockpit drill which I checked as he did it. He put flaps half down, closed the gills, switched on fuel booster pumps, unlocked the flying controls and put mixture controls in rich.

(7) I then tested the elevators, ailerons and rudders for complete freedom of movement to the limit of their range. They were completely free.

(8) I instructed the wireless operator to switch on generators.

(9) I then released the parking brake, turned into position and took off.

Question 6. — Did you see the 2nd Pilot release the flying controls locking lever strap ?

Answer — Yes.

Question 7. — How did he release the strap ?

Page 22.

-2-

Answer. He slipped it off the friction nut and I saw the locking lever go into the fully down position.

Question 8. What happened to the strap ?

Answer. I don't know in this instance, but generally it is left lying on the floor.

Question 9. How was the cockpit lighted.?

Answer. The lights were fully on and the cockpit was well illuminated while the cockpit drill was being carried out, but I turned them down for take-off.

Question 10. Was the Aldis lamp used for signalling before take-off ?

Answer. No;

Question 11. Where was it stowed ?

Answer. In the navigator's compartment.

Question 12. How did you get permission to take-off?

Answer. By a green light from the Airfield Controller.

Question 13. How did you keep Liberator AL.523 straight during its' take off run on this occasion ?

Answer. By throttles first and then rudders.

Question 14. Can you state how much rudder you used.?

Answer. A very slight amount.

Question 15. In previous evidence you stated that rudders, ailerons and elevators were definitely functioning correctly when the aircraft became airborne. Why are you so certain of this ?

Answer. First of all I had to pull the aircraft off the runway by a considerable movement of the control column backwards, and secondly, although I cannot actually remember operating the aileron or rudders in the air, I am certain I should have known if they had not been free.

Question 16. Did you take off by instruments ?

Answer. No, because there was good visibility and a good horizon, but I glanced at my airspeed indicator and altimeter from time to time.

Question 17. Why did you not feel for the control locking lever if you thought the controls were locked ?

Answer. Because if I had bent down to do that, I would not have been able to see the horizon.

Question 18; In what attitude was the aircraft when it struck the sea ?

Answer. Laterally level, about 15° - 20° nose down.

Question 19. Do you know what is the maximum permissible speed with flaps down for a Liberator Mk.II ?

Answer. 155 m.p.h. with flaps fully down.

Question 20. In previous evidence, you stated that your speed built up to 165 m.p.h. with flaps half down. Why did you do this ?

Answer. Normally I would allow my speed to build up to 155 m.p.h. but in this instance, as I could not pull the control column back, my speed built up to 165 m.p.h. before crashing.

39

Page 23.

-3-

Question 21. When you eased the control column forward to build up speed, did you notice the nose go down ?

Answer. Yes.

Question 22. Can you state whether there was any play in the controls of Liberator AL.523 (a) locked (b) unlocked ?

Answer. (a) I cannot remember. (b) I do not know, the controls of this aircraft were very heavy, and in view of this I think I should have noticed if there had been any play.

Question 23. Who raised the undercarriage on this occasion ?

Answer. I did.

Question 24. Is there an appreciable increase in speed when the undercarriage goes up in Mark II Liberators.?

Answer. While it is going up there is no increase, but when it is going up there is an appreciable increase.

Question 25. What type of Automatic Pilot was fitted to Liberator AL.523 ?

Answer. Sperry.

Question 26. In previous evidence, you stated that you were quite satisfied with the disposal of load prior to taking off on the night of the 4th July, 1943. Why were you satisfied ?

Answer. Firstly, because I had flown Liberator AL.523 from Cairo and the load was the same from Gibraltar with the exception that one additional passenger and his luggage was in the bomb bay, and this additional load made no difference because it was near the centre of gravity of the aircraft; and secondly, when taxying, the aircraft was well balanced on its' main wheels. If there is too much load in the nose she tends to ride on her nose wheel, and if there is too much load aft she tends to drop her tail.

Question 27. How do you know that the flying controls were in fact locked, when you entered the aircraft prior to starting up, or during taxying ?

Answer. First of all because when I got into the aircraft, I helped myself into the seat with the control column and it did not move. All the time I was taxying I had my left hand on the control column and it was quite rigid. Also whilst taxying and using the brakes I should have noticed at once if the rudders had not been locked, since the brake pedal is hinged to the toe end of the rudder pedal.

Question 28. Before entering Liberator AL.523 on the night of the 4th July, 1943 prior to starting up did you check over the exterior of the aircraft ?

Answer. Yes, I always do.

Question 29. Were any covers on or near the aircraft ?

Answer. I am positive when I examined the aircraft on this occasion, there were no covers of any description on or near the aircraft.

Question 30. Do you normally satisfy yourself that the occupants of the aircraft wear Mae West's and/or parachute harnesses.

Answer. Yes, normally I do.

Question 31. What action did you take on this occasion to satisfy yourself that the occupants of Liberator AL.523 were wearing Mae Wests ?

Answer. None.

Question 32. Who provides Mae Wests and parachutes for the passengers and instructs them in their use ?

Answer. A.D.R.U.

Page 24.

-4-

Question 33. Were you wearing a Mae West on this occasion ?

Answer. No. I had my Mae West behind my back where I normally carry it.

Question 34. What is the maximum play in the controls of any Liberator you have flown.

Answer. In elevators less than an inch movement in the control column, but in ailerons I can recollect no instance of play. In rudders, slight play when locked, but none when unlocked.

Signed Prchal F/Lt.

5th August, 1943.

29th Witness. Flight Lieutenant John Willis Buck, Acc.I, Branch, Air Ministry by special arrangement with the Chief Inspector of Accidents, states:-

I am an Inspector of Accidents and was detailed to investigate the accident to Liberator AL.523. I examined in detail the wreckage of the aircraft during the salvage operations and after it was brought ashore. The aircraft was salvaged in three portions, the tail unit, aft part of the fuselage and the main planes including the wreckage of the cockpit and all four engines.

I examined the tail plane, elevators and rudders. There was no evidence of any jamming in the elevators and rudders. All damage was consistent with impact or subsequent salvage operations. The elevator and rudder control surfaces and hinge lines were particularly examined for jamming by some external body. There was no evidence of this having occurred. The entire operating mechanism of the control surfaces were examined and no defect found which could not be attributed to the crash or salvage. The cables had parted under severe tension.

An examination of the pilot's flying controls was made. All sprockets and chains were subjected to a detailed examination. This examination showed no damage to the teeth or walls, of the sprockets. An examination of the chains showed them to be in good condition, there being no signs of over-riding or jamming on any of the links. Both chains were broken at the connecting link, but this was due to the impact of the crash. A complete examination of the control system showed no signs of any jamming previous to the crash.

An examination of the controls locking mechanism showed that all locking pins were disengaged. There was no evidence to show that the locks had been engaged at the moment of impact.

Both dinghies were properly stowed in their housings.

Signed. J.W. Buck.

Question 1. If the locking pins had been engaged at the moment of impact, what would you have expected to find ?

Answer. Signs of shearing or bending of the locking pins.

Question 2. Have you ever heard of a case in which a Liberator attempted to take off or took off with the flying controls locked ?

Answer. Yes, in one case where a Liberator attempted to take off with locked controls but never left the ground. The aircraft ran the full length of the aerodrome and crashed into a hangar at high speed.

Signed J.W. Buck
5.8.43.

40

Page 25.

-5-

30th Witness — Squadron Leader Roland John Falk R.A.E., Farnborough, states:-

I am Chief Test Pilot at the R.A.E., Farnborough and have carried out test flights at various loads including a long distance flight of eleven hours on all marks of Liberator aircraft. My total experience on the type is approximately 60 hours, and total flying experience approximately 4,800 hours.

Signed Roland Falk.

Question 1. With a correctly disposed load, do you consider a Liberator Mark II, with all up weight 54,600 lbs, could leave the ground with its' flying controls locked ?

Answer. It would be possible for a Liberator to take off with the controls locked provided that it reached a sufficiently high indicated speed. As this indicated speed is, however, in the neighbourhood of 180 m.p.h. a take off under these conditions is probably only a theoretical consideration.

Question 2. Would it be possible so to dispose the load that a Liberator aircraft with locked controls could take off in approximately 1100 yards in calm conditions?

Answer. Yes, but in my opinion, if the c.g. was aft to this extent, the aircraft would be unmanageable in any case. If it took off in this condition with the controls locked it would immediately assume a steep climbing attitude and stall. In my opinion this is not a practical possibility.

Question 3. Would it be possible to take a Liberator off with rudders only locked.

Answer. Yes. The steering on the initial stage of the run is done by manipulation of the throttle, and it is quite possible to meet conditions in which there would be no subsequent swing, and therefore there would be no need for rudder correction.

Question 4. Would it be possible for a pilot to hold the control column fully back without realising it had reached the end of its' travel ?

Answer. No. The travel is so great that the pilot would not possibly fail to realise it.

Question 5. Can you tell whether or not the load on a Liberator is correctly disposed whilst taxying ?

Answer. You cannot tell whether it is correctly disposed but an experienced Liberator pilot would know if it were dangerously disposed.

Question 6. If a Liberator aircraft were so loaded that it could take off in 1100 yds with all the flying controls locked, would this fact be obvious to the pilot when taxying ?

Answer. Yes.

Question 7. What is the altimeter position error correction on Liberators Mk.II ?

Answer. At 140 m.p.h. A.S.I. at ground level the correction to be applied to the altimeter reading is - 33 ft. This would not vary appreciably up to 500 ft.

Signed Roland Falk.

31st Witness. Flight Lieutenant Wallace Lynton Watson, R.A.F.Station, Lyneham, states:-

I am 'A' Flight Commander in 511 Squadron, and have just taken over the Flight from Squadron Leader Sach. I am also the Squadron instructor on Liberators and instructed Flight Lieutenant Prchal on Liberators by day and night. He went solo after 50 mins instruction by day and 20 mins by night. In my opinion he was an exceptional pupil, and of over 50 pilots which I have converted to Liberators, Flight

Page 26.

-6-

Lieutenant Prchal was easily the best.

Signed Lynton Watson, F/Lt.

Question 1. How do you interpret the flight limitation that flaps should not be down at speeds exceeding 155 m.p.h.

Answer. This applies to full flaps only and I have often exceeded the figure with half flaps on when making a circuit prior to coming in to land. When taking off with a heavy load, I always build up my speed to at least 165 m.p.h. before taking off any flap.

Question 2. What was the seating accomodation for passengers in Liberator AL.523.

Answer. When I flew it on the previous trip to the fatal one, there were six seats in the fuselage behind the bomb bay bulkhead. The balance of the passengers would be put in the bomb bay on mattresses.

Question 3. What method was there for securing passengers in Liberator AL.523 ?

Answer. Safety belts on the six seats none in the bomb bay.

Signed Lynton Watson, F/Lt.
5.8.43.

1st Witness. Flight Lieutenant Prchal recalled.

Question 1. Are you aware of the altimeter position error on Liberator II aircraft ?

Answer. Yes, I know about it but I never allow for it, becasue it is so small, except when doing blind landings.

Question 2. What is the position error ?

Answer. I think it is about -20ft. That is the reading on Liberator AL.616 which is my own aircraft.

Signed Prchal, F/Lt.

Additional conclusions as a result of the re-opening of the Inquiry into the accident involving Liberator AL.523 at Gibraltar on the 4th July, 1943.

The Court, accompanied by Flight Lieutenant Buck, A.I.B. representative, Wing Commander Dudzinski, Wing Commander Russell and Squadron Leader Everest, Liberator Conversion Unit, Beaulieu, visited the R.A.F. Station, Lyneham for the purpose of exploring the possibilities of the flying controls becoming jammed by the raising of the nose wheel.

A Liberator Mk.II, which O.C. 511 Squadron stated was similar to Liberator AL.523, was jacked up, and the undercarriage system was retracted several times and the nose wheel mechanism carefully examined, both from inside and outside the aircraft, at every stage of its' retraction.

At the conclusion of these tests the Court decided that such jamming of the flying controls by the nose wheel and/or nose wheel retracting mechanism was extremely unlikely and could not be considered as a possible cause of the accident.

41 The additional evidence of the 1st Witness, Flight Lieutenant Prchal, Squadron Leader Falk, Chief Test Pilot R.A.E. Farnborough and Flight Lieutenant Buck, A.I.B. Inspector, has confirmed the opinion of the Court that the elevator controls were jammed by some means other than the flying controls locking mechanism, but that there is no further evidence to show how this jamming occurred. Furthermore, this additional evidence shows that it is not a practical possibility for a Liberator

Page 27.

-7-

aircraft to leave the ground with the flying controls locked in the normal position under the conditions obtaining at the time of the accident. The Court consider that Flight Lieutenant Prchal was in no way to blame for the accident.

The all-up weight of Liberator AL.523 at take off from Cairo on 3rd July, 1943 was 54,313 lbs and this load was distributed as shown in exhibit E. One additional passenger only Col. Gralewski was taken up at Gibralter, as stated by the 10th Witness. He was seated in the bomb bay as stated by the 1st Witness.

The despatching organisation at R.A.F.Station, Lyneham, was examined by the Court and is as follows:-

On arrival, passengers are taken to the A.D.R.U. reception room where they are issued with a parachute and harness, flying clothing two blankets and Mae West and parachute bag. The Captain of the aircraft instructs them in abandonment and dinghy drill and they are then weighed with their kit. They are next briefed by the Intelligence, Customs, Security and Medical Officers. Finally they are taken to the aircraft and placed in their allotted positions by the duty officer of A.D.R.U.

This organisation is considered to be satisfactory and it is recommended that it should be carried out by all A.D.R. Units.

Attention is drawn to the fact that there is no method of securing passengers in the bomb bay of converted Liberator aircraft.

Group Captain P.G. Tweedie, Deputy Chief Investigation(Accidents) was present during the taking of the evidence of Flight Lieutenant Prchal recalled, Squadron Leader Falk, Flight Lieutenant Buck, A.I.B. and Flight Lieutenant Watson at Headquarters, Coastal Command.

President	V.G. ELTON. Group Captain.
Member	A.W. Kay, Wing Commander.
Member	D.M. Wellings Squadron Leader.

Exhibit E attached.

Page 28.

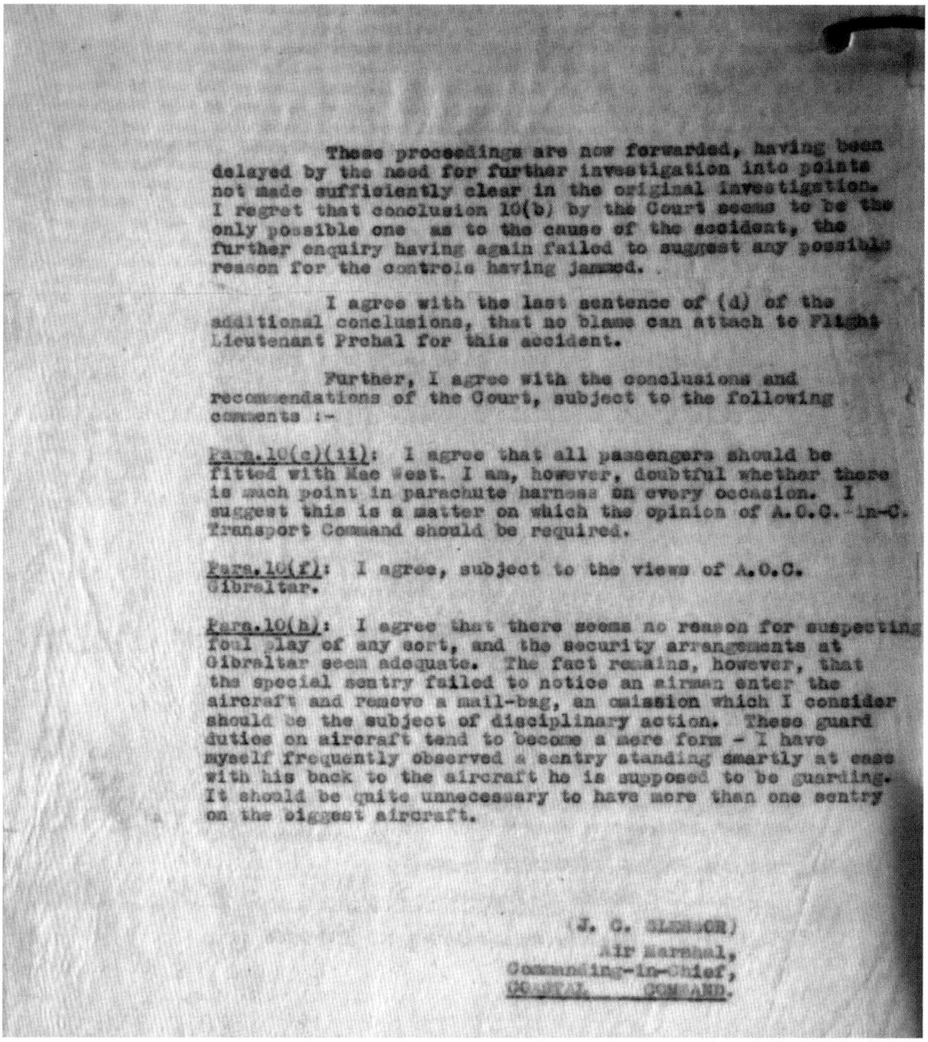

These proceedings are now forwarded, having been delayed by the need for further investigation into points not made sufficiently clear in the original investigation. I regret that conclusion 10(b) by the Court seems to be the only possible one as to the cause of the accident, the further enquiry having again failed to suggest any possible reason for the controls having jammed.

I agree with the last sentence of (d) of the additional conclusions, that no blame can attach to Flight Lieutenant Prchal for this accident.

Further, I agree with the conclusions and recommendations of the Court, subject to the following comments :-

Para.10(c)(ii): I agree that all passengers should be fitted with Mae West. I am, however, doubtful whether there is much point in parachute harness on every occasion. I suggest this is a matter on which the opinion of A.O.C.-in-C. Transport Command should be required.

Para.10(f): I agree, subject to the views of A.O.C. Gibraltar.

Para.10(h): I agree that there seems no reason for suspecting foul play of any sort, and the security arrangements at Gibraltar seem adequate. The fact remains, however, that the special sentry failed to notice an airman enter the aircraft and remove a mail-bag, an omission which I consider should be the subject of disciplinary action. These guard duties on aircraft tend to become a mere form - I have myself frequently observed a sentry standing smartly at ease with his back to the aircraft he is supposed to be guarding. It should be quite unnecessary to have more than one sentry on the biggest aircraft.

(J. C. SLESSOR)
Air Marshal,
Commanding-in-Chief,
COASTAL COMMAND.

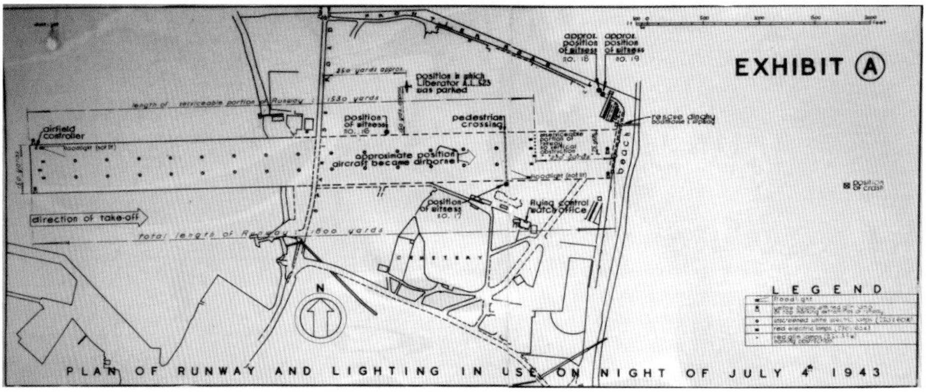

Pages 29 and 30.

BIBLIOGRAPHY AND SOURCES

PRIMARY SOURCES

Archiwum Akt Nowych (AAN) – Archives of New Records

Akta Władysława Sikorskiego, Sygnatura 204

Churchill Archives Centre

CHAR 20/110 Prime Minister's Personal Telegrams Serial No. T501/3-T600/3, April 1943

CHAR 20/111 Prime Minister's Personal Telegrams Serial No. T601/3-T700/3, May 1943

CHAR 20/114 Prime Minister's Personal Telegrams Serial No. T901/3-T100/3, 28 June 1943–10 July 1943

Flight Manuals

Air Ministry, Consolidated LB 30A and Liberator I Aeroplanes Four Twin Wasp R.1830 S3C4-G Aero-Engines, Air Publication 1867A, 5 February 1941

Air Ministry, Pilot and Flight Engineer's Notes Liberator III, V and VI. 3rd Edition, Air Publication 1867C, E, F & G.-P.N., February 1944

Air Ministry, Pilot's Notes for Liberator II Airplane Four Twin Wasp R.1830 S3C4G Engines, Air Publication 1867B, 21 May 1941

Air Ministry, Pilot's Notes General, Air Publication 2095, April 1943

Air Ministry, Pilot's Notes The Hudson III Aeroplane Two Cyclone Gr. 1820-G.205A Engines, Air Publication 1690 C, January 1941

Air Ministry, Pilot's Notes for Mitchell III Two Cyclone R-2600-29 Engines, Air Publication 2341C-P.N., May 1945

Commanding General, Army Air Forces, Pilot's Handbook of Flight Operating Instructions. Navy Model PB4Y-2 Airplane, AN 01-5EN-1, 15 April 1945

Consolidated Aircraft Corporation, Handbook of Operations and Flight Instructions for the Model LB-30B Bombardment Airplane, No. ZE-32-016, 28 February 1941

Consolidated Aircraft, Flight Manual B-24D Airplane, 15 September 1942

Fleet Air Wing, Headquarters Squadron, Transition Landplane Unit. Pilots Guide Consolidated "Liberator" PB4Y-1 type Aircraft

Flight Handbook, USAF Series, TB-25J Aircraft, T.O. 1B-25(T)J-1, 5 July 1957, aircorpslibrary.com

Headquarters AAF, Office of Flight Safety, C-87, Revised 1 May 1945

Headquarters AAF, Office of Flight Safety, Pilot Training Manual for the Liberator B-24. AAF Manual No. 50-12

The Chief of the Bureau of Aeronautics, Pilot's Handbook of Flight Operating Instructions, Navy Model RY-3 Airplane, AN 01-5CB-1, 1 December 1944

US Army Air Forces, Pilot's Flight Instructions for Army Models C-87, C-87A and C-87B Navy Models RY-1 and RY-2 Airplanes, AN 01-5CA-1, 15 December 1943 (Revised 5 July 1944)

Her Majesty's Stationery Office

The Royal Air Force Medical Services, Her Majesty's Stationery Office, 1955

Heritage Canada

William Lyon Mackenzie King: Memoranda and notes (J4): H-1522: https://heritage.canadiana.ca/view/oocihm.lac_reel_h1522/ Last accessed: 9 August 2023

Hoover Institution Library & Archives

TN: 96474. Title: Bohdan Kleczyński papers. Author: Kleczyński, Bohdan, 1902–1944.

Imperial War Museum (IWM)

The crew of a Lockheed Hudson Mark I, N7318, of No. 206 Squadron RAF which rescued the commander-in-chief of Free Polish Forces, General Władysław Sikorski and his staff from Bordeaux, France, in June 1940. © IWM CH 358, 1940-07. https://www.iwm.org.uk/collections/item/object/205208467

WALKER, CHARLES WILLIAM THOMAS (ORAL HISTORY), SOUND. © IWM 30271, Reel 9/23, 29 August 2007, https://www.iwm.org.uk/collections/item/object/80029753 Last accessed 10 August 2023

WALKER, CHARLES WILLIAM THOMAS (ORAL HISTORY), SOUND. © IWM 30271, Reel 13/23, 29 August 2007 https://www.iwm.org.uk/collections/item/object/80029753 Last accessed 10 August 2023

Interviews

Waterfield, Jack, Audio_11_05_2021_10_28_30 am, 5 November 2021, Garth Barnard

Waterfield, Jack, Audio_11_05_2021_11_30_31 am, 5 November 2021, Garth Barnard

Waterfield, Jack, Audio, 24 February 2022, Oskie Films

Memoirs

Anders, Władysław, *An Army in Exile: The Story of The Second Polish Corps*, Battery Press, 2004

Beurling, George, Roberts, Leslie, *Malta Spitfire: The Diary of an Ace Fighter Pilot*, Grub Street, 2011

Cazalet, Victor, *With Sikorski to Russia*, Curwen Press, 1942

Ciechanowski, Jan M, *Defeat in Victory*, Doubleday & Company, 1947

Knowles, Sydney, *A Diver in the Dark*, Woodfield Publishing, 2009

Lipski, Józef, Raczyński, Edward, Stroński, Stanisław *Trzy podróże gen. Sikorskiego do Ameryk*, Instytut Historyczny im. gen. Sikorskiego, 1949

Mikołajczyk, Stanisław, *The Rape of Poland: The Pattern of Soviet Aggression*, Arcole Publishing, 2017

Mitkiewicz, Leon, *Z gen. Sikorskim na obczy'znie: fragmenty wspomnień*, Instytut Literacki, 1968

Podoski, Victor, 'General Sikorski: Some Personal Reminiscences', *Queen's Quarterly*, Vol. 53, 1946, pp. 314–326

West, Bruce, *The Man Who Flew Churchill*, McGraw-Hill Ryerson, 1975

Mission Reports

Headquarters 98th Bombardment Group Sorties 1 May–31 May 1943, *Sortie Report. 6 May 1943 – 343rd Squadron, Type of Aircraft B-24D, Aircraft No. 112, Aircraft Letter U.* Van fleet, Captain S. C., Air Corps, Intelligence Officer, Accessed from https://www.taracopp.com/98th-Bombardment-Group-WWII/W-051943/i-QrNX8S2 Last accessed 10 August 2023

Navigational Information

JEPPESEN JeppView 3.5.2.0 LXGB (Gibraltar AB), 16 February 2008

Narodowe Archiwum Cyfrowe (NAC) The National Digital Archive

Gen Władysław Sikorski w kabinie pilota samolotu (Gen Władysław Sikorski in the pilot's cabin of the plane) https://www.szukajwarchiwach.gov.pl/en/jednostka/-/jednostka/5974766/obiekty/284956#opis_obiektu

Statki w miejscu katastrofy samolotu, którym leciał gen. Władysław Sikorski (Ships at the crash site of the plane of which General Sikorski flew) https://www.szukajwarchiwach.gov.pl/en/jednostka/-/jednostka/5919838/obiekty/303818 Last accessed 10 August 2023

Official Documents

Ministry of Defence, JSP 832, *Guide to Service Inquiries*, October 2008

Nichols, J, *Investigating Air Accidents*, House Of Representatives, Report No. 2383, 23 July 1942 https://books.google.ca/books?id=C6fhJiXp34oC

Office of the Historian, Foreign Service Institute, United States Department of State. *Foreign Relations of the United States: Diplomatic Papers, 1943, The British Commonwealth, Eastern Europe, the Far East, Volume III.* https://history.state.gov/historicaldocuments/frus1943v03

US Department of Transportation, Federal Aviation Administration, *Transport Water Impact and Ditching Performance*, DOT/FAA/AR-95/54, March 1996

United States, Munitions Board, Aircraft Committee, Subcommittee on Air Force-Navy-Civil Aircraft Design Criteria; United States. Army-Navy-Civil Committee on Aircraft Design Criteria. *Strength Of Metal Aircraft Elements. Anc-5 Bulletin*, 1951

Public Safety Canada

Report of the Royal Canadian Mounted Police for the Year Ended 31 March 1943 https://www.publicsafety.gc.ca/lbrr/archives/rcmp-rrcmp-1943-eng.pdf Last accessed 10 August 2023

Report of the Royal Canadian Mounted Police for the Year Ended 31 March 1945 https://www.publicsafety.gc.ca/lbrr/archives/rcmp-rrcmp-1945-eng.pdf Last accessed 10 August 2023

Reports

Aeroplane and Armament Experimental Establishment Boscombe Down, 3rd Part of Report No. A&AEE/769.a Liberator III. L.V.337,'Brief performance and tail buffet tests', 31 July 1942 http://www.wwiiaircraftperformance.org/B-24/B-24.html Last accessed 21 August 2023

Army Air Forces Headquarters, Air Technical Service Command, 'ATSC cold weather tests: winter 1944–1945' Army Air Forces Report No. 5230, Accessed from https://collections.nlm.nih.gov/catalog/nlm:nlmuid-101708855-bk Last accessed 10 August 2023

Fisher, L J, Hoffman, E L, 'Ditching Investigations of Dynamic Models and Effects of Design Parameters on Ditching Characteristics', Report 1347 and Technical Note 3946, National Advisory Committee for Aeronautics, 1958

Fisher, L J, Steiner, M F, 'Ditching Tests with a 1/16-Size Dynamic Model of the Army B-24 Airplane in Langley Tank No. 2 and on an outdoor catapult', Wartime Report L-620, National Advisory Committee for Aeronautics, 1945

Headquarters Eighth Air Force office of the Commanding General APO 634, 'Statistical Summary of Eighth Air Force Operations European Theater 17 Aug 1942–8 May 1945'

Smith, A G, Warren C H E, Wright, D F, 'Investigations of the Behaviour of Aircraft When Making a Forced Landing on Water (Ditching)' Ministry Of Supply Aeronautical Research Council, R. & M. No. 2917, Her Majesty's Stationery Office, 1957

Westfall, J R, 'Accelerations Measured at Center of Gravity and Along Span of the Wing of a B-24D Airplane in Landing Impacts', Report No. L-583, National Advisory Committee for Aeronautics, 1944

Westfall, J R, 'Measurements of Landing-Gear Forces and Horizontal-Tail Loads in Landing Tests of a Large Bomber-Type Airplane', Report No. 1140, National Advisory Committee for Aeronautics, 1946

War Department Air Corps Material Division, 'Acceptance Performance Tests', Memorandum Report PHQ-M-19-1401-A on Consolidated B-24D, airplane, A.C. No. 40–696, 22 May 1942, http://www.wwiiaircraftperformance.org/B-24/B-24.html Last accessed 21 August 2023

Service Bulletins

Field Service Bulletins, Consolidated Vultee Aircraft Corporation, Vol. 2 No. 1, 1943–4

Technical Manuals

Consolidated Vultee Aircraft Corporation, *Handbook of Erection and Maintenance Instructions for The Model LB-30 "Liberator II" Bombardment Airplane*, Air Publication 1867-B, 15 April 1941

Consolidated Vultee Aircraft Corporation, *Service and Training Manual Electricity B-24D Airplane*, 15 August 1942

Consolidated Vultee Aircraft Corporation, *Service and Instruction Manual Airplane General B-24 Bombardment Airplane*, Second Edition, 1944

Consolidated Vultee Aircraft Corporation, *Service and Instruction Manual Airplane General and Armament. PB4Y-2 Bombardment Airplane*, 1944

Ford Motor Company, Ford Airplane School, Cable Rigging (Surface Controls) Shop Theory Department, *B-24 E*, 5 June 1943, Benoit De Mulder personal collection

Minneapolis-Honeywell, *Here's How Operation of the C-1 Autopilot*, c.1944 Accessed from: https://aircorpslibrary.com/operation-of-the-c-1-autopilot/ Last accessed 10 August 2023

Pioneer Aircraft Instruments, Flight Security, *Pioneer Instruments, Bendix catalogue, manual for flight instruments*, c.1940, Accessed from https://aircorpslibrary.com/pioneer-aircraft-instruments/ Last accessed 10 August 2023

US Army Air Forces, *Aircraft Inspection and Maintenance Guide For B-24D, RB-24E, B-24G, B-24H and B-24J Aircraft*, Issue No. 1 (No. 00-20A-2-B-24), 20 July 1943, revised 1 May 1944

US Army Air Forces, *Erection and Maintenance Instructions for Army Models AT-18 and AT-18A*, T.O. No. 01-75KA-2, 20 August 1943

US Army Air Forces, *Erection and Maintenance Instructions for Army Models B-24D, G, H and J, RB-24C and E Navy Model PB4Y-1 British Models Liberator BIII, BIIIA, BIV, GRV, GRVI, and BVI*, T.O. No. 01-5EC-2, 20 July 1943, revised 1 July 1944

US Army Air Forces, *Index of Army-Navy Aeronautical Equipment – Instruments*, T.O. No. 05-1-67, 20 June 1944, Accessed from: https://aircorpslibrary.com/index-of-army-navy-aeronautical-equipment-instruments-oct15injw63/ Last accessed: 21 August 2023

US Army Air Forces, *Operation and Service Instructions for Automatic Pilot Type A-3*, T.O. No. 05-45AB-1, 15 October 1943, revised 10 September 1945

US Army Air Forces, *Operation and Service Instructions for Gyro Horizon Indicators (Sperry)*, AN 05-20GD-1, 15 February 1946

US Army Air Forces, *Service Instructions for Automatic Pilot Type A-3*, T.O. No. 05-45AB-2, 15 October 1943, revised 2 May 1946

US Army Air Forces, The Air Service Command, *Airplane Parts Catalog for Army Models B-24D and B-24J Navy Model PB4Y-1 British Models Liberators B III, B VI, B VIII, GR III, GR V, GR VI, and GR VIII*, AN 01-5E-4, 15 June 1944, revised 1 December 1944

US Army Air Forces, The Air Service Command, *Erection and Maintenance Instructions for The Model LB-30 "Liberator II" Bombardment Airplane*, T.O. No. 01-5ED-2, 30 December 1941, revised 1 May 1942

US Army Air Forces, The Air Service Command, *Handbook of Service Instructions for Models B-24C and B-24D Bombardment Airplanes*, T.O. No. 01-5EC-2, 20 January 1942

US Army Air Forces, The Air Service Command, *Parts Catalog for Models B-24 & B-24A Bombardment Airplanes*, T.O. No. 01-5EA-4, 1 September 1941, revised 1 January 1942

US Army Air Forces, The Air Service Command, *Parts Catalog For Army Models C-87, C-87A and AT-22 Navy Models RY-1 and RY-2 British Model Liberator C VII Airplanes*, T.O. No. 01-5-4, 25 August 1944, revised 10 March 1945

US Army Air Forces, The Air Service Command, *Preliminary Assembly Spare Parts List Consolidated Model LB-30 (British Liberator Airplane)*, T.O. No. 01-5ED-4, 30 December 1944

US Army Air Forces, The Air Service Command, *Repair Instructions For The Model LB-30 "Liberator II" Bombardment Airplane*, T.O. No. 01-5ED-3, 30 December 1941, revised 20 April 1942

US Department of Transportation, Federal Aviation Administration, *Airframe & Powerplant Mechanics: Airframe Handbook*, AC 65-15A, 1976

Wright Aeronautical Corporation, *Overhaul Manual Wright Aircraft Engines Cyclone 9 GC*, Third Edition, Part No. 114323-N3, October 1943

The National Archives (TNA), Kew

AIR 2/9234 Accident at Gibraltar to Liberator aircraft in which General Sikorski was killed: Court of Inquiry proceedings, 1943–1946

AIR 2/15113 General Sikorski, Prime Minister of Polish Government in Exile: court of inquiry into death in Liberator aircraft accident, Gibraltar, 4 July 1943; related papers, 1943–1972
AIR 8/779 Flying accident causing the death of General Sikorski, July 1943
AIR 10/2206 Flying Regulations for the Royal Air Force, 1938
AIR 27/293/15 24 Squadron Operations Record Book, 1 August–31 August 1940
AIR 27/604/11 68 Squadron Operations Record Book, 1 October–31 October 1941
AIR 27/604/12 68 Squadron Operations Record Book, 1 October–31 October 1941
AIR 27/604/13 68 Squadron Operations Record Book, 1 November–30 November 1941
AIR 27/604/14 68 Squadron Operations Record Book, 1 November–30 November 1941
AIR 27/604/15 68 Squadron Operations Record Book, 1 December–31 December 1941
AIR 27/604/17 68 Squadron Operations Record Book, 1 January–28 February 1942
AIR 27/604/19 68 Squadron Operations Record Book, 1 March–31 March 1942
AIR 27/1107/21 173 Squadron Operations Record Book, 1 May–30 June 1943
AIR 27/1107/22 173 Squadron Operations Record Book, 1 June–30 June 1943
AIR 27/1222/12 206 Squadron Operations Record Book, 1 June–30 June 1940
AIR 27/1223/67 206 Squadron Operations Record Book, 1 November–30 November 1943
AIR 27/1223/68 206 Squadron Operations Record Book, 1 November–30 November 1943
AIR 27/1675/43 307 Squadron Operations Record Book, 1 September–30 September 1942
AIR 27/1970/1 511 Squadron Operations Record Book, 1 October 1942–31 January 1943
AIR 27/1970/2 511 Squadron Operations Record Book, 1 January–31 January 1943
AIR 27/1970/4 511 Squadron Operations Record Book, 1 February–28 February1943
AIR 27/1970/6 511 Squadron Operations Record Book, 1 March–31 March 1943
AIR 27/1970/8 511 Squadron Operations Record Book, 1 April–30 April 1943
AIR 27/1970/10 511 Squadron Operations Record Book, 1 May–31 May 1943
AIR 27/1970/12 511 Squadron Operations Record Book, 1 June–30 June 1943
AIR 27/1970/14 511 Squadron Operations Record Book, 1 July–31 July 1943
AIR 27/1971 511 Squadron Operations Record Book Appendices, 1 October 1942–31 October 1945
AIR 28/306 RAF Station Gibraltar (North Front) Operations Record Book, January–December 1943
AIR 28/310 RAF Station Gibraltar (North Front) Operations Record Book, April–December 1943
AIR 29/893/1 Communication Flight, Habbaniya later Communications Flight, Iraq and Persia, then AHQ Communications Flight, Iraq with detachment at Baghdad, June 1943
AVIA 15/3012 Liberator aircraft: ditching safety
AVIA 15/3013 Liberator aircraft: ditching safety
CN 5/26 Court of Inquiry concerning accident to Liberator aircraft AL 523 at Gibraltar in which General Sikorski was killed: plan of runway and lighting in use on night of 4 July 1943 and details of aircraft components
FO 954/19B Private Office papers of Sir Anthony Eden, volume 19 (part B): Persia; Poland
KV 2/516 Secret Service Personal Files: General Władysław Sikorski and General Kazimierz Sosnkowski
KV 3/274 Secret Service Subject Files: Attempted sabotage on BOAC Liberator AM 262
KV 3/275 Secret Service Subject Files: Attempted sabotage on BOAC Liberator AM 262
KV 3/276 Secret Service Subject Files: Attempted sabotage on BOAC Liberator AM 262
TS 58/997 Crown privilege: Prchal v Irving and others, request for production of Court of Inquiry proceedings into the air crash at Gibraltar in 4 July 1943 in which General Sikorski and others were killed
WO 178 War Office: British Military Missions: War Diaries, Second World War, 26 Iraq, June 1942–December 1943

The Polish Institute and Sikorski Museum (PISM)

KOL.1/DCNW/40 & 40a, *Dziennik Czynności Naczelnego Wodza*, Glówczynski and Bowhill, Accident Report, Montreal, 30 November 1942

SECONDARY SOURCES

Books

Bartelski, Jan, *Disasters in the Air: Mysterious Air Disasters Explained*, Airlife, 2001

Bibel, George, *Beyond the Black Box: The Forensics of Airplane Crashes*, The John Hopkins University Press, 2008

Borovik, Genrikh, *The Philby Files: The Secret Life of the Master Spy Kim Philby*, Little, Brown, 1994

Christie, Carl A, Hatch, Fred, *Ocean Bridge: The History of RAF Ferry Command*, University of Toronto Press, 1995

Conway, H G, *Landing gear design*, Chapman & Hall, 1958

Grabowski, Franciszek, *Liberator AL523: Analiza Techniczna Katastrofy Gibraltarskiej*, Instytut Pamięci Narodowej–Komisja Ścigania Zbrodni przeciwko Narodowi Polskiemu, 2017

Gray, George W, *Frontiers of Flight: The Story of NACA Research*, A Polski Emu Knopf, 1948

Hale, Don, *The Final Dive: The Life and Death of 'Buster' Crabb*, Sutton Publishing, 2007

Instytut Historyczny im Gen. Sikorskiego, *Generał Sikorski w dziesiątą rocznicę śmierci.* [Including addresses in English and French], Instytut Historyczny im. gen. Sikorskiego, 1954

Irving, David, *Accident: The Death of General Sikorski*, William Kimber, 1967

Kennedy, Arthur R, Ridley, Jo Ann, *High Times Keeping 'em Flying: An Aviation Autobiography*, Fithian Press, 1992

Klimkowski, Jerzy, *Katastrofa w Gibraltarze. Kulisy śmierci generała Sikorskiego*, Śląsk, 1965

Koper, Sławomir, *Życie prywatne elit Drugiej Rzeczypospolitej*, Belona, 2009

Kukiel, Marian, *Generał Sikorski, żołnierż i maż stanu Polski walczacej*, Instytut Polski i Muzeum Im. Gen. Sikorskiego, 1981

Mulley, Clare, *The Spy Who Loved: The Secrets and Lives of Christine Granville*, St. Martin's Press, 2012

Osborne, Dave, *B-17 FORTRESS MASTERLOG*, Self-published master edit copy

Pallett, E H J, *Aircraft Instruments: Principles and Applications*, Longman Scientific & Technical, 1981

Polak, Bogusław, *Generał broni Władysław Sikorski – generał dywizji Władysław Anders Korespondencja 1941–1943 Wybór dokumentów*, Koszalin, 2000

Sanford, George, *Katyn and the Soviet Massacre of 1940: Truth, Justice and Memory*, Routledge, 2005

Sarner, Harvey, *General Anders and the Soldiers of The Second Polish Corps*, Brunswick Press, 1979

Sword, Keith, *Deportation and Exile: Poles in the Soviet Union, 1939–48*, Macmillan, 1996

Sword, Keith (ed.), *Sikorski: Soldier and Statesman: A Collection of Essays*, Orbis Books, 1990

Thompson, Carlos, *The Assassination of Winston Churchill*, Smythe, 1969

Tighe, Carl, *Tradition, literature and politics in East-Central Europe*, Routledge, 2021

Vincent, Carl, *Canada's Wings 2: The Liberator and Fortress*, Canada's Wings, 1975

Wood, Richard H, Sweginnis, Robert W, *Aircraft accident investigation*, Endeavor, 1995

Urbański, Peter, *To Live Well is to Hide Well: The Lizard Is Coming!*, Self-published, 2017

Journal and Magazine Articles

AIR FORCE: The Official Service Journal of the US Army Air Forces, Vol. 27 No. 6, June 1944

Air Tech: The Magazine of Aircraft Maintenance and Operation, Vol. 1 No. 1, October 1942

Dziennik Polski I Dziennik Żołnierza, 20 kwietnia 1946

Dockray, G H, Meadows, B, Smith, L, 'Cotton Waste', *Textile Research Journal*, Vol. 20 Issue 10, October 1950, pp. 684–718

Foot, M R D, 'The death of General Sikorski', *Intelligence and National Security*, Vol. 21 Issue 3, 2006, pp. 457–458

Grams, Grant, 'Enemies within our bosom: Nazi Sabotage in Canada', *Journal of Military and Strategic Studies*, Vol. 14 Nos. 3 & 4, 2012

Konopka, T, Gross, A, Woźniak, K, Kłys, M, 'Forensic medical examination of the corpse of General Władysław Sikorski, a putative victim of assassination in 1943', *Forensic Science International*, Vol. 202 Issues 1–3, 10 October 2010, pp. e29–e33

McClellan, J L, *B24 Draft*, 2005

Penava, Željko, Penava, Diana Š, Nakić, Marija, 'Woven Fabrics Behavior in Pure Shear', *Journal of Engineered Fibers and Fabrics*, Vol. 10, Issue 4, December 2015, pp. 114–124

Plane facts, Vol. 2 No. 6, June 1944
Ramsey, W G, 'The Death of General Sikorski', *After The Battle*, No. 20, pp. 1–18, 1978
Ramsey, W G, '1978 Sikorski Sequel – Seabed Site Investigation', *After The Battle*, No. 24, pp. 44–49, 1979
Różycki, Mieczysław Jan, 'Katastrofa Gibraltarska Droga do tragedii, część I', *Lotnictwo*, 1/2016, pp. 88-98, 2016
Tebinka, Jacek, 'Śmierć generała Władysława Sikorskiego w świetle nowych dokumentów brytyjskich', *Dzieje Najnowsze*, Vol. XXXIII, 2001, pp. 165–185
Zeszyt Sześćdziesiaty Piąty, Zeszyty Historyczne. TOM 379, 1 stycznia 1983
Zurowski, Michael, 'British Policy Towards the Polish Second Corps', *East European Quarterly*, XXVII, No. 3, September 1993, pp. 271–300

Online Sources

Aircraft Serial Number Search: http://users.rcn.com/jeremy.k/serialSearch.html Last accessed 11 August 2023
Aviation Safety Network: https://aviation-safety.net Last accessed 11 August 2023
B-24J Liberator: http://vintagetin.net/B-24Witchcraft/J/ Last accessed 11 August 2023
British Airways Heritage Collection: https://www.britishairways.com/en-us/information/about-ba/history-and-heritage Last accessed 11 August 2023
British Pathé and the Reuters Historical Collection: https://www.britishpathe.com Last accessed 11 August 2023
Čeští RAFRafáci – Czech RAF Crew [Czech language]: http://www.rafaci.cz/ Last accessed 11 August 2023
Environment Canada: https://climate.weather.gc.ca Last accessed 30 August 2023
Flight Manuals Online: https://www.flight-manuals-online.com/ Last accessed 11 August 2023
Footage Farm Ltd.: Post-WWII – Color, 1945, England: Lancaster Bombers & RAF Crew Mission Preparations. Jun45 https://footagefarm.com/reel-details/wwii/generic/post-wwii---color-1945-england--lancaster-bombers--raf-crew-mission-preparations--jun45 Last accessed 21 August 2023
Free Czechoslovak Air Force: https://fcafa.com/ Last accessed 11 August 2023
Generał Władysław Sikorski Polityk i zołnierz – General Władysław Sikorski Politician and soldier: https://ipn.gov.pl/strony-zewnetrzne/wystawy/general_wladyslaw_sikorski/wstep.html Last accessed 11 August 2023
History of BST: https://greenwichmeantime.com/daylight-saving-time/history-bst/ Last accessed 11 August 2023
Interview of Lieutenant Colonel Edward A Montgomery, USMC Night Fighter Operations in Great Britain in the Bureau of Aeronautics 9 June 1943: http://www.researcheratlarge.com/Aircraft/USMC_RAF_VMFN/ Last accessed 11 August 2023
Military aircraft crashes in the south-west Midlands – 1943 http://www.aviationarchaeology.org.uk/marg/crashes1943.htm Last accessed 14 August 2023
Narodowe Archiwum Cyfrowe (National Digital Archives – Polish language): https://www.nac.gov.pl/ Last accessed 11 August 2023
Polish Squadrons Remembered: http://www.polishsquadronsremembered.com Last accessed 11 August 2023
Swopes, B R, *AL503*, 2018 https://www.thisdayinaviation.com/2-june-1941/
The Cost of Silence: Normalization of Deviance and Groupthink: https://sma.nasa.gov/docs/default-source/safety-messages/safetymessage-normalizationofdeviance-2014-11-03b.pdf Last accessed 11 August 2023
The Polish Institute and Sikorski Museum (PISM): SIK 215 – Gen Sikorski's visit to the Middle East: https://www.youtube.com/watch?v=HzudSolBr34 Last accessed 30 August 203
USASC-USAAS-USAAC-USAAF-USAF Military Aircraft Serial Numbers – 1908 to Present: http://www.joebaugher.com/usaf_serials/usafserials.html Last accessed 11 August 2023
Walker, C W T, First-hand account of aspects of the death of General Sikorski in the crash of the Liberator AL523 at Gibraltar on July 4th 1943: http://www.microscopy-uk.org.uk/dww/sikorski/sikorski.html Last accessed 11 August 2023
Wings Over New Zealand forum: https://rnzaf.proboards.com/thread/22924/years-ago-today-lockheed-hudson?page=1&scrollTo=304031 Last accessed 30 August 2023

Podcasts and Television Documentaries

Milton, Giles, 'Episode 6: Fisherman John's Catch of the Day', *Cover Up: Ministry of Secrets*, 2023
'The Last B-24', *NOVA*, Season 45, Episode 15, PBS, 29 October 2018

NOTES

CHAPTER ONE

1. George Sanford, *Katyn and the Soviet Massacre of 1940: Truth, Justice and Memory*, Routledge, 2005, p. 21
2. Michael Zurowski 'British Policy Towards the Polish Second Corps', *East European Quarterly*, XXVII, No. 3, September 1993, p. 274. Anders planned on a force of 100,000 troops.
3. Keith Sword, *Deportation and Exile: Poles in the Soviet Union, 1939-48*, Macmillan, 1996, pp. 31–32
4. The National Archives (TNA): KV 2/516, 57b. and Instytut Historyczny Im Gen. Sikorskiego, *Generał Sikorski w dziesiątą rocznicę śmierci*, 1954, p. 26
   A memorandum report about Sikorski's visit by the 'Nationalities Branch of the US Offices of Strategic Services for the Director' concluded:
   "It would appear from the evidence cited above that if the creation of unified support for his government among American Poles was one of the objectives of General Sikorski's visit to the United States, his dual defense of the Polish National Council's resolution and the Russian-Polish 1941 treaty constituted a stumbling block which he did not succeed in surmounting. In fact during his stay in the United States the antagonism dividing the supporters and opponents of Sikorski seems to have become more bitter, and the nationalist papers' campaign against Sikorski himself to have become increasingly more violent."
   In three conversations with President Roosevelt, including conferences with Sumner Welles and military authorities, Sikorski presented Polish war and post-war aims. He recommended an offensive in the direction of the Balkans pointing out that control by military forces of the Belgrade-Warsaw axis would guarantee security of this region against future aggressions. He further emphasised that the Polish Eastern frontiers should remain intact, presented plans for a future Western frontier and Central European Federation of European nations extending from the Baltic to the Aegean Sea. Sikorski also requested that the Polish underground army should be recognised as a regular Allied army. He also took part in a meeting of the Allied War Council.
5. TNA: KV 2/516, 56b. Polish sources reported to British intelligence that Sikorski's visit was a total failure in that he claimed Roosevelt had agreed to the necessity of creating buffer states against the Soviet Union. When British ambassador to the USA, Lord Halifax, went to see Roosevelt he was informed that the whole thing was pure fiction on Sikorski's part.
6. Anders, Władysław, *An Army in Exile: The Story of The Second Polish Corps*, Battery Press, 2004, p. 93
7. Sanford, p. 94

8. TNA: CHAR 20/110/92-93, FO 954/19B/491, FO 954/19B/492 24 April 1943. Churchill telegrammed Stalin informing him that Eden had convinced Sikorski not to press for a Red Cross investigation in parallel with the German request as they would use it create a rift between the United Nations and break Polish-Soviet relations. Churchill also urged Stalin to abandon ideas of interrupting relations with the Poles. CHAR 20/111/8-9 28 April 1943. Churchill telegrammed Stalin expressing his disappointment at breaking relations with the Poles without giving time to inform him of results achieved with Sikorski, that the Poles had accepted the British view and wished to work loyally with him.
9. TNA: KV2/516, 61a. Capt F C Derbyshire. 27 March 1943 Report, General Sikorski's Position; 68a. Captain Derbyshire 19 April 1943 Report. "Theodor Zielinski, who is said to be in the Polish intelligence service, told Dr Angel that General Sikorski's position is continually growing worse. Some 30–40 Polish generals, i.e. practically all the Polish officers of high rank over here, are growing more emphatic in their demands that he should cease meddling in politics and confine himself to military affairs."; 13b. 22.4.41 Captain Derbyshire letter to Major Alley: "When Mr Savery (counsellor to the British Embassy to the Polish government) was asked if Sikorski would proclaim himself commander and chief and resign from government he replied Sikorski would never consent as he is an extremely vain and ambitious man always wishing to be in the limelight."
10. Tighe, Carl, *Tradition, literature and politics in East-Central Europe*, Routledge, 2021, pp. 91–93
11. TNA: FO 954/19B/539. From Minister of State Cairo To Foreign Office.
D. 9.56 p.m. July 3rd 1943.
R. 12.5 a.m. July 4th 1943.
"Prime Minister's message was personally delivered by Lord Moyne to General Sikorski who was highly gratified. General Sikorski left today direct for England. Although at one time there were indications of dangerous disagreement between Sikorski and Anders regarding [grp. undec.] unreliability of the Polish Army and certain senior appointments, these difficulties have now been surmounted. General position and results of visit can be regarded as satisfactory. General Sikorski before leaving told General Beaumont Nesbitt that he felt thoroughly satisfied and that he had been able to clear up many misunderstandings. Please inform Mr. Casey."
12. Anders, pp. 147-48; Sarner, Harvey, *General Anders and the Soldiers of the Second Polish Corps*, Brunswick Press, 1979, p. 153
13. TNA: AIR 27/1107/21; AIR 27/1107/22. Middle East air transport for Sikorski and his entourage was provided by No.173 Squadron RAF equipped with Lockheed Lodestar II.
14. Richard Gavin Gardiner Casey was the British Resident-Minister for the Middle East at the time.
15. TNA: CHAR 20/114/24
16. TNA: CHAR 20/114/43
17. Ciechanowski, Jan M., *Defeat in Victory*, Doubleday & Company, 1947, p. 174. Sikorski had telegrammed Ciechanowski in the days prior to 4 July 1943.
18. Office of the Historian, Foreign Service Institute, United States Department of State. *Foreign Relations of the United States: Diplomatic Papers, 1943, The British Commonwealth, Eastern Europe, the Far East, Volume III*, p. 427. Letter from Roosevelt to Sikorski on 7 June 1942; Mikołajczyk, Stanisław, *The Rape of Poland: The Pattern of Soviet Aggression*, Arcole Publishing, 2017, p. 70. Stanisław Mikołajczyk who was Sikorski's deputy prime minister wrote: "Before General Sikorski took off on his last flight – an inspection trip of our army in the Middle East – he asked both the British and American governments to intercede with Stalin and arrange for a Sikorski-Stalin meeting."
19. Ciechanowski, p. 174
20. Office of the Historian, Foreign Service Institute, et al. 424–25, 429–34, 438–39. Telegrams between Secretary of State Cordell Hull, American ambassador to the Soviet Union William Standley, Ambassador to the Polish government-in-exile Anthony Biddle, and Under Secretary of State Sumner Wells. The initiative emphasized the necessity for unity among the United Nations. The main objective being a formal resumption of diplomatic relations, endeavoring at the same time to remove as many grievances of the past as possible, and that no attempt be made to induce the Polish government to make changes in its government. It was further emphasized that should the Soviet government raise any discussion in general terms of rapprochement based on reconstitution of the Polish cabinet, the basic policy of the American government was to be clearly explained. That the question of relief and evacuation of Polish citizens should be discussed along the lines of earlier agreements. And lastly that fundamental questions of citizenship were to be avoided in preliminary conversations as it was feared they would lead to discussions of frontier problems and a deadlock in

negotiations; 16 June 1943, Hull to Standley. Cordell Hull summarized the initiative's justification to William Standley in the following terms:

> "The proposed step by step approach was advanced with a view to building up confidence between the Polish and the Soviet governments and a hope of prevailing upon the Soviet government 'to view the matter primarily in the light of its importance in the prosecution of the war'. Under present circumstances I feel we have little chance of prevailing upon the Soviet government to bring itself to view the question in 'the light of a settlement of the complex post-war problems on a just and equitable basis'. At the same time I feel that we must always be vigilant and prepared fully to support the Poles should it become evident that a gradual capitulation of the Polish government to the basic demands of the Soviet government was being maneuvered."

21. Sword, Keith (ed.), *Sikorski: Soldier and Statesman: A Collection of Essays*, Orbis Books, 1990, p. 151. "At about seven o'clock on Sunday morning, 4 July, Mr Maisky arrived at Gibraltar airfield. His aircraft, a Soviet one with a Soviet crew, was wheeled to a spot on the apron not far from Sikorski's Liberator, and a maintenance party of airmen was detailed to service it."
22. TNA: AIR 28/306, 251. The registration for this BOAC Liberator was G-AGFR.
23. TNA: AIR 28/310, 169. G-AGFR is recorded departing at 12:03 to Cairo West via Marble Arch.
24. *Zeszyt Sześćdziesiaty Piąty, Zeszyty Historyczne*. TOM 379, 1 stycznia 1983, p.103
25. TNA: AIR 27-1971, 2
26. Ministry Of Defence. JSP 832, 1, 2, 23, 24

CHAPTER TWO

27. It is unknown what name Bronislaw Urbański used while on Gibraltar or if he was on the sentry's list of people allowed aboard or near AL523. According to Peter Urbański's book his father went by an assumed name and Polish officer rank. Despite security measures on North Front's apron there were obvious lapses and instances where people approached AL523 and not challenged by sentries. Whether Urbański was on any list of personnel allowed near the aircraft is unknown.
28. Urbański, Peter, *To Live Well is to Hide Well: The Lizard Is Coming!*, Self-published, 2017, pp. 62–71
29. Ibid, pp. 107–9
30. Tighe, pp. 91-93
31. Mulley, Clare, *The Spy Who Loved: The Secrets and Lives of Christine Granville*, St. Martin's Press, 2012, pp. 107, 121–22; Sarner, pp. 152–53
32. Koper, Sławomir, *Życie prywatne elit Drugiej Rzeczypospolitej*, Belona, 2009, p. 246
33. Edward Rydz-Śmigły was a Polish politician, statesman, Marshal of Poland, and commander-in-chief of Poland's armed forces from 1935 to 1939.
34. Mulley, pp. 122, 144
35. Polish author Jerzy Rostkowski in his 2016 book *Swiat Muszkieterów (The World of Musketeers)* suggested final approval for high-level executions such as Witkowski had to go through Poland's commander-in-chief in London, General Sikorski.
36. Tighe, pp. 91–93
37. TNA: AIR 28/310. RAF North Front's ORB war diaries for May, June, and July 1943 list multiple transport flights arriving and departing daily between Britain, North Africa, and the Middle East. Among these flights were aircraft from the RAF's Nos. 24, 216, and 511 Transport Squadrons, BOAC (British Overseas Airways Corporation) flights, and USAAF transport flights; any of which could have served as a possible expedient means for Urbański to enter Gibraltar.
38. TNA: TS 58/997, 351. Klimkowski, Jerzy, *Katastrofa w Gibraltarze. Kulisy śmierci generała Sikorskiego*, Śląsk, 1965, pp. 134, 136–37.
    It is doubtful that Klimkowski had any knowledge that an assassin was being positioned in Gibraltar for an attempt on Sikorski. In 1965 Klimkowski published a book in Poland where he suggested that the crash was engineered by the British with Churchill's approval as part of British support for General Ander's opposition to Sikorski. Klimkowski alleged that Prchal was given a special British co-pilot, a senior intelligence officer, with no flying experience. He further alleges that shortly after take-off Prchal deliberately descended and

flew 30 feet above the water for 650 yards then turned off the engines. He and the co-pilot then jumped out of the Liberator which flew another 70 yards and crashed. Prchal was rescued wearing his life jacket while the co-pilot swam away and was never seen again. In addition to the deliberate crash Klimkowski hypothesized that a bomb hidden in a box of chocolates given to Zofia Leśniowska just prior to her boarding exploded seconds before impact and was the reason her body was never found.

39. *Zeszyt Sześćdziesiaty Piąty, Zeszyty Historyczne*, p. 97
40. TNA: KV 2/516, 35a, 39a, 41c, 42x
41. Interview of Lieutenant Colonel Edward A. Montgomery, USMC Night Fighter Operations in Great Britain in the Bureau of Aeronautics 9 June 1943, pp. 5, 7
42. TNA: AIR 27/604/11 through AIR 27/604/19
43. Free Czechoslovak Air Force Associates: https://fcafa.com/2012/02/01/eduard-prchal/
44. TNA: AIR 2/9234, p. 2
45. TNA: AIR 27/1970/1 through AIR 27/1970/14
46. Free Czechoslovak Air Force Associates
47. *Plane facts*, Vol. 2 No. 6, June 1944, p. 9
48. *AIR FORCE: The Official Service Journal of the US Army Air Forces*, Vol. 27 No. 6, June 1944, p. 38
49. Dockray, G H. Meadows, B. Smith, L., 'Cotton Waste', *Textile Research Journal*, Vol. 20 Issue 10, October 1950, p. 689
50. Penava, Željko, Penava, Diana Š, Nakić, Marija, 'Woven Fabrics Behavior in Pure Shear', *Journal of Engineered Fibers and Fabrics*, Vol. 10, Issue 4, December 2015, pp. 117–18, 122
51. US Army Air Forces, The Air Service Command. *Repair Instructions for The Model LB-30 "Liberator II" Bombardment Airplane*, T.O. No. 01-5ED-3, 30 December 1941, revised 20 April 1942, p. 8; US Department of Transportation, AC 65-15A, pp. 165–66
52. US Army Air Forces, T.O. No. 01-5ED-3, p. 47
53. It was impractical to manufacture the replica from sheet aluminium due to material cost, hardware, and tooling requirements. All described material was obtained inexpensively from a local hardware supplier.
54. TNA: AIR 2/9234, p. 3

CHAPTER THREE

55. Thompson, Carlos, *The Assassination of Winston Churchill*, Smythe, 1969, p. 299
56. Ibid., pp. 173–74
57. Ibid., p. 324
58. Ibid., p. 297
59. Swopes, B R, (2018) AL503. https://www.thisdayinaviation.com/2-june-1941/
60. Nichols, J, *Investigating Air Accidents*, House Of Representatives, Report No. 2383, 23 July 1942, p. 14. The transcript did not indicate which of the two control column sprockets had been jammed by the machine screw.
61. TNA: AIR 2/9234, p. 25
62. TNA: AIR 2/15113, 11
63. Irving, David, *Accident: The Death of General Sikorski*, William Kimber, 1967, pp. 190-92. Irving in his first edition had suggested that a mailbag possibly caught in the nose undercarriage and was pressed against the flight controls when retracted.
64. TNA: AIR 2/15113, 27-29, 34. The theory put forward by Falk and Llewellyn was referred to as 'the falling mailbag'.
65. Ibid., 16. William Kimber & Co. Limited had disassociated itself from the publication of Irving's German-language book. They sent a letter to the German publisher advising them that a new theory put forward by Falk and Llewellyn was seen to be the conclusive explanation for the crash as both gentlemen were viewed as experienced and knowledgeable on the subject.
66. Ibid., 16, 31-34.

67. Air Ministry, *Pilot's Notes for Liberator II Airplane Four Twin Wasp R.1830 S3C4G Engines*, Air Publication 1867B, 21 May 1941, p. 8
68. Consolidated Vultee Aircraft Corporation, *Service and Instruction Manual Airplane General B-24 Bombardment Airplane*, Second Edition, 1944, p.52
69. US Army Air Forces, The Air Service Command, *Handbook of Service Instructions for Models B-24C and B-24D Bombardment Airplanes*, T.O. No. 01-5EC-2, 20 January 1942, p. 328
70. *Field Service Bulletins*, Consolidated Vultee Aircraft Corporation, Vol. 2 No. 1, 1943–4, p.99
71. Army Air Forces Headquarters, Air Technical Service Command, 'ATSC cold weather tests: winter 1944–1945' Army Air Forces Report No. 5230, pp. 108, 184, 204
72. *Field Service Bulletins*, Consolidated Vultee Aircraft Corporation, pp. 144–45
73. TNA: AIR 2/9234, p. 26
74. US Army Air Forces, *Erection and Maintenance Instructions for Army Models B-24D, G, H and J, RB-24C and E Navy Model PB4Y-1 British Models Liberator BIII, BIIIA, BIV, GRV, GRVI, and BVI*, T.O. No. 01-5EC-2, 20 July 1943, revised 1 July 1944, p.328
75. Ford Motor Company, Ford Airplane School, Cable Rigging (Surface Controls) Shop Theory Department, *B-24 E*, 5 June 1943, Benoit De Mulder personal collection, p. 43
76. US Army Air Forces, T.O. No. 01-5EC-2, p. 326
77. Air Ministry, Air Publication 1867B, p. 8. The original LB30 Pilot Handbook (published 28 February 1941) described the operational locking sequence as rudder, elevator, and aileron. In the revised edition (21 May 1941), the sequence was changed to rudder, aileron, and elevator.
78. TNA: AIR 2/9234, p. 22
79. TNA: AIR 2/9234, p. 17
80. Instytut Historyczny Im Gen. Sikorskiego, p. 32
81. Consolidated Vultee Aircraft Corporation, *Service and Instruction Manual Airplane General B-24 Bombardment Airplane*, pp. 183–85
82. Air Ministry, Air Publication 1867B., 9. Though Prchal prior to take-off had sent his flight engineer to the bomb bay to switch on the hydraulic booster pump, the only way to make its pressure available in an emergency was to open emergency shut off valves at the pump and the reservoir.
83. Thompson, p. 312
84. Ramsey, W G, 'The Death of General Sikorski', *After The Battle*, No. 20, pp. 1–18, p. 7
85. US Army Air Forces, The Air Service Command, *Airplane Parts Catalog for Army Models B-24D and B-24J Navy Model PB4Y-1 British Models Liberators B III, B VI, B VIII, GR III, GR V, GR VI, and GR VIII*, AN 01-5E-4, 15 June 1944, revised 1 December 1944, p.60
86. Conway, H G, *Landing gear design*, Chapman & Hall, 1958, pp. 162–63, 313
87. Ibid., pp. 141–42, 163
88. US Army Air Forces, T.O. 01-5EC-2, p. 96
89. US Army Air Forces, *Aircraft Inspection and Maintenance Guide For B-24D, RB-24E, B-24G, B-24H and B-24J Aircraft*, Issue No. 1 (No. 00-20A-2-B-24), 20 July 1943, revised 1 May 1944, p. 14
90. McClellan, J L, *B24 Draft*, 2005, p. 25
91. Różycki, Mieczysław Jan, 'Katastrofa Gibraltarska Droga do tragedii, część I', *Lotnictwo*, 1/2016, 2016, p. 98. "Radio telegraphist [...] Kenneth Brooks was on board. According to him, the machine was lying at a maximum distance of 200 to 300 yards from [...] the beach, turned upside down."
92. Thompson, p. 310.
    In a letter to Carlos Thompson, Prchal described a confrontation he had with David Irving during a television interview in Toronto on 10 March 1968. Prchal was convinced that AL523 had indeed overturned: "Then we had an argument about the entry of the plane into the water. He obviously does not know the term 'on even keel', as used in the court of inquiry report. His statement was that the plane landed on its belly. I have to return to the court of inquiry statement: fifteen to twenty degrees nose down on even keel, meaning that the plane didn't hit the water with one wing down. On TV Irving insisted that it was a belly-landing. So I asked the moderator for a picture of the plane in the water, and with a close-up camera, I made the following statement: 'I am absolutely sure that any expert can see from this picture how it happened. The plane hit the water with the nose-section first. After the impact, this section (including the pilot's cockpit) separated from the plane completely. Then the centre section and the tail unit broke into two pieces and the wing turned

upside down. You could have this picture analysed by an expert who does not know anything about this accident and I am sure that he would say the same thing.'"

93. Ramsey, W G, 'The Death of General Sikorski', p. 7
94. Bibel, George, *Beyond the Black Box: The Forensics of Airplane Crashes*, The John Hopkins University Press, 2008, pp. 52–4
95. Headquarters 98th Bombardment Group Sorties 1 May–31 May 1943, *Sortie Report. 6 May 1943 – 343rd Squadron, Type of Aircraft B-24D, Aircraft No. 112, Aircraft Letter U*. Van fleet, Captain S. C., Air Corps, Intelligence Officer, p. 2
96. TNA: AVIA 15/3013, 59-61; *An Analysis of Water Landings by Thirteenth Air Force Bombers*.
    An instance of a Liberator overturning is recorded by the Thirteenth Air Force on 28 July 1943 when a B-24D ran out of fuel while attempting to land. Flaps were set to half, airspeed 100 mph, tail slightly down, sea conditions choppy. The undercarriage hit first, plane turned nose down, tail up and completely over. The fuselage broke at bulkhead 6, tail and wings floated for about 10–15 seconds, top turret fell out as plane turned over. Attitude of airplane while afloat was bottom side up.
    Two further instances recorded on pages 59–61 describe Thirteenth Air Force ditchings where the Liberator nearly overturned but instead floated with the fuselage near vertical.
    7 July 1943. a B-24D ditched with full flaps, airspeed 95 mph, tail well down. Nose crushed, top turret fell in, ball turret crushed against bulkhead 6. The aircraft floated nose down, tail up.
    11 November 1943 a B-24D ditched with no flaps, airspeed 100 mph, tail slightly down. The nose and several engines sheared off, tail assembly from 1 ft. behind waist window was gone. Aircraft floated with the fuselage straight up.
    An earlier instance is recorded in AVIA 15/3012, p. 270, of a Costal Command Liberator III ditching on 8 August 1942 off Tory Island, Ireland. The aircraft struck tail first at 130 mph, tail assembly and rear turret were torn off. Nose struck second, violence of the impact left the aircraft floating with the rear fuselage pointing up at a steep angle.
97. 'The Last B-24', *NOVA*, Season 45, Episode 15, PBS, 29 October 2018
98. Wood, Richard H, Sweginnis, Robert W, *Aircraft accident investigation*, Endeavor, 1995, pp. 33–34
99. Smith, A G, Warren C H E, Wright, D F, *Investigations of the Behaviour of Aircraft When Making a Forced Landing on Water (Ditching)*, 1957, Ministry Of Supply Aeronautical Research Council, R. & M. No. 2917. London: Her Majesty's Stationery Office, p.14
100. Fisher, L J, Steiner, M F, 'Ditching Tests with a 1/16-Size Dynamic Model of the Army B-24 Airplane in Langley Tank No. 2 and on an outdoor catapult', Wartime Report L-620, National Advisory Committee for Aeronautics, 1945 Report L-620, p. 2
101. Fisher, L J, Hoffman, E L, 'Ditching Investigations of Dynamic Models and Effects of Design Parameters on Ditching Characteristics', Report 1347 and Technical Note 3946, National Advisory Committee for Aeronautics, 1958, p. 15
102. Pioneer Aircraft Instruments, Flight Security, *Pioneer Instruments, Bendix catalogue, manual for flight instruments*, c.1940, 'Sensitive Altimeters'
103. US Army Air Forces. T.O. No. 01-5ED-4, p. 106
104. *Pioneer Instruments, Bendix catalogue, manual for flight instruments*, 'Airspeed Indicator Type table'
105. US Army Air Forces, T.O. No. 01-5ED-4, p. 106
106. Ibid.
107. Ibid.
108. Ibid.
109. US Army Air Forces, *Index of Army-Navy Aeronautical Equipment – Instruments*, T.O. No. 05-1-67, 20 June 1944, p. 141
110. TNA: AIR 2/9234, pp. 4, 23, 27
111. Aeroplane and Armament Experimental Establishment Boscombe Down. 3rd Part of Report No. A&AEE/769,a. Liberator III. L.V.337. *Brief performance and tail buffet tests*. 31 July 1942, Figure 2
112. Pallett, E H J, *Aircraft Instruments: Principles and Applications*, Longman Scientific & Technical, 1981, pp. 55–57
113. War Department Air Corps Material Division. PHQ-M-19-1401-A, 5
114. TNA: AIR 2/9234, p. 26

115. Aeroplane and Armament Experimental Establishment Boscombe Down. Report No. A.&A.E.E./769,a., Figure 3
116. TNA: AIR 2/9234, pp. 9–10
117. Grabowski, Franciszek, *Liberator AL523: Analiza Techniczna Katastrofy* Gibraltarskiej, Instytut Pamięci Narodowej–Komisja Ścigania Zbrodni przeciwko Narodowi Polskiemu, 2017, p. 62
118. Ibid., pp. 81, 83–84, 88
119. Bibel, p. 37
120. US Department of Transportation, Federal Aviation Administration, *Transport Water Impact and Ditching Performance*, DOT/FAA/AR-95/54, March 1996, pp. 7–9
121. Headquarters Eight Air Force office of the Commanding General APO 634., 54
122. Air Ministry, Air Publication 1867C., 51
123. Fisher, Report 1347, p. 204
124. Fisher, Technical Note 3946, p. 15
125. Thompson, p. 295
126. TNA: AIR 2/9234, p. 3
127. Ibid., p. 7
128. War Department Air Corps Material Division. PHQ-M-19-1401-A, 5
129. Aeroplane and Armament Experimental Establishment Boscombe Down. Report No. A.&A.E.E./769,a., Figure 3.
130. *Air Tech: The Magazine of Aircraft Maintenance and Operation*, Vol. 1 No. 1, October 1942
An article written by RAF Captain Charles Kennett titled 'Wind, Sand And Trouble' outlined the hazards experienced by RAF ground crews in Africa and Middle East Command due to the prevalent heat and sand.

> "The pitot tube, as most Air Tech readers know, is away from any disturbance set up by the air screw and has an air intake so that the air pressure against the aircraft in flight will register the pressure on a diaphragm. This pressure is recorded on the dial of the speed indicator, so that the pilot will know his actual flying speed. Desert dust passing through small-drilled holes in the pitot tube will, owing to the delicate adjustment to the air speed indicator, cause reading which may be as much as twenty to fifty mph in error. This discrepancy, in the event of a landing on sand in a heat haze might easily cause a pilot to come in too fast, overshoot, and nose over when applying the brakes. Sand will also creep into the sensitive altimeter, the barometric pressure again causing faulty readings."

131. Air Ministry, Air Publication 2341C-P.N., p. 21
132. Ibid., p. 34
133. Consolidated Vultee Aircraft Corporation. Volume 2, Number 3, 37. Service bulletin MCR 585 issued 15 January 1944 and incorporated on B-24J models describes installation of a cockpit selector valve to be utilized when icing conditions render exterior static openings inoperative.
134. US Army Air Forces, T.O. No. 01-5EC-2, p. 279
135. Consolidated Vultee Aircraft Corporation. PB4Y-2 Bombardment Airplane, pp. 168–69
136. The Chief of the Bureau of Aeronautics. (AN 01-5CB-1), 73.
137. Ibid., p. 73
138. US Army Air Forces, *Operation and Service Instructions for Gyro Horizon Indicators (Sperry)*, AN 05-20GD-1, 15 February 1946, p. 1
139. Headquarters AAF. No. 50-12, 60
140. Consolidated Vultee Aircraft Corporation. Volume 2, Number 20, 280.
141. Irving, p. 174
142. Thompson, p. 245
143. Consolidated Vultee Aircraft Corporation. Volume 2, Number 20, 280
144. Headquarters AAF. No. 50-12, 75
145. Headquarters AAF. Pilot Training Manual For The Liberator B-24, 18
146. Thompson, p. 301
147. TNA: AIR 2/9234, p. 16
148. Thompson, p. 304

149. US Army Air Forces, AN 01-5E-4, p. 95
150. US Army Air Forces, T.O. 01-5EC-2, p. 314
151. United States, Munitions Board, Aircraft Committee, Subcommittee on Air Force-Navy-Civil Aircraft Design Criteria; United States. Army-Navy-Civil Committee on Aircraft Design Criteria, *Strength Of Metal Aircraft Elements*, Anc-5 Bulletin, 1951, p. 42
152. TNA: AIR 2/9234, p. 17
153. US Army Air Forces, T.O. 01-5EC-2, p. 327
154. US.MB.AC. et al., 1951, 42
155. Waterfield, Audio_11_05_2021_10_28_30 am, 40:10.
156. US Army Air Forces, T.O. No. 01-5EC-2, p. 128
157. Air Ministry, Air Publication 1867B., 41
158. TNA: AIR 2/9234, p. 10
159. Ibid., p. 14
160. US Army Air Forces, The Air Service Command, *Erection and Maintenance Instructions for The Model LB-30 "Liberator II" Bombardment Airplane*, T.O. No. 01-5ED-2, 30 December 1941, revised 1 May 1942, p. 114
161. TNA: AIR 2/9234, p. 22
162. Air Ministry, Air Publication 2095, 72
163. Grabowski, p. 51
164. Headquarters AAF, No. 50-12, 41
165. Consolidated Aircraft. Flight Manual B-24D Airplane, 138
166. US Army Air Forces. T.O. No. 01-5ED-2, p. 152
167. US Army Air Forces, *Operation and Service Instructions for Automatic Pilot Type A-3*, T.O. No. 05-45AB-1, 15 October 1943, revised 10 September 1945, pp. 23–24
168. Air Ministry, Air Publication 2095, p. 73
169. US Army Air Forces, *Service Instructions for Automatic Pilot Type A-3*, T.O. No. 05-45AB-2, 15 October 1943, revised 2 May 1946, p. 64. The overpower valves were adjusted to operate and relieve at 75% of automatic pilot operating pressure.
170. US Army Air Forces. T.O. No. 05-45AB-1, p. 8
171. Ibid., pp. 9–10
172. Gray, George W, *Frontiers of Flight: The Story of NACA Research*, A A Knopf, 1948, p. 170
173. McClellan, pp. 8–9
174. Westfall, J R, (1946). National Advisory Committee for Aeronautics, *Measurements of Landing-Gear Forces and Horizontal-Tail Loads in Landing Tests of a Large Bomber-Type Airplane*, Report No. 1140. Washington: NACA. pp. 2, 9, 11

    "During the NACA tests [...] [the] maximum tail response was found to occur in normal landings as a result of resonance with fore-and-aft vibration of the landing gear when both main wheels touched simultaneously and vibrated in phase. The airplane was equipped with a 25g stabilizer, that is, one designed for an ultimate static load of 25 times the weight of the tail assembly. A number of stabilizer failures, apparently caused by loads imposed as a result of landing impacts, [had] been reported for earlier models of the airplane that were equipped with 15g stabilizers. [...] A statistical analysis of the stabilizer-load data indicated [...] that about one landing in 100 would develop the maximum stabilizer load measured during the tests (50 per cent of the design yield bending moment). It might be pointed out that 50 per cent of the design yield bending moment for the 25g stabilizer would be about 83 per cent of the design yield bending moment for the 15g stabilizer, with which early models of the airplane were equipped and on which several stabilizer failures were experienced in service."

175. TNA: AIR 27/1970/1 to AIR 27/1970/14.
    From No. 511 Squadron diaries the recorded time flown by AL523 from 8 December 1942 to 3 July 1943 totalled approximately 450 airframe hours. During that time there were forty-eight take-offs and landings. The hours accumulated on AL523 prior to 8 December 1942 is unknown. What is known is that it was flown from San Diego and taken on charge in Dorval on 16 October 1941. It was then flown from Dorval to Gander on 27 October, Gander to Scottish Aviation Ltd (SAL) Prestwick on 28 October, SAL Prestwick to Control Research Development at Royal Aircraft Establishment (RAE) Farnborough on 25 November, RAE Farnborough

to SAL Prestwick on 11 May 1942 as service pilot for special trials, SAL Prestwick on 23 May for transport modifications, transferred to No. 511 Squadron on 29 November 1942. The accumulated hours flown from 16 October 1941 to 29 November 1942 can only be estimated with a possible tally of between 75 and 150 airframe hours with twelve or more take-offs and landings.

176. Foot, M R D, 'The death of General Sikorski', *Intelligence and National Security*, Vol. 21 Issue 3, 2006, p.458
177. TNA: AIR 2/9234, p. 9
178. Bartelski, Jan, *Disasters in the Air: Mysterious Air Disasters Explained*, Airlife, 2001, pp. 51–53
179. Ibid., p. 52
180. Ibid., pp. 40–41
181. Walker, C W T, First-hand account of aspects of the death of General Sikorski in the crash of the Liberator AL523 at Gibraltar on July 4th, 1943, 2014, p. 2
182. Sarner, p. 155
183. Tebinka, Jacek, 'Śmierć generała Władysława Sikorskiego w świetle nowych dokumentów brytyjskich', Dzieje Najnowsze, Vol. XXXIII, 2001, p. 170
184. Borovik, Genrikh, *The Philby Files: The Secret Life of the Master Spy Kim Philby*, Little, Brown, 1994, pp. 196–209, 216–17
185. US Army Air Forces, T.O. No. 01-5EC-2, p. 320
186. TNA: AIR 2/9234, p. 17
187. Air Ministry. 1867B, pp. 43–46
188. Headquarters AAF. No. 50-12, p. 31
189. US Army Air Forces. No. 00-20A-2-B-24, pp. 16–17
190. Ibid., pp. 16–17
191. TNA: AIR 2/9234, p. 4
192. Ibid., 5 August 1943, 1
193. Air Ministry. 1867B, p. 45

CHAPTER FOUR

194. Sword, *Sikorski: Soldier and Statesman: A Collection of Essays*, p. 153; Thompson, p. 56. Sikorski had referred to Łubieński as captain due to his pending promotion from lieutenant upon return to England.
195. Różycki, pp. 97–98. HSL 181 arrived at the crash scene at approximately 11:14 pm.
196. Sword, *Sikorski: Soldier and Statesman: A Collection of Essays*, p. 154; Thompson, pp. 54–55
197. Thompson, p. 415
198. Konopka, T., Gross, A., Woźniak, K., Kłys, M., 'Forensic medical examination of the corpse of General Władysław Sikorski, a putative victim of assassination in 1943', *Forensic Science International*, Vol. 202 Issues 1–3, 10 October 2010, p. e31
199. TNA: AIR 2/15113, pp. 70–71; AIR 27/1970/14; AIR 28/306, pp. 217–18. There is some confusion as to whether General Spaatz's aircraft was a USAAF Liberator or Fortress. Group Captain Frederick W Winterbotham who was also a passenger on this aircraft recounted in a letter dated 10 January1972 to then Air Marshal Sir John Slessor that it was a Liberator. From North Front's operations record book a lone B-17 was logged arriving in Gibraltar from the UK on 3 July 1943 but not departing. On 4 July 1943 a B-17 was recorded arriving from Maison Blanche, Algeria and later departing on a return trip to Maison Blanche. On 5 July 1943 a B-17 was recorded departing for the UK. Presumably Scrope, Clutterbuck, and Winterbotham had flown in earlier from Maison Blanche and transferred to another USAAF B-17 or continued their trip in the same aircraft departing the following day, 5 July, due to AL523's accident. The only aircraft to depart for the UK on 4 July, with exception of AL523, were a BOAC Dakota and a No. 511 Squadron Albemarle. The only Liberator recorded departing for the UK on 5 July was AL584 from No. 511 Squadron along with two Armstrong Whitworth Albemarles from the same unit.
200. TNA: AIR 27/1970/14, 1; AIR 28/306, 217. Along with General Spaatz's Fortress, four Liberators were present in Gibraltar on 4 July. Along with AL523 there was a No. 511 Squadron Liberator I AM914 which departed at 08:49 hours local time (GMT + 2 hours) for Cairo West, a BOAC Liberator G-AGFR (Ambassador Maisky) to

Cairo West via Marble Arch airfield Libya, and an unknown refors (reinforcement) Liberator that departed to Ras el Ma in Morocco.

201. Adrian Scrope email 13 January 2015 at 10:24 pm
202. Knowles, Sydney, *A Diver in the Dark*, Woodfield Publishing, 2009, p. 43
203. Irving, pp. 63, 205. Irving alleged that there had been at least one case of spirits or sherry per person, and a general laxity among crew and passengers in purchasing large quantities of duty-free whisky and sherry to bring back to England.
204. Thompson, p. 31
205. Ibid., p. 339. According to Irving, Łubieński had allegedly told Rolf Hochhuth that Quayle had told someone that the Poles had killed themselves by buying too much sherry. Thompson asked Quayle if these were his words which Quayle vehemently denied having said. Irving never produced evidence of this allegation.
206. Hale, Don, *The Final Dive: The Life and Death of 'Buster' Crabb*, Sutton Publishing, 2007, pp. 90–91. In this book there is mention of 30 to 40 broken cases of alcohol among AL523's underwater wreckage which he attributes to an uncited National Archives document. Further research within TNA file TS 58/997 *Crown privilege: Prchal v Irving and others [et al]* revealed that Hale likely quoted from a letter dated 12 February 1969 addressed to then Prime Minister Harold Wilson from David Irving. The letter contained allegations of liquor smuggling and 30 to 40 liquor crates that Irving could not substantiate and offered no proof. The letter also included SOE wireless operator Douglas Martin's questionable and unlikely crash account. He further claimed to have witnesses who said that Prchal had told them he had lied during the court of inquiry to cover his crew's smuggling activities and mistake by his co-pilot. These claims could not be substantiated as neither witness would come forward publicly.
207. Walker, p. 3
208. WALKER, CHARLES WILLIAM THOMAS (ORAL HISTORY), SOUND. © IWM 30271, Reel 13/23, 29 August 2007
209. Walker, pp. 3-4, IWM 30271, Reel 13/23, 13:34-14:35. Charles had observed there were no aircrew present during the loading and that Sikorski's entourage were milling about nearby. When he asked the guard standing by the tail who's overseeing the loading, the guard replied, "they are".
210. IWM 30271, Reel 13/23. 09:43: "The aircraft itself was white." 11:15: "This white aircraft.". An image of a No. 511 Squadron Liberator AL522 clearly shows its side and upper surfaces painted in a green and brown temperate land scheme with lighter coloured under surfaces painted sky or azure. It is notable that No. 172 Squadron's Wellingtons were painted white which may explain Charles misidentifying the Liberators colour. 11:56: "It was a beautiful evening as well, and it was pretty light." 27:26: "It was daylight." David Walker's research on sky conditions made it clear it was quite dark that evening.
211. TNA. AVIA 15/3012, 16. Conversion of Liberator Mark II Bombers to Transport Aircraft. Minutes of meeting held at the Air Ministry, Bush House at 1500 Hours on Thursday, 20 May 1943.
Camouflage, 12. (i) Upper surface - Temperate Sea Scheme. (ii) Under Surfaces - Azure Blue.
212. IWM 30271, Reel 13/23, 13:50: "And as I looked in, of course the doors were open, and I saw two rods at the back." 24:38: "Two tubes and every so often there would be knuckle joints [...] universal knuckle joints [...] that would follow around the shape of the aircraft." It was firmly established in Chapter Three that the Liberator's flight controls were primarily cable operated including those of the elevator. The only system that remotely resembled what Charles described were rudder control rods found exclusively within the horizontal stabilizer.
213. Ibid., 13:16, "the tailgate was down and the level of the floor of the lorry was the same level where they were putting things into the aircraft." There were no side doors on this model Liberator only fuselage side hatches on either side which on other versions mounted a machine gun for a waist gunner which AL523 did not have. It should also be noted that the bottom sill of the fuselage side hatch was approximately six feet off the ground and far higher than the lowered tailgate and floor of any truck then in use on Gibraltar. The described loading arrangement more closely resembles the loading of a Douglas C-47 Dakota which had a much broader and lower fuselage side door designed for the loading of bulk cargo.
214. TNA: AIR 27/1971, 2., Beurling, George, Roberts, Leslie, *Malta Spitfire: The Diary of an Ace Fighter Pilot*, Grub Street, 2011, p. 221. According to David Walker his father was posted to Gibraltar on 19 November 1942, curiously Charles' description shares similarities to the crash of Liberator AL516 which overshot Gibraltar's eastern runway on landing, stalled and crashed into the sea 200 yards off the east runway at 09:23 hours GMT on 31 October 1942. Several on board were being ferried back to the UK after serving as fighter pilots in the defence of Malta. Of the 34 occupants 17 were killed or drowned. Given the darkness and 700-yard

distance of AL523's crash location from the runway end, plus it's tail breaking off on impact, raises doubts as to whether the crash described by Charles was AL523.

215. TNA: AVIA 15/3012, p. 16; AVIA 15/3013, p. 291

216. TNA: AVIA 15/3012, p. 13; AVIA 15/3013, pp. 288–90. A decision to install a rear fuselage port side-loading door along with other extensive modifications came into effect on 27 May 1943. The installation was scheduled to be incorporated on four new Liberator IIs that were to be delivered to No. 511 Squadron after modification at Scottish Aviation in Prestwick. The aircraft to be modified were AL559, AL545, AL619, and AL635. Door dimensions were 4'6" in height and 3'6" in width.

217. AIR 28/306, p. 221, 8 July 1943 "Landing from Ras el Ma at 15:32 in strong West crosswind Dakota FD.888 of 24 Squadron over-ran the runway and went into the sea just off the western end. The crew of 4 and 13 passengers were uninjured. The pilot was 1066901 Sgt Francis J S."

218. Thompson, p. 417. This myth was perpetuated by David Irving. "As late as October 1968, Irving had expressed his doubts that Squadron Leader Herring had really drowned, and said that in his opinion, he had been swept away and landed on some foreign coast. (It is clear that, given the Irving letter to *Der Spiegel*, this belief of his was fortified by Douglas F Martin's account of a man standing on the wing of the Liberator shortly after the crash ... or 'ditching'.)"

219. WALKER, CHARLES WILLIAM THOMAS (ORAL HISTORY), SOUND. © IWM 30271, Reel 9/23, 29 August 2007, 18:45. Walker would send home oranges and bananas in tin boxes on Wellingtons going back to the UK for major servicing.

220. During the Second World War, British clocks were put forward an extra hour in the summer to maximize the benefits of natural light. The GMT +2 hours rule (Double British Summer Time) was repeated in 1947, when Britain was in the grip of post-war austerity.

221. Walker, C W T, First-hand account of aspects of the death of General Sikorski in the crash of the Liberator AL523 at Gibraltar on July 4th 1943
David Walker, http://www.microscopy-uk.org.uk/dww/sikorski/sikorski.html

222. Waterfield, Jack. Audio_11_05_2021_10_28_30 am, 41:00

223. Ibid., 40:10

224. Waterfield, Jack. Audio, 24 February 2022, Oskie Films, 07:31:59, 07:37:10

225. Ibid., 17:17:50

226. *Dziennik Polski I Dziennik Żołnierza*, 20 kwietnia 1946, p. 2

227. Waterfield, Jack. Audio_11_05_2021_10_28_30 am, 41:00, 42:18

228. Thompson, p. 224

229. Ibid., p. 226

230. TNA: AIR 2/9234, p. 9, Sword, *Sikorski: Soldier And Statesman*, p. 153; Thompson, pp. 279, 309

231. Thompson, pp. 271–72

232. Ibid., p. 282. In Martin's original letter to Irvine he wrote: "The 'figure' on the wing appeared almost as soon as the plane settled on the water before the searchlights came on and remained until the wing dipped into the water; during this time the searchlights came on."

233. JEPPESEN JeppView 3.5.2.0 LXGB, plate 10-9, plate 19-10. Single flashing white light at 3000' (914m), single flashing light at 6000' (1829m) and 9000' (2743m) from sea wall.

234. Ramsey, W G, '1978 Sikorski Sequel – Seabed Site Investigation', *After The Battle*, No. 24, 1979, p.49
After The Battle magazine in November 1977 sponsored recovery of a propeller from the AL523 crash location which turned out to be a Hamilton Standard propeller not used on early model Liberators like AL523 which was fitted with Curtiss-Wright propellers. It was later determined by the Accidents and Investigations Branch at Farnborough that it came from a Douglas DC-3 (Dakota) or Boeing B-17. The propeller is currently on display as part of the Sikorski Memorial in Gibraltar.

235. Only two known crashes of B-17s near Gibraltar are recorded neither of which could have been the source of the recovered propeller given their distance from Gibraltar.
AIR 28/309, 17 November 1942, p.133. From UK, Transit In. "Nine B-17s landed between 15:32 and 17:34. 1 Crashed in sea off Gibraltar."
Osborne, Dave. B-17 FORTRESS MASTERLOG, p. 62. The above mentioned B-17 was 42-2969 from the USAAF 97th Bombardment Group en route to Maison Blanche via Gibraltar 17 November 1942 which suffered engine fire and crashed in the Bay of Biscay. All eleven crew and passengers were killed.
AIR 28/306, 402; http://www.rafcommands.com/database/serials/details.php?uniq=FK208;

Osborne, p. 38. Crash of a B-17 near Gibraltar on 29 November 1943 when a Coastal Command Fortress IIa FK208 while on approach to RAF Gibraltar crashed into the sea off Punta Carnero, south of Algeciras, seven miles west of Gibraltar. All eight crewmembers were killed.

Two addition Douglas Dakota crashes are recorded at Gibraltar. Registration 43-15298 possibly accounts for the recovered propeller in 1977 though there are no details as to which runway this aircraft was using during take-off. Registration 41-7856 is recorded as having burnt out and could not have therefore crashed into the sea.

https://avsafety.net/database/record.php?id=19421111-0; AIR 28/309, 112. November 11, 1942. USAAF Douglas C-47, 41-7856. "Crashed during take-off from Gibraltar and burnt out. The aircraft was overloaded. All aircraft movements were delayed."

https://avsafety.net/database/record.php?id=19440720-0; http://www.joebaugher.com/usaf_serials/1943_2.html. USAAF Douglas C-47A, 43-15298. "Crashed just as it becomes airborne departing RAF North Front, Gibraltar en route to Canino, Italy 20 July 44 [4 crew KIA: 4 passengers returned to duty]."

236. Thompson, p. 246. Prchal's right leg was in a cast, he had pain in the left when putting weight on it using crutches. X-rays afterward revealed his left leg was broken but had started to mend.
237. TNA: AIR 2/9234, p. 15
238. TNA: AIR 2/9234, RAF Form 412, 1B
239. TNA: TS 58/997, 161. J E Cornish. Permanent Under Secretary's Department Foreign and Commonwealth Office. A factual account of the death General Sikorski
240. TNA: AIR 8/779, pp. 34, 36, 38
241. Thompson, p. 281
242. Jaroslav Prokop had been a wireless air gunner with No. 311 (Czechoslovak) Squadron RAF from January 1945 to 12 August 1945. http://www.rafaci.cz/?sekce1=cs_letci&sekce2=letci_z_vysociny#prokop_jaroslav
243. TNA: TS 58/997, p. 296
244. Irving, p. 229
245. Thompson, p. 322. Presumably Prokop had heard this from Prchal or other former pilots who had flown VIPs during the war.
246. Thompson, pp. 319–22
247. TNA: AIR 27/1970/16, No. 511 Squadron Diary. Flt Lt Swabey on strength 30 August 1943, p. 16; AIR 27/1970/17, No. 511 Squadron Diary. Flt Lt Swabey on strength 1 September 1943, p. 1
248. TNA: TS 58/997, p. 295
249. Ibid., p. 296
250. Thompson, p. 325
251. Free Czechoslovak Air Force: https://fcafa.com/2010/10/07/josef-rechka/
252. Thompson, p. 328
253. Thompson, p. 249. Prchal's mention of others having been court-martialled for smuggling is interesting as it speaks to his underlying concern at the time and stands out in stark contrast to VIPs who faced no penalty for doing the same.
254. TNA: AIR 2/9234, p. 15. Sach was the 26th witness.
255. Thompson, p. 42
256. Thompson, p. 61
257. Sword, *Sikorski: Soldier And Statesman*, p. 150. Łubieński described VIP smuggling in the following terms:

    > "While with normal Transport Command aircraft ferrying passengers to Britain from the Middle East, officers of the RAF station's No. 27 ADRU would board the aircraft, check off its passengers and cargo against the aircraft manifest – Form 1256 – and search the plane for contraband or unauthorized passengers, with VIP planes these procedures were not so rigorously applied."

258. Ibid., pp. 181–82
259. Ibid., pp. 294, 299
260. TNA: TS 58/997, p. 303
261. Ibid., pp. 300, 304. The government report noted how Irving's dealings with the Air Historical Branch (AHB) were at times deceitful. "Experience gained by members of AHB in their dealings with Irving indicate that he is sometime less than scrupulous in reporting information which purports to support his point of

view. Contacts with AHB have been quoted to some witnesses in a manner suggesting official backing for his enquiries. He seems inclined to quote opinion as proof – a tendency shown both in the letter and in his recent appearances in David Frost's programmes on TV." Draft letter from PUS (Parliamentary Under Secretary) to Sir Burke Trend.

262. Ibid., p. 331. Klimkowski alleged Prchal was given a special British second pilot.

263. AAN: *Akta Władyslawa Sikorskiego*, Sygnatura. 204, 17th February 1969, pp. 3–6 (R W L Hooper)

264. Knowles, p. 43

265. Milton, Giles, 'Episode 6: Fisherman John's Catch of the Day', *Cover Up: Ministry of Secrets*, 2023

266. Instytut Historyczny Im Gen. Sikorskiego, pp. 11–12; https://www.britishpathe.com/video/polish-premier-here The French registration for this aircraft was F-AQBL.

267. According to a chronology of Sikorski's political and travel itinerary for this period he left France by plane on 17 May and returned on 20 May while an Imperial War Museum image cites Sikorski having left France on 10 May in a No. 206 Squadron Hudson. A review of No. 206 Squadron diaries for June 1940 makes no reference to having flown Sikorski out of France though it may simply have not been recorded.
Instytut Historyczny Im Gen. Sikorskiego, p. 14. Sikorski left for London by a plane sent to his disposal by the British government.
IWM, ©IWM CH 358. A captioned image held by the IWM describes a "Lockheed Hudson Mark I, N7318, of No. 206 Squadron RAF which rescued the commander-in-chief of Free Polish Forces, General Władysław Sikorski and his staff from Bordeaux, France, in June 1940."; TNA: AIR 27/1222/12. The first recorded flight of Hudson N7318 was on 18 June 1940 when it flew a reconnaissance along the Dutch coast from 20:50 to 23:55.

268. Instytut Historyczny Im Gen. Sikorskiego, pp. 14–15. Sikorski was as taken to Libourne to issue last orders referring to the evacuation. Returned to London with General Sosnkowski and officers of the general staff.

269. British Airways Speedbird Centre, BOAC's movement chart, documents, and log for June 1940. G-AFKZ departed Poole at 09:41 arriving Lake Biscarosse at 13:29, departed 21 June at 04:45 arriving in Poole at 09:37.

270. Sword, *Sikorski: Soldier And Statesman*, pp. 160–61

271. Ibid., p. 163

272. British Airways Speedbird Centre, BOAC's Movement Chart, documents, and log for June 1940.

273. TNA: AIR 27/293/1. The aircraft registration was G-AGAZ.

274. Cazalet, Victor, *With Sikorski to Russia*, Curwen Press, 1942, p. 21

275. Ibid, pp. 15–16

276. Ibid., p. 9

277. Thompson, pp. 128, 279, 405

278. Thompson, pp. 259–260; Cazalet, pp. 26–27

279. Thompson, p. 6. Rolf Hochhuth claimed this landing had been an attempt on Sikorski's life.

280. Ibid., p. 128. The times and locations were transcribed and translated directly to Carlos Thompson from the diary of General Sikorski as recorded by Captain Janusz Ticzkiewicz-Lacki, ADC to General Sikorski who also accompanied him during that flight.
Tuesday, 25th November 1941
09:00 Start from Bagdad
12:00 Forced landing on a field near Hammadan.
14:20 After refilling with petrol brought from Hammadan by military lorry, start for further flight.
16:45 Landing in Teheran.

281. Ibid., pp. 260–61

282. Ibid., pp. 261–62

283. British Airways Speedbird Centre, email Wed 2022-08-24 5:38 AM.
Information from the BOAC's Movement Chart for January 1942:
3 January 1942 Flight No. EW10 C Class G-AFCT 'Champion'
Departed Malta 2315Z
Arrived Gibraltar 0725Z on 4 January
Departed Gibraltar 1008Z on 6 January
Arrived Belem 1135Z on 6 January
Arrived Poole 1630Z on 6 January.

284. Cazalet, p. 8

285. William Lyon Mackenzie King: Memoranda and notes (J4): H-1522: https://heritage.canadiana.ca/view/oocihm.lac_reel_h1522/ images 257, 259, 278, 261–2
286. Instytut Historyczny imienia Generala Sikorskiego, pp. 17–18. Sikorski's first trip to Canada and the United States occurred from 24 March 1941 to 9 May 1941; Podoski, Victor, 'General Sikorski: Some Personal Reminiscences', Queen's Quarterly, Vol. 53, 1946, pp. 316–17. Victor Podoski was consul-general of Poland to Canada during the Second World War. Podoski met Sikorski in Halifax, the general having travelled on the battleship HMS *Revenge* from Britain on his first trip to Canada and the United States.
287. Colonel Protasewicz would later head the Polish Sixth Bureau in London that processed intelligence from the Polish Underground Army.
288. Mitkiewicz, Leon, *Z gen. Sikorskim na obczy'znie: fragmenty wspomnień*, Instytut Literacki, 1968, p. 235
289. TNA: KV 3/274 Secret Service Subject Files: Attempted sabotage on BOAC Liberator AM 262, p. 56
290. TNA: KV 3/274, p. 106
291. Mitkiewicz, pp. 251–52; TNA: KV 3/274, pp. 28, 36. Upon arrival in Montreal the matter was brought to the attention of Lieutenant Colonel Ilinski of the Polish Military Mission and they conferred with Air Marshal Bowhill. A decision was reached that nothing would be said and that the bomb should be taken to Washington to be examined by their G-2.
292. Mitkiewicz, pp. 257–58
293. TNA: KV 3/274, pp. 101–2; Mitkiewicz, pp. 258–59
294. TNA: KV 3/274, pp. 59, 78, 92
295. Ibid., 95, 98.
296. TNA: KV 3/276 Secret Service Subject Files: Attempted sabotage on BOAC Liberator AM 262, p. 45. Statement by 2nd Lieutenant Eugeniusz Jurewicz, Polish Army engineers.
297. TNA: KV 3/275 Secret Service Subject Files: Attempted sabotage on BOAC Liberator AM 262, pp. 59–61
298. TNA: KV 3/275, pp. 59–62; TNA: KV 3/276, p. 69
299. TNA: KV 3/274, pp. 44. Royal Canadian Mounted Police report, April 18, 1942. After a flight arrives the Equipment Checking section in Montreal closely inspect flares, parachutes, harnesses, and mattresses removed from the aircraft. Covers of mattresses showing any signs of scorching or burning would have been set aside for further examination.
300. TNA: KV 3/274, pp. 66, 102
301. TNA: KV 3/276, pp. 39–40
302. Ibid., pp. 30–36
303. TN: 96474. Title: Bohdan Kleczyński papers. Author: Kleczyński, Bohdan, 1902–1944
Death certificate from Royal Infirmary Edinburgh, Bohdan Kleczyński papers, box 1, Hoover.
304. Thompson, pp. 211–12; TNA: KV 3/274, p. 80. Note from Lieutenant Commander J Senter, SOE, April 13, 1942; TNA: KV 3/275, p. 3. Director General Sir David Petrie notes, paragraph 6.
305. Death certificate from Royal Infirmary Edinburgh, Bohdan Kleczyński papers, box 1, Hoover. Institution Library & Archives; Thompson, pp. 329–30.
306. Irving, p. 157. Irving cites this information having been provided by Michal Protasewicz in July 1967; Thompson, pp. 6, 21, 104, 329. Hochhuth made identical claims adding that Kleczyński had been pushed.
307. http://www.polishsquadronsremembered.com/307/307_faces_1.html; TNA: AIR 27/1675/43. The aircraft registration was EW-V flown by Wing Commander Jan Michalowski.
308. PISM, KOL.1/DCNW/40 & 40a. Glówczynski and Bowhill, Accident Report, Montreal, 30 November 1942, 1; West, Bruce, *The Man Who Flew Churchill*, McGraw-Hill Ryerson, 1975, p. 183
309. Instytut Historyczny Im Gen. Sikorskiego, pp. 26, 29.XI.1942 – 13.I.1943
310. Ciechanowski, p. 122. Sikorski's second transatlantic flight had been particularly stressful. Just before noon on 30 November, his aide-de-camp called Ambassador Jan Ciechanowski in Washington reporting the general's plane had just landed in Montreal after a "somewhat jumpy flight" and that he wished to speak with him. Ciechanowski recorded:

> "General Sikorski asked me what arrangements I had made for the first days of his visit. I said I had just heard from Mr. Summerlin that the president wished me to bring him to tea at the White House straight from the airport on that very day. 'I am not even shaved,' said Sikorski, 'and as I am to leave for Washington immediately, I will not even have time for a bath and change of uniform. Could you not explain this to the president and ask him to agree to receive

me tomorrow? I will then be better prepared to meet him.' I laughed as I assured the general that the president certainly would not hold it against him if he appeared unshaved and travel stained."

311. PISM: KOL.1/DCNW/40 & 40a, 2-4
312. Ibid., 4.
313. Ciechanowski, p. 123; Kukiel, Marian, *Generał Sikorski, żołnierż i mąż stanu Polski walczacej*. Londyn: Instytut Polski i Muzeum Im. Gen. Sikorskiego, 1981, pp. 212–13
314. Thompson, p. 265
315. http://www.rafcommands.com/forum/showthread.php?4455-Hudson-loss-in-Canada-4
316. PISM: KOL.1/DCNW/40 & 40a, 4. The pilot of Hudson BW409 was Captain H J Bowen, an experienced American civilian pilot. Bowen was running both engines, waiting for his passengers, when he discovered that one of the petrol lines was not working properly. He stopped the engines and removed the fuel fill caps to confirm if both tanks were full. Group Captain Powell came out inquiring of Bowen if his aircraft was serviceable. After confirming the tanks were full Powell chose to run the engines himself in a final check of the aircraft's general condition before take-off.
317. Ibid., 4. The report stated all spark plugs were brand new, had been tested prior to installation and had performed without problem during engine run-ups and magneto checks prior to take-off. Conditions for carburettor icing were noted by Air Chief Marshal Frederick Bowhill commander of RAF Ferry Command in Montreal.
318. Aviation Safety Network: https://aviation-safety.net/wikibase/wiki.php?id=74088
319. Military aircraft crashes in the south west Midlands – 1943 http://www.aviationarchaeology.org.uk/marg/crashes1943.htm
320. Wings over New Zealand forum: https://rnzaf.proboards.com/thread/22924/years-ago-today-lockheed-hudson?page=1&scrollTo=304031
321. Environment Canada https://climate.weather.gc.ca
322. Air Ministry (Air Publication 1690 C), 2, 16; US Army Air Forces (T.O. No. 01-75KA-2), 111, 152, 323; Wright Aeronautical Corporation (Part No. 114323-N3), 27. Early model Lockheed Hudsons were powered by versions of the Wright Cyclone R-1820-87 engine fitted with a Bendix Stromberg Injection PD12H3 carburettor. Though the Bendix design was considered inherently non-icing it was not impervious to ice accumulation. Lockheed incorporated a carburettor anti-icer system to de-ice and prevent ice formation in the carburettor. This was accomplished by injecting alcohol through four nozzles into the air intake duct just above the carburettor. In addition two alternate air intakes were provided. One supplied warm air from around the exhaust collector that could be selected during icing conditions. The other supplied filtered air for use during landing and take-off, the hot air intake was normally used only for cruise power settings.
323. Irving, pp. 158–61; PISM: KOL.1/DCNW/40 & 40a, pp. 1–5; Christie, Carl A, Hatch, Fred, *Ocean Bridge: The History of RAF Ferry Command*, University of Toronto Press, 1995, p. 394
324. Kennedy, Arthur R, Ridley, Jo Ann, High Times Keeping 'em Flying: An Aviation Autobiography, Fithian Press, 1992, p. 102
325. Ibid., p. 103
326. Irving, pp. 148-60; Thompson, p. 6. David Irving attempted to suggest the March 1942 incendiary incident and December 1942 engine failure were related. Rolf Hochhuth suggested the March 1942 incident to be one of three assassination attempts on Sikorski. "Did you know that there were three, before they succeeded in Gibraltar? One in Montreal, that time over the Atlantic and the third in Hamadan, in his flight to Persia, where he miraculously survived a crash-landing."
327. The term prederat, spelled *preterite* or *preterit*, is a grammatical tense or verb form serving to denote events that took place or were completed in the past; in some languages, such as Spanish, French, and English, it is equivalent to the simple past tense.
328. Thompson, p. 265
329. Report of the Royal Canadian Mounted Police for the Year Ended March 31, 1943. *Suspected Sabotage*, p. 35
330. Report of the Royal Canadian Mounted Police for the Year Ended March 31, 1945. *Suspected Sabotage*, p. 29
331. Ibid., *Cases outside of Canada*, p. 30
332. Grams, Grant, 'Enemies within our bosom: Nazi Sabotage in Canada', *Journal of Military and Strategic Studies*, Vol. 14 Issues 3 & 4, 2012, pp. 10–11, 13–19

333. TNA: AIR 27/1970/10; Sword, *Sikorski: Soldier and Statesman*, pp. 147–48

334. TNA: AIR 27/1107/21; AIR 27/1107/22

335. Polak, Bogusław, *Generał broni Władysław Sikorski – generał dywizji Władysław Anders Korespondencja 1941–1943 Wybór dokumentów*, Koszalin, 2000, pp. 303-305. From General Sikorski's itinerary 1 June to 16 June 1943; Instytut Historyczny Im Gen. Sikorskiego, pp. 30–32. Chronology of General Sikorski's trip to the Middle East from 25 May 1943 to 4 July 1943; Sword, *Sikorski: Soldier and Statesman: A Collection of Essays*, p. 148. Last week of June Sikorski was resting in Beirut. Locations and dates were obtained from these sources along with squadron ORBs.

336. TNA: AIR 29/893/1. The ORB entry for 11 June 1943 records HK862 flying from Baghdad to Kirkuk, to Qizil Ribat and return.

337. TNA: AIR 29/893/1. There is no record in the ORB war diary of a 13 June 1943 flight from Qizil Ribat to Baghdad. HK862 is recorded having flown on 14 June from Baghdad to Habbaniya and return; Polak, p. 305. "Sunday, June 13, 1943. time. 1500 Departure from Baghdad. Honour company at the airport with an orchestra. Present according to the orders of the Base and Stages commander; TNA: WO 178/23. 26 BMM PAIFORCE, War Diary, Qizil Ribat, June 13, 1943. "Gen SIKORSKI leaves by aeroplane to stay at BAGHDAD as guest of HRH The Regent."; The Polish Institute and Sikorski Museum (PISM): SIK 215 – Gen Sikorski's visit to the Middle East: https://www.youtube.com/watch?v=HzudSolBr34, 16:39. Sikorski is filmed stepping out of a DH.98 Dragon Rapide during his Middle East visit in June 1943.
Given that 26 BMM (British Military Mission) and Sikorski's itinerary record him departing Qizil Ribat for Baghdad on 13 June. The AIR 29/893/1 ORB war diary discrepancy can only be assumed to have been due to transposed or missing flight log entries. It is recorded that DH.98 HK862, Valentia 8063 and 3599 flew from 12 June to 18 June exclusively between Baghdad, Habbaniya and Baghdad, sometimes twice a day; the abbreviation do for ditto used consecutively for repetitive destinations. It is presumed Sikorski flew to Baghdad in HK862 on 13 June 1943.

338. TNA: AIR 27/1107/21. The first flight to Beirut is recorded departing Heliopolis the morning of 18 June 1943 carrying a Colonel Lees, Commander Courtney, and five passengers. General Sikorski's itinerary incorrectly lists him arriving in Syria on 17 June 1943 when in fact the ORB records him arriving at Heliopolis Egypt on this day. It is presumed General Sikorski and his party were among the five passengers departing Heliopolis for Beirut on 18 June 1943.

339. TNA: AIR 27/1107/22. ORB entry for 27 June. EW990 and crew overnighted in Beirut, departed with Sikorski party the morning of 28 June for Heliopolis via Lydda.

340. TNA: AIR 27/1107/22. Typical routes for these round-trip flights were Heliopolis–Lydda–Beirut–Lydda–Heliopolis; Heliopolis–Beirut–Adana–Lydda–Heliopolis; Heliopolis–Lydda–Beirut–Nicosia–Beirut–Lydda–Heliopolis; Heliopolis–Lydda–Beirut–Lydda–Heliopolis.

341. TNA: AIR 27/1107/22. The engine on EW989 was changed in Lydda, and aircraft returned to Heliopolis on 1 July 1943.

342. Ibid. ORB entry for 27 June 1943.

343. Ciechanowski, p. 135. Poland's ambassador to the United States Jan Ciechanowski in his memoirs recorded after the Montreal accident, "As I sat listening to Sikorski's comments, I noted the expression of grave concern on his handsome, virile, and still youthful face. Suddenly the plane accident in Montreal flashed through my mind. It was Sikorski's third narrow escape since the beginning of the war. I was filled with a premonition that this Polish soldier-statesman, so typical of our people, was a man exposed to great personal danger and that I might perhaps never see him again."

344. Thompson, pp. 247–48. "Until General Sikorski made me that present, I was not aware that he preferred me to other pilots. On the way to the Middle East, when we made our stopover in Cairo, I stayed at the same hotel as he, the Mena House, by the Pyramids, and there I had occasion to talk to him several times, sitting outside on the hotel terrace." [...]"During the flight from Cairo to Gibraltar, General Sikorski came several times to the flight-deck and I myself visited him several times in the passenger section. He gave it to me then. His present was a great surprise to me, although I must say I felt the same regard for him; he was a cordial, warm-hearted man, full of easy authority and dignity."

345. Thompson, Appendix C, 2. Prchal outwardly appeared quite normal prior to departure according to General Mason Macfarlane the then governor of Gibraltar. "I knew the pilot – a Czech named Perzl [Prchal] – quite well, having flown with him on two or three previous occasions, while the second pilot was finishing warming up the engines and doing preliminary cock-pit checks, I had at least five minutes talk with him outside the aircraft. He was absolutely normal, and in-fact, the best type of pre-war civilian airline pilot, which we had always known him to be."

346. The Cost of Silence: Normalization of Deviance and Groupthink: https://sma.nasa.gov/docs/default-source/safety-messages/safetymessage-normalizationofdeviance-2014-11-03b.pdf. Diane Vaughan, 1996. Professor Vaughan is a sociologist who examined the chronology of events that led to the Challenger Space Shuttle accident. She reconstructed the cultural and sociological context of events and decisions that culminated in the disaster.

347. AAN: *Akta Władyslawa Sikorskiego*, Sygnatura 204, pp. 2–25, 27. Sir Robin Hooper was member of a British government committee chaired by Sir Burke Trend. The committee had been formed in mid-January to address a parliamentary question raised by Labour opposition member Mr Woodrow Wyatt on 13 January 1969 "about co-ordination between the relevant government departments in inquiries into air accidents" which suggested British complicity in the death of General Sikorski. This was followed by a 31 January 1969 article by Chapmen Pincher in the *Daily Express* demanding Whitehall disclose the full report on the Sikorski crash. The committee's objective was to re-examine the accident and formulate a draft reply for Prime Minister Wilson that addressed Wyatt's question. A review of the case soundly refuted claims of British complicity with Prime Minister Wilson stating in parliament on 11 February 1969 that there was no evidence to imply that the crash at Gibraltar was anything more than a genuine accident and that the House refused to entertain any contrary assumption.

348. TNA: AIR 10/2206, A.P. 1640/G.1., 18

349. https://footagefarm.com/reel-details/wwii/generic/post-wwii---color-1945-england--lancaster-bombers--raf-crew-mission-preparations--jun45

EPILOGUE

350. Vincent, Carl, *Canada's Wings 2: The Liberator and Fortress*, Canada's Wings, 1975, p. 129

351. TNA: TS 58/997, 345–46. Walter Lock was a representative for the Ministry of War Transport in the Persian Gulf and chairman of the Basra War Transport Committee. His body was never found. Harry Pinder was a Royal Navy warrant telegraphist and was being posted back to the UK at the time of the crash. His body was buried at sea.

352. It is unclear from Walker's account whether it was Polish military personnel who were supervising and loading AL523 or if it was Polish military personnel who were supervising RAF personnel in the loading.

353. TNA: AIR 28/306, 248. Along with the launch of a six-man dinghy, a four-man canoe was also launched at 23:30 hrs and assisted with rescue operations. These four individuals were identified as Lieutenant E G Cruikshank RA, two airmen – AC Lindsay and AC Mason – and Stafford R E M E.

354. Mieczysław Różycki is an aviation researcher from Poland. He is critical of authors who conduct suspect research and weave conspiracy theories into their narratives. In 2016 he investigated circumstances surrounding the Gibraltar crash and published his findings in the Polish aviation magazine *Lotnictwo*. He concluded AL523 was likely overloaded and exceeded the take-off weight limit set by the manufacturer and RAF Transport Command. From estimates and comparative data he calculated the take-off weight to be about 63,000 lbs requiring a 1,600-yard take-off run, Gibraltar's airstrip at the time was only 1,530 yards long. He also acknowledged minor smuggling by aircrew was widespread and that VIP baggage was not checked or weighed resulting in pilots having to estimate aircraft weight. Gibraltar was also known for bad weather due to winds and sea currents, accidents were frequent which included other Liberators in 1942 and 1943. The 63,000 lbs that Różycki estimates possibly reflects the three-ton capacity classification (6,720 lbs) of the truck described in Charles Walker's account and added in excess to the 56,000 lbs maximum take-off weight quoted in Air Publication 1867-B Pilot Notes Liberator II.

INDEX